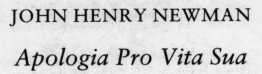

JOHN HENRY NEWMAN

Apologia Pro Vita Sua

*Edited, with an Introduction and Notes, by
William Oddie*

J M Dent
London
Charles E. Tuttle Co.
Rutland, Vermont
EVERYMAN'S LIBRARY

Textual editing, introduction and commentary
© William Oddie 1993
This edition first published in Everyman by J M Dent
1993

All rights reserved

Photoset by Deltatype Ltd, Ellesmere Port, Cheshire
Printed in Great Britain by
The Guernsey Press Co. Ltd, Guernsey, C.I.
for
J M Dent Ltd
Orion Publishing Group
Orion House
5 Upper St Martin's Lane
London WC2H 9EA
and
Charles E. Tuttle Co. Inc.
28 South Main Street
Rutland, Vermont
05701 – USA

British Library Cataloguing-in-Publication Data is
available upon request.

ISBN 0 460 87232 X

CONTENTS

JOHN HENRY NEWMAN, who became the most powerful influence over the Oxford movement in the Church of England, and then one of the seminal minds in modern Roman Catholicism, was born into an Evangelical household on February 21, 1801. He underwent a conversion experience at the age of 14; he was educated at Trinity College, Oxford, and elected to a fellowship of Oriel at 21. In 1825, he was ordained to the Anglican priesthood; three years later he became Vicar of St Mary the Virgin, the Oxford University Church. At this time he fell under the influence of Hurrell Froude and John Keble, whose Assize Sermon (1833) was the effective beginning of the Oxford movement.

Newman was the movement's strongest intellectual influence, through the *Tracts for the Times*, his sermons, and his classic statement of Tractarian doctrine, the *Lectures on the Prophetical Office of the Church* (1837).

In 1838–9, Newman and Keble published Hurrell Froude's *Literary Remains*, in which the Reformation was strongly denounced; this, together with Tract XC (1841) and other signs of the movement's supposed Papist tendencies brought on a crisis and a period of withdrawal during which Newman came to see that his view of the Church was embodied only by Rome.

He was received into the Roman Catholic Church in 1845. Two years later, he was ordained priest; the same year he published the *Essay on the Development of Christian Doctrine*. He founded the Birmingham Oratory in 1848. He was at first suspect to Catholic rigorists, who wrongly (and ironically) suspected him of liberalism. A period of frustration and misunderstanding came to an end with the publication of the *Apologia* in 1864. In 1870 he published perhaps his most important contribution to theology, *An Essay in Aid of a Grammar of Assent*. His stature in the Catholic Church was acknowledged when at the age of 78 he was made a Cardinal by Pope Leo XIII. He died at Birmingham on August 11, 1890.

CHRONOLOGY OF NEWMAN'S LIFE

Year	Age	Life
1801		Born February 21
1808	7	Goes to Ealing School
1816	15	Converted to Evangelical Christianity
1817	16	Undergraduate at Trinity College, Oxford
1820	19	B.A. Degree
1822	21	Elected to Oriel fellowship
1825	24	Becomes vice-principal of Alban Hall; takes Holy Orders
1826	25	Becomes tutor at Oriel
1828	27	Meets Hurrell Froude; becomes Vicar of St Mary's
1830	29	Newman and Froude deprived of Oriel tutorships
1832	31	Tour of Southern Europe
1833	32	Returns to England; *Arians of the Fourth Century*; *Tracts for the Times* begins
1834	33	*Parochial and Plain sermons* (1834–42)
1837	36	*Prophetical Office of the Church*
1838	37	Appointed editor of *The British Critic*; *Lectures on Justification*
1841	40	*Tract XC*; condemned by University authorities
1842	41	Newman withdraws to Littlemore

Year	Literary Context	Historical Events
1801	Tennyson b.	Suppression of Irish Parliament; Act of Union between Great Britain and Ireland
1803		Napoleonic Wars begin
1814	Wordsworth: *The Excursion*; Byron: *The Corsair*; Scott: *Waverley*	
1815	Coleridge: *Kubla Khan* published	Battle of Waterloo; Corn Law; Congress of Vienna restores Papal States
1818	Byron: *Don Juan*	
1820	Scott: *Ivanhoe*; Keats: *Ode to a Nightingale*	Accession of George IV; Cato St conspiracy
1821	Keats d.: James Mill: *Elements of Political Economy*	
1822	Shelley d.	
1827	Keble: *The Christian Year*; William Blake d.	
1829		Catholic Emancipation
1830	Hazlitt d.; Cobbett: *Rural Rides*	July Revolution; Accession of William IV
1832	Walter Scott d.	Reform Act
1833	Carlyle: *Sartor Resartus*	Keble Assize sermon; Factory Act
1834		New Poor Law; Parliament burns down
1837	Hurrell Froude: *Literary Remains*	Accession of Queen Victoria
1838		Rise of Chartism
1839	Darwin: *Voyage of the Beagle*	Bedchamber plot; Birmingham riots; Penny postage Act
1841		Robert Peel becomes Prime Minister
1842		Chartist riots; Lord Ashley's Act protecting women and children in mines

Year	Literary Context	Historical Events
1843	Carlyle: *Past and Present*; J. S. Mill: *System of Logic*	
1844	Disraeli: *Coningsby*	
1845		Maynooth grant
1846	Edward Lear: *Book of Nonsense*	Repeal of Corn Laws, Election of Pius IX
1847	Emily Brontë: *Jane Eyre*; Thackeray: *Vanity Fair*; Charlotte Brontë: *Wuthering Heights*	
1848	Dickens: *Dombey and Son*; Kingsley: *Yeast*; Mrs Gaskell: *Mary Barton*	Gorham judgement; European revolutions
1850	Dickens: *David Copperfield*; Tennyson: *In Memoriam*	Restoration of Catholic Hierarchy in England causes anti-Catholic sentiment
1851	Ruskin: *Stones of Venice*	Ecclesiastical titles Act forbidding Catholic use of names of existing dioceses
1853	Matthew Arnold: *The Scholar Gipsy*	Crimean War begins (ends '56)
1854	Dickens: *Hard Times*	
1855	Trollope: *The Warden*	Daily Telegraph founded
1857	George Eliot: *Scenes of clerical life*	Indian Mutiny
1858		India transferred to Crown; Jews admitted to Parliament
1859	Darwin: *Origin of species*; J. S. Mill: *On Liberty*	
1860	Wilkie Collins: *Woman in White*; Dickens: *Great Expectations*; Ruskin: *Unto this last Essays and Reviews*	Unification of Italy; loss of most Papal States; discovery of the source of the Nile
1863	Kingsley: *Water Babies*	
1864	Tolstoi: *War and Peace*; Trollope: *Small House at Allington*	Pius IX: *Syllabus of Errors*
1865	Lewis Carroll: *Alice in Wonderland*; Rudyard Kipling b.; W. B. Yeats b.	Assassination of Abraham Lincoln
1866	Kingsley: *Hereward the Wake*; Dostoyevsky: *Crime and Punishment*	Treaty of Vienna; invention of Dynamite
1867	Marx: *Das Kapital*, Vol I	Reform Bill

Year	Age	Life
1870	69	*Essay in aid of a Grammar of Assent*
1875	74	*Letter to the Duke of Norfolk*
1877	76	Elected to honorary fellowship of Trinity College, Oxford
1879	78	Receives Cardinal's Hat from Pope Leo XIII
1890	89	Dies in Birmingham, August 11

Year	Literary Context	Historical Events
1869	Matthew Arnold: *Culture and Anarchy*; J. S. Mill: *On the Subjection of Women*	Foundation of Girton College, Cambridge; Abolition of debtors prisons
1870	Death of Charles Dickens; Disraeli: *Lothair*	Vatican Council, Pius IX 'Prisoner of the Vatican', Franco-Prussian War
1874	G. K. Chesterton b.	
1875	Kingsley d.	Purchase of Suez Canal
1877	Henry James: *The American*	
1878	Thomas Hardy: *The Return of the Native*	Election of Leo XIII
1879	Ibsen: *A Doll's House*	Trotsky and Stalin b.; British Zulu War
1880	George Eliot d.; Lytton Strachey b.	
1881	Thomas Carlyle d.	
1890	Oscar Wilde: *The Picture of Dorian Gray*	Charles De Gaulle b.; First Electric power station; Forth Bridge opened

INTRODUCTION

No literary work of the nineteenth century so stubbornly resists classification as Newman's *Apologia*. It is generally thought of as a 'spiritual autobiography': yet it hardly approaches (except as an intellectual question) the mystery of man's relationship with God; as an autobiography it is notably deficient in the usual biographical details. It can seem at first sight – especially outside its original polemical context – simply to be a plain and rational account of the development of Newman's ideas about the nature and identity of the Church. And yet we are aware as we read that such an assessment will not do, that it fails to register the deeper resonances of feeling and perception contained in the text, but declared only when they rise irresistibly to the surface – as in the valedictory passage at the end of the last chapter (which George Eliot confessed she could not read without tears).

We are thus faced from the outset with a text whose character is ambiguous. Despite the self-consciously cerebral character of the main body of the work, nowhere in Christian literature is there a more moving personal testimony to the passion with which Catholics – especially, perhaps, converts – have fallen in love with their Church. The deliberate narrowness of focus, too, – on the intellectual development of a single individual – has a curiously paradoxical effect: Newman is so deeply engaged in the spiritual crisis of his times that the more closely we focus on him, the more we become involved in his world.

Newman's own relationship with God – face-to-face or *solus cum solo*, as he himself puts it – is the starting point of the journey; though his conversion to Christian faith is briefly described, it is not the real subject of his mental history. The *Apologia* is a story of *Fides quaerens intellectum*, of a faith which has already been received – before the action begins – searching for an understanding of its own consequences. For Newman, the search takes the form of a particular question: where, amid the confused welter of holiness and corruption that is the history of Christendom, is to be found the true Church, the Church instituted by Christ and given the authority to speak in his name ? The work's central section is thus a kind of drama of the mind: it is – in a certain sense literally – the story of Newman's quest for the holy grail.

The intellectual excitement of the journey is at times intense. History is no dead study for Newman; the third century is as vivid to him as the nineteenth. He knows that somewhere the past contains the key that will unlock the secret of his quest. When the discovery comes, it is a moment of high drama: we can imagine it, almost, made into an operatic *tour de force* by Verdi or Donizetti. The scene is Newman's study in Oxford. A friend has pointed out to him a passage from an article by Wiseman in the *Dublin Review*, comparing Anglicanism with the Donatist heresy. At first, he is unimpressed. Then his friend points out a quotation from St Augustine:

'Securus judicat orbis terrarum.' He repeated these words again and again, and, when he was gone, they kept ringing in my ears. 'Securus judicat orbis terrarum': they were words which went beyond the occasion of the Donatists. . . . What a light was hereby thrown on every controversy in the Church! Not that, for the moment the multitude may not falter in their judgement . . . but that the deliberate judgement, in which the whole Church at length rests and acquiesces, is an infallible prescription and a final sentence against such portions of it as protest and secede. Who can account for the impressions which are made in him ? For a mere sentence, the words of St Augustine, struck me with a power which I never had felt from any words before. . . . 'Securus judicat orbis terrarum!' By those great words of the ancient Father . . . the theory of the *Via Media* was absolutely pulverised. (p. 174)'

'Securus judicat orbis terrarum': the settled judgement of the universal Church (rather than that of breakaway factions) has authority in matters of faith and doctrine (see note to p. 174).

It is hardly possible to read such a passage without a clear perception of Newman's intellect as being wholly impelled and impregnated by faith. The *Apologia*, we can say, represents in English literature a striking reversal of what T. S. Eliot called the 'dissociation of sensibility', that separation of feeling and thought, of the heart and the mind, that Eliot believed took place in English culture during the seventeenth century. Newman possessed the most impressive analytical intellect of any Churchman of his age; yet there is no incongruity that his motto should be 'Cor ad Cor Loquitur' (heart speaks to heart). Nor do we feel that Newman's heart represents some kind of mitigation for any coldness in his mind: the Wordsworthian language of 'the feeling intellect' is entirely appropriate here.

Newman wrote the *Apologia* in response to a crude personal attack, and the circumstances are more than usually important to a critical discernment of the work as a whole. They form more than any mere subtext: in its first appearances, first as a series of pamphlets then as a book, lengthy sections of passionate and brilliant polemic and argument are presented at the beginning and end as an intrinsic part of the text itself. The *Apologia* was composed under pressure, in a kind of creative white heat; Newman was writing as if for his life, to meet a crisis he had dimly foreseen but for which, in the event, he was unprepared, particularly in the form it actually took. It is at least arguable that the original text of the *Apologia*, which came fresh out of the furnace (rather than the extensively depolemicised later editions), is actually the most authentic – the text that most accurately displays the work's underlying character and intention.

Before developing such an argument, it is also necessary to say that the *Apologia* represents considerably more than a response to an immediate crisis. The ground had been long prepared by years of misunderstanding and apparent failure. The incomprehension of his fellow-Anglicans had been compounded by his 'perversion' to Rome; he had expected no better. But after his reception, he was to meet with years of frustration, made harder by the suspicions of his fellow Catholics. His attempts to found a Catholic University in Dublin had failed because of the lack of cooperation of the Irish hierarchy; Cardinal Wiseman's suggestion that he should prepare a translation of the Bible had similarly foundered for lack of support; Newman's editorship of the Catholic periodical *The Rambler* had even brought accusations of heresy. By 1863, Newman was looking back wistfully at the time when, as an Anglican, he was recognised as having a 'remarkable mission': 'How am I changed even in look', he wrote in his journal; '. . . Persons who would naturally look towards me,

converts who would naturally consult me, are stopped by some
light or unkind word said against me. I am *passé*, in decay . . .'

Then occurred the train of events which dramatically and
permanently reversed Newman's situation. The story was
recorded in the first two parts of the first edition of the *Apologia*
(excluded from the main text until now in every subsequent
edition but one) and there is little need to describe what happened
in detail (see p. 3 ff.) In a review in Macmillan's Magazine of two
volumes of J. A. Froude's *History of England* (an example of the
generally anti-Catholic bias of English historiography), Charles
Kingsley indulged in a sideways lunge which because of
Newman's reaction to it was to become famous:

> Truth, for its own sake, had never been a virtue with the Roman clergy.
> Father Newman informs us that it need not, and on the whole ought
> not to be; that cunning is the weapon which heaven has given to the
> Saints wherewith to withstand the brute male force of the wicked
> world which marries and is given in marriage.'

Newman drew the matter to the publisher's attention; Kingsley
compounded his error by writing a statement for the next issue of
the magazine which, under the guise of being an apology, gave the
impression that Newman had withdrawn the statement which
Kingsley claimed he had made. When Newman asked him where
he had ever said that truth was no virtue with the Roman clergy,
Kingsley referred him, without any specific reference, to one of his
Anglican sermons.

Newman was not pacified; now he moved onto the offensive.
He published his correspondence with Kingsley, together with his
own sardonic comments, in a pamphlet. It was a response both
Swiftian in its brilliance and devastating in its effect. Its full power
can only be appreciated in its context, but more than one writer
on the *Apologia* has been unable to resist quoting the following
passage for its characteristically Newmanian combination of
intellectual verve, sardonic wit, and perfect control of tone and
language; it is Newman in his most exquisitely comic satirical
vein. When and where, asks Newman, did he say that truth for its
own sake was no virtue ? 'Let us have the passage':

> Mr Kingsley relaxes: 'Do you know, I like your *tone*. From your *tone* I
> rejoice, greatly rejoice, to be able to believe that you did not mean what
> you said.'
>
> I rejoin: '*Mean* it! I maintain I never *said* it, whether as a Protestant
> or as a Catholic.'

Mr Kingsley replies: 'I waive that point.'

I object: 'Is it possible! What? waive the main question! I either said it or I didn't. You have made a monstrous charge against me; direct, distinct, public. You are bound to prove it as directly, as distinctly, as publicly; – or to own you can't.'

'Well,' says Mr Kingsley, 'if you are quite sure you did not say it, I'll take your word for it; I really will.'

My *word*! I am dumb. Somehow, I had thought that it was my *word* that happened to be on trial. The *word* of a Professor of lying that he does not lie!

But Mr Kingsley re-assures me: 'We are both gentlemen,' he says: 'I have done as much as one English gentleman can expect from another.'

I begin to see: he thought me a gentleman at the very time that he said I taught lying on a system . . .

Newman's pamphlet appeared in February; towards the end of the same month appeared a review by R. H. Hutton, a former Unitarian now an Anglican, in the *Spectator* (see pages 420 to 424). It was, says Ian Ker in his definitive critical biography, 'a turning point . . . it was not what [Newman] was accustomed to read.' Hutton wrote of Kingsley's 'rough but manly intellect', and commented that 'a more opportune Protestant ram for Father Newman's sacrificial knife could scarcely have been found.' It was already becoming clear that Kingsley was no match for his victim; he would have been wise to have let the matter drop. But about five weeks after Newman's pamphlet appeared Kingsley's reply, 'What, then does Dr Newman mean?' There could now be no doubt: Kingsley's accusation had been no careless mistake; it was, on the contrary, the result of a long and deeply-felt distaste for the Catholic religion and for Newman personally.

There was no question of leaving matters as they stood. Kingsley had to be answered; and in his answer, Newman now had the opportunity to clear away the misunderstanding of his motives that had begun to dog him long before he became a Catholic; he wrote to Keble that it was the book he had 'for years wished to write'. The strength of the case he had to answer, he told a supporter '*as directed rhetorically* to the popular mind lies in the antecedent prejudice *that I was a Papist while I was an Anglican.*' The only way, Newman thought, to destroy this notion would be 'to give my history, and the history of my mind, from 1822 or earlier, down to 1845.' Another inseparable aim emerged unavoidably as he began work; not only to defend his own integrity but also that of the Catholic clergy in general: both had been assailed in Kingsley's original accusation, and now in his pamphlet.

The burden of work Newman imposed on himself in order to answer Kingsley before the affair was forgotten was crushing. To reach as many people as possible, his self-defence appeared in weekly pamphlets. The first appeared on April 21; the seventh (entitled 'General answer to Mr Kingsley') on June 2. Two weeks later the last and eighth pamphlet appeared, entitled 'Answer in Detail to Mr Kingsley'. The first two and the last two pamphlets were openly apologetic or polemical, their purpose being to put Kingsley in his place and to defend the Catholic religion against some common misunderstandings; the central part of the series consisted of the four parts described by Newman as a history of his mind. It was, he wrote after the astonishing feat was completed, 'the most arduous work . . . I ever had in my life', and 'one of the most terrible trials that I have had'.

Its effect, however, was immediate. *Blackwood*'s magazine summed up the general reaction: that Kingsley had been 'entirely and wantonly the aggressor'. Most devastatingly for Kingsley, it concluded that Newman had always cared more for the truth, and declared that 'we do not distrust one word of all that he has written about himself.' The *Edinburgh Review* spoke of Newman's 'honest allegiance to truth'. Samuel ('Soapy Sam') Wilberforce, Bishop of Oxford, magisterially handed down the general verdict: 'the post-mortem examination of his life is complete . . . All lies perfectly open and the foul taint is nowhere.'

There was, however, a certain sympathy for Kingsley. Everybody agreed that he had brought his troubles on himself; but there was no doubt that his defeat had been crushing. After reading Newman's 'tremendous handling of his opponent in the introduction and conclusion of the *Apologia*', Newman's fellow oratorian, Fr Ignatius Dudley Rider wrote that it was 'impossible, whatever one's sympathies, to avoid a sense of honest pity for the victim as for one condemned though by his own rashness to fight with gods or with the elements.' The exuberance and acid wit of Newman's polemic had found its mark; but Kingsley had hardly stinted himself in his own attack: 'Deliberately, after 20 years of thought, I struck as hard as I could', he wrote to Alexander Macmillan afterwards. Kingsley was unattractively bitter in defeat, referring to Newman as 'one who, like a treacherous ape, lifts to you meek and suppliant eyes, till he thinks he has you within his reach, and then springs, gibbering and biting, at your face.'

Newman had been resolute and bloody in battle; now he was magnanimous in victory. The angry tone of his reply had been as much a matter of calculation as of genuine resentment; he was well aware from his own experience that unless he wrote with the 'keen feeling' which he really had, 'though it is ordinarily one's duty not to show it', people would not believe him. Now he had won, it was not only possible but necessary for Newman to set aside his 'keen feeling'. To have kept the controversy alive in subsequent editions of the *Apologia* during his own lifetime would have been to crow over his vanquished opponent. Newman had nothing against Kingsley; and though many readers thoroughly enjoyed his discomfiture, others had been uneasy at the spectacle.

It was, in the circumstances of the time, inevitable that the balance of the text should be as radically altered as it was in the second and all subsequent editions. Parts 1 and 2, Newman explained, 'as being for the most part directly controversial' were omitted; of the Appendix – the often brilliantly witty and argumentative 'Answer in Detail to Mr Kingsley's Accusations' – about half was cut out for the same reason. He also removed all mention of Kingsley's name from the 'autobiographical' parts of the book.

Just how radical the effect of this revision was becomes clear when we reflect that the large sections of the original text which Newman removed are not peripherally but centrally concerned with the origins and underlying motivation of the work itself. This raises real critical questions about how the text is to be read. The *Apologia*, says Ian Ker in his definitive biography, writing of the text as generally received,

> is unique among Newman's published works, not only in its form and content, but also in its style and tone. This is not surprising when one considers that far from attempting to persuade by argument, the main autobiographical part of the book convinces by deliberately abandoning all argument in favour of facts, by adopting an almost dry documentation in the place of polemical rhetoric in order to prove the integrity of the author's own life. It is thus a curious anomaly that the very book on which Newman's literary reputation is usually presumed principally to rest, itself so strikingly differs from his other works of

controversy, which give him so distinctive a place in the history of English literature. Its power lies in the (almost) disconcertingly calm, limpid tone of the author's conversational, indeed confidential voice.

This is acutely observed. Beneath the calm and limpid surface, however, Newman the controversialist is never far away, his sword only partly sheathed. We can note first, that Newman himself makes clear that the motivation underlying parts 3 to 6 (which became chapters 1 to 4) is precisely the same as that of the first two more overtly polemical parts: it is to prove Kingsley and his other detractors wrong over the central charge that he was dishonest. He had to overcome, he wrote, 'the antecedent prejudice *that I was a Papist while I was an Anglican*'; the only way of doing this was 'to give my history, and the history of my mind, from 1822 or earlier, down to 1845.'

Once we replace these chapters in their original context, what Fr Ker perceptively calls the 'curious anomaly' which sets the *Apologia* apart from his other works of controversy becomes more clearly a matter of tone and strategy than of genre; the anomalous character of the work as a whole, in fact, largely disappears. For, as we proceed, we now see unavoidably that Newman's restraint in these central four chapters is not the restraint of a man who has decided that there is no argument. Step by step, as he establishes that his present forthright opinions – opinions deeply offensive to many of his readers – may be honestly held by a rational and learned man, he is also arguing for the opinions themselves: self-revelation and apologetics are woven seamlessly together. This did not pass unnoticed at the time; The High Church *Quarterly Review* warned its readers that: 'never is he more a controversialist than when he avoids controversy. There is more force in the burning words he drops, impregnated with the fire of his own inner life, than in the closest of his studied arguments.'

Hence, his account of the effect on him of Augustine's words 'securus judicat orbis terrarum' – which for him 'pulverise' the claims of the Church of England (not an eirenic turn of phrase) – is more than a mere self-justification: they are an implied but delicate invitation to follow Newman on his journey to Rome. The very caution with which he describes his own halting progress is a reassurance that what he is describing is no strange exotic bewitchment, that a plain commonsense Englishman need have no mistrust of being drawn on by Newman's arguments, that he can withdraw freely at any stage.

'I had to determine', Newman relates of his reaction to St Augustine's words, 'its logical value, and its bearing on my duty . . . perhaps some new light was coming upon me. He who has seen a ghost cannot be as if he had never seen it. The heavens had opened and closed again. The thought for the moment had been, "the Church of Rome will be found right after all. . . ." ' Here, if anywhere, for all that Newman describes it as a passing 'thought for the moment', is the work's principal theme, often recalled, the origin of many variations: 'The Church of Rome will be found right after all.'

There are, of course, changes in key and tempo between the different sections of the work, for instance between the four chapters of narrative and the final chapter; but all is held together by this underlying theme and purpose. A failure to perceive this has led to some odd mistakes. More than one critic, for example, has identified this particular transition as an actual change in genre, even a 'generic crisis'. Jerome H. Buckley describes it as a 'sudden shift' from 'self-history' to apology: that is to 'an exercise in interested advocacy defending a system or creed, *rather than* a single life, from attack or neglect.' (my italics) In fact, we can make no such clear distinction: for as we have seen, in defending the rationality and honesty of his own acceptance of this particular 'system or creed', Newman is defending the rationality and honesty of the 'system or creed' itself. Buckley explains the supposed 'sudden shift' by pointing to the fact that this final chapter is 'adapted from' the pamphlet 'General Answer to Mr Kingsley'. But of course, *all* the chapters that precede it are similarly 'adapted from' the original polemical pamphlets; and the very title *Apologia pro Vita Sua* ought by itself to establish the apologetic character of the work – including the parts to do with Newman's life – as a whole.

To adjust our reading of the *Apologia* in this way, is not only to add a dimension to our understanding of the text; it is to recover a more fully-rounded picture of the man himself. The *Apologia* more than any of his other works has influenced the modern perception of Newman, who is seen today not only as an essentially eirenic and unifying figure but also as an uncontroversial one. There is, perhaps, a sense in which Newman's cuts in the text have had a distorting, even a sentimentalizing effect on our perceptions of him, amounting almost to a kind of unintended self-bowdlerization. For, though Newman, of course, never forgot that Christ came to bring peace in the hearts of men, he remembered, too, the paradox that he came also 'to bring not peace but a sword'.

The nearer Newman approaches beatification, the greater the risk that he will become an unreal and somewhat anaemic 'plaster saint' in the modern imagination. He himself disliked books 'which chop up a Saint into chapters of faith, hope and charity'; and he pointed out that the Saints of the early Church 'rather than writing formal doctrinal treatises . . . write controversy'. Not only that, they 'mix up their own persons . . . with the didactic or polemical works which engaged them.' This predates the *Apologia* by four years; but Newman could have been writing about himself.

To recover Newman the controversialist is to make him more and not less relevant to our own times. Our own age, no less than his, is one of passionate (and unavoidable) ecclesiastical conflict in the English-speaking world, and the underlying themes of today's controversies are in some ways remarkably similar to those of Newman's day. In the most obvious controversy of all for Anglicanism for instance – the question of women's ordination – the arguments against the movement increasingly converged on the central perception which, for Newman himself, had been the test of Anglicanism's authenticity a century and a half before: 'Securus judicat orbis terrarum': in Newman's words, 'the deliberate judgement, in which the whole Church at length rests and acquiesces, is an infallible prescription and a final sentence against such portions of it as protest and secede'. For a substantial minority of Anglicans the independent decision to ordain women by the Church of England's General Synod was a conscious rejection of that 'deliberate judgement' and a final act of secession from 'the whole Church'. What was at stake for them was, in the end, the question whether or not the Church of England – in fact rather than simply in theory – accepted the faith and order of Catholic christendom.

Underlying the Synod's deliberations was the wider question of the way in which, for those who can be seen as Newman's spiritual descendants, contemporary liberal Protestantism had become a mere reflection of secular progressive attitudes, of what St Paul called 'the wisdom of this world'. Here, in a sense, is the most Newmanian theme of all, a controversy in which Newman's perceptions of the nature of theological liberalism are only now reaching their full relevance to the crisis of Western Christendom in the Industrial age. Among the principles of this liberalism, he said, were these: 'That truth and falsehood in religion are but a matter of opinion; that one doctrine is as good as another; . . . that there is no truth; that we are not more acceptable to God by believing this than by believing that; . . . that it is enough if we sincerely hold what we profess; that our merit lies in seeking, not in possessing; . . . that we may safely trust to ourselves in matters of Faith; and need no other guide . . .'

For Newman, in the end, the question was this: is Christianity, or is it not, a religion whose principles were revealed by God? Liberalism, he wrote in the 1865 appendix to the *Apologia*, 'is the mistake of subjecting to human judgement those revealed doctrines which are in their nature beyond and independent of it . . .' (p. 387). Whether or not Newman was right to see Liberalism thus defined as a 'mistake' is still the question underlying most theological controversy in the Western world.

William Oddie, 1993

A NOTE ON THIS EDITION

To publish an edition of Newman's *Apologia* is to face a familiar problem in an acute form. Newman's great work ran into several editions: which one do we choose to reprint? As I discuss in the Introduction, the first edition of 1864 is radically different from later editions in that it was written in the heat of controversy, and contains much controversial material which Newman removed from all subsequent revisions. Newman described this radical surgery in his Preface to the 1865 edition (on which all subsequent editions were based):

> The original work consisted of seven Parts, which were published in series on consecutive Thursdays, between 21 April and 2 June. An Appendix, in answer to specific allegations urged against me in the Pamphlet of Accusation, appeared on 16 June. Of these Parts 1 and 2, as being for the most part directly controversial, are omitted in this Edition, excepting the latter pages of Part 2, which are subjoined to this Preface as being necessary for the due explanation of the subsequent five Parts. These (being [Parts] 3, 4, 5, 6, 7, of the Apologia), are here numbered [i.e. in 1865] as Chapters 1, 2, 3, 4, 5 respectively. Of the Appendix, about half has been omitted, for the same reason as has led to the omission of Parts 1 and 2.

One would normally accept an author's later refinements of his own text as definitive: but if we do that here, we remove the *Apologia* from a particularly fascinating historical context, one which is equally essential whether we seek to understand the work for the light it throws on Newman and his times, or to read it for its continuing and striking relevance to the intellectual and ecclesiastical controversies of our own age.

The simplest solution for this particular difficulty would have been to return to the original edition of 1864. But this would be to lose the hundreds of small refinements that Newman made in the second edition, and which gave us the version best known today; it would also mean that we would lose the new material of various kinds – from the odd sentence or short passage here and there, to such essential matter as the *Note on Liberalism* added in 1865.

In this edition I have tried to have the best of both worlds. My aim has been to achieve a text which combines clarity and completeness, and my general working principle has been to include wherever appropriate both old material excised and new material added. I have restored the structure of the first edition, as well as all the cuts of controversial material made with the suppression of Parts 1 and 2, and much of the original Appendix (which appears here as Appendix A). I have also included the most important part of the material which appeared for the first time in 1865, the *Note on Liberalism*; this appears here as Appendix B. To these Appendices, I have added those on the Church of England and the University of Oxford first published in the French edition of 1866: these appear as Appendix C.

In the *Apologia* proper (Parts 3–7, Chapters 1–5), I have for the most part adhered closely to the text of 1865; but though editorial interference with this text has been minimal, some restorations have been made.

I have reversed some changes in the text made in order to obscure its controversial origins. Such restorations can sometimes make sense of passages which otherwise seem puzzling: for example, Newman's assertion in the 1865 edition that his 'accusers' have founded charges of reserve and economy on a particular passage in his *History of the Arians*. But, though Kingsley may well have followed others in pointing to this passage, it seems clear that Newman is thinking mainly of him; and, indeed, the 1864 text has 'accuser'. Newman, having won the argument, is here avoiding undue vindictiveness by blurring the focus. In a few cases where (for this or other personal reasons) changes involve a loss of concreteness of this kind, they are reversed.

A few short passages are restored because they help explain or articulate the text, and were not replaced by new material. In a small number of cases, too, I have opted for the 1864 variant where a change of usage has made the meaning less clear rather than more so for a modern reader, e.g. 'acknowledge' (1864) rather than 'own' (1865). I have also added information still being withheld in 1865, but added in later editions: thus 'the friend' [consulted by Newman over leaving the Church of England] becomes 'Mr Keble'. Such interferences with Newman's pain-staking revision of Parts 3 to 7 have been few; and they have only been made where some clarification of meaning or context seemed to me to be the result. I have given the part numbers of 1864 as well as the chapter numbers of 1865, with the dates of the original pamphlets, at the beginning of each chapter. Chapter titles are those of 1865 except for the last: Part VII in 1864 was entitled 'General Answer to Mr Kingsley'; this became Chapter V in 1865 and was entitled 'The Position of my mind since 1845'. Both titles are informative, so I have taken the liberty of eliding them.

In accordance with modern usage, long quotations have been indented and set without quotation marks; I have, however, resisted the modern practice of eliminating in Victorian texts initial Capitals and italics where they are used to provide emphasis.

In annotating the text, I have avoided asterisks or other indications that a note is provided, leaving it up to the reader to judge whether he/she needs to refer to the note. The purpose of the notes is to give help where obstacles to unimpeded reading tend to arise (particularly, perhaps, where Patristic controversies are evoked as dramatic parallels for controversies of Newman's own day). Such statements as 'I saw my face in that mirror, and I was a monophysite' tend to be puzzling to the general reader, and it has been my principal aim to give a basic minimum of unobtrusive guidance to a number of passages where such difficulties arise. The notes are therefore not intended as an exhaustive textual commentary; where the plain meaning of the text is clear, I have generally avoided comment, though I have offered some brief supplementary information about, for instance, such important figures as Hurrell Froude, Keble and Pusey. Latin and Greek passages are translated and quotations are, if possible, identified. Probably the best way to use the notes would be for the reader quickly to scan through them at the outset to ascertain whether they contain any information he/she does not already possess. The reader should note that the notes, for obvious reasons, deal only with Chapters 1–5, Parts 3–7.

MR KINGSLEY AND DR NEWMAN

A Correspondence on the Question whether Dr Newman
teaches that Truth is No Virtue?

MR KINGSLEY AND DR NEWMAN
A CORRESPONDENCE

I

Extract from a Review of Froude's History of England, vols vii and viii, in Macmillan's Magazine for January 1864, signed 'C. K.'

Pages 216, 217

The Roman religion had, for some time past, been making men not better men, but worse. We must face, we must conceive honestly for ourselves, the deep demoralization which had been brought on in Europe by the dogma that the Pope of Rome had the power of creating right and wrong; that not only truth and falsehood, but morality and immorality, depended on his setting his seal to a bit of parchment. From the time that indulgences were hawked about in his name, which would issue pardon for any man, '*etsi matrem Dei violavisset*', the world in general began to be of that opinion. But the mischief was older and deeper than those indulgences. It lay in the very notion of the dispensing power. A deed might be a crime, or no crime at all — like Henry the Eighth's marriage of his brother's widow —according to the will of the Pope. If it suited the interest or caprice of the old man of Rome *not* to say the word, the doer of a certain deed would be burned alive in hell for ever. If it suited him, on the other hand, to say it, the doer of the same deed would go, sacramentis munitus, to endless bliss. What rule of morality, what eternal law of right and wrong, could remain in the hearts of men born and bred under the shadow of so hideous a deception ?

And the shadow did not pass at once, when the Pope's authority was thrown off. Henry VIII evidently thought that if the Pope could make right and wrong, perhaps he could do likewise. Elizabeth seems to have fancied, at one weak moment, that the Pope had the power of making her marriage with Leicester right, instead of wrong.

Moreover, when the moral canon of the Pope's will was gone, there was for a while no canon of morality left. The average morality of Elizabeth's reign was not so much low, as capricious, self-willed, fortuitous; magnificent one day in virtue, terrible the next in vice. It was not till more than one generation had grown up and died with the Bible in their hands, that Englishmen and Germans began to understand (what Frenchmen and Italians did not understand) that they were to be judged by the everlasting laws of a God who was no respecter of persons.

So, again, of the virtue of truth. Truth, for its own sake, had never been a virtue with the Roman clergy. Father Newman informs us that it need not, and on the whole ought not to be; that cunning is the weapon which Heaven has given to the saints wherewith to withstand the brute male force of the wicked world which marries and is given in marriage. Whether his notion be doctrinally correct or not, it is at least historically so.

Ever since Pope Stephen forged an epistle from St Peter to Pepin, King of the Franks, and sent it with some filings of the saint's holy chains, that he might bribe him to invade Italy, destroy the Lombards, and confirm to him the 'Patrimony of St Peter'; ever since the first monk forged the first charter of his monastery, or dug the first heathen Anglo-Saxon out of his barrow, to make him a martyr and a worker of miracles, because his own minister did not 'draw' as well as the rival minster ten miles off – ever since this had the heap of lies been accumulating, spawning, breeding fresh lies, till men began to ask themselves whether truth was a thing worth troubling a practical man's head about, and to suspect that tongues were given to men, as claws to cats and horns to bulls, simply for purposes of offence and defence.

II

Dr Newman *to* Messrs Macmillan and Co.

The Oratory, Dec. 30, 1863.

Gentlemen,

I do not write to you with any controversial purpose, which would be preposterous; but I address you simply because of your special interest in a Magazine which bears your name.

That highly respected name you have associated with a Magazine, of which the January number has been sent to me by this morning's post, with a pencil mark calling my attention to page 217.

There, apropos of Queen Elizabeth, I read as follows:

Truth, for its own sake, had never been a virtue with the Roman clergy. Father Newman informs us that it need not, and on the whole ought not to be; that cunning is the weapon which Heaven has given to the saints wherewith to withstand the brute male force of the wicked world which marries and is given in marriage. Whether his notion be doctrinally correct or not, it is at least historically so.

There is no reference at the foot of the page to any words of mine, much less any quotation from my writings, in justification of this statement.

I should not dream of expostulating with the writer of such a passage, nor with the editor who could insert it without appending evidence in proof of its allegations. Nor do I want any reparation from either of them. I neither complain of them for their act, nor should I thank them if they reversed it. Nor do I even write to you with any desire of troubling you to send me an answer. I do but wish to draw the attention of yourselves, as gentlemen, to a grave and gratuitous slander, with which I feel confident you will be sorry to find associated a name so eminent as yours.

I am, Gentlemen,
Your obedient Servant,
(Signed) John H. Newman.

III

The REV. CHARLES KINGSLEY *to* DR NEWMAN.

Eversley Rectory, January 6, 1864.

REVEREND SIR,

I have seen a letter of yours to Mr Macmillan, in which you complain of some expressions of mine in an article in the January number of Macmillan's Magazine.

That my words were just, I believed from many passages of your writings; but the document to which I expressly referred was one of your Sermons on 'Subjects of the Day', No. XX, in the volume published in 1844, and entitled 'Wisdom and Innocence'.

It was in consequence of that Sermon, that I finally shook off the strong influence which your writings exerted on me; and for much of which I still owe you a deep debt of gratitude.

I am most happy to hear from you that I mistook (as I understand from your letter) your meaning; and I shall be most happy, on your showing me that I have wronged you, to retract my accusation as publicly as I have made it.

I am, Reverend Sir,
Your faithful Servant,
(Signed) CHARLES KINGSLEY.

IV

DR NEWMAN *to the* REV. CHARLES KINGSLEY.

The Oratory, Birmingham,
January 7, 1864.

REVEREND SIR,

I have to acknowledge your letter of the 6th, informing me that you are the writer of an article in Macmillan's Magazine, in which I am mentioned, and referring generally to a Protestant sermon of mine, of seventeen pages, published by me, as Vicar of St Mary's, in 1844, and treating of the bearing of the Christian towards the world, and of the character of the reaction of that bearing upon him; and also, referring to my works *passim*; in justification of your statement, categorical and definite, that

'Father Newman informs us that truth for its own sake need not, and on the whole ought not to be, a virtue with the Roman clergy.'

I have only to remark, in addition to what I have already said with great sincerity to Messrs Macmillan and Co., in the letter of which you speak, and to which I refer you, that, when I wrote to them, no person whatever, whom I had ever seen or heard of, had occurred to me as the author of the statement in question. When I received your letter, taking upon yourself the authorship, I was amazed.

I am, Reverend Sir,
Your obedient Servant,
(Signed) JOHN H. NEWMAN.

V

DR NEWMAN *to* X. Y., ESQ.[1]

The Oratory, January 8, 1864.

DEAR SIR,

I thank you for the friendly tone of your letter of the 5th just received, and I wish to reply to it with the frankness which it invites. I have heard from Mr Kingsley, avowing himself, to my extreme astonishment, the author of the passage about which I wrote to Messrs Macmillan. No one, whose name I had ever heard, crossed my mind as the writer in their Magazine: and, had any one said that it was Mr Kingsley, I should have laughed in his face. Certainly, I saw the initials at the end; but, you must recollect, I live out of the world; and, I must own, if Messrs Macmillan will not think the confession rude, that, as far as I remember, I never before saw even the outside of their Magazine. And so of the Editor: when I saw his name on the cover, it conveyed to me absolutely no idea whatever. I am not defending myself, but merely stating what was the fact; and as to the article, I said to myself, 'Here is a young scribe, who is making himself a cheap reputation by smart hits at safe objects.'

All this will make you see, not only how I live out of the world, but also how wanton I feel it to have been in the parties concerned

---

[1] A gentleman who interposed between Mr Kingsley and Dr Newman.

thus to let fly at me. Were I in active controversy with the Anglican body, or any portion of it, as I have been before now, I should consider untrue assertions about me to be in a certain sense a rule of the game, as times go, though God forbid that I should indulge in them myself in the case of another. I have never been very sensitive of such attacks; rarely taken notice of them. Now, when I have long ceased from controversy, they continue: they have lasted incessantly from the year 1833 to this day. They do not ordinarily come in my way: when they do, I let them pass through indolence. Sometimes friends send me specimens of them; and sometimes they are such as I am bound to answer, if I would not compromise interests which are dearer to me than life. The January number of the Magazine was sent to me, I know not by whom, friend or foe, with the passage on which I have animadverted, emphatically, not to say indignantly, scored against. Nor can there be a better proof that there was a call upon me to notice it, than the astounding fact that you can so calmly (excuse me) 'confess plainly' of yourself, as you do, 'that you had read the passage, and did not even think that I or any of my communion would think it unjust.'

Most wonderful phenomenon! An educated man, breathing English air, and walking in the light of the nineteenth century, thinks that neither I nor any members of my communion feel any difficulty in allowing that 'Truth for its own sake need not, and on the whole ought not to be, a virtue with the Roman clergy'; nay, that they are not at all surprised to be told that 'Father Newman had informed' the world, that such is the standard of morality acknowledged, acquiesced in, by his co-religionists! But, I suppose, in truth, there is nothing at all, however base, up to the high mark of Titus Oates, which a Catholic may not expect to be believed of him by Protestants, however honourable and hardheaded. However, dismissing this natural train of thought, I observe on your avowal as follows; and I think what I shall say will commend itself to your judgment as soon as I say it.

I think you will allow then, that there is a broad difference between a virtue, considered in itself as a principle or rule, and the application or limits of it in human conduct. Catholics and Protestants, in their view of the substance of the moral virtues, agree, but they carry them out variously in detail; and in particular instances, and in the case of particular actors or writers, with but indifferent success. Truth is the same in itself and in substance to Catholic and Protestant; so is purity: both virtues are to be referred to that moral sense which is the natural possession of us all. But when we come to the question in detail, whether this or that act in particular is conformable to the rule of truth, or again to the rule of purity; then sometimes there is a difference of opinion between individuals, sometimes between schools, and sometimes between religious communions. I, on my side, have long thought, even before I was a Catholic, that the Protestant system, as such, leads to a lax observance of the rule of purity; Protestants think that the Catholic system, as such, leads to a lax observance of the rule of truth. I am very sorry that they should think so, but I cannot help it; I lament their mistake, but I bear it as I may. If Mr Kingsley had said no more than this, I should not have felt it necessary to criticize such an ordinary remark. But, as I should be committing a crime, heaping dirt upon my soul, and storing up for myself remorse and confusion of face at a future day, if I applied my abstract belief of the latent sensuality of Protestantism, on *à priori* reasoning, to individuals, to living persons, to authors and men of name, and said (not to make disrespectful allusion to the living) that Bishop Van Mildert, or the Rev. Dr Spry, or Dean Milner, or the Rev. Charles Simeon 'informs us that chastity for its own sake need not be, and on the whole ought not to be, a virtue with the Anglican clergy', and then, when challenged for the proof, said, '*Vide* Van Mildert's Bampton Lectures and Simeon's Skeleton Sermons *passim*'; and, as I should only make the matter still worse, if I pointed to flagrant instances of paradoxical divines or of bad clergymen among Protestants, as, for instance, to that popular London preacher at the end of last century who advocated polygamy in print; so, in like manner, for a writer, when he is criticizing definite historical facts of the sixteenth century, which stand or fall on their own merits, to go out of his way to have a fling at an unpopular name, living but 'down', and boldly to say to those who know no better, who know nothing but what he tells them, who take their tradition of historical facts from him, who do not know *me* – to say of *me*, 'Father Newman *informs* us that Truth for its own sake *need not be, and on the whole ought not to be,* a virtue with the Roman clergy', and to be thus brilliant and antithetical (save the mark!) in the very cause of Truth, is a proceeding of so special a character as to lead me to exclaim, after the pattern of the celebrated saying, 'O Truth, how many lies are told in thy name!'

Such being the state of the case, I think I shall carry you along with me when I say, that, if there is to be any explanation in the Magazine of so grave an inadvertence, it concerns the two gentlemen who are responsible for it, of what complexion that explanation shall be. For me, it is not I who ask for it; I look on mainly as a spectator, and shall praise or blame, according to my best judgment, as I see what they do. Not that, in so acting, I am implying a doubt of all that you tell me of them; but 'handsome is, that handsome does'. If they set about proving their point, or, should they find that impossible, if they say so, in either case I shall call them *men*. But – bear with me for harbouring a suspicion which Mr Kingsley's letter to me has inspired – if they propose merely to smooth the matter over by publishing to the world that I have 'complained', or that 'they yield to my letters, expostulations, representations, explanations', or that 'they are quite ready to be convinced of their mistake, if I will convince them', or that 'they have profound respect for me, but really they are not the only persons who have gathered from my writings what they have said of me', or that 'they are unfeignedly surprised that I should visit in their case what I have passed over in the case of others', or that 'they have ever had a true sense of my good points, but cannot be expected to be blind to my faults', if this be the sum total of what they are to say, and they ignore the fact that the *onus probandi* of a very definite accusation lies upon them, and that they have no right to throw the burden upon others, then, I say with submission, they had better let it all alone, as far as I am concerned, for a half-measure settles nothing.

January 10 – I will add, that any letter addressed to me by Mr Kingsley, I account public property; not so, should you favour me with any fresh communication yourself.

I am, Dear Sir,
Yours faithfully,
(Signed) JOHN H. NEWMAN.

VI

The REV. CHARLES KINGSLEY *to* DR NEWMAN.

Eversley Rectory, January 14, 1864.

REVEREND SIR,

I have the honour to acknowledge your answer to my letter. I have also seen your letter to Mr X. Y. On neither of them shall I make any comment, save to say, that, if you fancy that I have attacked you because you were, as you please to term it, 'down', you do me a great injustice; and also, that the suspicion expressed in the latter part of your letter to Mr X. Y., is needless.

The course, which you demand of me, is the only course fit for a gentleman; and, as the tone of your letters (even more than their language) make me feel, to my very deep pleasure, that my opinion of the meaning of your words was a mistaken one, I shall send at once to Macmillan's Magazine the few lines which I inclose.

You say, that you will consider my letters as public. You have every right to do so.

> I remain, Reverend Sir,
> Yours faithfully,
> (Signed) C. KINGSLEY.

VII

[This will appear in the next number]

TO THE EDITOR OF MACMILLAN'S MAGAZINE.

SIR,

In your last number I made certain allegations against the teaching of the Rev. Dr Newman, which were founded on a Sermon of his, entitled 'Wisdom and Innocence' (the sermon will be fully described, as to[1] . . .).

Dr Newman has, by letter, expressed in the strongest terms, his denial of the meaning which I have put upon his words.

---

[1] Here follows a word or half-word, which neither I nor any one else to whom I have shown the MS can decypher. I have at p. 13 filled in for Mr Kingsley what I understood him to mean by 'fully'. – J. H. N.

No man knows the use of words better than Dr Newman; no man, therefore, has a better right to define what he does, or does not, mean by them.

It only remains, therefore, for me to express my hearty regret at having so seriously mistaken him; and my hearty pleasure at finding him on the side of Truth, in this, or any other, matter.

(Signed) CHARLES KINGSLEY.

VIII

DR NEWMAN *to the* REV. CHARLES KINGSLEY.

The Oratory, January 17, 1864.

REVEREND SIR,

Since you do no more than announce to me your intention of inserting in Macmillan's Magazine the letter, a copy of which you are so good as to transcribe for me, perhaps I am taking a liberty in making any remarks to you upon it. But then, the very fact of your showing it to me seems to invite criticism; and so sincerely do I wish to bring this painful matter to an immediate settlement, that, at the risk of being officious, I avail myself of your courtesy to express the judgment which I have carefully formed upon it.

I believe it to be your wish to do me such justice as is compatible with your duty of upholding the consistency and quasi-infallibility which is necessary for a periodical publication; and I am far from expecting any thing from you which would be unfair to Messrs Macmillan and Co. Moreover, I am quite aware, that the reading public, to whom your letter is virtually addressed, cares little for the wording of an explanation, provided it be made aware of the fact that an explanation has been given.

Nevertheless, after giving your letter the benefit of both these considerations, I am sorry to say I feel it my duty to withhold from it the approbation which I fain would bestow.

Its main fault is, that, quite contrary to your intention, it will be understood by the general reader to intimate, that I have been confronted with definite extracts from my works, and have laid before you my own interpretations of them. Such a proceeding I have indeed challenged, but have not been so fortunate as to bring about.

But besides, I gravely disapprove of the letter as a whole. The grounds of this dissatisfaction will be best understood by you, if I place in parallel columns its paragraphs, one by one, and what I conceive will be the popular reading of them.

This I proceed to do.

> I have the honour to be,
> Reverend Sir,
> Your obedient Servant,
> (Signed) JOHN H. NEWMAN.

Mr Kingsley's Letter.	*Unjust, but too probable, popular rendering of it.*
1. Sir – In your last number I made certain allegations against the teaching of the Rev. Dr Newman, which were founded on a Sermon of his, entitled 'Wisdom and Innocence', preached by him as Vicar of St Mary's, and published in 1844.	
2. Dr Newman has, by letter, expressed in the strongest terms his denial of the meaning which I have put upon his words.	2. I have set before Dr Newman, as he challenged me to do, extracts from his writings, and he has affixed to them what he conceives to be their legitimate sense, to the denial of that in which I understood them.
3. No man knows the use of words better than Dr Newman; no man, therefore, has a better right to define what he does, or does not, mean by them.	3. He has done this with the skill of a great master of verbal fence, who knows, as well as any man living, how to insinuate a doctrine without commiting himself to it.
4. It only remains, therefore, for me to express my hearty regret at having so seriously mistaken him, and my hearty pleasure at finding him on the side of Truth, in this or any other matter.	4. However, while I heartily regret that I have so seriously mistaken the sense which he assures me his words were meant to bear, I cannot but feel a hearty pleasure also, at having brought him, for once in a way, to confess that after all truth is a Christian virtue.

IX

REV. CHARLES KINGSLEY *to* DR NEWMAN.

Eversley Rectory, January 18, 1864.

REVEREND SIR,

I do not think it probable that the good sense and honesty of the British Public will misinterpret my apology, in the way in which you expect.

Two passages in it, which I put in in good faith and good

feeling, may, however, be open to such a bad use, and I have written to Messrs Macmillan to omit them; viz the words, 'No man knows the use of words better than Dr Newman'; and those, 'My hearty pleasure at finding him in the truth (*sic*) on this or any other matter'.

As to your Art. 2, it seems to me, that, by referring publicly to the Sermon on which my allegations are founded, I have given, not only you, but every one an opportunity of judging of their injustice. Having done this, and having frankly accepted your assertion that I was mistaken, I have done as much as one English gentleman can expect from another.

> I have the honour to be,
> Reverend Sir,
> Your obedient Servant,
> (Signed) CHARLES KINGSLEY.

X

DR NEWMAN *to* MESSRS MACMILLAN & CO.

The Oratory, January 22, 1864.

GENTLEMEN,

Mr Kingsley, the writer of the paragraph to which I called your attention on the 30th of last month, has shown his wish to recall words, which I considered a great affront to myself, and a worse insult to the Catholic priesthood. He has sent me the draft of a Letter which he proposes to insert in the February number of your Magazine; and, when I gave him my criticisms upon it, he had the good feeling to withdraw two of its paragraphs.

However, he did not remove that portion of it, to which, as I told him, lay my main objection.

That portion ran as follows:

Dr Newman has by letter expressed in the strongest terms his denial of the meaning which I have put upon his words.

My objection to this sentence, which (with the addition of a reference to a Protestant sermon of mine, which he says formed the ground of his assertion, and of an expression of regret at having mistaken me) constitutes, after the withdrawal of the two paragraphs, the whole of his proposed letter, I thus explained to him:

> Its [the proposed letter's] main fault is, that, quite contrary to your intention, it will be understood by the general reader to intimate, that I have been confronted with definite extracts from my works, and have laid before you my own interpretation of them. Such a proceeding I have indeed challenged, but have not been so fortunate as to bring about.

In answer to this representation, Mr Kingsley wrote to me as follows:

> It seems to me, that, by referring publicly to the sermon, on which my allegations are founded, I have given, not only you, but every one, an opportunity of judging of their injustice. Having done this, and having frankly accepted your assertion that I was mistaken, I have done as much as one English gentleman can expect from another.

I received this reply the day before yesterday. It disappointed me, for I had hoped that, with the insertion of a letter from him in your Magazine for February, there would have been an end of the whole matter. However, I have waited forty-eight hours, to give time for his explanation to make its full, and therefore its legitimate impression on my mind. After this interval, I find my judgment of the passage just what it was.

Moreover, since sending to Mr Kingsley that judgment, I have received a letter from a friend at a distance, whom I had consulted, a man about my own age, who lives out of the world of theological controversy and contemporary literature, and whose intellectual habits especially qualify him for taking a clear and impartial view of the force of words. I put before him the passage in your January number, and the writer's proposed letter in February;[1] and I asked him whether I might consider the letter sufficient for its purpose, without saying a word to show him the leaning of my own mind. He answers:

> In answer to your question, whether Mr Kingsley's proposed reparation is sufficient, I have no hesitation in saying, Most decidedly not. Without attempting to quote any passage from your writings which justifies in any manner the language which

[1] viz as it is given above, p. 12. – J. H. N.

he has used in his review, he leaves it to be inferred that the representation, which he has given of your statements and teaching in the sermon to which he refers, is the fair and natural and primary sense of them, and that it is only by your declaring that you did not mean what you really and in effect said, that he finds that he had made a false charge.

This opinion thus given came to me, I repeat, *after* I had sent to Mr Kingsley the letter of objection, of which I have quoted a portion above. You will see that, though the two judgments are independent of each other, they in substance coincide.

It only remains for me then to write to you again; and, in writing to you now, I do no more than I did on the 30 December. I bring the matter before you, without requiring from you any reply.

> I am, Gentlemen,
> Your obedient Servant,
> (Signed) JOHN H. NEWMAN.

XI

Letter of Explanation from MR KINGSLEY, *as it stands in Macmillan's Magazine for February* 1864, p. 368.

TO THE EDITOR OF MACMILLAN'S MAGAZINE.

SIR,

In your last number I made certain allegations against the teaching of Dr John Henry Newman, which I thought were justified by a Sermon of his, entitled 'Wisdom and Innocence' (Sermon 20 of 'Sermons bearing on Subjects of the Day'). Dr Newman has by letter expressed in the strongest terms, his denial of the meaning which I have put upon his words. It only remains, therefore, for me to express my hearty regret at having so seriously mistaken him.

> Yours faithfully,
> (Signed) CHARLES KINGSLEY.

Eversley, January 14, 1864.

XII

Reflections on the above.

I shall attempt a brief analysis of the foregoing correspondence; and I trust that the wording which I shall adopt will not offend against the gravity due both to myself and to the occasion. It is impossible to do justice to the course of thought evolved in it without some familiarity of expression.

Mr Kingsley begins then by exclaiming – 'O the chicanery, the wholesale fraud, the vile hypocrisy, the conscience-killing tyranny of Rome! We have not far to seek for an evidence of it. There's Father Newman to wit: one living specimen is worth a hundred dead ones. He, a Priest writing of Priests, tells us that lying is never any harm.'

I interpose: 'You are taking a most extraordinary liberty with my name. If I have said this, tell me when and where.'

Mr Kingsley replies: 'You said it, Reverend Sir, in a Sermon which you preached, when a Protestant, as Vicar of St Mary's, and published in 1844; and I could read you a very salutary lecture on the effects which that Sermon had at the time on my own opinion of you.'

I make answer: 'Oh . . . *Not*, it seems, as a Priest speaking of Priests – but let us have the passage.'

Mr Kingsley relaxes: 'Do you know, I like your *tone*. From your *tone* I rejoice, greatly rejoice, to be able to believe that you did not mean what you said.'

I rejoin: '*Mean* it! I maintain I never *said* it, whether as a Protestant or as a Catholic.'

Mr Kingsley replies: 'I waive that point.'

I object: 'Is it possible! What? waive the main question! I either said it or I didn't. You have made a monstrous charge against me; direct, distinct, public. You are bound to prove it as directly, as distinctly, as publicly – or to own you can't.'

'Well,' says Mr Kingsley, 'if you are quite sure you did not say it, I'll take your word for it; I really will.'

My *word*! I am dumb. Somehow I thought that it was my *word* that happened to be on trial. The *word* of a Professor of lying, that he does not lie!

But Mr Kingsley re-assures me: 'We are both gentlemen,' he

says: 'I have done as much as one English gentleman can expect from another.'

I begin to see: he thought me a gentleman at the very time that he said I taught lying on system. After all, it is not I, but it is Mr Kingsley who did not mean what he said. 'Habemus confitentem reum.'

So we have confessedly come round to this, preaching without practising; the common theme of satirists from Juvenal to Walter Scott! 'I left Baby Charles and Steenie laying his duty before him,' says King James of the reprobate Dalgarno: 'O Geordie, jingling Geordie, it was grand to hear Baby Charles laying down the guilt of dissimulation, and Steenie lecturing on the turpitude of incontinence.'

While I feel then that Mr Kingsley's February explanation is miserably insufficient in itself for his January enormity, still I feel also that the Correspondence, which lies between these two acts of his, constitutes a real satifaction to those principles of historical and literary justice to which he has given so rude a shock.

Accordingly, I have put it into print, and make no further criticism on Mr Kingsley.

J. H. N.

'WHAT, THEN, DOES DR NEWMAN MEAN?'

A Reply
to
A Pamphlet lately published by Dr Newman
by the
Rev. Charles Kingsley

'WHAT, THEN, DOES DR NEWMAN MEAN?'

Dr Newman has made a great mistake. He has published a correspondence between himself and me, with certain 'Reflexions' and a title-page, which cannot be allowed to pass without a rejoinder.

Before commenting on either, I must give a plain account of the circumstances of the controversy, which seem to have been misunderstood in several quarters. In the January number of *Macmillan's Magazine*, I deliberately and advisedly made use of these words:

> Truth, for its own sake, had never been a virtue with the Roman clergy. Father Newman informs us that it need not, and, on the whole, ought not to be; that cunning is the weapon which Heaven has given to the saints wherewith to withstand the brute male force of the wicked world which marries and is given in marriage.

This accusation I based upon a considerable number of passages in Dr Newman's writings, and especially on a sermon entitled 'Wisdom and Innocence', and preached by Dr Newman as Vicar of St Mary's, and published as No. XX of his 'Sermons on Subjects of the Day'.

Dr Newman wrote, in strong but courteous terms, to Messrs Macmillan and Co. complaining of this language as a slander. I at once took the responsibility on myself, and wrote to Dr Newman.

I had been informed (by a Protestant) that he was in weak health, that he wished for peace and quiet, and was averse to controversy; I therefore felt some regret at having disturbed him: and this regret was increased by the moderate and courteous tone of his letters, though they contained, of course, much from which I differed. I addressed to him the following letter, of which, as I trust every English gentleman will feel, I have no reason to be ashamed:

REVEREND SIR,

I have seen a letter of yours to Mr Macmillan, in which you complain of some expressions of mine in an article in the January number of *Macmillan's Magazine*.

That my words were just, I believed from many passages of your writings; but the document to which I expressly referred was one of your sermons on "Subjects of the Day", No. XX in the volume published in 1844, and entitled "Wisdom and Innocence".

It was in consequence of that sermon that I finally shook off the strong influence which your writings exerted on me, and for much of which I still owe you a deep debt of gratitude.

I am most happy to hear from you that I mistook (as I understand from your letter) your meaning; and I shall be most happy, on your showing me that I have wronged you, to retract my accusation as publicly as I have made it.

I am, Rev. Sir,
Your faithful servant,
CHARLES KINGSLEY.

I received a very moderate answer from Dr Newman, and a short correspondence ensued, which ended in my inserting in the February number of *Macmillan's Magazine* the following apology:

To the Editor of 'MACMILLAN'S MAGAZINE'.

SIR,

In your last number I made certain allegations against the teaching of Dr John Henry Newman, which I thought were justified by a sermon of his, entitled "Wisdom and Innocence" (Sermon XX of "Sermons bearing on Subjects of the Day"). Dr Newman has, by letter, expressed in the strongest terms his denial of the meaning which I have put upon his words. It only remains, therefore, for me to express my hearty regret at having so seriously mistaken him.

Yours faithfully,
CHARLES KINGSLEY.

My object had been throughout to avoid war, because I thought Dr Newman wished for peace. I therefore dropped the question of the meaning of 'many passages of his writings', and confined myself to the sermon entitled 'Wisdom and Innocence', simply to give him an opportunity of settling the dispute on that one ground.

But whether Dr Newman lost his temper, or whether he thought that he had gained an advantage over me, or whether he wanted a more complete apology than I chose to give, whatever, I say, may have been his reasons, he suddenly changed his tone of courtesy and dignity for one of which I shall only say that it shows sadly how the atmosphere of the Romish priesthood has degraded his notions of what is due to himself; and when he published (as I am much obliged to him for doing) the whole correspondence, he appended to it certain reflexions, in which he attempted to convict me of not having believed the accusations which I had made.

There remains for me, then, nothing but to justify my mistake, as far as I can.

I am, of course, precluded from using the sermon entitled 'Wisdom and Innocence' to prove my words. I have accepted Dr Newman's denial that it means what I thought it did: and Heaven forbid that I should withdraw my word once given, at whatever disadvantage to myself. But more. I am informed by those from whose judgment on such points there is no appeal, that '*en hault courage*' and strict honour, I am also precluded, by the terms of my explanation, from using any other of Dr Newman's past writings to prove my assertion. I have declared Dr Newman to have been an honest man up to the 1st of February 1864. It was, as I shall show, only Dr Newman's fault that I ever thought him to be anything else. It depends entirely on Dr Newman whether he shall sustain the reputation which he has so recently acquired. If I give him thereby a fresh advantage in this argument, he is most welcome to it. He needs, it seems to me, as many advantages as possible. But I have a right, in self-justification, to put before the public so much of that sermon, and of the rest of Dr Newman's writings, as will show why I formed so harsh an opinion of them and him, and why I still consider that sermon (whatever may be its meaning) as most dangerous and misleading. And I have a full right to do the same by those 'many passages of Dr Newman's writings' which I left alone at first, simply because I thought that Dr Newman wished for peace.

First, as to the sermon entitled 'Wisdom and Innocence'. It must be remembered always that it is not a Protestant, but a Romish sermon. It is occupied entirely with the attitude of 'the world' to 'Christians' and 'the Church'. By the world appears to be signified, especially, the Protestant public of these realms. What Dr Newman means by Christians, and the Church, he has not left in doubt; for in the preceding sermon (XIX p. 328) he says:

> But, if the truth must be spoken, what are the humble monk, and the holy nun, and other regulars, as they are called, but Christians after the very pattern given us in Scripture? What have they done but this – continue in the world the Christianity of the Bible? Did our Saviour come on earth suddenly, as He will one day visit, in whom would He see the features of the Christians He and His apostles left behind them, but in them? Who but these give up home and friends, wealth and ease, good name and liberty of will, for the kingdom of heaven? Where shall we find the image of St Paul, or St Peter, or St John, or of Mary the mother of Mark, or of Philip's daughters, but in those who, whether they remain in seclusion, or are sent over the earth, have calm faces, and sweet plaintive voices, and spare frames, and gentle manners, and hearts weaned from the world, and wills subdued; and for their meekness meet with insult, and for their purity with slander, and for their gravity with suspicion, and for their courage with cruelty . . .

This is his definition of Christians. And in the sermon itself he sufficiently defines what he means by 'the Church' in two 'notes' of her character, which he shall give in his own words (Sermon XX, p. 316):

> What, for instance, though we grant that sacramental confession and the celibacy of the clergy do tend to consolidate the body politic in the relation of rulers and subjects, or, in other words, to aggrandize the priesthood? for how can the Church be one body without such relation? . . .

Monks and nuns the only perfect Christians; sacramental confession, and the celibacy of the clergy notes of the Church; the laity in relation to the clergy of subjects to rulers. What more? If I, like others, on the strength of Dr Newman's own definitions, gave to his advice to Christians concerning 'wisdom', 'prudence', 'silence', the meaning which they would have in the mouth of a

Romish teacher – St Alfonso da Liguori, for instance – whom can Dr Newman blame for the mistake, save himself?

But to the sermon itself; the test of which is from Matthew x 16. It begins by stating that the Church has been always helpless and persecuted, in proportion to its purity. Dr Newman, then asks, how Christians are to defend themselves if they might not fight? and answers, 'They were allowed the arms, that is, the arts, of the defenceless.' He shows how the weaker animals are enabled to defend themselves by various means, among which he enumerates 'natural cunning, which enables them to elude or even to destroy their enemies.' He goes on to show how the same holds good in our own species in the case of 'a captive, effeminate race'; of 'slaves'; of 'ill-used and oppressed children'; of the 'subjects of a despot'. 'They exercise the inalienable right of self-defence in such methods as they best may; only, since human nature is unscrupulous, guilt or innocence is all the same to them, if it works their purpose.'

He goes on to point out the analogy between these facts and the conduct fit for Christians.

> The servants of Christ are forbidden to defend themselves by violence; but they are not forbidden other means: direct means are not allowed, but others are even commanded. For instance, foresight, 'beware of men': avoidance, 'when they persecute you in one city, flee into another': prudence and skill, as in the text, 'Be ye wise as serpents.'

The mention of the serpent reminds him of the serpent in Paradise; and he says,

> Considering that the serpent was chosen by the enemy of mankind as the instrument of his temptations in Paradise, it is very remarkable that Christ should choose it as the pattern of wisdom for His followers. It is as if He appealed to the whole world of sin, and to the bad arts by which the feeble gain advantages over the strong. It is as if He set before us the craft and treachery, the perfidy of the slave, and bade us extract a lesson even from so great an evil. It is as if the more we are forbidden violence, the more we are exhorted to prudence; as if it were our bounden duty to rival the wicked in endowments of mind, and to excel them in their exercise.

Dr Newman then goes on to assert, that 'if there be one reproach more than another which has been cast upon' the Church, 'it is that of fraud and cunning.' He quotes the imputations of craftiness and deceitfulness thrown upon St Paul, and even of 'deceit' upon our Lord himself. He then says that 'Priestcraft has ever been considered the badge, and its imputation as a kind of note, of the Church.' He asserts that the accusation has been, save in a few exceptions, unfounded; and that 'the words "craft" and "hypocrisy" are but the version of "wisdom" and "harmlessness" in the language of the world.'

It is remarkable, however, that not only is harmlessness the corrective of wisdom, securing it against the corruption of craft and deceit, as stated in the text: but innocence, simplicity, implicit obedience to God, tranquillity of mind, contentment, these and the like virtues are in themselves a sort of wisdom; I mean, they produce the same results as wisdom, because God works for those who do not work for themselves; and thus they especially incur the charge of craft at the hands of the world, because they pretend to so little, yet effect so much. This circumstance admits dwelling on.

He then goes on to mention seven heads:

First, sobriety, self-restraint, control of word and feeling, which religious men exercise, have about them an appearance of being artificial, because they are not natural; and of being artful, because artificial

and adds shortly after, that

those who would be holy and blameless, the sons of God, find so much in the world to unsettle and defile them, that they are necessarily forced upon a strict self-restraint, lest they should receive injury from such intercourse with it as is unavoidable; and this self-restraint is the first thing which makes holy persons seem wanting in openness and manliness.

Next he points out that 'religious men are a mystery to the world; and being a mystery, they will in mere self-defence be called by the world mysterious, dark, subtle, designing.' Next, that 'it is very difficult to make the world understand the difference between an outward obedience and an inward assent.' He then instances the relations between the early Christians and the heathen magistrates; and adds, that 'when religious men outwardly conform, on the score of duty, to the powers that be, the world is easily led into the mistake that they have renounced their opinions, as well as submitted their actions; and it feels or affects surprise, to find that their opinions remain; and it considers, or calls this, an inconsistency, or a duplicity': with more to the same purpose.

Next, the silent resignation of Christians is set forth as a cause of the world's suspicion; and 'so is their confidence, in spite of their apparent weakness, their cause will triumph.'

Another cause of the world's suspicion is, the unexpected success of religious men.

Another, that the truth has in itself the power of spreading, without instruments, 'making the world impute' to secret management that uniformity, which is nothing but the echo of the One Living and True Word.

Another, that when Christians prosper, contrary to their own expectations, 'it looks like deceit to show surprise, and to disclaim the work themselves.'

And lastly, because God works for Christians, and they are successful, when they only mean to be dutiful.

But what duplicity does the world think it, to speak of conscience, or honour, or propriety, or delicacy, or to give other tokens of personal motives, when the event seems to show that a calculation of results has been the actuating principle at bottom. It is God who designs, but His servants seem designing. . . .

Dr Newman then goes on to point out how

Jacob is thought worldly wise in his dealings with Laban, whereas he was a 'plain man', simply obedient to the angel. . . . Moses is sometimes called sagacious and shrewd in his measures or his law, as if wise acts might not come from the source of wisdom. . . . Bishops have been called hypocritical in submitting and yet opposing themselves to the civil power, in a matter of plain duty, if a popular movement was the consequence; and then hypocritical again, if they did their best to repress it. And, in like manner, theological doctrine or ecclesiastical usages are styled politic if they are but salutary; as if the Lord of the Church, who has willed her sovereignty, might not effect it by secondary causes. What, for instance, though we grant that sacramental confession and the celibacy of the clergy do tend to consolidate the body politic in the relation of rulers and subjects, or, in other words, to aggrandise the priesthood? For how can the Church be one body without such relation; and why should not He, who has decreed that there should be unity, take measures to secure it?

The reason of these suspicions on the part of the world is then stated to be, that 'men do not like to hear of the interposition of Providence in the affairs of the world; and they invidiously ascribe ability and skill to His agents, to escape the thought of an Infinite Wisdom and an Almighty Power. . . .'

The sermon then closes with a few lines of great beauty, in that style which has won deservedly for Dr Newman the honour of being the most perfect orator of this generation; but they have no reference to the question in hand, save the words, 'We will glory in what they disown.'

I have tried conscientiously to give a fair and complete digest of this, to me, very objectionable and dangerous sermon. I have omitted no passage in which Dr Newman guards himself against the conclusions which I drew from it; and none, I verily believe, which is required for the full understanding of its general drift. I have abstained from all comment as I went on, in order not to prejudice the minds of my readers. But I must now turn round and ask, whether the mistake into which Dr Newman asserts me to have fallen was not a very reasonable one; and whether the average of educated Englishmen, in reading that sermon, would not be too likely to fall into the same? I put on it, as I thought, the plain and straightforward signification. I find I am wrong; and nothing is left for me but to ask, with some astonishment, What, then, did the sermon mean? Why was it preached? To insinuate that a Church which had sacramental confession and a celibate clergy was the only true Church? Or to insinuate that the admiring young gentlemen who listened to him stood to their fellow-countrymen in the relation of the early Christians to the heathen Romans? Or that Queen Victoria's Government was to the Church of England what Nero's or Diocletian's was to the Church of Rome? It may have been so. I know that men used to suspect Dr Newman – I have been inclined to do so myself – of writing a whole sermon, not for the sake of the text or of the matter, but for the sake of one single passing hint – one phrase, one epithet, one little barbed arrow which, as he swept magnificently past on the stream of his calm eloquence, seemingly unconscious of all presences, save those unseen, he delivered unheeded, as with his finger-tip, to the very heart of an initiated hearer, never to be withdrawn again. I do not blame him for that. It is one of the highest triumphs of oratoric power, and may be employed honestly and fairly, by any person who has the skill to do it honestly and fairly. But then – Why did he entitle his sermon 'Wisdom and Innocence'?

What, then, could I think that Dr Newman meant? I found a preacher bidding Christians imitate, to some undefined point, the 'arts' of the basest of animals and of men, and even of the Devil himself. I found him, by a strange perversion of Scripture, insinuating that St Paul's conduct and manner were such as naturally to bring down on him the reputation of being a crafty deceiver. I found him – horrible to have to say it – even hinting the same of One greater than St Paul. I found him denying or explaining away the existence of that priestcraft which is a notorious fact to every honest student of history; and justifying (as far as I can understand him) that double-dealing by which prelates, in the middle age, too often played off alternately the sovereign against the people and the people against the sovereign, careless which was in the right, as long as their own power gained by the move. I found him actually using of such (and, as I thought, of himself and his party likewise) the words, 'They yield outwardly; to assent inwardly were to betray the faith. Yet they are called deceitful and double-dealing, because they do as much as they can, and not more than they may.' I found him telling Christians that they will always seem 'artificial', and 'wanting in openness and manliness'; that they will always be 'a mystery' to the world, and that the world will always think them rogues; and bidding them glory in what the world (*i.e.* the rest of their fellow-countrymen) disown, and say with Mawworm, 'I like to be despised.'

Now how was I to know that the preacher, who had the reputation of being the most acute man of his generation, and of having a specially intimate acquaintance with the weaknesses of the human heart, was utterly blind to the broad meaning and the plain practical result of a sermon like this, delivered before fanatic and hot-headed young men, who hung over his every word? That he did not foresee that they would think that they obeyed him, by becoming affected, artificial, sly, shifty, ready for concealments and equivocations? That he did not foresee that they, hearing his words concerning priestcraft and double-dealing, and being engaged in the study of the Medieval Church, they consider the same chicanery allowed to them which they found practised but too often by the Medieval Church? or even go to the Romish casuists, to discover what amount of cunning did or did not come under Dr Newman's one passing warning against craft and deceit? In a word, that he did not foresee that the natural result of the sermon on the minds of his disciples would be, to make them suspect that truth was not a virtue for its own sake, but only for the sake of the spread of 'catholic opinions', and the 'salvation of their own souls'; and that cunning was the weapon which Heaven had allowed to them to defend themselves against the persecuting Protestant public?

All England stood round in those days, and saw that this would be the outcome of Dr Newman's teaching. How was I to know that he did not see it himself?

And as a fact, his teaching had this outcome. Whatever else it did, it did this. In proportion as young men absorbed it into themselves, it injured their straightforwardness and truthfulness. The fact is notorious to all England. It spread misery and shame into many an English home. The net practical result of Dr Newman's teachings on truthfulness cannot be better summed up than by one of his own disciples, Mr Ward, who, in his 'Ideal of a Christian Church', page 382, says thus:

> Candour is rather an intellectual than a moral virtue, and by no means either universally or distinctively characteristic of the saintly mind.

Dr Newman ought to have told his disciple, when he wrote those words, that he was on the highroad to the father of lies; and he ought to have told the world, too, that such was his opinion; unless he wished it to fall into the mistake into which I fell — namely, that he had wisdom enough to know the practical result of his words, and therefore meant what they seemed to say.

Dr Newman has nothing to blame for that mistake, save his own method. If he would (while a member of the Church of England) persist (as in this sermon) in dealing with matters dark, offensive, doubtful, sometimes actually forbidden, at least according to the notions of the great majority of English Churchmen; if he would always do so in a tentative, paltering way, seldom or never letting the world know how much he believed, how far he intended to go; if, in a word, his method of teaching was a suspicious one, what wonder if the minds of men were filled with suspicions of him? What wonder if they said of him (as he so naïvely, in one of his letters, expresses his fear that they will say again), 'Dr Newman has the skill of a great master of verbal fence, who knows, as well as any man living, how to insinuate a doctrine without committing himself to it?' If he told the world, as he virtually does in this sermon, 'I know that my conduct looks like cunning; but it is only the "arts" of the defenceless': what wonder if the world answered, 'No. It is what it seems. That is just what we call cunning; a habit of mind which, once indulged, is certain to go on from bad to worse, till the man becomes — like too many of the medieval clergy who indulged in it — utterly untrustworthy.' Dr Newman, I say, has no one to blame but himself. The world is not so blind but that it will soon find out an honest man if he will take the trouble of talking and acting like one. No one would have suspected him to be an honest man, if he had not perversely chosen to assume a style which (as he himself confesses) the world always associates with dishonesty.

When, therefore, Dr Newman says (p. 10 of his pamphlet) that 'he supposes, in truth, there is nothing at all, however base, up to the high mark of Titus Oates, which a Catholic may not expect to be believed of him by Protestants, however honourable and hard-headed', he is stating a mere phantom of his own brain. It is not so. I do not believe it ever was so. In the days when Jesuits were inciting fanatics to assassinate Queen Elizabeth, and again in the days of the Gunpowder Plot, there was deservedly a very strong feeling against Romish priests, and against a few laymen who were their dupes; and it was the recollection of that which caused the 'Titus Oates' tragedy, which Dr Newman so glibly flings in our teeth, omitting (or forgetting) that Oates' villany would have been impossible without the preceding villanies of Popish fanatics, and that he was unmasked, condemned, and punished by the strong and great arm of British law. But there was never, I believe, even in the worst times, any general belief that Catholics, simply as such, must be villains.

There is none now. The Catholic laity of these realms are just as much respected and trusted as the Protestants, when their conduct justifies that respect and trust, as it does in the case of all save a few wild Irish; and so are the Romish priests, as long as they show themselves good and honest men, who confine themselves to the care of their flock. If there is (as there is) a strong distrust of certain Catholics, it is restricted to the proselytizing priests among them; and especially to those who, like Dr Newman, have turned round upon their mother-Church (I had almost said their mother-country) with contumely and slander. And I confess, also, that this public dislike is very rapidly increasing, for reasons which I shall leave Dr Newman and his advisers to find out for themselves.

I go on now to other words of Dr Newman, from which (as I told him in my first letter) I had conceived an opinion unfavourable to his honesty.

I shall be expected to adduce, first and foremost, the too notorious No. 90 of 'Tracts for the Times'. I shall not do so. On reading that tract over again, I have been confirmed in the opinion which I formed of it at first, that, questionable as it was, it was not meant to be consciously dishonest; that some few sayings in it were just and true; that many of its extravagances were pardonable, as the natural fruit of a revulsion against the popular cry of those days, which called on clergymen to interpret the Articles only in their Calvinistic sense, instead of including under them (as their wise framers intended) not only the Calvinistic, but the Anglican form of thought. There were pages in it which shocked me, and which shock me still. I will instance the commentaries on the 5th, on the 7th, on the 9th, and on the 12th Articles; because in them Dr Newman seemed to me trying to make the Articles say the very thing which (I believe) the Articles were meant not to say. But I attributed to him no intentional dishonesty. The fullest licence of interpretation should be given to every man who is bound by the letter of a document. The *animus imponentium* should be heard of as little as possible, because it is almost certain to become merely the *animus interpretantium*. And more: Every excuse was to be made for a man struggling desperately to keep himself in what was, in fact, his right place, to remain a member of the Church of England, where Providence had placed him, while he felt himself irresistibly attracted towards Rome. But I saw in that tract a fearful danger for the writer. It was but too probable, that if he continued to demand of that subtle brain of his, such *tours de force* as he had all but succeeded in performing, when he tried to show that the Article against 'the sacrifice of masses' 'did not speak against the mass itself', he would surely end in one or other of two misfortunes. He would either destroy his own sense of honesty – *i.e.* conscious truthfulness – and become a dishonest person; or he would destroy his common sense – *i.e.* unconscious truthfulness, and become the slave and puppet seemingly of his own logic, really of his own fancy, ready to believe anything, however preposterous, into which he could, for the moment, argue himself. I thought, for years past, that he had become the former; I now see that he has become the latter.

I beg pardon for saying so much about myself. But this is a personal matter between Dr Newman and me, and I say what I say simply to show, not Dr Newman, but my fellow-Protestants, that my opinion of him was not an 'impulsive' or 'hastily-formed one'. I know his writings of old, and now. But I was so far just to him, that No. 90, which made all the rest of England believe him a dishonest man, had not the same effect on me.

But again –

I found Dr Newman, while yet (as far as could be now discovered) a member of the Church of England, aiding and abetting the publication of certain 'Lives of the English Saints', of which I must say, that no such public outrage on historic truth, and on plain common sense, has been perpetrated in this generation. I do not intend to impute to any of the gentlemen who wrote these lives – and more than one of whom, I believe, I knew personally – the least deliberate intention to deceive. They said what they believed; at least, what they had been taught to believe that they ought to believe. And who had taught them? Dr Newman can best answer that question. He had, at least, that power over them, and in those days over hundreds more, which genius can always command. He might have used it well. He might have made those 'Lives of Saints', what they ought to have been, books to turn the hearts of the children to the Fathers, and to make the present generation acknowledge and respect the true sanctity which there was, in spite of all mistakes, in those great men of old – a sanctity founded on true virtue and true piety, which required no tawdry super-structure of lying and ridiculous wonders. He might have said to the author of the 'Life of St Augustine', when he found him, in the heat and haste of youthful fanaticism, outraging historic truth and the law of evidence: 'This must not be. Truth for its own sake is a more precious thing than any purpose, however pious and useful, which we may have in hand.' But when I found him allowing the world to accept, as notoriously sanctioned by him, such statements as are found in that life, was my mistake a hasty, or far-fetched, or unfounded one, when I concluded that he did not care for truth for its own sake, or teach his disciples to regard it as a virtue? I found that 'Life of St Augustine' saying, that though the pretended visit of St Peter to England wanted historic evidence,

> yet it has undoubtedly been received as a pious opinion by the Church at large, as we learn from some often-quoted words of St Innocent I (who wrote AD 416), that St Peter was instrumental in the conversion of the West generally. And this sort of argument, though it ought to be kept quite distinct from documentary and historic proof, and will form no substitute for such proof with those who stipulate for something like legal accuracy in inquiries of this nature, will not be without its effect upon devout minds, accustomed to rest in the thought of God's watchful guardianship over His Church.

And much more in the same tone, which is worthily, and consistently summed up by the question:

> On what evidence do we put faith in the existence of St George, the patron of England? Upon such, assuredly, as an acute critic or skilful pleader might easily scatter to the winds; the belief of prejudiced or credulous witnesses; the unwritten record of empty pageants and bauble decorations. On the side of scepticism might be exhibited a powerful array of suspicious legends and exploded acts. Yet, after all, what Catholic is there but would count it a profaneness to question the existence of St George?

When I found Dr Newman allowing his disciples – members, even then, of the Protestant Church of England – in page after page, in Life after Life, to talk nonsense of this kind, which is not only sheer Popery, but saps the very foundation of historic truth, was it so wonderful that I conceived him to have taught and thought like them?

But more. I found, that although the responsibility of these Saints' Lives was carefully divided and guarded by anonymousness, and by Dr Newman's advertisement in No. 1, that the different lives would be 'published by their respective authors on their own responsibility', yet that Dr Newman had, in what I must now consider merely a moment of amiable weakness, connected himself formally with one of the most offensive of those Lives, and with its most ridiculous statements. I speak of the 'Life of St Walburga'. There is, in all the Lives, the same tendency to repeat childish miracles, to waive the common laws of evidence, to say to the reader, 'You must believe all or nothing.' But some of them, the writers, for instance, of Vol. IV, which contains, among others, a charming life of St Neot – treat the stories openly as legends and myths, and tell them as they stand, without asking the reader, or themselves, to believe them altogether. The method is harmless enough, if the legends had stood alone; but dangerous enough, when they stand side by side with stories told in earnest, like that of St Walburga. In that, not only has the writer expatiated upon some of the most nauseous superstitions of the middle age, but Dr Newman has, in a preface signed with his initials, solemnly set his seal to the same.

The writer – an Oxford scholar, and, as far as I know, then a professed member of the Church of England – dares to tell us of such miracles as these:

How a little girl, playing with a ball near the monastery, was punished for her over-fondness for play, by finding the ball stick to her hand, and, running to St Walburga's shrine to pray, had the ball immediately taken off.

How a woman who would spin on festival-days in like manner found her distaff cling to her hand, and had to beg of St Walburga's bone, before she could get rid of it.

How a man who came into the church to pray, 'irreverently kept his rough gauntlets, or gloves, on his hands, as he joined them in the posture of prayer'. How they were miraculously torn off, and then, when he repented, 'restored by a miracle'. 'All these,' says the writer, 'have the character of a gentle mother correcting the idleness and faults of careless and thoughtless children with tenderness.'

But the most remarkable and lasting miracle, attesting the holy Walburga's sanctity, is that which reckons her among the saints who are called 'Elæophori', or 'unguentiferous', becoming almost in a literal sense, olive-trees in the courts of God. These are they from whose bones a holy oil distils. That oil of charity and gentle mercy which graced them while alive, and fed in them the flame of universal love at their death, still permeates their bodily remains.

After quoting the names of male saints who have possessed this property, the author goes on to detail how this holy oil fell, in drops, sometimes the size of a hazel-nut, sometimes of a pea, into the silver bowl beneath the stone slab. How, when the state of Aichstadt was laid under an interdict, the holy oil ceased, 'until the Church regained its rights', and so forth, and so forth; and then, returning to his original image, metaphor, illustration, proof, or whatever else it may be called by reasoners such as he and Dr Newman, he says that the same flow of oil or dew is related of this female saint and that − women whose souls, like that of Walburga, were touched 'with true compassion; whose bosom, like hers, melted by divine love, was filled with the milk of human kindness' &c. I can quote no more. I really must recollect that my readers and I are living in the nineteenth century.

And to all this stuff and nonsense, more materialist than the dreams of any bone-worshipping Buddhist, Dr Newman puts a preface, in which he says of the question whether the 'miracles recorded in these narratives' (*i.e.* in the whole series, this being only No. II), especially those contained in the life of St Walburga, 'are to be received as matter of fact': that 'in this day, and under our present circumstances, we can only reply, that there is no reason why they should not be. They are the kind of facts proper to ecclesiastical history, just as instances of sagacity or daring, personal prowess, or crime, are the facts proper to secular history.' Verily, his idea of 'secular history' is almost as degraded as his idea of 'ecclesiastical'.

He continues: 'There is nothing, then, *prima facie*, in the miraculous accounts in question to repel a properly-taught or religiously-disposed mind': only, it has the right of rejecting or accepting them according to the evidence. No doubt; for (as he himself confesses) Mabillon, like many sensible Romanists, has found some of these miracles too strong for his 'acute nostril', and has, therefore, been reproved by Basnage for 'not fearing for himself, and warning the reader'.

But what evidence Dr Newman requires, he makes evident at once. He, at least, will 'fear for himself', and swallow the whole as it comes.

'As to the miracles ascribed to St Walburga, it must be remembered that she is one of the principal saints of her age and country'; and then he goes on to quote the authorities for these miracles. They begin nearly 100 years after her death, with one Wolfhard, a monk. Then follows, more than 400 years after,

Philip, Bishop of Aichstadt, the disinterested witness who tells the story of the holy oil ceasing during the interdict, who tells the world how, 'From her virgin limbs, *maxime pectoralibus,* flows this sacred oil, which, by the grace of God and the intercession of the blessed Virgin Walburga, illuminates the blind, makes the deaf hear', &c., and of which he says that he himself once drank a whole cup, and was cured forthwith. Then come the nuns of this same place, equally disinterested witnesses, after the invention of printing; then one Rader, in 1615; and one Gretser, in 1620. But what has become of the holy oil for the last 240 years, Dr Newman does not say.

In his 'Lectures on the present position of Catholics in England, addressed to the brothers of the Oratory', in 1851, he has again used the same line of sophism. Argument I cannot call it, while such a sentence as this is to be found: (p. 295) 'Is the tower of London shut against sight-seers, because the coats of mail or pikes there may have half legendary tales connected with them? Why, then, may not the country people come up in joyous companies, singing and piping, to see the holy coat at Treves?' To see, forsooth! To worship, Dr Newman would have said, had he known (as I take for granted he does not) the facts of that imposture. He himself, meanwhile, seems hardly sure of the authenticity of the holy coat. He (p. 298) 'does not see why it may not have been what it professes to be'. It may 'have been' so, no doubt, but it certainly is not so now; for the very texture and material of the thing prove it to be spurious. However, Dr Newman 'firmly believes that portions of the true Cross are at Rome and elsewhere, that the crib of Bethlehem is at Rome', &c. And more than all; he thinks it 'impossible to withstand the evidence which is brought for the liquefaction of the blood of St Januarius, at Naples, and for the motion of the eyes of the pictures of the Madonna in the Roman States.'

How art thou fallen from heaven, O Lucifer, son of the Morning!

But when I read these outrages upon common sense, what wonder if I said to myself, 'This man cannot believe what he is saying?'

I believe I was wrong. I have tried, as far as I can, to imagine to myself Dr Newman's state of mind; and I see now the possibility of a man's working himself into that pitch of confusion, that he can persuade himself, by what seems to him logic, of anything whatsoever which he wishes to believe; and of his carrying self-deception to such perfection that it becomes a sort of frantic honesty, in which he is utterly unconscious, not only that he is deceiving others, but that he is deceiving himself.

But I must say, If this be 'historic truth', what is historic falsehood? If this be honesty, what is dishonesty? If this be wisdom, what is folly?

I may be told, But this is Roman Catholic doctrine. You have no right to be angry with Dr Newman for believing it. I answer, this is not Roman Catholic doctrine, any more than belief in miraculous appearances of the Blessed Virgin, or the miracle of the stigmata, on which two matters I shall say something hereafter. No Roman Catholic, as far as I am aware, is bound to believe these things. Dr Newman has believed them of his own free will. He is anxious, it would seem, to show his own credulity. He has worked his mind, it would seem, into that morbid state, in which nonsense is the only food for which it hungers. Like the sophists of old, he has used reason to destroy reason. I had thought that, like them, he had preserved his own reason, in order to be able to destroy that of others. But I was unjust to him, as he says. While he tried to destroy others' reason, he was at least fair enough to destroy his own. That is all that I can say. Too many prefer the charge of insincerity to that of insipience – Dr Newman seems not to be of that number.

But more. In connexion with this said life of St Walburga, Dr Newman has done a deed, over which I might make merry, if that were my wish. But I am not a wit, like Dr Newman.

In page 77, we find the following wonderful passage:

> Illuminated men . . . to them the evil influence of Satanic power is horribly discernible . . . and the only way to express their keen perception of it is to say, that they see upon the countenances of the slaves of sin, the marks, and lineaments, and stamp of the evil one; and they smell with their nostrils the horrible fumes which arise from their vices and uncleansed hearts, driving good angels from them in dismay, and attracting and delighting devils. It is said of the holy Sturme, a disciple and companion of Winfred, that in passing a horde of unconverted Germans, as they were bathing and gambolling in a stream, he was so overpowered by the intolerable scent which arose from them, that he nearly fainted away. And no doubt such preternatural discernments are sometimes given to saints.

– and a religious reason is given for it which I shall not quote. I should be ashamed to use the sacred name in the same page with such materialist nonsense.

Now this 'no doubt' seemed as convincing to Dr Newman as to the author. The fly which his disciple had heedlessly cast over the turbid waters of his brain was too fine to be resisted; and he rose at it, heavily but surely, and has hooked himself past remedy. For into his lectures, given before the Catholic University of Ireland, published in 1859, he has inserted, at page 96, on the authority of 'an Oxford writer', the whole passage which relates to St Sturme, word for word.

I thought, when I was in my former mind as to Dr Newman, that he had gone out of his way to tell this fable, in order to intimate to the young gentlemen who had the blessing of his instructions, that they need care nothing for 'truth for its own sake', in the investigation of a miracle, but take it on any anonymous authority, provided only it made for the Catholic faith. And when I saw that I was wrong, I was sorely puzzled as to why my old friend St Sturme (against whom I do not say a word) had thus been dragged unceremoniously into a passage on National Literature, which had nothing whatsoever to do with him. But I am not bound to find motives for Dr Newman's eccentricities.

But now comes the worst part of the matter. Dr Newman has been taken in. There is no miracle. There never was any in the original document. There is none in Mabillon who quotes it. It is a sheer invention of the ardent Oxford writer.

The story appears first in the Life of St Sturme, by his contemporary and friend St Eigils. It may be found in Pertz's 'Monumenta Critica'; and a most charming sketch of medieval missionary life it is; all the more so because one can comfortably believe every word of it, from its complete freedom (as far as I recollect) from signs and wonders.

The original passage sets forth how St Sturme rides on his donkey, and wishing for a place where to found Fulda Abbey, came to a ford where the Sclavonians (not Germans, as the Oxford writer calls them) were bathing, on the way to the fair at Mentz, '*whose naked bodies the animal on which he rode fearing, began to tremble, and the man of God himself shuddered (exhorruit) at their evil smell.*' They mocked him, and went about to hurt him; but Divine providence kept them back, and he went on in safety.

That is all. There is not a hint of a miracle. A horde of dirty savages, who had not, probably, washed for a twelve-month, smelt very strong, and St Sturme had a nose. As for his 'nearly fainting away', that is a 'devout imagination'.

Really, if Dr Newman or the 'Oxford writer' had been monks of more than one Roman Catholic nation, one might have excused their seeing something quite miraculous in any man's being shocked at his fellow-creatures' evil smell; but in Oxford gentlemen, accustomed to the use of soap and water, it is too bad.

Besides, to impute a miracle in this case, is clearly to put the saint, in virtue, below his own donkey; for while the saint was only shocked at the odour, the donkey did what the saint should have done (in imitation of many other saints before and since), and expressed his horror at the impropriety of the *déshabille* of the 'miscreants'. Unless we are to understand a miracle – and why not ? – in the donkey's case likewise; not indeed expressed, but understood as a matter of course by 'properly-taught and religiously-disposed minds'; and piously hold that the virtue of the saint (which seems, from monkish writings, to be some kind of gas or oil) diffused itself through the saddle into the inmost recesses of the donkey's frame, and imbued him for the moment, through the merits of St Sturme, with a preternatural and angelic modesty ?

Which if we shall believe, we shall believe something not a whit more ridiculous than many a story told in these hapless volumes.

What can I say, again, of Dr Newman's 'Lectures on Anglican Difficulties', published in 1850, save what I have said already ? That if I, like hundreds more, have mistaken his meaning and intent, he must blame not me, but himself. If he will indulge in subtle paradoxes, in rhetorical exaggerations; if, whenever he touches on the question of truth and honesty, he will take a perverse pleasure in saying something shocking to plain English notions, he must take the consequences of his own eccentricities.

He tells us, for instance, in Lecture VIII that the Catholic Church

holds it better for sun and moon to drop from heaven, for the earth to fail, and for all the many millions on it to die of starvation in extremest agony, as far as temporal affliction goes, than that one soul, I will not say should be lost, but should commit one single venial sin, should tell one wilful untruth, or should steal one poor farthing without excuse.

And this in the face of those permissions to deception, which may be seen formalized and detailed in the works of the Romish casuists, and especially in those of the great Liguori, whose books have received the public and solemn sanction of the Romish see. In one only way can Dr Newman reconcile this passage with the teaching of his Church; namely, by saying that the licence given to equivocation, even on oath, is so complete, that to tell a downright lie is the most superfluous and therefore most wanton of all sins.

But how will he reconcile it with the statement with which we meet a few pages on, that the Church 'considers consent, though quick as thought, to a single unchaste wish as indefinitely more heinous than any lie that can possibly be fancied; that is when viewed, of course, in itself, and apart from its causes, motives, and consequences ?' Heaven forbid that any man should say that such consent is anything save a great and mortal sin: but how can we reconcile this statement with the former one, save by the paradox, that it is a greater crime to sin like an animal, than like the Devil the Father of Lies ?

Indeed, the whole teaching of this lecture and the one following it concerning such matters is, I confess, so utterly beyond my comprehension, that I must ask, in blank astonishment, What does Dr Newman mean ? He assures us so earnestly and indignantly that he is an honest man, believing what he says, that we in return are bound, in honour and humanity, to believe him; but still – What does he mean ?

He says:

> Take a mere beggar woman, lazy, ragged, and filthy, and not over-scrupulous of truth – (I do not say she has arrived at perfection) – but if she is chaste, sober, and cheerful, and goes to her religious duties (and I am not supposing at all an impossible case), she will, in the eyes of the Church, have a prospect of heaven, quite closed and refused to the State's pattern-man, the just, the upright, the generous, the honourable, the conscientious, if he be all this, not from a supernatural power (I do not determine whether this is likely to be the fact, but I am contrasting views and principles) – not from a supernatural power, but from mere natural virtue (Lecture VIII 207).

I must ask again, What does Dr Newman mean by this astounding passage ? What I thought that he meant, when I first read it, some twelve years ago, may be guessed easily enough. I said, This man has no real care for truth. Truth for its own sake is no virtue in his eyes, and he teaches that it need not be. I do not say that now: but this I say, that Dr Newman, for the sake of exalting the magical powers of his Church, has committed himself unconsciously to a statement which strikes at the root of all morality. If he answer, that such is the doctrine of his Church concerning 'natural virtues', as distinguished from 'good works performed by God's grace', I can only answer, So much the worse for his Church. The sooner it is civilized off the face of the earth, if this be its teaching, the better for mankind. For as for his theory that it may be a 'natural virtue', I value it as little as I trust every honest Englishman will do. I hold it to be utterly antiscriptural; to border very closely (in theological language) on the Pelagian heresy. Every good gift and every perfect gift comes down from God above. Without Him no man does a right deed, or thinks a right thought; and when Dr Newman says otherwise, he is doing his best (as in this passage) to make the 'State's pattern-man' an atheist, as well as to keep the beggar-woman a lying barbarian. What Dr Newman may have meant to teach by these words, I cannot say; but what he has taught practically is patent. He has taught the whole Celtic Irish population, that as long as they are chaste (which they cannot well help being, being married almost before they are men and women) and sober (which they cannot well help being, being too poor to get enough whisky to make them drunk), and 'go to their religious duties' – an expression on which I make no comment – they may look down upon the Protestant gentry who send over millions to feed them in famine; who found hospitals and charities to which they are admitted freely; who try to introduce among them capital, industry, civilization, and, above all, that habit of speaking the truth, for want of which they are what they are, and are likely to remain such, as long as they have Dr Newman for their teacher – that they may look down, I say, on the Protestant gentry as cut off from God, and without hope of heaven, because they do their duty by mere 'natural virtue'.

And Dr Newman has taught them, too, in the very same page,[1] that they may confess 'to the priest thefts which would sentence

---

[1] Lecture VIII 207

the penitent to transportation if brought into a court of justice; but which the priest knows too' (and it is to be remembered that the priest is bound to conceal his knowledge of the crime), 'in the judgment of the Church, might be pardoned on the man's private contrition, without any confession at all.'

If I said that Dr Newman has, in this page, justified, formally and deliberately, some of the strongest accusations brought by the Exeter Hall party against the Irish priests, I should be answered (and possibly with temporary success) by some of those ingenious special pleadings with which, in spite of plain fact and universal public opinion, black is made to appear, if not white, yet still grey enough to do instead. But this I will say, that if the Roman Catholic hierarchy in these realms had had any sense of their own interests (as far as standing well with the British nation is concerned), they would, instead of sending the man who wrote those words to teach in an Irish Catholic university, have sent him to the furthest mission among the savages of the South Seas.

The next lecture, the ninth, contains matter more liable still to be mistaken; and equally certain, mistaken or not, to shock common sense. It is called, 'The Religious Character of Catholic Countries no Prejudice to the Sanctity of the Church'. By the religious character, we find, is meant what we should call the irreligious character — the tendency to profanity, blasphemy, imposture, stealing, lying. These are not my accusations, but Dr Newman's. He details them all with charming *naïveté*, and gives (as we shall see) most picturesque and apposite instances. But this he holds 'is no prejudice to the sanctity of the Church', because the Church considers that 'faith and works are separable', and that all these poor wretches, though they have not works, have at least faith, 'caused directly by a supernatural influence from above', and are therefore, unless I have lost utterly the clue to the intent of Dr Newman's sophistries, *ipso facto* infinitely better off than Protestants. What he means by the separableness of faith and works is clear enough. A man, he says, 'may be gifted with a simple, undoubting, cloudless, belief that Christ is in the Blessed Sacrament, and yet commit the sacrilege of breaking open the tabernacle, and carrying off the consecrated particles for the sake of the precious vessel containing them.'

At which most of my readers will be inclined to cry: 'Let Dr Newman alone, after that. What use in arguing with a man who has argued himself into believing that? He had a human reason once, no doubt: but he has gambled it away, and left no common ground on which he and you, or we either, can meet him.'

True: so true, that I never would have written these pages, save because it was my duty to show the world, if not Dr Newman, how the mistake of his not caring for truth arose; and specially how this very lecture fostered that mistake. For in it, after using the blasphemy and profanity which he confesses to be so common in Catholic countries, as an argument for, and not against, the 'Catholic Faith', he takes a seeming pleasure in detailing instances of dishonesty on the part of Catholics, as if that were the very form of antinomianism which was most strongly and perpetually present to his mind, and which needed most to be palliated and excused. 'The feeble old woman, who first genuflects before the Blessed Sacrament, and then steals her neighbour's handkerchief or prayer-book, who is intent on his devotions' – she is very wrong, no doubt: but 'she worships, and she sins: she kneels because she believes; she steals because she does not love. She may be out of God's grace; she is not altogether out of His sight.'

Heaven forbid that we should deny those words. That, at least, is a doctrine common to Romanist and to Protestant: but while Dr Newman, with a kind of desperate audacity, will dig forth such scandals as notes of the 'Catholic Church', he must not wonder at his motive for so doing being mistaken.

His next instance is even more wanton and offensive, and so curious that I must quote it at length:

You come out again and mix in the idle and dissipated throng, and you fall in with a man in a palmer's dress, selling false relics, and a credulous circle of customers buying them as greedily, as though they were the supposed Franch laces and India silks of a pedlar's basket. One simple soul has brought of him a cure for the rheumatism or ague, which might form a case of conscience. It is said to be a relic of St Cuthbert, but only has virtue at sunrise, and when applied with three crosses to the head, arms, and feet. You pass on to encounter a rude son of the Church, more like a showman than a religious, recounting to the gaping multitude some tale of a vision of the invisible world, seen by Brother Augustine of the Friar Minors, or by a holy Jesuit preacher who died in the odour of sanctity, and sending round his bag to collect pence for the souls in purgatory; and of some appearance of Our Lady (the like of which has really been before and since), but on no authority except popular report, and in no shape but that which popular caprice has given it. You go forward, and you find preparations proceeding for a great pageant or mystery; it is a high festival, and the incorporated trades have each undertaken their special religious celebration. The plumbers and glaziers are to play the Creation; the barbers the call of Abraham; and at night is to be the grandest performance of all, the Resurrection and Last Judgment, played by the carpenters, masons, and blacksmiths. Heaven and hell are represented – saints, devils, and living men; and the *chef d'oeuvre* of the exhibition is the display of fireworks to be let off as the *finale*. 'How unutterably profane!' again you cry. Yes, profane to you, my dear brother –profane to a population which only half believes; not profane to those who believe wholly, who one and all have a vision within which corresponds with what they see, which resolves itself into, or rather takes up into itself, the external pageant, whatever be the moral condition of each individual composing the mass. They gaze, and in drinking in the exhibition with their eyes they are making one continuous and intense act of faith (Lecture IX 236, 237).

The sum of which is, that for the sake of the 'one continuous and intense act of faith' which the crowd is performing, 'the rude son of the Church, more like a showman than a religious' – in plain English, the brutal and lying monk, is allowed to continue his impostures without interruption; and the moral which Dr Newman draws is, that though his miraculous appearance of our Lady may be a lie, yet 'the like thereof has been before and since'.

After which follows a passage – of which I shall boldly say, that I trust that it will arouse in every English husband, father, and brother, who may read these words, the same feelings which it roused in me; and express my opinion, that it is a better compliment to Dr Newman to think that he did not believe what he said, than to think that he did believe it:

> You turn to go home, and in your way you pass through a retired quarter of the city. Look up at those sacred windows; they belong to the Convent of the Perpetual Adoration, or to the poor Clares, or to the Carmelites of the Reform of St Theresa, or to the Nuns of the Visitation. Seclusion, silence, watching, adoration, is their life day and night. The

Immaculate Lamb of God is ever before the eyes of the
worshippers; or, at least, the invisible mysteries of faith ever
stand out, as if in bodily shape, before their mental gaze. Where
will you find such a realized heaven upon earth ? Yet that very
sight has acted otherwise on the mind of a weak sister; and the
very keenness of her faith and wild desire of approaching the
object of it has led her to fancy or to feign that she has received
that singular favour vouchsafed only to a few elect souls; and
she points to God's wounds, as imprinted on her hand, and feet,
and side, though she herself has been instrumental in their
formation (Lecture IX 237, 238).

There are occasions on which courtesy or reticence is a crime, and
this one of them. A poor girl, cajoled, flattered, imprisoned,
starved, maddened, by such as Dr Newman and his peers, into
that degrading and demoralising disease, hysteria, imitates on her
own body, from that strange vanity and deceit which too often
accompany the complaint, the wounds of our Lord; and all that
Dr Newman has to say about the matter is, to inform us that the
gross and useless portent is 'a singular favour vouchsafed only to a
few elect souls'. And this is the man who, when accused of
countenancing falsehood, puts on first a tone of plaintive and
startled innocence, and then one of smug self-satisfaction – as
who should ask, 'What have I said ? What have I done ? Why am I
upon my trial ?' On his trial ? If he be on his trial for nothing else,
he is on his trial for those words; and he will remain upon his trial
as long as Englishmen know how to guard the women whom God
has committed to their charge. If the British public shall ever need
informing that Dr Newman wrote that passage, I trust there will
be always one man left in England to inform them of the fact, for
the sake of the ladies of this land.

Perhaps the most astounding specimens of Dr Newman's
teaching are to be found, after all, in the two sermons which end
his 'Discourses addressed to Mixed Congregations', published in
1849; 'The Glories of Mary for the sake of her Son'; and 'On the
fitness of the Glories of Mary'. Of the mis-quotations of Scripture,
of the sophisms piled on sophisms, of these two sermons, I have
no room wherein to give specimens. All I ask is, that they should
be read; read by every man who thinks it any credit to himself to
be a rational being. But two culminating wonders of these two
sermons I must point out. The first is the assertion that the Blessed

Virgin 'had been inspired, the first of womankind, to dedicate her virginity to God'. As if there had not been Buddhist nuns (if not others) centuries before Christianity. As if (allowing the argument that they dedicated their virginity to a false God) there were the slightest historic proof that the Blessed Virgin dedicated hers before the Incarnation. The second is in a sermon which professes to prove logically the 'fitness' of the Immaculate Conception, and is filled (instead of logic) with traditions which are utterly baseless. I allude to the assertion that 'the world' – *i.e.* all who do not belong to the Romish Church – 'blasphemes' Mary. I make no comment. All I ask, again, of my readers, is to read these two sermons.

But what, after all, does Dr Newman teach concerning truth ? What he taught in 1843, and what he (as far as I can see) teaches still, may be seen in his last sermon in a volume entitled, 'Chiefly on the Theory of Religious Belief', called a sermon 'On the Theory of Developments in Religious Doctrine'. I beg all who are interested in this question to read that sermon (which I had overlooked till lately); and to judge for themselves whether I exaggerate when I say that it tries to undermine the grounds of all rational belief for the purpose of substituting blind superstition. As examples: speaking of 'certain narratives of martyrdoms', and 'alleged miracles', he says (p. 345): 'If the alleged facts did not occur, they ought to have occurred, if I may so speak.' Historic truth is thus sapped; and physical truth fares no better.

> Scripture says (p. 350) that the sun moves, and that the earth is stationary; and science that the earth moves, and the sun is comparatively at rest. How can we determine which of these statements is the very truth, till we know what motion is ? If our idea of motion be but an accident of our present senses neither proposition is true, and both are true; neither true philosophically, both true for certain purposes in the system in which they are respectively found; and physical science will have no better meaning when it says that the earth moves, than plain astronomy when it says that the earth is still.

Quorsum hæc ? What is the intent of this seemingly sceptic method, pursued through page after page ? To tell us that we can know nothing certainly, and therefore must take blindly what 'The Church' shall choose to teach us. For the Church, it would seem, is not bound to tell us, indeed cannot tell us, the whole truth. We are to be treated like children, to whom (at least to those with whom Dr Newman has come in contact) it is necessary to:

> dispense and 'divide' the word of truth, if we would not have it changed, as far as they are concerned, into a word of falsehood. And so, again as regards savages, or the ignorant, or weak, or narrow-minded, our representations must take a certain form, if we are to gain admission into their minds at all, and to reach them. (p. 343)

This method of teaching by half-truths Dr Newman calls 'economy'; and justifies it (if I understand his drift), by the instances of 'mythical representations', legends, and so forth, 'which, if they did not occur, ought to have occurred.' 'Many a theory or view of things,' he goes on –

> on which an institution is founded, or a party held together, is of the same kind. Many an argument, used by zealous and earnest men, has this economical character, being not the very ground on which they act (for they continue in the same course, though it be refuted), yet, in a certain sense, a representation of it, a proximate description of their feelings in the shape of argument, on which they can rest, to which they can recur when perplexed, and appeal when they are questioned (p. 345)

After which startling words, Dr Newman says – and it is really high time – 'In this reference to accommodation or economy in human affairs, I do not meddle with the question of casuistry, viz. which of such artifices, as it may be called, are innocent, or where the "line is to be drawn."'

A hasty reader might say, that herein is an open justification of equivocation and dishonest reticence. But he would be mistaken. The whole sermon is written in so tentative a style, that it would be rash and wrong to say that Dr Newman intends to convey any lesson by it, save that the discovery of truth is an impossibility. Only once, and in a note, he speaks out.

> Hence it is not more than an hyperbole to say that, in certain cases, a lie is the nearest approach to truth. This seems the meaning for instance, of St Clement, when he says 'He (the Christian) both thinks and speaks the truth, unless when, at any time, in the way of treatment, as a physician toward his

patients, so for the welfare of the sick he will be false, or will tell a falsehood, as the sophists speak.' (p. 342).

If St Clement said that, so much the worse for him. He was a great and good man. But he might have learned from his Bible that no lie was of the truth, and that it is ill stealing the devil's tools to do God's work withal.

Be that as it may. What Dr Newman teaches is clear at last, and I see now how deeply I have wronged him. So far from thinking truth for its own sake to be no virtue, he considers it a virtue so lofty, as to be unattainable by man, who must therefore, in certain cases, take up with what-it-is-no-more-than-a-hyperbole-to-call lies; and who, if he should be so lucky as to get any truth into his possession, will be wise in 'economizing' the same, and 'dividing it', so giving away a bit here and a bit there, lest he should waste so precious a possession.

That this is Dr Newman's opinion at present, there can be no manner of doubt. What he has persuaded himself to believe about St Walburga's oil, St Sturme's nose, St Januarius' blood, and the winking Madonna's eyes, proves sufficiently that he still finds, in certain cases, what-it-is-no-more-than-a-hyperbole-to-call-lies, the nearest approach which he can make to truth; while, as to the right of economizing and dividing truth, I shall shortly bring forward two instances of his having done so to such an extent, that very little of poor truth remains after the dismemberment.

And yet I do not call this conscious dishonesty. The man who wrote that sermon was already past the possibility of such a sin. It is simple credulity, the child of scepticism. Credulity, frightened at itself, trying to hide its absurdity alike from itself and from the world by quibbles and reticences which it thinks prudent and clever; and, like the hunted ostrich, fancying that because it thrusts its head into the sand, its whole body is invisible.

And now, I have tried to lead my readers along a path to which some of them, I fear, have objected.

They have fallen, perhaps, into the prevailing superstition that cleverness is synonymous with wisdom. They cannot believe that (as is too certain) great literary, and even barristerial ability, may co-exist with almost boundless silliness: but I can find no other explanation of the phenomena than that which I have just given. That Dr Newman thinks that there is no harm in 'economy', and 'dividing the truth', is evident; for he has employed it again in his comments on the correspondence. He has employed twice, as the most natural and innocent thing possible, those 'arts of the defenceless' which require so much delicacy in the handling lest 'liberal shepherds give a grosser name', and call them cunning or even worse.

I am, of course, free to make my own comments on them, as on all other words of Dr Newman's printed since the 1st of February, 1864, on which day my apology was published. I shall certainly take the sense of the British public on the matter. Though Dr Newman may be 'a mystery' to them, as he says 'religious men' always are to the world, yet they possess quite common sense enough to see what his words are, even though his intention be, as it is wont to be, obscure.

They recollect the definitions of the 'Church' and 'Christians', on the ground of which I called Sermon XX a Romish sermon?

Dr Newman does not apply to it that epithet. He called it, in his letter to me of 7 January (published by him), a 'Protestant' one. I remarked that, but considered it a mere slip of the pen. Besides, I have now nothing to say to that letter. It is to his 'Reflexions' in page 17 which are open ground to me, that I refer. In them he deliberately repeats the epithet 'Protestants'; only he, in an utterly imaginary conversation, puts it into my mouth, 'which you preached when a Protestant.' I call the man who preached that sermon a Protestant? I should have sooner called him a Buddhist. At that very time he was teaching his disciples to scorn and repudiate that name of Protestant, under which, for some reason or other, he now finds it convenient to take shelter. If he forgets, the world does not, the famous article in the *British Critic* (the then organ of his party), of three years before – July, 1841 – which, after denouncing the name of Protestant, declared the object of the party to be none other than the 'Unprotestantising' the English Church.

But Dr Newman convicts himself. In the sermon before, as I have shown, monks and nuns are spoken of as the only true Bible Christians, and in the sermon itself a celibate clergy is made a note of the Church. And yet Dr Newman goes on to say that he was not then 'a priest, speaking of priests.' Whether he were a priest himself matters little to the question; but if he were not speaking of priests, and those Romish ones, when he spoke of a celibate clergy, of whom he was speaking? But there is no use in wasting words on this 'economical' statement of Dr Newman's. I shall only say that there are people in the world whom it is very difficult to help. As soon as they are got out of one scrape, they walk straight into another.

But Dr Newman has made, in my opinion, another and a still greater mistake. He has committed, on the very title-page of his pamphlet, an 'economy' which some men will consider a very serious offence. He has there stated that the question is, 'Whether Dr Newman teaches that truth is no virtue.' He has repeated this misrepresentation in a still stronger form at page 17 where he has ventured to represent me as saying 'Dr Newman tells us that lying is never any harm.' He has economised the very four words of my accusation, which make it at least a reasonable one; namely – '*For its own sake.*'

I never said what he makes me say, or anything like it. I never was inclined to say it. Had I ever been, I should be still more inclined to say it now.

But Dr Newman has shown 'wisdom' enough of that serpentine type which is his professed ideal in what he has done, and has been so economic of truth, and 'divided' the truth so thoroughly, that really there is very little of it left.

For while no one knew better than he the importance of the omission, none knew better that the public would not do so; that they would never observe it; that, if I called their attention to it, they would smile, and accuse me of word-splitting and raising metaphysical subtleties. Yes, Dr Newman is a very economical person. So, when I had accused him and the Romish clergy of teaching that 'truth is no virtue, for its own sake', he simply economized the last four words, and said that I accused him and them of teaching that 'truth is no virtue.'

This, in Dr Newman, the subtle dialectician, is, indeed, an 'enormity', as he chooses to call my accusation of him. No one better knows the value of such limitations. No one has, sometimes fairly, sometimes unfairly, made more use of them. No man, therefore, ought to have been more careful of doing what he has done.

Dr Newman tries, by cunning sleight-of-hand logic, to prove that I did not believe the accusation when I made it. Therein he is mistaken. I did believe it, and I believed, also, his indignant denial. But when he goes on to ask, with sneers, Why I should believe his denial, if I did not consider him trustworthy in the first instance ? – I can only answer, I really do not know. There is a great deal to be said for that view, now that Dr Newman has become (one must needs suppose) suddenly, and since the 1st of February, 1864, a convert to the economic views of St Alfonso da Liguori and his compeers. I am henceforth in doubt and fear, as much as an honest man can be, concerning every word Dr Newman may write. How can I tell that I shall not be the dupe of some cunning equivocation, of one of the three kinds laid down as permissible by the blessed St Alfonso da Liguori and his pupils even when confirmed with an oath, because 'then we do not deceive our neighbour, but allow him to deceive himself?'[1] – The whole being justified by the example of Christ, 'who answered, "I go not up to this feast", subintelligendo, "openly". For,' say the casuists, 'if there were no such restrictions (on the telling of truth), there would be no means of concealing secrets, which one could not open without loss or inconvenience; but this would be no less pernicious to human society than a lie itself.' It is admissible, therefore, to use words and sentences which have a double signification, and leave the hapless hearer to take which of them he may choose. What proof have I, then, that by 'mean it! I never said it!' Dr Newman does not signify, 'I did not say it: but I did mean it?'

Or again, how can I tell that I may not in this pamphlet have made an accusation, of the truth of which Dr Newman is perfectly conscious; but that as I, a heretic Protestant, have no business to make it, he has a full right to deny it? For what says Neyraguet, after the blessed St Alfonso da Luguori? That 'a criminal or witness, being interrogated by a judge contrary to law, may swear that he knows not of the crime; meaning, that he knows not of a crime of which he may be lawfully questioned.'

These are hard words. If Dr Newman shall complain of them, I can only remind him of the fate which befel the stork caught among the cranes, even though the stork had not done all he could to make himself like a crane, as Dr Newman has, by 'economising' on the very title-page of his pamphlet.

I know perfectly well that truth – 'veracity, as they call it' – is a virtue with the Romish moralists; that it is one of the cardinal virtues, the daughters of justice, like benevolence, courtesy,

---

[1] I quote from Scavini, tom. ii page 232, of the Paris edition, and from Neyraguet, p. 141, two compendiums of Liguori which are (or were lately) used, so I have every reason to believe – one at Oscott, the other at Maynooth.

gratitude, and so forth; and is proved to be such because there is a *naturalis honestas* in it, and also that without it society could not go on. Lying, on the other hand, though not one of the seven 'capital' sins, which are pride, avarice, luxury (unchastity), gluttony, anger, envy, and acedia (lukewarmness), is yet held to be always a sin, when direct. It is proved to be such from Scripture, from the fathers, and from natural reason, because 'truth is an essential perfection of the Divine nature.' So far well. But a lie is a venial sin, if it 'neither hurts our neighbour or God gravely, or causes a grave scandal'; as no lie told in behalf of the Catholic faith can well do, though one wise Pope laid it down that it was a sin to tell a lie, even for the sake of saving a soul. But though it were a sin, the fact of its being a venial one seems to have gained for it, as yet, a very slight penance. Meanwhile, as a thousand venial sins can never make one mortal one, a man may be a habitual liar all his life long, without falling into mortal sin. Moreover, though 'formal simulation', when 'one signifies by outward act something different to what he has in his mind,' is illicit, as a lie, yet 'material simulation', or stratagem, is not so. 'For when one does something, not intending the deception of another, but some end of his own, then it is allowable on cause; although, from other circumstances, men might conjecture that the act was done for another end. So Joshua fled lawfully, not meaning fear, but that he might draw the enemy further from the city of Hai.' From which one can gather, that Romish casuists allow the same stratagems to man against his neighbours, in peaceable society, which Protestant public opinion allows (and that with a growing compunction) only to officers in war, against the enemies of their country. Considering this fact, and the permission of equivocation, even on oath, it is somewhat difficult to expect that the Romish moralists, at least, hold truth to be a virtue for its own sake, or to deny that they teach cunning to be the weapons of the weak against the strong.

Yes – I am afraid that I must say it once more – Truth is not honoured among these men for its own sake. There are, doubtless, pure and noble souls among them, superior, through the grace of God, to the official morality of their class: but in their official writings, and in too much of their official conduct, the great majority seem never, for centuries past, to have perceived that truth is the capital virtue, the virtue of all virtues, without which all others are hollow and rotten; and with which there is hope for a man's repentance and conversion, in spite of every vice, if only he remains honest. They have not seen that facts are the property not of man, to be 'economized' as man thinks fit, but of God, who ordereth all things in heaven and earth; and that therefore not only every lie, but every equivocation, every attempt at deception, is a sin, not against man, but against God; they have not seen that no lie is of the truth, and that God requires truth, not merely in outward words, but in the inward parts; and that therefore the first and most absolute duty of every human being is to speak and act the exact truth; or if he wish to be silent, to be silent, courageously and simply, and take the risk, trusting in God to protect him, as long as he remains on God's side in the universe, by scorning to sully his soul by stratagem or equivocation. Had they seen this; had they not regarded truth as a mere arbitrary command of God, which was not binding in doubtful cases, they would never have dared to bargain with God as to how little truth He required of men; and to examine and define (to the injury alike of their own sense of honour, and that of their hearers) how much deception He may be reasonably supposed to allow.

Is this last Dr Newman's view of truth? I hope not. I hope that he, educated as an English gentleman and Oxford scholar, is at variance with the notions formally allowed by the most popular and influential modern Doctor of his Church. But that there is some slight difference between his notions of truth and ours he has confessed – in a letter to 'X. V. Esqre',[1] which he has printed in his 'Correspondence'. For there he says

> I think that you will allow that there is a broad difference between a virtue, considered as a principle or rule, and the applications and limits of it in human conduct. Catholics and Protestants, in their view of the substance of the moral virtues, agree; but they carry them out variously in detail. (p. 8)

He then gives us to understand, that this is the case as to truth; that Catholics differ from Protestants as to 'whether this or that act in particular is conformable to the rule of truth.'

I beg to say, that in these words Dr Newman has made another great mistake. He has calumniated, as far as my experience goes, the Catholic gentry of these realms. I am proud to say, as far as I have had the honour and pleasure of their acquaintance, that

---

[1] ['X. V.' for 'X. Y.', so in first and third editions of Kingsley's pamphlet.]

there is no difference whatsoever, of detail or other, between their truthfulness and honour, and the truthfulness and honour of the Protestant gentry among whom they live, respected and beloved, in spite of all religious differences, simply because they are honest gentlemen and noble ladies. But if Dr Newman will limit his statement to the majority of the Romish priesthood, and to those hapless Irish Celts over whom they rule, then we will willingly accept it as perfectly correct. There is a very wide difference in practical details between their notions of truth and ours; and what that difference is, I have already pointed out. It is notorious enough in facts and practice. It may be seen at large by any one who chooses to read the Romish Moral Theologians. And if Dr Newman, as a Catholic priest, includes himself in his own statement, that is his act, not mine.

And so I leave Dr Newman, only expressing my fear, that if he continues to 'economize' and 'divide' the words of his adversaries as he has done mine, he will run great danger of forfeiting once more his reputation for honesty.

CHARLES KINGSLEY

APOLOGIA PRO VITA SUA

Being

A Reply to a Pamphlet
Entitled

'What, then, does Dr Newman Mean?'

PART I

Mr Kingsley's Method of Disputation
Published as a Pamphlet, Thursday, April 21, 1864.

I cannot be sorry to have forced Mr Kingsley to bring out in fulness his charges against me. It is far better that he should discharge his thoughts upon me in my lifetime, than after I am dead. Under the circumstances I am happy in having the opportunity of reading the worst that can be said of me by a writer who has taken pains with his work and is well satisfied with it. I account it a gain to be surveyed from without by one who hates the principles which are nearest to my heart, has no personal knowledge of me to set right his misconceptions of my doctrine, and who has some motive or other to be as severe with me as he can possibly be.

And first of all, I beg to compliment him on the motto in his Title-page; it is felicitous. A motto should contain, as in a nutshell, the contents, or the character, or the drift, or the *animus* of the writing to which it is prefixed. The words which he has taken from me are so apposite as to be almost prophetical. There cannot be a better illustration than he thereby affords of the aphorism which I intended them to convey. I said that it is not more than an hyperbolical expression to say that in certain cases a lie is the nearest approach to truth. Mr Kingsley's pamphlet is emphatically one of such cases as are contemplated in that proposition. I really believe, that his view of me is about as near an approach to the truth about my writings and doings, as he is capable of taking. He has done his worst towards me; but he has also done his best. So far well; but, while I impute to him no malice, I unfeignedly think, on the other hand, that, in his invective against me, he as faithfully fulfils the other half of the proposition also.

This is not a mere sharp retort upon Mr Kingsley, as will be seen, when I come to consider directly the subject, to which the words of his motto relate. I have enlarged on that subject in various passages of my publications; I have said that minds in different states and circumstances cannot understand one another, and that in all cases they must be instructed according to their capacity, and, if not taught step by step, they learn only so much the less; that children do not apprehend the thoughts of grown people, nor savages the instincts of civilization, nor blind men the perceptions of sight, nor pagans the doctrines of Christianity, nor men the experiences of Angels. In the same way, there are people of matter-of-fact, prosaic minds, who cannot take in the fancies of poets; and others of shallow, inaccurate minds, who cannot take in the ideas of philosophical inquirers. In a Lecture of mine I have illustrated this phenomenon by the supposed instance of a foreigner, who, after reading a commentary on the principles of English Law, does not get nearer to a real apprehension of them than to be led to accuse Englishmen of considering that the Queen is impeccable and infallible, and that the Parliament is omnipotent. Mr Kingsley has read me from beginning to end in the fashion in which the hypothetical Russian read Blackstone; not, I repeat, from malice, but because of his intellectual build. He appears to be so constituted as to have no notion of what goes on in minds very different from his own, and moreover to be stone-blind to his ignorance. A modest man or a philosopher would have scrupled to treat with scorn and scoffing, as Mr Kingsley does in my own instance, principles and convictions, even if he did not acquiesce in them himself, which had been held so widely and for so long – the beliefs and devotions and customs which have been the religious life of millions upon millions of Christians for nearly twenty centuries – for this in fact is the task on which he is spending his pains. Had he been a man of large or cautious mind, he would not have taken it for granted that cultivation must lead every one to see things precisely as he sees them himself. But the narrow-minded are the more prejudiced by very reason of their narrowness. The Apostle bids us 'in malice be children, but in understanding be men.' I am glad to recognize in Mr Kingsley an illustration of the first half of this precept; but I should not be honest, if I ascribed to him any sort of fulfilment of the second.

I wish I could speak as favourably either of his drift or of his method of arguing, as I can of his convictions. As to his drift, I think its ultimate point is an attack upon the Catholic Religion. It is I indeed, whom he is immediately insulting – still, he views me only as a representative, and on the whole a fair one, of a class or caste of men, to whom, conscious as I am of my own integrity, I ascribe an excellence superior to mine. He desires to impress upon the public mind the conviction that I am a crafty, scheming man, simply untrustworthy; that, in becoming a Catholic, I have just found my right place; that I do but justify and am properly interpreted by the common English notion of Roman casuists and confessors; that I was secretly a Catholic when I was openly professing to be a clergyman of the Established Church; that so far from bringing, by means of my conversion, when at length it openly took place, any strength to the Catholic cause, I am really a burden to it – an additional evidence of the fact, that to be a pure, german, genuine Catholic, a man must be either a knave or a fool.

These last words bring me to Mr Kingsley's method of disputation, which I must criticize with much severity – in his drift he does but follow the ordinary beat of controversy, but in his mode of arguing he is actually dishonest.

He says that I am either a knave or a fool, and (as we shall see by and by) he is not quite sure which, probably both. He tells his readers that on one occasion he said that he had fears I should 'end in one or other of two misfortunes.'

'He would either,' he continues, 'destroy his own sense of honesty, i.e. conscious truthfulness – and become a dishonest person; or he would destroy his common sense, i.e. unconscious truthfulness, and become the slave and puppet seemingly of his own logic, really of his own fancy . . . I thought for years past that he had become the former; I now see that he has become the latter.' (pp. 32–33). Again, 'When I read these outrages upon common sense, what wonder if I said to myself, "This man cannot believe what he is saying?" ' (p. 37). Such has been Mr Kingsley's state of mind till lately, but now he considers that I am possessed with a spirit of 'almost boundless silliness', of 'simple credulity, the child of scepticism', of 'absurdity' (p. 49), of a 'self-deception which has become a sort of frantic honesty' (p. 38). And as to his fundamental reason for this change, he tells us, he really does not know what it is (p. 51). However, let the reason be what it will, its upshot is intelligible enough. He is enabled at once, by this professed change of judgment about me, to put forward one of these alternatives, yet to keep the other in reserve – and this he actually does. He need not commit himself to a definite accusation against me, such as requires definite proof and admits of definite refutation; for he has two strings to his bow – when he is thrown off his balance on the one leg, he can recover himself by the use of the other. If I demonstrate that I am not a knave, he may exclaim, 'Oh, but you are a fool!' and when I demonstrate that I am not a fool, he may turn round and retort, 'Well, then, you are a knave.' I have no objection to reply to his arguments in behalf of either alternative, but I should have been better pleased to have been allowed to take them one at a time.

But I have not yet done full justice to the method of disputation, which Mr Kingsley thinks it right to adopt. Observe this first – He means by a man who is 'silly' not a man who is to be pitied, but a man who is to be *abhorred*. He means a man who is not simply weak, and incapable, but a moral leper; a man who, if not a knave, has every thing bad about him except knavery: nay, rather, has together with every other worst vice, a spice of knavery to boot. *His* simpleton is one who has become such, in judgment for his having once been a knave. *His* simpleton is not a born fool, but a self-made idiot, one who has drugged and abused himself into a shameless depravity; one, who, without any misgiving or remorse, is guilty of drivelling superstition, of reckless violation of sacred things, of fanatical excesses, of passionate inanities, of unmanly audacious tyranny over the weak, meriting the wrath of fathers and brothers. This is that milder judgment, which he seems to pride himself upon as so much charity; and, as he expresses it, he 'does not know' why. This is what he really meant in his letter to me of January 14, when he withdrew his charge of my being dishonest. He said, 'The *tone* of your letters, even more than their language, makes me feel, *to my very deep pleasure*' – what? that you have gambled away your reason, that you are an intellectual sot, that you are a fool in a frenzy. And in his Pamphlet, he gives us this explanation why he did not say this to my face, viz. that he had been told that I was 'in weak health,' and was 'averse to controversy' (p. 21). He 'felt some regret for having disturbed me.'

But I pass on from these multiform imputations, and confine myself to this one consideration, viz. that he has made any fresh imputation upon me at all. He gave up the charge of knavery; well and good: but where was the logical necessity of his bringing another? I am sitting at home without a thought of Mr Kingsley; he wantonly breaks in upon me with the charge that I had '*informed*' the world 'that Truth for its own sake *need not* and on the whole *ought not to be* a virtue with the Roman clergy.' When challenged on the point he cannot bring a fragment of evidence in proof of his assertion, and he is convicted of false witness by the voice of the world. Well, I should have thought that he had now nothing whatever more to do. 'Vain man!' he seems to make answer, 'what simplicity in you to think so! If you have not broken one commandment, let us see whether we cannot convict you of the breach of another. If you are not a swindler or forger, you are guilty or arson or burglary. By hook or by crook you shall not escape. Are *you* to suffer or *I* ? What does it matter to you who are going off the stage, to receive a slight additional daub upon a character so deeply stained already ? But think of me, the immaculate lover of Truth, so observant (as I have told you, p. 23) of "*hault courage* and strict honour" – and (*aside*) – "and not as this publican" – do you think I can let you go scot free instead of myself ? No; *noblesse oblige*. Go to the shades, old man, and boast that Achilles sent you thither.'

But I have not even yet done with Mr Kingsley's method of disputation. Observe secondly – when a man is said to be a knave or a fool, it is commonly meant that he is *either* the one *or* the other; and that – either in the sense that the hypothesis of his being a fool is too absurd to be entertained; or, again, as a sort of contemptuous acquittal of one, who after all has not wit enough to be wicked. But this is not at all what Mr Kingsley proposes to himself in the antithesis which he suggests to his readers. Though he speaks of me as an utter dotard and fanatic, yet all along, from the beginning of his Pamphlet to the end, he insinuates, he proves from my writings, and at length in his last pages he openly pronounces, that after all he was right at first, in thinking me a conscious liar and deceiver.

Now I wish to dwell on this point. It cannot be doubted, I say, that, in spite of his professing to consider me as a dotard and driveller, on the ground of his having given up the notion of my being a knave, yet it is the very staple of his Pamphlet that a knave after all I must be. By insinuation, or by implication, or by question, or by irony, or by sneer, or by parable, he enforces again and again a conclusion which he does not categorically enunciate.

For instance (1) p. 28. 'I know that men *used to suspect Dr Newman*, I have been inclined to do so myself, of writing a whole sermon . . . for the sake of one single passing hint, one phrase, one epithet, one little barbed arrow which . . . he delivered unheeded, as with his finger tip, to the very heart of an initiated hearer, *never to be withdrawn again.*'

(2) p. 29. 'How *was* I to know that the preacher, who had the reputation of being the most *acute* man of his generation, and of having a specially intimate acquaintance with the weaknesses of the human heart, was utterly blind to the broad meaning and the plain practical result of a sermon like this, delivered before fanatic and hot-headed young men, who hung upon his every word? That he did not *foresee* that they would think that they obeyed him, *by becoming affected, artificial, sly, shifty, ready for concealments and equivocations?*'

(3) p. 31. 'No one *would have* suspected him to be a dishonest man, if he had not perversely chosen to *assume a style* which (as he himself confesses) the world always associates with dishonesty.'

(4) p. 40. '*If* he will indulge in subtle paradoxes, in rhetorical exaggerations; if, *whenever he touches on the question of truth and honesty*, he will take a perverse pleasure in saying something shocking to plain English notions, he *must take the consequences of his own eccentricities.*'

(5) pp. 43, 44. 'At which most of my readers will be inclined to cry: "Let Dr Newman alone, after that. . . . He had a human reason once, no doubt: but he has gambled it away." . . . True: so true, &c.'

(6) p. 44. He continues: 'I should never have written these pages, save because it was my duty to show the world, if not Dr Newman, how the mistake (!) of his *not caring* for truth *arose.*'

(7) p. 46. 'And this is the man, who when accused of countenancing falsehood, puts on first a tone of *plaintive* (!) and startled innocence, and then one of smug self-satisfaction — as who should ask, "What have I said? What have I done? Why am I on my trial?".'

(8) p. 49. 'What Dr Newman teaches is clear at last, and *I see now how deeply I have wronged him.* So far from thinking truth for its own sake to be no virtue, *he considers it a virtue so lofty as to be unattainable by man.*'

(9) pp. 50, 51. 'There is no use in wasting words on this "economical" statement of Dr Newman's. I shall only say that there are people in the world whom it is very difficult to *help.* As soon as they are got out of one scrape, they walk straight into another.'

(10) p. 51. 'Dr Newman has shown "wisdom" enough of that *serpentine* type which is his professed ideal . . . Yes, Dr Newman is a very economical person.'

(11) p. 51. 'Dr Newman *tries*, by *cunning sleight-of-hand logic*, to prove that I did not believe the accusation when I made it.'

(12) p. 52. 'These are hard words. If Dr Newman shall complain of them, I can only remind him of the fate which befel the stork caught among the cranes, *even though* the stork had *not* done all he could to make himself like a crane, *as Dr Newman has*, by 'economising' on the very title-page of his pamphlet.'

These last words bring us to another and far worse instance of these slanderous assaults upon me, but its place is in a subsequent page.

Now it may be asked of me, 'Well, why should not Mr Kingsley take a course such as this? It was his original assertion that Dr Newman was a professed liar, and a patron of lies; he spoke somewhat at random; granted; but now he has got up his references and he is proving, not perhaps the very thing which he said at first, but something very like it, and to say the least quite as bad. He is now only aiming to justify morally his original assertion; why is he not at liberty to do so?'

Why should he *not* now insinuate that I am a liar and a knave! he had of course a perfect right to make such a charge, if he chose; he might have said, 'I was virtually right, and here is the proof of it', but this he has not done, but on the contrary has professed that he no longer draws from my works, as he did before, the inference of my dishonesty. He says distinctly, p. 37, 'When I read these outrages upon common sense, what wonder if I said to myself, "This man cannot believe what he is saying?" *I believe I was wrong.*' And in p. 42, 'I said, This man has no real care for truth. Truth for its own sake is no virtue in his eyes, and he teaches that it need not be. *I do not say that now.*' And in p. 49, 'I do not call this conscious dishonesty; the man who wrote that sermon *was already past the possibility* of such a sin.'

Why should he *not!* because it is on the ground of my not being a knave that he calls me a fool; adding to the words just quoted, '[My readers] have fallen perhaps into the prevailing superstition that cleverness is synonymous with wisdom. They cannot believe that (as is too certain) great literary and even barristerial ability may co-exist with almost boundless silliness.'

Why should he *not!* because he has taken credit to himself for that high feeling of honour which refuses to withdraw a concession which once has been made; though, (wonderful to say!) at the very time that he is recording this magnanimous resolution, he lets it out of the bag that his relinquishment of it is only a profession and a pretence; for he says, p. 23: 'I have accepted Dr Newman's denial that [the Sermon] means what I thought it did; and *heaven forbid*' (oh!) 'that I should withdraw my word once given, *at whatever disadvantage to myself.*' Disadvantage! but nothing can be advantageous to him which is *untrue*; therefore in proclaiming that the concession of my honesty is a disadvantage to him, he thereby implies unequivocally that there is some probability still, that I am *dis*honest. He goes on, 'I am informed by those from whose judgment on such points there is no appeal, that "*en hault courage*", and strict honour, I am also *precluded*, by the *terms* of my explanation, from using any other of Dr Newman's past writings to prove my assertion.' And then, 'I have declared Dr Newman to have been an honest man up to the 1st of February, 1864; it was, as I shall show, only Dr Newman's fault that I ever thought him to be anything else. It depends entirely on Dr Newman whether he shall *sustain* the reputation which he has so recently acquired' (by diploma of course from Mr Kingsley). 'If I give him thereby a fresh advantage in this argument, he is *most welcome* to it. He needs, it seems to me, *as many advantages as possible.*'

What a princely mind! How loyal to his rash promise, how delicate towards the subject of it, how conscientious in his interpretation of it! I have no thought of irreverence towards a Scripture Saint, who was actuated by a very different spirit from Mr Kingsley's, but somehow since I read his Pamphlet words have been running in my head, which I find in the Douay version thus: 'Thou hast also with thee Semei the son of Gera, who cursed me with a grievous curse when I went to the camp, but I swore to him, saying, I will not kill thee with the sword. Do not thou hold him guiltless. But thou art a wise man and knowest what to do with him, and thou shalt bring down his grey hairs with blood to hell.'

Now I ask, Why could not Mr Kingsley be open? If he intended still to arraign me on the charge of lying, why could he not say so as a man? Why must he insinuate, question, imply, and use sneering and irony, as if longing to touch a forbidden fruit, which still he was afraid would burn his fingers, if he did so? Why must he 'palter in a double sense', and blow hot and cold in one breath?

He first said he considered me a patron of lying; well, he changed his opinion; and as to the logical ground of this change, he said that, if any one asked him what it was, he could only answer that *he really did not know*. Why could not he change back again, and say he did not know why ? He had quite a right to do so; and then his conduct would have been so far straightforward and unexceptional. But no – in the very act of professing to believe in my sincerity, he takes care to show the world that it is a profession and nothing more. That very proceeding which at p. 29 he lays to my charge (whereas I detest it) of avowing one thing and thinking another, that proceeding he here exemplifies himself; and yet, while indulging in practices as offensive as this, he ventures to speak of his sensitive admiration of 'hault courage and strict honour!'. 'I forgive you, Sir Knight,' says the heroine in the Romance, 'I forgive you as a Christian.' 'That means,' said Wamba, 'that she does not forgive him at all.' Mr Kingsley's word of honour is about as valuable as in the jester's opinion was the Christian charity of Rowena. But here we are brought to a further specimen of Mr Kingsley's method of disputation, and having duly exhibited it, I shall have done with him.

It is his last, and he has intentionally reserved it for his last. Let it be recollected that he professed to absolve me from his original charge of dishonesty up to February 1. And further, he implies that, *at the time when he was writing*, I had not *yet* involved myself in any fresh acts suggestive of that sin. He says that I have had a great *escape* of conviction, that he hopes I shall take warning, and act more cautiously. 'It depends entirely,' he said, 'on *Dr Newman, whether* he shall *sustain* the reputation which he has so recently acquired' (p. 23). Thus, in Mr Kingsley's judgment, I was *then*, when he wrote these words, *still* innocent of dishonesty, for a man cannot sustain what he actually has not got; *only he could not be sure of my future*. Could not be sure! Why at this very time he had already noted down valid proofs, as he thought them, that I *had* already forfeited the character which he contemptuously accorded to me. He had cautiously said '*up* to February 1st', *in order* to reserve the Title-page and last three pages of my Pamphlet, which were not published till February 12, and out of these four pages, which he had *not* whitewashed, he had *already* forged charges against me of dishonesty at the very time that he implied that as yet there was nothing against me. When he gave me that plenary condonation, as it seemed to be, he had already done his best that I should never enjoy it. He knew well at p. 23, what he meant to say at pp. 51 and 52. At best indeed I was only out upon ticket of leave; but that ticket was a pretence; he had made it forfeit when he gave it. But he did not say so at once, first, because between p. 23 and p. 51 he meant to talk a great deal about my idiotcy and my frenzy, which would have been simply out of place, had he proved me too soon to be a knave again; and next, because he meant to exhaust all those insinuations about my knavery in the past, which 'strict honour' did not permit him to countenance, in order thereby to give colour and force to his direct charges of knavery in the present, which 'strict honour' *did* permit him to handsel. So in the fifth act he gave a start, and found to his horror that, in my miserable four pages, I had committed the 'enormity' of an 'economy', which in matter of fact he had got by heart before he began the play. Nay, he suddenly found two, three, and (for what he knew) as many as four profligate economies in that Title-page and those Reflections, and he uses the language of distress and perplexity at this appalling discovery.

Now why this *coup de théâtre ?* The reason soon breaks on us. Up to February 1, he could not categorically arraign me for lying, and therefore could not involve me (as was so necessary for his case), in the popular abhorrence which is felt for the casuists of Rome: but, as soon as ever he could openly and directly pronounce (saving his 'hault courage and strict honour') that I am guilty of three or four new economies, then at once I am made to bear, not only my own sins, but the sins of other people also, and, though I have been condoned the knavery of my antecedents, I am guilty of the knavery of a whole priesthood instead. So the hour of doom for Semei is come, and the wise man knows what to do with him – he is down upon me with the odious names of 'St Alfonso da Liguori', and 'Scavini' and 'Neyraguet', and 'the Romish moralists', and their 'compeers and pupils', and I am at once merged and whirled away in the gulph of notorious quibblers, and hypocrites, and rogues.

But we have not even yet got at the real object of the stroke, thus reserved for his *finale*. I really feel sad for what I am obliged now to say. I am in warfare with him, but I wish him no ill – it is very difficult to get up resentment towards persons whom one has never seen. It is easy enough to be irritated with friends or foes, *vis-à-vis*; but, though I am writing with all my heart against what he has said of me, I am not conscious of personal unkindness towards himself. I think it necessary to write as I am writing, for my own sake, and for the sake of the Catholic Priesthood; but I wish to impute nothing worse to Mr Kingsley than that he has been furiously carried away by his feelings. But what shall I say of the upshot of all this talk of my economies and equivocations and the like ? What is the precise *work* which it is directed to effect ? I am at war with him; but there is such a thing as legitimate warfare: war has its laws; there are things which may fairly be done, and things which may not be done. I say it with shame and with stern sorrow – he has attempted a great transgression; he has attempted (as I may call it) to *poison the wells*. I will quote him and explain what I mean.

Dr Newman tries, by cunning sleight-of-hand logic, to prove that I did not believe the accusation when I made it. Therein he is mistaken. I did believe it, and I believed also his indignant denial. But when he goes on to ask with sneers, why I should believe his denial, if I did not consider him trustworthy in the first instance ? I can only answer, I really do not know. There is a *great deal* to be said for *that* view, *now that* Dr Newman has become (one must needs suppose) *suddenly* and *since* the 1st of February, 1864, a convert to the *economic* views of St Alfonso da Liguori and his compeers. I am *henceforth* in doubt and *fear*, as much as any honest man can be, *concerning every word* Dr Newman may write. *How can I tell that I shall not be the dupe of some cunning equivocation*, of one of the three kinds laid down as permissible by the blessed Alfonso da Liguori and his pupils, even when confirmed by an oath, because 'then we do not deceive our neighbour, but allow him to deceive himself ?' . . . It is admissible, therefore, to use words and sentences which have a double signification, and leave the hapless hearer to take which of them he may choose. *What proof have I, then, that by* 'mean it ? I never said it!' *Dr Newman does not signify*, I did not say it, but I did mean it ? (pp. 51, 52).

Now these insinuations and questions shall be answered in their proper places; here I will but say that I scorn and detest lying, and quibbling, and double-tongued practice, and slyness, and cunning, and smoothness, and cant, and pretence, quite as much as any Protestants hate them; and I pray to be kept from the snare of them. But all this is just now by the bye; my present subject is

Mr Kingsley; what I insist upon here, now that I am bringing this portion of my discussion to a close, is this unmanly attempt of his, in his concluding pages, to cut the ground from under my feet – to poison by anticipation the public mind against me, John Henry Newman, and to infuse into the imaginations of my readers, suspicion and mistrust of every thing that I may say in reply to him. This I call *poisoning the wells*.

'I am henceforth in *doubt and fear*,' he says, 'as much as any *honest* man can be, *concerning every word* Dr Newman may write. *How can I tell that I shall not be the dupe of some cunning equivocation?* . . . What proof have I, that by "mean it? I never said it!" Dr Newman does not signify, "I did not say it, but I did mean it" ?'

Well, I can only say, that, if his taunt is to take effect, I am but wasting my time in saying a word in answer to his foul calumnies; and this is precisely what he knows and intends to be its fruit. I can hardly get myself to protest against a method of controversy so base and cruel, lest in doing so, I should be violating my self-respect and self-possession; but most base and most cruel it is. We all know how our imagination runs away with us, how suddenly and at what a pace – the saying, 'Caesar's wife should not be suspected', is an instance of what I mean. The habitual prejudice, the humour of the moment, is the turning-point which leads us to read a defence in a good sense or a bad. We interpret it by our antecedent impressions. The very same sentiments, according as our jealousy is or is not awake, or our aversion stimulated, are tokens of truth or of dissimulation and pretence. There is a story of a sane person being by mistake shut up in the wards of a Lunatic Asylum, and that, when he pleaded his cause to some strangers visiting the establishment, the only remark he elicited in answer was, 'How naturally he talks! you would think he was in his senses.' Controversies should be decided by the reason; is it legitimate warfare to appeal to the misgivings of the public mind and to its dislikings? Any how, if Mr Kingsley is able thus to practise upon my readers, the more I succeed, the less will be my success. If I am natural, he will tell them, 'Ars est celare artem'; if I am convincing, he will suggest that I am an able logician; if I show warmth, I am acting the indignant innocent; if I am calm, I am thereby detected as a smooth hypocrite; if I clear up difficulties, I am too plausible and perfect to be true. The more triumphant are my statements, the more certain will be my defeat.

So will it be if Mr Kingsley succeeds in his manoeuvre; but I do not for an instant believe that he will. Whatever judgment my readers may eventually form of me from these pages, I am confident that they will believe me in what I shall say in the course of them. I have no misgiving at all, that they will be ungenerous or harsh with a man who has been so long before the eyes of the world; who has so many to speak of him from personal knowledge; whose natural impulse it has ever been to speak out; who has ever spoken too much rather than too little; who would have saved himself many a scrape, if he had been wise enough to hold his tongue; who has ever been fair to the doctrines and arguments of his opponents; who has never slurred over facts and reasonings which told against himself; who has never given his name or authority to proofs which he thought unsound, or to testimony which he did not think at least plausible; who has never shrunk from confessing a fault when he felt that he had committed one; who has ever consulted for others more than for himself; who has given up much that he loved and prized and could have retained, but that he loved honesty better than name, and Truth better than dear friends.

And now I am in a train of thought higher and more serene than any which slanders can disturb. Away with you, Mr Kingsley, and fly into space. Your name shall occur again as little as I can help, in the course of these pages. I shall henceforth occupy myself not with you, but with your charges.

PART II

True Mode of meeting Mr Kingsley
Published as a Pamphlet, Thursday, April 28, 1864.

What shall be the special imputation, against which I shall throw myself in these pages, out of the thousand and one which my accuser directs upon me? I mean to confine myself to one, for there is only one about which I much care – the charge of Untruthfulness. He may cast upon me as many other imputations as he pleases, and they may stick on me, as long as they can, in the course of nature. They will fall to the ground in their season.

And indeed I think the same of the charge of Untruthfulness, and I select it from the rest, not because it is more formidable, but because it is more serious. Like the rest, it may disfigure me for a time, but it will not stain: Archbishop Whately used to say, 'Throw dirt enough, and some will stick'; well, will stick, but not, will stain. I think he used to mean 'stain', and I do not agree with him. Some dirt sticks longer than other dirt; but no dirt is immortal. According to the old saying, Prævalebit Veritas. There are virtues indeed, about which the world is not fitted to judge or to uphold, such as faith, hope, and charity: but it can judge about Truthfulness; it can judge about the natural virtues, and Truthfulness is one of them. Natural virtues may also become supernatural; Truthfulness is such; but that does not withdraw it from the jurisdiction of mankind at large. It may be more difficult in this or that particular case for men to take cognizance of it, as it may be difficult for the Court of Queen's Bench at Westminster to try a case fairly, which took place in Hindoostan; but that is a question of capacity, not of right. Mankind has the right to judge of Truthfulness in the case of a Catholic, as in the case of a Protestant, of an Italian, or of a Chinese. I have never doubted, that in my hour, in God's hour, my avenger will appear, and the world will acquit me of untruthfulness, even though it be not while I live.

Still more confident am I of such eventual acquittal, seeing that my judges are my own countrymen. I consider, indeed, Englishmen the most suspicious and touchy of mankind; I think them unreasonable, and unjust in their seasons of excitement; but I had rather be an Englishman (as in fact I am), than belong to any other race under heaven. They are as generous, as they are hasty and burly; and their repentance for their injustice is greater than their sin.

For twenty years and more I have borne an imputation, of which I am at least as sensitive, who am the object of it, as they can be, who are only the judges. I have not set myself to remove it, first, because I never have had an opening to speak, and, next, because I never saw in them the disposition to hear. I have wished to appeal from Philip drunk to Philip sober. When shall I pronounce him to be himself again ? If I may judge from the tone of the public press, which represents the public voice, I have great reason to take heart at this time. I have been treated by contemporary critics in this controversy with great fairness and gentleness, and I am grateful to them for it. However, the decision of the time and mode of my defence has been taken out of my hands; and I am thankful that it has been so. I am bound now as a duty to myself, to the Catholic cause, to the Catholic Priesthood, to give account of myself without any delay, when I am so rudely and circumstantially charged with Untruthfulness. I accept the challenge; I shall do my best to meet it, and I shall be content when I have done so.

I confine myself then, in these pages, to the charge of Untruthfulness; and I hereby cart away, as so much rubbish, the impertinences, with which the Pamphlet of Accusation swarms. I shall not think it necessary here to examine, whether I am 'worked into a pitch of confusion', or have 'carried self-deception to perfection', or am 'anxious to show my credulity', or am 'in a morbid state of mind', or 'hunger for nonsense as my food', or 'indulge in subtle paradoxes' and 'rhetorical exaggerations', or have 'eccentricities' or teach in a style 'utterly beyond' my Accuser's 'comprehension', or create in him 'blank astonishment' or 'exalt the magical powers of my Church', or have 'unconsciously committed myself to a statement which strikes at the root of all morality', or 'look down on the Protestant gentry as without hope of heaven', or 'had better be sent to the furthest' Catholic 'mission among the savages of the South seas', than 'to teach in an Irish Catholic University', or have 'gambled away my reason', or adopt 'sophistries', or have published 'sophisms piled upon sophisms', or have in my sermons 'culminating wonders', or have a 'seemingly sceptical method', or have 'barristerial ability' and 'almost boundless silliness' or 'make great mistakes', or am 'a subtle dialectician', or perhaps have 'lost my temper', or 'misquote Scripture', or am 'antiscriptural', or 'border very closely on the Pelagian heresy' – pp. 21, 23, 38, 39, 42, 47, 48, 49, 50, 54.

These all are impertinences; and the list is so long that I am almost sorry to have given them room which might be better used. However, there they are, or at least a portion of them; and having noticed them thus much, I shall notice them no more.

Coming then to the subject, which is to furnish the staple of my publication, the question of my Truthfulness, I first direct attention to the passage which the Act of Accusation contains at p. 24 and p. 50. I shall give my reason presently, why I begin with it.

My accuser is speaking of my Sermon on Wisdom and Innocence, and he says, 'It must be *remembered always* that it is not a Protestant, but a Romish sermon' (p. 24).

Then at p. 50 he continues, 'Dr Newman does not apply to it that epithet. He called it in his letter to me of the 7th of January (published by him), a "Protestant" one. I remarked that, but considered it a mere slip of the pen. Besides, I have now nothing to say to that letter. It is to his "Reflections", in p. 20, which are open ground to me, that I refer. In them he deliberately repeats the epithet "Protestant": only he, in an utterly imaginary conversation, puts it into my mouth, "which you preached when a Protestant". I call the man who preached that Sermon a Protestant? I should have sooner called him a Buddhist. *At that very time he was teaching his disciples to scorn* and repudiate that name of Protestant, under which, for some reason or other, he *now finds it convenient to take shelter*. If *he* forgets, the world does not, the famous article in the British Critic (the then organ of his party), of three years before, July 1841, which, after denouncing the name of Protestant, declared the object of the party to be none other than the "*unprotestantizing*" of the English Church.'

In this passage my accuser asserts or implies, 1. that the Sermon, on which he originally grounded his slander against me in the January No. of the Magazine, was really and in matter of fact a 'Romish' Sermon; 2. that I ought in my Pamphlet to have acknowledged this fact; 3. that I didn't. 4. That I actually called it instead a Protestant Sermon. 5. That at the time when I published it, twenty years ago, I should have denied that it was a Protestant Sermon. 6. By consequence, I should in that denial have avowed that it was a 'Romish' Sermon; 7. and therefore, not only, when I was in the Established Church, was I guilty of the dishonesty of preaching what at the time I knew to be a 'Romish' Sermon, but now too, in 1864, I have committed the additional dishonesty of calling it a Protestant Sermon. If my accuser does not mean this, I submit to such reparation as I owe him for my mistake, but I cannot make out that he means any thing else.

Here are two main points to be considered; 1. I in 1864 have called it a Protestant Sermon. 2. He in 1844 and now has styled it a Popish Sermon. Let me take these two points separately.

1. Certainly, when I was in the English Church, I *did* disown the word 'Protestant', and that, even at an earlier date than my Accuser names; but just let us see whether this fact is any thing at all to the purpose of his accusation. Last January 7th I spoke to this effect: 'How can you prove that *Father* Newman informs us of a certain thing about the Roman Clergy,' by referring to a *Protestant* Sermon of the Vicar of St Mary's? My Accuser answers me thus: 'There's a quibble! why, *Protestant* is *not* the word which you would have used when at St Mary's, and yet you use it now!' Very true; I do; but what on earth does this matter to my *argument*? how does this word 'Protestant', which I used, tend in any degree to make my argument a quibble? What word *should* I have used twenty years ago instead of 'Protestant'? 'Roman' or 'Romish'? by no manner of means.

My accuser indeed says that 'it must always be remembered that it is not a Protestant *but* a Romish Sermon.' He implies, and, I suppose, he thinks, that not to be a Protestant is to be a Roman; he may say so, if he pleases, but so did not say that large body who have been called by the name of Tractarians, as all the world knows. The movement proceeded on the very basis of denying that position which my Accuser takes for granted that I allowed. It ever said, and it says now, that there is something *between* Protestant and Romish; that there is a 'Via Media' which is neither the one nor the other. Had I been asked twenty years ago, what the doctrine of the Established Church was, I should have answered, 'Neither Romish *nor* Protestant, *but* "Anglican" or "Anglo-catholic." ' I should never have granted that the Sermon was Romish; I should have denied, and that with an internal denial, quite as much as I do now, that it was a Roman or Romish Sermon. Well then, substitute the word 'Anglican' or 'Anglo-catholic' for 'Protestant' in my question, and see if the argument is a bit the worse for it — thus: 'How can you prove that *Father* Newman informs us a certain thing about the Roman Clergy, by referring to an *Anglican* or *Anglo-catholic* Sermon of the Vicar of St Mary's ?' The cogency of the argument remains just where it was. What have I gained in the argument, what has he lost, by my having said, not 'an Anglican Sermon', but 'a Protestant Sermon ?'. What dust then is he throwing into our eyes!

For instance: in 1844 I lived at Littlemore; two or three miles distant from Oxford; and Littlemore lies in three, perhaps in four, distinct parishes, so that of particular houses it is difficult to say, whether they are in St Mary's, Oxford, or in Cowley, or in Iffley, or in Sandford, the line of demarcation running even through them. Now, supposing I were to say in 1864, that 'twenty years ago I did not live in Oxford, *because* I lived out at Littlemore, in the parish of Cowley'; and if upon this there were letters of mine produced dated Littlemore, 1844, in one of which I said that 'I lived, not in Cowley, but at Littlemore, in St Mary's parish', how would that prove that I contradicted myself, and that therefore after all I must be supposed to have been living in Oxford in 1844 ? The utmost that would be proved by the discrepancy, such as it was, would be, that there was some confusion either in me, or in the state of the fact as to the limits of the parishes. There would be no confusion about the place or spot of my residence. I should be saying in 1864, 'I did not live in Oxford twenty years ago, because I lived at Littlemore in the Parish of Cowley.' I should have been saying in 1844, 'I do not live in Oxford, because I live in St Mary's, Littlemore.' In either case I should be saying that my *habitat* in 1844 was *not* Oxford, but Littlemore; and I should be giving the same reason for it. I should be proving an *alibi*. I should be naming the same place for the *alibi*; but twenty years ago I should have spoken of it as St Mary's, Littlemore, and today I should have spoken of it as Littlemore in the Parish of Cowley.

And so as to my Sermon; in January, 1864, I called it a *Protestant* Sermon, and not a Roman; but in 1844 I should, if asked, have called it an *Anglican* Sermon, and not a Roman. In both cases I should have denied that it was Roman, and that on the ground of its being something else; though I should have called that something else, then by one name, now by another. The doctrine of the *Via Media* is a *fact*, whatever name we give to it; I, as a Roman Priest, find it more natural and usual to call it Protestant: I, as an Oxford Vicar, thought it more exact to call it Anglican; but, whatever I then called it, and whatever I now call it, I mean one and the same object by my name, and therefore not another object – viz. not the Roman Church. The argument, I repeat, is sound, whether the *Via Media* and the Vicar of St Mary's be called Anglican or Protestant.

This is a specimen of what my Accuser means by my 'Economies'; nay, it is actually one of those special two, three, or four, committed after February 1, which he thinks sufficient to connect me with the shifty casuists and the double-dealing moralists, as he considers them, of the Catholic Church. What a 'Much ado about nothing!'.

2. But, whether or no he can prove that I in 1864 have committed any logical fault in calling my Sermon on Wisdom and Innocence a Protestant Sermon, he is and has been all along, most firm in the belief himself that a Romish Sermon it is; and this is the point on which I wish specially to insist. It is for this cause that I made the above extract from his Pamphlet, not merely in order to answer him, though, when I had made it, I could not pass by the attack on me which it contains. I shall notice his charges one by one by and by; but I have made this extract here in order to insist and to dwell on this phenomenon – viz. that he does consider it an undeniable fact, that the Sermon is 'Romish' – meaning by 'Romish' not 'savouring of Romish doctrine' merely, but 'the work of a real Romanist, of a conscious Romanist.' This belief it is which leads him to be so severe on me, for now calling it 'Protestant'. He thinks that, whether I have committed any logical self-contradition or not, I am very well aware that, when I wrote it, I ought to have been elsewhere, that I was a conscious Romanist, teaching Romanism – or if he does not believe this himself, he wishes others to think so, which comes to the same thing; certainly I prefer to consider that he thinks so himself, but, if he likes the other hypothesis better, he is welcome to it.

He believes then so firmly that the Sermon was a 'Romish Sermon', that he pointedly takes it for granted, before he has adduced a syllable of proof of the matter of fact. He *starts* by saying that it is a fact to be 'remembered'. 'It *must* be *remembered always*,' he says, 'that it is not a Protestant, but a Romish Sermon,' p. 24. Its Romish parentage is a great truth for the memory, not a thesis for inquiry. Merely to refer his readers to the Sermon is, he considers, to secure them on his side. Hence it is that, in his letter of January 18, he said to me, 'It seems to me, that, by *referring* publicly to the Sermon on which my allegations are founded, I have given every one *an opportunity of judging of their injustice*', that is, an opportunity of seeing that they are transparently just. The notion of there being a *Via Media*, held all along by a large party in the Anglican Church, and now at least not less than at any former time, is too subtle for his intellect. Accordingly, he thinks it was an allowable figure of speech – not more, I suppose, than an 'hyperbole' – when referring to a Sermon of the Vicar of St Mary's in the Magazine, to say that it was the writing of a Roman Priest; and as to serious arguments to prove the point, why, they may indeed be necessary, as a matter of form, in an Act of Accusation, such as his Pamphlet, but they are superfluous to the good sense of any one who will only just look into the matter himself.

Now, with respect to the so-called arguments which he ventures to put forward in proof that the Sermon is Romish, I shall answer them, together with all his other arguments, in the latter portion of this Reply; here I do but draw the attention of the reader, as I have said already, to the phenomenon itself, which he exhibits, of an unclouded confidence that the Sermon is the writing of a virtual member of the Roman communion, and I do so because it has made a great impression on my own mind, and has suggested to me the course that I shall pursue in my answer to him.

I say, he takes it for granted that the Sermon is the writing of a virtual or actual, of a conscious Roman Catholic; and is impatient at the very notion of having to prove it. Father Newman and the Vicar of St Mary's are one and the same: there has been no change of mind in him; what he believed then he believes now, and what he believes now he believed then. To dispute this is frivolous; to distinguish between his past self and his present is subtlety, and to ask for proof of their identity is seeking opportunity to be sophistical. This writer really thinks that he acts a straightforward honest part, when he says 'A Catholic Priest informs us in his Sermon on Wisdom and Innocence preached at St Mary's', and he thinks that I am the shuffler and quibbler when I forbid him to do so. So singular a phenomenon in a man of undoubted ability has struck me forcibly, and I shall pursue the train of thought which it opens.

It is not my present accuser alone who entertains, and has entertained, so dishonourable an opinion of me and of my writings. It is the impression of large classes of men; the impression twenty years ago and the impression now. There has been a general feeling that I was for years where I had no right to be; that I was a 'Romanist' in Protestant livery and service; that I was doing the work of a hostile Church in the bosom of the English Establishment, and knew it, or ought to have known it. There was no need of arguing about particular passages in my writings, when the fact was so patent, as men thought it to be.

First it was certain, and I could not myself deny it, that I scouted the name 'Protestant'. It was certain again, that many of the doctrines which I professed were popularly and generally known as badges of the Roman Church, as distinguished from the faith of the Reformation. Next, how could I have come by them? Evidently, I had certain friends and advisers who did not appear; there was some underground communication between Stony-hurst or Oscott and my rooms at Oriel. Beyond a doubt, I was advocating certain doctrines, not by accident, but on an under-standing with ecclesiastics of the old religion. Then men went further, and said that I had actually been received into that religion, and withal had leave given me to profess myself a Protestant still. Others went even further, and gave it out to the world, as a matter of fact, of which they themselves had the proof in their hands, that I was actually a Jesuit. And when the opinions which I advocated spread, and younger men went further than I, the feeling against me waxed stronger and took a wider range.

And now indignation arose at the knavery of a conspiracy such as this – and it became of course all the greater, in consequence of its being the received belief of the public at large, that craft and intrigue, such as they fancied they beheld with their own eyes, were the very instruments to which the Catholic Church has in these last centuries been indebted for her maintenance and extension.

There was another circumstance still, which increased the irritation and aversion felt by the large classes, of whom I have been speaking, against the preachers of doctrines, so new to them and so unpalatable; and that was, that they developed them in so measured a way. If they were inspired by Roman theologians (and this was taken for granted), why did they not speak out at once ? Why did they keep the world in such suspense and anxiety as to what was coming next, and what was to be the upshot of the whole ? Why this reticence, and half-speaking, and apparent indecision ? It was plain that the plan of operations had been carefully mapped out from the first, and that these men were cautiously advancing towards its accomplishment, as far as was safe at the moment; that their aim and their hope was to carry off a large body with them of the young and the ignorant; that they meant gradually to leaven the minds of the rising genera-tion, and to open the gates of that city, of which they were the sworn defenders, to the enemy who lay in ambush outside of it. And when in spite of the many protestations of the party to the contrary, there was at length an actual movement among their disciples, and one went over to Rome, and then another, the worst anticipations and the worst judgments which had been formed of them received their justification. And lastly, when men first had said of me, 'You will see, *he* will go, he is only biding his time, he is waiting the word of command from Rome', and, when after all, after my arguments and denunciations of former years, at length I did leave the Anglican Church for the Roman, then they said to each other, 'It is just as we said: we knew it would be so.'

This was the state of mind of masses of men twenty years ago, who took no more than an external and commonsense view of what was going on. And partly the tradition, partly the effect of that feeling, remains to the present time. Certainly I consider that, in my own case, it is the great obstacle in the way of my being favourably heard, as at present, when I have to make my defence. Not only am I now a member of a most un-English communion, whose great aim is considered to be the extinction of Protestant-ism and the Protestant Church, and whose means of attack are popularly supposed to be unscrupulous cunning and deceit, but besides, how came I originally to have any relations with the Church of Rome at all ? did I, or my opinions, drop from the sky ? how came I, in Oxford, *in gremio Universitatis*, to present myself to the eyes of men in that full-blown investiture of Popery ? How could I dare, how could I have the conscience, with warnings, with prophecies, with accusations against me, to persevere in a path which steadily advanced towards, which ended in, the religion of Rome? And how am I now to be trusted, when long ago I was trusted, and was found wanting?

It is this which is the strength of the case of my Accuser against me – not his articles of impeachment which he has framed from my writings, which I shall easily crumble into dust, but the bias of the court. It is the state of the atmosphere; it is the vibration all around, which will more or less echo his bold assertion of my dishonesty; it is that prepossession against me, which takes it for granted that, when my reasoning is convincing it is only ingenious, and that when my statements are unanswerable, there is always much put out of sight or hidden in my sleeve; it is that plausible, but cruel conclusion to which men are so apt to jump, that when much is imputed, something must be true, and that it is more likely that one should be to blame, than that many should be mistaken in blaming him – these are the real foes which I have to fight, and the auxiliaries to whom my Accuser makes his advances.

Well, I must break through this barrier of prejudice against me, if I can; and I think I shall be able to do so. When first I read the Pamphlet of Accusation, I almost despaired of meeting effectively such a heap of misrepesentations and such a vehemence of animosity. What was the good of answering first one point, and then another, and going through the whole circle of its abuse; when my answer to the first point would be forgotten, as soon as I got to the second? What was the use of bringing out half a hundred separate principles or views for the refutation of the separate counts in the Indictment, when rejoinders of this sort would but confuse and torment the reader by their number and their diversity? What hope was there of condensing into a pamphlet of a readable length, matter which ought freely to expand itself into half a dozen volumes? What means was there, except the expenditure of interminable pages, to set right even one of that series of 'single passing hints', to use my Assailant's own language which, 'as with his finger tip, he had delivered' against me?

All those separate charges of his had their force in being illustrations of one and the same great imputation. He had already a positive idea to illuminate his whole matter, and to stamp it with force and to quicken it with an interpretation. He called me a *liar* – a simple, a broad, an intelligible, to the English public a plausible arraignment; but for me, to answer in detail charge one by reason one, and charge two by reason two, and charge three by reason three, and so on through the whole string both of accusations and replies, each of which was to be independent of the rest, this would be certainly labour lost as regards any effective result. What I needed was a corresponding antagonist unity in my defence, and where was that to be found ? We see, in the case of commentators on the prophecies of Scripture, an exemplification of the principle on which I am insisting; viz. how much more powerful even a false interpretation of the sacred text is than none at all – how a certain key to the visions of the Apocalypse, for instance, may cling to the mind (I have found it so in my own case), because the view, which it opens on us, is positive and objective, in spite of the fullest demonstration that it really has no claim upon our belief. The reader says, 'What else can the prophecy mean ?' just as my Accuser asks, 'What, then, does Dr Newman mean ?' . . . I reflected, and I saw a way out of my perplexity.

Yes, I said to myself, his very question is about my *meaning*; 'What does Dr Newman mean ?' It points in the very same direction as that into which my musings had turned me already. He asks what I *mean*; not about my words, not about my arguments, not about my actions, as his ultimate point, but about that living intelligence, by which I write, and argue, and act. He asks about my Mind and its Beliefs and its sentiments; and he shall be answered – not for his own sake, but for mine, for the sake of the Religion which I profess, and of the Priesthood in which I am unworthily included, and of my friends and of my foes, and of that general public which consists of neither one nor the other, but of well-wishers, lovers of fair play, sceptical cross-questioners, interested inquirers, curious lookers-on, and simple strangers, unconcerned yet not careless about the issue – for the sake of all these he shall be answered.

My perplexity had not lasted half an hour. I recognized what I had to do, though I shrank from both the task and the exposure which it would entail. I must, I said, give the true key to my whole life; I must show what I am, that it may be seen what I am not, and that the phantom may be extinguished which gibbers instead of me. I wish to be known as a living man, and not as a scarecrow which is dressed up in my clothes. False ideas may be refuted indeed by argument, but by true ideas alone are they expelled. I will vanquish, not my Accuser, but my judges. I will indeed answer his charges and criticisms on me one by one, lest any one should say that they are unanswerable, but such a work shall not be the scope nor the substance of my reply. I will draw out, as far as may be, the history of my mind; I will state the point at which I began, in what external suggestion or accident each opinion had its rise, how far and how they were developed from within, how they grew, were modified, were combined, were in collision with each other, and were changed; again how I conducted myself towards them, and how, and how far, and for how long a time, I thought I could hold them consistently with the ecclesiastical engagements which I had made and with the position which I held. I must show – what is the very truth – that the doctrines which I held, and have held for so many years, have been taught me (speaking humanly) partly by the suggestions of Protestant friends, partly by the teaching of books, and partly by the action of my own mind: and thus I shall account for that phenomenon which to so many seems so wonderful, that I should have left 'my kindred and my father's house' for a Church from which once I turned away with dread – so wonderful to them! as if forsooth a Religion which has flourished through so many ages, among so many nations, amid such varieties of social life, in such contrary classes and conditions of men, and after so many revolutions, political and civil, could not subdue the reason and overcome the heart, without the aid of fraud in the process and the sophistries of the schools.

What I had proposed to myself in the course of half an hour, I determined on at the end of ten days. However, I have many difficulties in fulfilling my design. How am I to say all that has to be said in a reasonable compass ? And then as to the materials of my narrative; I have no autobiographical notes to consult, no written explanations of particular treatises or of tracts which at the time gave offence, hardly any minutes of definite transactions or conversations, and few contemporary memoranda, I fear, of the feelings or motives under which from time to time I acted. I have an abundance of letters from friends with some copies or drafts of my answers to them, but they are for the most part unsorted, and, till this process has taken place, they are even too numerous and various to be available at a moment for my purpose. Then, as to the volumes which I have published, they would in many ways serve me, were I well up in them; but though

I took great pains in their composition, I have thought little about them, when they were once out of my hands, and, for the most part, the last time I read them has been when I revised their last proof sheets.

Under these circumstances my sketch will of course be incomplete. I now for the first time contemplate my course as a whole; it is a first essay, but it will contain, I trust, no serious or substantial mistake, and so far will answer the purpose for which I write it. I purpose to set nothing down in it as certain, for which I have not a clear memory, or some written memorial, or the corroboration of some friend. There are witnesses enough up and down the cuntry to verify, or correct, or complete it; and letters moreover of my own in abundance, unless they have been destroyed.

Moreover, I mean to be simply personal and historical: I am not expounding Catholic doctrine, I am doing no more than explaining myself, and my opinions and actions. I wish, as far as I am able, simply to state facts, whether they are ultimately determined to be for me or against me. Of course there will be room enough for contrariety of judgment among my readers, as to the necessity, or appositeness, or value, or good taste, or religious prudence, of the details which I shall introduce. I may be accused of laying stress on little things, of being beside the mark, of going into impertinent or ridiculous details, of sounding my own praise, of giving scandal; but this is a case above all others, in which I am found to follow my own lights and to speak out my own heart. It is not at all pleasant for me to be egotistical; nor to be criticized for being so. It is not pleasant to reveal to high and low, young and old, what has gone on within me from my early years. It is not pleasant to be giving to every shallow or flippant disputant the advantage over me of knowing my most private thoughts. I might even say the intercourse between myself and my Maker. But I do not like to be called to my face a liar and a knave: nor should I be doing my duty to my faith or to my name, if I were to suffer it. I know I have done nothing to deserve such an insult; and if I prove this, as I hope to do, I must not care for such incidental annoyances as are involved in the process.

PART III

History of my Religious Opinions to the Year 1833
Published as a Pamphlet, Thursday, May 5, 1864

CHAPTER I

It may easily be conceived how great a trial it is to me to write the following history of myself; but I must not shrink from the task. The words, 'Secretum meum mihi', keep ringing in my ears; but as men draw towards their end, they care less for disclosures. Nor is it the least part of my trial, to anticipate that upon first reading what I have written, my friends may consider much in it irrelevant to my purpose; yet I cannot help thinking that, viewed as a whole, it will effect what I propose to myself in giving it to the public.

I was brought up from a child to take great delight in reading the Bible; but I had no formed religious convictions till I was fifteen. Of course I had a perfect knowledge of my Catechism.

After I was grown up, I put on paper such recollections of the thoughts and feelings on religious subjects, which I had at the time that I was a child and a boy. Out of these I select two, which are at once the most definite among them, and also have a bearing on my later convictions.

In the paper to which I have referred, written either in the Long Vacation of 1820, or in October, 1823, the following notices of my school days were sufficiently prominent in my memory for me to consider them worth recording: 1. 'I used to wish the Arabian Tales were true: my imagination ran on unknown influences, on magical powers, and talismans. . . . I thought life might be a dream, or I an Angel, and all this world a deception, my fellow-angels by a playful device concealing themselves from me, and deceiving me with the semblance of a material world.'

Again, 'Reading in the Spring of 1816 a sentence from [Dr

Watts's] "Remnants of Time", entitled "the Saints unknown to the world", to the effect, that "there is nothing in their figure or countenance to distinguish them", &c. &c., I supposed he spoke of Angels who lived in the world, as it were disguised.'

2. The other remark is this: 'I was very superstitious, and for some time previous to my conversion' [when I was fifteen] 'used constantly to cross myself on going into the dark.'

Of course I must have got this practice from some external source or other; but I can make no sort of conjecture whence; and certainly no one had ever spoken to me on the subject of the Catholic religion, which I only knew by name. The French master was an *émigré* Priest, but he was simply made a butt, as French masters too commonly were in that day, and spoke English very imperfectly. There was a Catholic family in the village, old maiden ladies we used to think; but I knew nothing about them but their name. I have of late years heard that there were one or two Catholic boys in the school; but either we were carefully kept from knowing this, or the knowledge of it made simply no impression on our minds. My brother will bear witness how free the school was from Catholic ideas.

I had once been into Warwick Street Chapel, with my father, who, I believe, wanted to hear some piece of music; all that I bore away from it was the recollection of a pulpit and a preacher, and a boy swinging a censer.

When I was at Littlemore, I was looking over old copy-books of my school days, and I found among them my first Latin verse-book; and in the first page of it, there was a device which almost took my breath away with surprise. I have the book before me now, and have just been showing it to others. I have written in the first page, in my schoolboy hand, 'John H. Newman, February 11th, 1811, Verse Book'; then follow my first Verses. Between 'Verse' and 'Book' I have drawn the figure of a solid cross upright, and next to it is, what may indeed be meant for a necklace, but what I cannot make out to be any thing else than a set of beads suspended, with a little cross attached. At this time I was not quite ten years old. I suppose I got these ideas from some romance, Mrs Radcliffe's or Miss Porter's; or from some religious picture; but the strange thing is, how, among the thousand objects which meet a boy's eyes, these in particular should so have fixed themselves in my mind, that I made them thus practically my own. I am certain there was nothing in the churches I attended, or the prayer books I read, to suggest them. It must be recollected that Anglican churches and prayer books were not decorated in those days as I believe they are now.

When I was fourteen, I read Paine's Tracts against the Old Testament, and found pleasure in thinking of the objections which were contained in them. Also, I read some of Hume's Essays; and perhaps that on Miracles. So at least I gave my father to understand; but perhaps it was a brag. Also, I recollect copying out some French verses, perhaps Voltaire's, in denial of the immortality of the soul, and saying to myself something like 'How dreadful, but how plausible!'.

When I was fifteen (in the autumn of 1816), a great change of thought took place in me. I fell under the influences of a definite Creed, and received into my intellect impressions of dogma, which, through God's mercy, have never been effaced or obscured. Above and beyond the conversations and sermons of the excellent man, long dead, the Rev. Walter Mayers, of Pembroke College, Oxford, who was the human means of this beginning of divine faith in me, was the effect of the books which he put into my hands, all of the school of Calvin. One of the first books I read, was a work of Romaine's; I neither recollect the title nor the contents, except one doctrine, which of course I do not include among those which I believe to have come from a divine source, viz. the doctrine of final perseverance. I received it at once, and believed that the inward conversion of which I was conscious (and of which I still am more certain than that I have hands and feet) would last into the next life, and that I was elected to eternal glory. I have no consciousness that this belief had any tendency whatever to lead me to be careless about pleasing God. I retained it till the age of twenty-one, when it gradually faded away; but I believe that it had some influence on my opinions, in the direction of those childish imaginations which I have already mentioned, viz. in isolating me from the objects which surrounded me, in confirming me in my mistrust of the reality of material phenomena, and making me rest in the thought of two and two only absolute and luminously self-evident beings, myself and my Creator – for while I considered myself predestined to salvation, my mind did not dwell upon others, as fancying them simply passed over, not predestined to eternal death. I only thought of the mercy to myself.

The detestable doctrine last mentioned is simply denied and

abjured, unless my memory strangely deceives me, by the writer who made a deeper impression on my mind than any other, and to whom (humanly speaking) I almost owe my soul – Thomas Scott of Aston Sandford. I so admired and delighted in his writings, that, when I was an undergraduate, I thought of making a visit to his Parsonage, in order to see a man whom I so deeply revered. I hardly think I could have given up the idea of this expedition, even after I had taken my degree; for the news of his death in 1821 came upon me as a disappointment as well as a sorrow. I hung upon the lips of Daniel Wilson, afterwards Bishop of Calcutta, as in two sermons at St John's Chapel he gave the history of Scott's life and death. I had been possessed of his 'Force of Truth' and Essays from a boy; his Commentary I bought when I was an undergraduate.

What, I suppose, will strike any reader of Scott's history and writings, is his bold unworldliness and vigorous independence of mind. He followed truth wherever it led him, beginning with Unitarianism, and ending in a zealous faith in the Holy Trinity. It was he who first planted deep in my mind that fundamental Truth of religion. With the assistance of Scott's Essays, and the admirable work of Jones of Nayland, I made a collection of Scripture texts in proof of the doctrine, with remarks (I think) of my own upon them, before I was sixteen; and a few months later I drew up a series of texts in support of each verse of the Athanasian Creed. These papers I have still.

Besides his unworldliness, what I also admired in Scott was his resolute opposition to Antinomianism, and the minutely practical character of his writings. They show him to be a true Englishman, and I deeply felt his influence; and for years I used almost as proverbs what I considered to be the scope and issue of his doctrine, 'Holiness rather than peace', and 'Growth is the only evidence of life'.

Calvinists make a sharp separation between the elect and the world; there is much in this that is cognate or parallel to the Catholic doctrine; but they go on to say, as I understand them, very differently from Catholicism – that the converted and the unconverted can be discriminated by man, that the justified are conscious of their state of justification, and that the regenerate cannot fall away. Catholics on the other hand shade and soften the awful antagonism between good and evil, which is one of their dogmas, by holding that there are different degrees of justification, that there is a great difference in point of gravity between sin and sin, that there is the possibility and the danger of falling away, and that there is no certain knowledge given to any one that he is simply in a state of grace, and much less that he is to persevere to the end – of the Calvinistic tenets the only one which took root in my mind was the fact of heaven and hell, divine favour and divine wrath, of the justified and the unjustified. The notion that the regenerate and the justified were one and the same, and that the regenerate, as such, had the gift of perseverance, remained with me not many years, as I have said already.

This main Catholic doctrine of the warfare between the city of God and the powers of darkness was also deeply impressed upon my mind by a work of a character very opposite to Calvinism, Law's 'Serious Call'.

From this time I have given a full inward assent, and belief to the doctrine of eternal punishment, as delivered by our Lord Himself, in as true a sense as I hold that of eternal happiness; though I have tried in various ways to make that truth less terrible to the intellect.

Now I come to two other works, which produced a deep impression on me in the same autumn of 1816, when I was fifteen years old, each contrary to each, and planting in me the seeds of an intellectual inconsistency which disabled me for a long course of years. I read Joseph Milner's Church History, and was nothing short of enamoured of the long extracts from St Augustine, St Ambrose, and the other Fathers which I found there. I read them as being the religion of the primitive Christians: but simultaneously with Milner I read Newton on the Prophecies, and in consequence became most firmly convinced that the Pope was the Antichrist predicted by Daniel, St Paul, and St John. My imagination was stained by the effects of this doctrine up to the year 1843; it had been obliterated from my reason and judgment at an earlier date; but the thought remained upon me as a sort of false conscience. Hence came that conflict of mind, which so many have felt besides myself – leading some men to make a compromise between two ideas, so inconsistent with each other – driving others to beat out the one idea or the other from their minds – and ending in my own case, after many years of intellectual unrest, in the gradual decay and extinction of one of them – I do not say in its violent death, for why should I not have murdered it sooner, if I murdered it at all ?

I am obliged to mention, though I do it with great reluctance, another deep imagination, which at this time, the autumn of 1816, took possession of me – there can be no mistake about the fact – viz. that it would be the will of God that I should lead a single life. This anticipation, which has held its ground almost continuously ever since – with the break of a month now and a month then, up to 1829, and, after that date, without any break at all – was more or less connected, in my mind, with the notion, that my calling in life would require such a sacrifice as celibacy involved; as, for instance, missionary work among the heathen, to which I had a great drawing for some years. It also strengthened my feeling of separation from the visible world, of which I have spoken above.

In 1822 I came under very different influences from those to which I had hitherto been subjected. At that time, Mr Whately, as he was then, afterwards Archbishop of Dublin, for the few months he remained in Oxford, which he was leaving for good, showed great kindness to me. He renewed it in 1825, when he became Principal of Alban Hall, making me his Vice-Principal and Tutor. Of Dr Whately I will speak presently, for from 1822 to 1825 I saw most of the present Provost of Oriel, Dr Hawkins, at that time Vicar of St Mary's; and, when I took orders in 1824 and had a curacy in Oxford, then, during the Long Vacations, I was especially thrown into his company. I can say with a full heart that I love him, and have never ceased to love him; and I thus preface what otherwise might sound rude, that in the course of the many years in which we were together afterwards, he provoked me very much from time to time, though I am perfectly certain that I have provoked him a great deal more. Moreover, in me such provocation was unbecoming, both because he was the Head of my College, and because, in the first years that I knew him, he had been in many ways of great service to my mind.

He was the first who taught me to weigh my words, and to be cautious in my statements. He led me to that mode of limiting and clearing my sense in discussion and in controversy, and of distinguishing between cognate ideas, and of obviating mistakes by anticipation, which to my surprise has been since considered, even in quarters friendly to me, to savour of the polemics of Rome. He is a man of most exact mind himself, and he used to snub me severely, on reading, as he was kind enough to do, the first Sermons that I wrote, and other compositions which I was engaged upon.

Then as to doctrine, he was the means of great additions to my belief. As I have noticed elsewhere, he gave me the 'Treatise on Apostolical Preaching', by Sumner, afterwards Archbishop of Canterbury, from which I was led to give up my remaining Calvinism, and to receive the doctrine of Baptismal Regeneration. In many other ways too he was of use to me, on subjects semi-religious and semi-scholastic.

It was Dr Hawkins too who taught me to anticipate that, before many years were over there would be an attack made upon the books and the canon of Scripture. I was brought to the same belief by the conversation of Mr Blanco White, who also led me to have freer views on the subject of inspiration than were usual in the Church of England at the time.

There is one other principle, which I gained from Dr Hawkins, more directly bearing upon Catholicism, than any that I have mentioned; and that is the doctrine of Tradition. When I was an Undergraduate, I heard him preach in the University Pulpit his celebrated sermon on the subject, and recollect how long it appeared to me, though he was at that time a very striking preacher; but, when I read it and studied it as his gift, it made a most serious impression upon me. He does not go one step, I think, beyond the high Anglican doctrine, nay he does not reach it; but he does his work thoroughly, and his view was in him original, and his subject was a novel one at the time. He lays down a proposition, self-evident as soon as stated, to those who have at all examined the structure of Scripture, viz. that the sacred text was never intended to teach doctrine, but only to prove it, and that, if we would learn doctrine, we must have recourse to the formularies of the Church; for instance to the Catechism, and to the Creeds. He considers, that, after learning from them the doctrines of Christianity, the inquirer must verify them by Scripture. This view, most true in its outline, most fruitful in its consequences, opened upon me a large field of thought. Dr Whately held it too. One of its effects was to strike at the root of the principle on which the Bible Society was set up. I belonged to its Oxford Association; it became a matter of time when I should withdraw my name from its subscription-list, though I did not do so at once.

It is with pleasure that I pay here a tribute to the memory of the

Rev. William James, then Fellow of Oriel; who, about the year 1823, taught me the doctrine of Apostolical Succession, in the course of a walk, I think, round Christ Church meadow: I recollect being somewhat impatient of the subject at the time.

It was at about this date, I suppose, that I read Bishop Butler's Analogy; the study of which has been to so many, as it was to me, an era in their religious opinions. Its inculcation of a visible Church, the oracle of truth and a pattern of sanctity, of the duties of external religion, and of the historical character of Revelation, are characteristics of this great work which strike the reader at once; for myself, if I may attempt to determine what I most gained from it, it lay in two points, which I shall have an opportunity of dwelling on in the sequel; they are the underlying principles of a great portion of my teaching. First, the very idea of an analogy between the separate works of God leads to the conclusion that the system which is of less importance is economically or sacramentally connected with the more momentous system, and of this conclusion the theory, to which I was inclined as a boy, viz. the unreality of material phenomena, is an ultimate resolution. At this time I did not make the distinction between matter itself and its phenomena, which is so necessary and so obvious in discussing the subject. Secondly, Butler's doctrine that Probability is the guide of life, led me, at least under the teaching to which a few years later I was introduced, to the question of the logical cogency of Faith, on which I have written so much. Thus to Butler I trace those two principles of my teaching, which have led to a charge against me both of fancifulness and of scepticism.

And now as to Dr Whately. I owe him a great deal. He was a man of generous and warm heart. He was particularly loyal to his friends, and to use the common phrase, 'all his geese were swans'. While I was still awkward and timid in 1822, he took me by the hand, and acted towards me the part of a gentle and encouraging instructor. He, emphatically, opened my mind, and taught me to think and to use my reason. After being first noticed by him in 1822, I became very intimate with him in 1825, when I was his Vice-Principal at Alban Hall. I gave up that office in 1826, when I became Tutor of my College, and his hold upon me gradually relaxed. He had done his work towards me or nearly so, when he had taught me to see with my own eyes and to walk with my own feet. Not that I had not a good deal to learn from others still, but I influenced them as well as they me, and co-operated rather than merely concurred with them. As to Dr Whately, his mind was too different from mine for us to remain long on one line. I recollect how dissatisfied he was with an Article of mine in the London Review, which Blanco White, good-humouredly, only called Platonic. When I was diverging from him in opinion (which he did not like), I thought of dedicating my first book to him, in words to the effect that he had not only taught me to think, but to think for myself. He left Oxford in 1831; after that, as far as I can recollect, I never saw him but twice – when he visited the University; once in the street in 1834, once in a room in 1838. From the time that he left, I have always felt a real affection for what I must call his memory; for at least from the year 1834, he made himself dead to me. He had practically indeed given me up from the time that he became Archbishop in 1831; but in 1834 a correspondence took place between us, which, though conducted in the most friendly language on both sides, was the expression of differences of opinion which acted as a final close to our intercourse. My reason told me that it was impossible that we could have got on together longer, had he stayed in Oxford; yet I loved him too much to bid him farewell without pain. After a few years had passed, I began to believe that his influence on me in a higher respect than intellectual advance (I will not say through his fault) had not been satisfactory. I believe that he has inserted sharp things in his later works about me. They have never come in my way, and I have not thought it necessary to seek out what would pain me so much in the reading.

What he did for me in point of religious opinion, was, first, to teach me the existence of the Church, as a substantive body or corporation; next to fix in me those anti-Erastian views of Church polity, which were one of the most prominent features of the Tractarian movement. On this point, and, as far as I know, on this point alone, he and Hurrell Froude intimately sympathized, though Froude's development of opinion here was of a later date. In the year 1826, in the course of a walk, he said much to me about a work then just published, called 'Letters on the Church by an Episcopalian'. He said that it would make my blood boil. It was certainly a most powerful composition. One of our common friends told me, that, after reading it, he could not keep still, but went on walking up and down his room. It was ascribed at once to Whately; I gave eager expression to the contrary opinion; but I found the belief of Oxford in the affirmative to be too strong for me; rightly or wrongly I yielded to the general voice; and I have never heard, then or since, of any disclaimer of authorship on the part of Dr Whately.

The main positions of this able essay are these; first that Church and State should be independent of each other – he speaks of the duty of protesting 'against the profanation of Christ's kingdom, by that *double usurpation*, the interference of the Church in temporals, of the State in spirituals', p. 191; and, secondly, that the Church may justly and by right retain its property, though separated from the State. 'The clergy,' he says p. 133, 'though they ought not to be the hired servants of the Civil Magistrate, may justly retain their revenues; and the State, though it has no right of interference in spiritual concerns, not only is justly entitled to support from the ministers of religion, and from all other Christians, but would, under the system I am recommending, obtain it much more effectually.' The author of this work, whoever he may be, argues out both these points with great force and ingenuity, and with a thorough-going vehemence, which perhaps we may refer to the circumstance, that he wrote, not *in propriâ personâ*, and as thereby answerable for every sentiment that he advanced, but in the professed character of a Scotch Episcopalian. His work had a gradual, but a deep effect on my mind.

I am not aware of any other religious opinion which I owe to Dr Whately. For his special theological tenets I had no sympathy. In the next year, 1827, he told me he considered that I was Arianizing. The case was this: though at that time I had not read Bishop Bull's *Defensio* nor the Fathers, I was just then very strong for that ante-Nicene view of the Trinitarian doctrine, which some writers, both Catholic and non-Catholic, have accused of wearing a sort of Arian exterior. This is the meaning of a passage in Froude's *Remains*, in which he seems to accuse me of speaking against the Athanasian Creed. I had contrasted the two aspects of the Trinitarian doctrine, which are respectively presented by the Athanasian Creed and the Nicene. My criticisms were to the effect that some of the verses of the former Creed were unnecessarily scientific. This is a specimen of a certain disdain for Antiquity which had been growing on me now for several years. It showed itself in some flippant language against the Fathers in the Encyclopaedia Metropolitana, about whom I knew little at the time, except what I had learnt as a boy from Joseph Milner. In writing on the Scripture Miracles in 1825–6, I had read Middleton on the Miracles of the early Church, and had imbibed a portion of his spirit.

The truth is, I was beginning to prefer intellectual excellence to moral; I was drifting in the direction of the liberalism of the day. I was rudely awakened from my dream at the end of 1827 by two great blows – illness and bereavement.

In the beginning of 1829, came the formal break between Dr Whately and me; the affair of Mr Peel's attempted re-election was the occasion of it. I think in 1828 or 1827 I had voted in the minority, when the Petition to Parliament against the Catholic Claims was brought into Convocation. I did so mainly on the views suggested to me by the theory of the Letters of an Episcopalian. Also I disliked the bigoted 'two bottle orthodox', as they were invidiously called. Accordingly I took part against Mr Peel, on a simple academical, not at all an ecclesiastical or a political ground; and this I professed at the time. I considered that Mr Peel had taken the University by surprise, that his friends had no right to call upon us to turn round on a sudden, and to expose ourselves to the imputation of time-serving, and that a great University ought not to be bullied even by a great Duke of Wellington. Also by this time I was under the influence of Keble and Froude; who, in addition to the reasons I have given, disliked the Duke's change of policy as dictated by liberalism.

Whately was considerably annoyed at me, and he took a humourous revenge, of which he had given me due notice beforehand. As head of a house, he had duties of hospitality to men of all parties; he asked a set of the least intellectual men in Oxford to dinner, and men most fond of port: he made me one of this party; placed me between Provost This and Principal That, and then asked me if I was proud of my friends. However, he had a serious meaning in his act; he saw, more clearly than I could do, that I was separating from his own friends for good and all.

Dr Whately attributed my leaving his *clientela* to a wish on my part to be the head of a party myself. I do not think that this charge was deserved. My habitual feeling then and since has been, that it was not I who sought friends, but friends who sought me. Never man had kinder or more indulgent friends than I have had, but I expressed my own feeling as to the mode in which I gained them, in this very year 1829, in the course of a copy of verses. Speaking of my blessings, I said, 'Blessings of friends, which to my door, *unasked, unhoped,* have come'. They have come, they have gone; they came to my great joy, they went to my great grief. He who gave, took away. Dr Whately's impression about me, however, admits of this explanation –

During the first years of my residence at Oriel, though proud of my College, I was not quite at home there. I was very much alone, and I used often to take my daily walk by myself. I recollect once meeting Dr Copleston, then Provost, with one of the Fellows. He turned round, and with the kind courteousness which sat so well on him, made me a bow and said, 'Numquam minus solus, quàm cùm solus.' At that time indeed (from 1823) I had the intimacy of my dear and true friend Dr Pusey, and could not fail to admire and revere a soul so devoted to the cause of religion, so full of good works, so faithful in his affections; but he left residence when I was getting to know him well. As to Dr Whately himself, he was too much my superior to allow of my being at my ease with him; and to no one in Oxford at this time did I open my heart fully and familiarly. But things changed in 1826. At that time I became one of the Tutors of my College, and this gave me position; besides, I had written one or two Essays which had been well received. I began to be known. I preached my first University Sermon. Next year I was one of the Public Examiners for the BA degree. In 1828 I became Vicar of St Mary's. It was to me like the feeling of spring weather after winter; and, if I may so speak, I came out of my shell; I remained out of it till 1841.

The two persons who knew me best at that time are still alive, beneficed clergymen, no longer my friends. They could tell better than any one else what I was in those years. From this time my tongue was, as it were, loosened, and I spoke spontaneously and without effort. One of the two, Mr Rickards, said of me, I have been told, 'Here is a fellow who, when he is silent, will never begin to speak; and when he once begins to speak, will never stop.' It was at this time that I began to have influence, which steadily increased for a course of years. I gained upon my pupils, and was in particular intimate and affectionate with two of our proba-tioner Fellows, Robert Isaac Wilberforce (afterwards Arch-deacon) and Richard Hurrell Froude. Whately then, an acute man, perhaps saw around me the signs of an incipient party, of which I was not conscious myself. And thus we discern the first elements of that movement afterwards called Tractarian.

The true and primary author of it, however, as is usual with great motive-powers, was out of sight. Having carried off as a mere boy the highest honours of the University, he had turned from the admiration which haunted his steps, and sought for a better and holier satisfaction in pastoral work in the country. Need I say that I am speaking of John Keble? The first time that I was in a room with him was on occasion of my election to a fellowship at Oriel, when I was sent for into the Tower, to shake hands with the Provost and Fellows. How is that hour fixed in my memory after the changes of forty-two years, forty-two this very day on which I write! I have lately had a letter in my hands, which I sent at the time to my great friend, John William Bowden, with whom I passed almost exclusively my Undergraduate years. 'I had to hasten to the Tower,' I say to him, 'to receive the congratulations of all the Fellows. I bore it till Keble took my hand, and then felt so abashed and unworthy of the honour done me, that I seemed desirous of quite sinking into the ground.' His had been the first name which I had heard spoken of, with reverence rather than admiration, when I came up to Oxford. When one day I was walking in High Street with my dear earliest friend just mentioned, with what eagerness did he cry out, 'There's Keble!' and with what awe did I look at him! Then at another time I heard a Master of Arts of my college give an account how he had just then had occasion to introduce himself on some business to Keble, and how gentle, courteous, and unaffected Keble had been, so as almost to put him out of countenance. Then too it was reported, truly or falsely, how a rising man of brilliant reputation, the present Dean of St Paul's, Dr Milman, admired and loved him, adding, that somehow he was strangely unlike any one else. However, at the time when I was elected Fellow of Oriel he was not in residence, and he was shy of me for years in consequence of the marks which I bore upon me, of the evangelical and liberal schools. At least so I have ever thought. Hurrell Froude brought us together about 1828: it is one of the sayings preserved in his 'Remains', – 'Do you know the story of the murderer who had done one good thing in his life? Well; if I was ever asked what good deed I had ever done, I should say that I had brought Keble and Newman to understand each other.'

The Christian Year made its appearance in 1827. It is not necessary, and scarcely becoming, to praise a book which had already become one of the classics of the language. When the general tone of religious literature was so nerveless and impotent, as it was at that time, Keble struck an original note and woke up in the hearts of thousands a new music, the music of a school, long unknown in England. Nor can I pretend to analyze, in my own instance, the effect of religious teaching so deep, so pure, so beautiful. I have never till now tried to do so; yet I think I am not wrong in saying, that the two main intellectual truths which it brought home to me, were the same two, which I had learned from Butler, though recast in the creative mind of my new master. The first of these was what may be called, in a large sense of the word, the Sacramental system; that is, the doctrine that material phenomena are both the types and the instruments of real things unseen – a doctrine, which embraces in its fulness, not only what Anglicans, as well as Catholics, believe about Sacraments properly so called; but also the article of 'the Communion of Saints'; and likewise the Mysteries of the faith. The connexion of this philosophy of religion with what is sometimes called 'Berkeleyism' has been mentioned above; I knew little of Berkeley at this time except by name; nor have I ever studied him.

On the second intellectual principle which I gained from Mr Keble, I could say a great deal; if this were the place for it. It runs through very much that I have written, and has gained for me many hard names. Butler teaches us that probability is the guide of life. The danger of this doctrine, in the case of many minds, is, its tendency to destroy in them absolute certainty, leading them to consider every conclusion as doubtful, and resolving truth into an opinion, which it is safe indeed to obey or to profess, but not possible to embrace with full internal assent. If this were to be allowed, then the celebrated saying, 'O God, if there be a God, save my soul, if I have a soul!' would be the highest measure of devotion – but who can really pray to a Being, about whose existence he is seriously in doubt?

I considered that Mr Keble met this difficulty by ascribing the firmness of assent which we give to religious doctrine, not to the probabilities which introduced it, but to the living power of faith and love which accepted it. In matters of religion, he seemed to say, it is not merely probability which makes us intellectually certain, but probability as it is put to account by faith and love. It is faith and love which give to probability a force which it has not in itself. Faith and love are directed towards an Object; in the vision of that Object they live; it is that Object, received in faith and love, which renders it reasonable to take probability as sufficient for internal conviction. Thus the argument from Probability, in the matter of religion, became an argument from Personality, which in fact is one form of the argument from Authority.

In illustration, Mr Keble used to quote the words of the Psalm: 'I will guide thee with mine *eye*. Be ye not like to horse and mule, which have no understanding; whose mouths must be held with bit and bridle, lest they fall upon thee.' This is the very difference, he used to say, between slaves, and frieds or children. Friends do not ask for literal commands; but, from their knowledge of the speaker, they understand his half-words, and from love of him they anticipate his wishes. Hence it is, that in his poem for St Bartholomew's Day, he speaks of the 'Eye of God's word': and in the note quotes Mr Miller, of Worcester College, who remarks, in his Bampton Lectures, on the special power of Scripture, as having 'this Eye, like that of a portrait, uniformly fixed upon us, turn where we will.' The view thus suggested by Mr Keble, is brought forward in one of the earliest of the 'Tracts for the Times'. In No. 8 I say, 'The Gospel is a Law of Liberty. We are treated as sons, not as servants; not subjected to a code of formal commandments, but addressed as those who love God, and wish to please Him.'

I did not at all dispute this view of the matter, for I made use of it myself; but I was dissatisfied, because it did not go to the root of the difficulty. It was beautiful and religious, but it did not even profess to be logical; and accordingly I tried to complete it by considerations of my own, which are implied in my University Sermons, Essay on Ecclesiastical Miracles, and Essay on Development of Doctrine. My argument is in outline as follows: that that absolute certitude which we were able to possess, whether as to the truths of natural theology, or as to the fact of a revelation, was the result of an *assemblage* of concurring and converging probabilities, and that, both according to the constitution of the human mind and the will of its Maker; that certitude was a habit of mind, that certainty was a quality of propositions; that probabilities which did not reach to logical certainty might suffice for a mental certitude; that the certitude thus brought about in measure and strength the certitude which was created by the strictest scientific demonstration; and that to possess such certitude might in given cases and to given individuals be a plain duty, though not to others in other circumstances –

Moreover, that as there were probabilities which sufficed for certitude, so there were other probabilities which were legitimately adapted to create opinion; that it might be quite as much a matter of duty in given cases and to given persons to have about a fact an opinion of a definite strength and consistency, as in the case of greater or of more numerous probabilities it was a duty to have a certitude; that accordingly we were bound to be more or less sure, on a sort of (as it were) graduated scale of assent, viz. according as the probabilities attaching to a professed fact were brought home to us, and, as the case might be, to entertain about it a pious belief, or a pious opinion, or a religious conjecture, or at least, a tolerance of such belief, or opinion, or conjecture in others; that on the other hand, as it was a duty to have a belief, of more or less strong texture, in given cases, so in other cases it was a duty not to believe, not to opine, not to conjecture, not even to tolerate the notion that a professed fact was true, inasmuch as it would be credulity or superstition, or some other moral fault, to do so. This was the religion of Private Judgement in religion; that is, of a Private Judgment, not formed arbitrarily and according to one's fancy or liking, but conscientiously, and under a sense of duty.

Considerations such as these throw a new light on the subject of Miracles, and they seem to have led me to re-consider the view which I had taken of them in my Essay in 1825–6. I do not know what was the date of this change in me, nor of the train of ideas on which it was founded. That there had been already great miracles, as those of Scripture, as the Resurrection, was a fact establishing the principle that the laws of nature had sometimes been suspended by their Divine Author; and since what had happened once might happen again, a certain probability, at least no kind of improbability, was attached to the idea, taken in itself, or miraculous intervention in later times, and miraculous accounts were to be regarded in connexion with the verisimilitude, scope, instrument, character, testimony, and circumstances, with which they presented themselves to us; and, according to the final result of those various considerations, it was our duty to be sure, or to believe, or to opine, or to surmise, or to tolerate, or to reject, or to denounce. The main difference between my Essay on Miracles in 1826 and my Essay in 1842 is this: that in 1826 I considered that miracles were sharply divided into two classes, those which were to be received, and those which were to be rejected; whereas in

1842 I saw that they were to be regarded according to their greater or less probability, which was in some cases sufficient to create certitude about them, in other cases only belief or opinion.

Moreover, the argument from Analogy, on which this view of the question was founded, suggested to me something besides, in recommendation of the Ecclesiastical Miracles. It fastened itself upon the theory of Church History which I had learned as a boy from Joseph Milner. It is Milner's doctrine, that upon the visible Church come down from above, at certain intervals, large and temporary *Effusions* of divine grace. This is the leading idea of his work. He begins by speaking of the day of Pentecost, as marking 'the first of those *Effusions* of the Spirit of God, which from age to age have visited the earth since the coming of Christ' Vol. i. p. 3. In a note he adds that 'in the term "Effusion" there is *not* here included the idea of the miraculous or extraordinary operations of the Spirit of God'; but still it was natural for me, admitting Milner's general theory, and applying to it the principle of analogy, not to stop short at his abrupt *ipse dixit*, but boldly to pass forward to the conclusion, on other grounds plausible, that, as miracles accompanied the first effusion of grace, so they might accompany the later. It is surely a natural and on the whole, a true anticipation (though of course there are exceptions in particular cases), that gifts and graces go together, now, according to the ancient Catholic doctrine, the gift of miracles was viewed as the attendant and shadow of transcendent sanctity: and moreover, since such sanctity was not of every day's occurrence, nay further, since one period of Church history differed widely from another, and, as Joseph Milner would say, there have been generations or centuries of degeneracy or disorder, and times of revival, and since one region might be in the mid-day of religious fervour, and another in twilight or gloom, there was no force in the popular argument, that, because we did not see miracles with our own eyes, miracles had not happened in former times, or were not now at this very time taking place in distant places – but I must not dwell longer on a subject, to which in a few words it is impossible to do justice.

Hurrell Froude was a pupil of Keble's, formed by him, and in turn reacting upon him. I knew him first in 1826, and was in the closest and most affectionate friendship with him from about 1829 till his death in 1836. He was a man of the highest gifts – so truly

many-sided, that it would be presumptuous in me to attempt to
describe him, except under those aspects in which he came before
me. Nor have I here to speak of the gentleness and tenderness of
nature, the playfulness, the free elastic force and graceful
versatility of mind, and the patient winning considerateness in
discussion, which endeared him to those to whom he opened his
heart; for I am all along engaged upon matters of belief and
opinion, and am introducing others into my narrative, not for
their own sake, or because I love and have loved them, so much as
because, and so far as, they have influenced my theological views.
In this respect then, I speak of Hurrell Froude – in his intellectual
aspect – as a man of high genius, brimful and overflowing with
ideas and views, in him original, which were too many and strong
even for his bodily strength, and which crowded and jostled
against each other in their effort after distinct shape and
expression. And he had an intellect as critical and logical as it was
speculative and bold. Dying prematurely, as he did, and in the
conflict and transition-state of opinion, his religious views never
reached their ultimate conclusion, by the very reason of their
multitude and their depth. His opinions arrested and influenced
me, even when they did not gain my assent. He professed openly
his admiration of the Church of Rome, and his hatred of the
Reformers. He delighted in the notion of an hierarchical system,
of sacerdotal power and of full ecclesiastical liberty. He felt scorn
of the maxim, 'The Bible and the Bible only is the religion of
Protestants'; and he gloried in accepting Tradition as a main
instrument of religious teaching. He had a high severe idea of the
intrinsic excellence of Virginity; and he considered the Blessed
Virgin its great Pattern. He delighted in thinking of the Saints; he
had a vivid appreciation of the idea of sanctity, its possibility and
its heights; and he was more than inclined to believe a large
amount of miraculous interference as occurring in the early and
middle ages. He embraced the principle of penance and mortifica-
tion. He had a deep devotion to the Real Presence, in which he had
a firm faith. He was powerfully drawn to the Medieval Church,
but not to the Primitive.

He had a keen insight into abstract truth; but he was an
Englishman to the backbone in his severe adherence to the real
and the concrete. He had a most classical taste, and a genius for
philosophy and art; and he was fond of historical inquiry, and the
politics of religion. He had no turn for theology as such. He set no

sufficient value on the writings of the Fathers, on the detail or development of doctrine, on the definite traditions of the Church viewed in their matter, on the teaching of the Ecumenical Councils, or on the controversies out of which they arose. He took an eager courageous view of things on the whole. I should say that his power of entering into the minds of others did not equal his other gifts; he could not believe, for instance, that I really held the Roman Church to be Antichristian. On many points he would not believe but that I agreed with him, when I did not. He seemed not to understand my difficulties. His were of a different kind, the contrariety between theory and fact. He was a high Tory of the Cavalier stamp, and was disgusted with the Toryism of the opponents of the Reform Bill. He was smitten with the love of the Theocratic Church; he went abroad and was shocked by the degeneracy which he thought he saw in the Catholics of Italy.

It is difficult to enumerate the precise additions to my theological creed which I derived from a friend to whom I owe so much. He taught me to look with admiration towards the Church of Rome, and in the same degree to dislike the Reformation. He fixed deep in me the idea of devotion to the Blessed Virgin, and he led me gradually to believe in the Real Presence.

There is one remaining source of my opinions to be mentioned, and that far from the least important. In proportion as I moved out of the shadow of that Liberalism which had hung over my course, my early devotion towards the Fathers returned; and in the Long Vacation of 1828 I set about to read them chronologically, beginning with St Ignatius and St Justin. About 1830 a proposal was made to me by Mr Hugh Rose, who with Mr Lyall (afterwards Dean of Canterbury) was providing writers for a Theological Library, to furnish them with a History of the Principal Councils. I accepted it, and at once set to work on the Council of Nicæa. It was to launch myself on an ocean with currents innumerable; and I was drifted back first to the ante-Nicene history, and then to the Church of Alexandria. The work at last appeared under the title of *The Arians of the Fourth Century*; and of its 422 pages, the first 117 consisted of introductory matter, and the Council of Nicæa did not appear till the 254th, and then occupied at most twenty pages.

I do not know when I first learnt to consider that Antiquity was the true exponent of the doctrines of Christianity and the basis of the Church of England; but I take it for granted that the works of Bishop Bull, which at this time I read, were my chief introduction to this principle. The course of reading, which I pursued in the composition of my volume, was directly adapted to develop it in my mind. What principally attracted me in the ante-Nicene period was the great Church of Alexandria, the historical centre of teaching in those times. Of Rome for some centuries comparatively little is known. The battle of Arianism was first fought in Alexandria; Athanasius, the champion of the truth, was Bishop of Alexandria; and in his writings he refers to the great religious names of an earlier date, to Origen, Dionysius, and others, who were the glory of its see, or of its school. The broad philosophy of Clement and Origen carried me away; the philosophy, not the theological doctrine; and I have drawn out some features of it in my volume, with the zeal and freshness, but with the partiality, of a neophyte. Some portions of their teaching, magnificent in themselves, came like music to my inward ear, as if the response to ideas, which, with little external to encourage them, I had cherished so long. These were based on the mystical or sacramental principle, and spoke of the various Economics or Dispensations of the Eternal. I understood these passages to mean that the exterior world, physical and historical, was but the manifestation to our senses of realities greater than itself. Nature was a parable: Scripture was an allegory: pagan literature, philosophy, and mythology, properly understood, were but a preparation for the Gospel. The Greek poets and sages were in a certain sense prophets; for 'thoughts beyond their thought to those high bards were given.' There had been a directly divine dispensation granted to the Jews; but there had been in some sense a dispensation carried on in favour of the Gentiles. He who had taken the seed of Jacob for His elect people, had not therefore cast the rest of mankind out of His sight. In the fulness of time both Judaism and Paganism had come to nought; the outward framework, which concealed yet suggested the Living Truth, had never been intended to last, and it was dissolving under the beams of the Sun of Justice which shone behind it and through it. The process of change had been slow; it had been done not rashly, but by rule and measure, 'at sundry times and in divers manners', first one disclosure and then another, till the whole evangelical doctrine was brought into full manifestation. And thus room was made for the anticipation of further and deeper disclosures, of truths still under the veil of the letter, and in their season to be revealed. The visible world still remains without its divine interpretation; Holy Church in her sacraments and her hierarchical appointments, will remain, even to the end of the world, only a symbol of those heavenly facts which fill eternity. Her mysteries are but the expressions in human language of truths to which the human mind is unequal. It is evident how much there was in all this in correspondence with the thoughts which had attracted me when I was young, and with the doctrine which I have already associated with the Analogy and the Christian Year.

It was, I suppose, to the Alexandrian school and to the early Church that I owe in particular what I definitely held about the Angels. I viewed them, not only as the ministers employed by the Creator in the Jewish and Christian dispensations, as we find on the face of Scripture, but as carrying on, as Scripture also implies, the Economy of the Visible World. I considered them as the real causes of motion, light, and life, and of those elementary principles of the physical universe, which, when offered in their developments to our senses, suggest to us the notion of cause and effect, and of what are called the laws of nature. I have drawn out this doctrine in my Sermon for Michaelmas day, written in 1831. I say of the Angels, 'Every breath of air and ray of light and hate, every beautiful prospect, is as it were, the skirts of their garments, the waving of the robes of those whose faces see God.' Again, I ask what would be the thoughts of a man who, 'when examining a flower, or a herb, or a pebble, or a ray of light, which he treats as something so beneath him in the scale of existence, suddenly discovered that he was in the presence of some powerful being who was hidden behind the visible things he was inspecting – who, though concealing his wise hand, was giving them their beauty, grace, and perfection, as being God's instrument for the purpose – nay, whose robe and ornaments those objects were, which he was so eager to analyze ?' and I therefore remark that 'we may say with grateful and simple hearts with the Three Holy Children, "O all ye works of the Lord, &c., &c., bless ye the Lord, praise Him, and magnify Him for ever.".'

Also, besides the hosts of evil spirits, I considered there was a middle race, δαιμόνια, neither in heaven, nor in hell; partially fallen, capricious, wayward; noble or crafty, benevolent or malicious, as the case might be. These beings gave a sort of inspiration or intelligence to races, nations, and classes of men.

Hence the action of bodies politic and associations, which is often so different from that of the individuals who compose them. Hence the character and the instinct of states and governments, of religious communities and communions. I thought these assemblages had their life in certain unseen Powers. My preference of the Personal to the Abstract would naturally lead me to this view. I thought it countenanced by the mention of 'the Prince of Persia' in the Prophet Daniel; and I think I considered that it was of such intermediate beings that the Apocalypse spoke when it introduced 'the Angels of the Seven Churches'.

In 1837 I made a further development of this doctrine. I said to an intimate and dear friend, Samuel Francis Wood, in a letter which came into my hands on his death, 'I have an idea. The mass of the Fathers, (Justin, Athenagoras, Irenæus, Clement, Tertullian, Origen, Lactantius, Sulpicius, Ambrose, Nazianzen) hold that, though Satan fell from the beginning, the Angels fell before the deluge, falling in love with the daughters of men. This has lately come across me as a remarkable solution of a notion which I cannot help holding. Daniel speaks as if each nation had its guardian Angel. I cannot but think that there are beings with a great deal of good in them, yet with great defects, who are the animating principles of certain institutions, &c., &c. . . . Take England, with many high virtues, and yet a low Catholicism. It seems to me that John Bull is a spirit neither of heaven nor hell . . . Has not the Christian Church, in its parts, surrendered itself to one or other of these simulations of the truth ? . . . How are we to avoid Scylla and Charybdis and go straight on to the very image of Christ ?' &c., &c.

I am aware that what I have been saying will, with many men, be doing credit to my imagination at the expense of my judgment – 'Hippoclides doesn't care'; I am not setting myself up as a pattern of good sense or of any thing else: I am but giving a history of my opinions, and that, with the view of showing that I have come by them through intelligible processes of thought and honest external means. The doctrine indeed of the Economy has in some quarters been itself condemned as intrinsically pernicious, as if leading to lying and equivocation, when applied, as I have applied it in my remarks upon it in my History of the Arians, to matters of conduct. My answer to this imputation I postpone to the concluding pages of my Volume.

While I was engaged in writing my work upon the Arians, great events were happening at home and abroad, which brought out into form and passionate expression the various beliefs which had so gradually been winning their way into my mind. Shortly before, there had been a Revolution in France; the Bourbons had been dismissed: and I held that it was unchristian for nations to cast off their governors, and, much more, sovereigns who had the divine right of inheritance. Again, the great Reform Agitation was going on around me as I wrote. The Whigs had come into power; Lord Grey had told the Bishops to set their house in order, and some of the Prelates had been insulted and threatened in the streets of London. The vital question was, how were we to keep the Church from being liberalized? There was such apathy on the subject in some quarters, such imbecile alarm in others; the true principles of Churchmanship seemed so radically decayed, and there was such distraction in the councils of the Clergy. Blomfield, the Bishop of London of the day, an active and open-hearted man, had been for years engaged in diluting the high orthodoxy of the Church by the introduction of members of the Evangelical body into places of influence and trust. He had deeply offended men who agreed in opinion with myself, by an off-hand saying (as it was reported) to the effect that belief in the Apostolical succession had gone out with the Non-jurors. 'We can count you,' he said to some of the gravest and most venerated persons of the old school. And the Evangelical party itself, with their late successes, seemed to have lost that simplicity and unworldliness which I admired so much in Milner and Scott. It was not that I did not venerate such men as Ryder, the then Bishop of Lichfield, and others of similar sentiments, who were not yet promoted out of the ranks of the Clergy, but I thought little of them as a class. I thought the Evangelicals played into the hands of the Liberals. With the Establishment thus divided and threatened, thus ignorant of its true strength, I compared that fresh vigorous Power of which I was reading in the first centuries. In her triumphant zeal on behalf of that Primeval Mystery, to which I had had so great a devotion from my youth, I recognized the movement of my Spiritual Mother. 'Incessu patuit Dea.' The self-conquest of her Ascetics, the patience of her Martyrs, the irresistible determination of her Bishops, the joyous swing of her advance, both exalted and abashed me. I said to myself, 'Look on this picture and on that'; I felt affection for my own Church, but not tenderness; I felt dismay at her prospects, anger and scorn at her do-nothing perplexity. I thought that if Liberalism once got a footing within her, it was sure of the victory in the event. I saw that Reformation principles were powerless to rescue her. As to leaving her, the thought never crossed my imagination; still I ever kept before me that there was something greater than the Established Church, and that that was the Church Catholic and Apostolic, set up from the beginning, of which she was but the local presence and the organ. She was nothing, unless she was this. She must be dealt with strongly, or she would be lost. There was need of a second reformation.

At this time I was disengaged from College duties, and my health had suffered from the labour involved in the composition of my Volume. It was ready for the Press in July 1832, though not published till the end of 1833. I was easily persuaded to join Hurrell Froude and his Father, who were going to the south of Europe for the health of the former.

We set out in December 1832. It was during this expedition that my Verses which are in the Lyra Apostolica were written – a few indeed before it, but not more than one or two of them after it. Exchanging, as I was, definite Tutorial work, and the literary quiet and pleasant friendships of the last six years, for foreign countries and an unknown future, I naturally was led to think that some inward changes, as well as some larger course of action, were coming upon me. At Whitchurch, while waiting for the down mail to Falmouth, I wrote the verses about my Guardian Angel, which begin with these words: 'Are these the tracks of some unearthly Friend?' and which go on to speak of 'the vision' which haunted me – that vision is more or less brought out in the whole series of these compositions.

I went to various coasts of the Mediterranean, parted with my friends at Rome; went down for the second time to Sicily without companion, at the end of April, and got back to England by Palermo in the early part of July. The strangeness of foreign life threw me back into myself; I found pleasure in historical sites and beautiful scenes, not in men and manners. We kept clear of Catholics throughout our tour. I had a conversation with the Dean of Malta, a most pleasant man, lately dead; but it was about the Fathers, and the Library of the great church. I knew the Abbate Santini, at Rome, who did no more than copy for me the Gregorian tones. Froude and I made two calls upon Monsignore (now Cardinal) Wiseman at the Collegio Inglese, shortly before we left Rome. Once we heard him preach at a church in the Corso.

I do not recollect being in a room with any other ecclesiastics, except a Priest at Castro-Giovanni in Sicily, who called on me when I was ill, and with whom I wished to hold a controversy. As to Church Services, we attended the Tenebræ, at the Sestine, for the sake of the Miserere; and that was all. My general feeling was, 'All, save the spirit of man, is divine'. I saw nothing but what was external; of the hidden life of Catholics I knew nothing. I was still more driven back into myself, and felt my isolation. England was in my thoughts solely, and the news from England came rarely and imperfectly. The Bill for the Suppression of the Irish Sees was in progress, and filled my mind. I had fierce thoughts against the Liberals.

I was the success of the Liberal cause which fretted me inwardly. I became fierce against its instruments and its manifestations. A French vessel was at Algiers; I would not even look at the tricolour. On my return, though forced to stop twenty-four hours at Paris, I kept indoors the whole time, and all that I saw of that beautiful city, was what I saw from the Diligence. The Bishop of London had already sounded me as to my filling one of the Whitehall preacherships, which he had just then put on a new footing; but I was indignant at the line which he was taking, and from my Steamer I had sent home a letter declining the appointment by anticipation, should it be offered to me. At this time I was specially annoyed with Dr Arnold, though it did not last into later years. Some one, I think, asked, in conversation at Rome, whether a certain interpretation of Scripture was Christian? it was answered that Dr Arnold took it; I interposed, 'But is *he* a Christian?'. The subject went out of my head at once; when afterwards I was taxed with it I could say no more in explanation, than (what I believe was the fact) that I must have had in mind some free views of Dr Arnold about the Old Testament – I thought I must have meant, 'Arnold answers for the interpretation, But who is to answer for Arnold?'. It was at Rome too that we began the Lyra Apostolica which appeared monthly in the British Magazine. The motto shows the feeling of both Froude and myself at the time: we borrowed from M. Bunsen a Homer, and Froude chose the words in which Achilles, on returning to the battle, says, 'You shall know the difference, now that I am back again.'

Especially when I was left by myself, the thought came upon me that deliverance is wrought, not by the many but by the few, not by bodies but by persons. Now it was, I think, that I repeated to myself the words, which had ever been dear to me from my school days, 'Exoriare aliquis!' — now too, that Southey's beautiful poem of Thalaba, for which I had an immense liking, came forcibly to my mind. I began to think that I had a mission. There are sentences of my letters to my friends to this effect, if they are not destroyed. When we took leave of Monsignore Wiseman, he had courteously expressed a wish that we might make a second visit to Rome; I said with great gravity, 'We have a work to do in England.' I went down at once to Sicily, and the presentiment grew stronger. I struck into the middle of the island, and fell ill of a fever at Leonforte. My servant thought that I was dying, and begged for my last directions. I gave them, as he wished; but I said, 'I shall not die.' I repeated, 'I shall not die, for I have not sinned against light. I have not sinned against light.' I never have been able to make out at all what I meant.

I got to Castro-Giovanni, and was laid up there for nearly three weeks. Towards the end of May I set off for Palermo, taking three days for the journey. Before starting from my inn in the morning of 26 or 27 May, I sat down on my bed, and began to sob bitterly. My servant, who had acted as my nurse, asked what ailed me. I could only answer him, 'I have a work to do in England.'

I was aching to get home; yet for want of a vessel I was kept at Palermo for three weeks. I began to visit the Churches, and they calmed my impatience, though I did not attend any services. I knew nothing of the Presence of the Blessed Sacrament there. At last I got off in an orange boat, bound for Marseilles. We were becalmed a whole week in the Straits of Bonifacio. Then it was that I wrote the lines, 'Lead, kindly light', which have since become well known. I was writing verses the whole time of my passage. At length I got to Marseilles, and set off for England. The fatigue of travelling was too much for me, and I was laid up for several days at Lyons. At last I got off again, and did not stop night or day (excepting the compulsory delay at Paris) till I reached England, and my mother's house. My brother had arrived from Persia only a few hours before. This was on the Tuesday. The following Sunday July 14th, Mr Keble preached the Assize Sermon in the University Pulpit. It was published under the title of 'National Apostasy'. I have ever considered and kept the day, as the start of the religious movement of 1833.

PART IV

History of my Religious Opinions from 1833 to 1839
Published as a Pamphlet, Thursday, 12 May 1864.

CHAPTER II

In spite of the foregoing pages, I have no romantic story to tell; but have written them, because it is my duty to tell things as they took place. I have not exaggerated the feelings with which I returned to England, and I have no desire to dress up the events which followed, so as to make them in keeping with the narrative which has gone before. I soon relapsed into the every-day life which I had hitherto led; in all things the same, except that a new object was given me. I had employed myself in my own rooms in reading and writing, and in the care of a Church, before I left England, and I returned to the same occupations when I was back again. And yet perhaps those first vehement feelings which carried me on were necessary for the beginning of the Movement; and afterwards, when it was once begun, the special need of me was over.

When I got home from abroad, I found that already a movement had commenced in opposition to the specific danger which at that time was threatening the religion of the nation and its Church. Several zealous and able men had united their counsels, and were in correspondence with each other. The principal of these were Mr Keble, Hurrell Froude, who had reached home long before me, Mr William Palmer of Dublin and Worcester College (not Mr William Palmer of Magdalen, who is now a Catholic), Mr Arthur Perceval, and Mr Hugh Rose.

To mention Mr Hugh Rose's name is to kindle in the minds of those who knew him, a host of pleasant and affectionate remembrances. He was the man above all others fitted by his cast of mind and literary powers to make a stand, if a stand could be made, against the calamity of the times. He was gifted with a high and large mind, and a true sensibility of what was great and beautiful; he wrote with warmth and energy; and he had a cool head and cautious judgment. He spent his strength and shortened his life, Pro Ecclesia Dei, as he understood that sovereign idea. Some years earlier he had been the first to give warning, I think from the University Pulpit at Cambridge, of the perils to England which lay in the biblical and theological speculations of Germany. The Reform agitation followed, and the Whig Government came into power; and he anticipated in their distribution of Church patronage the authoritative introduction of liberal opinions into the country – by 'liberal' I mean liberalism in *religion*, for questions of politics, as such, do not come into this narrative at all. He feared that by the Whig party a door would be opened in England to the most grievous of heresies, which never could be closed again. In order under such grave circumstances to unite Churchmen together, and to make a front against the coming danger, he had in 1832 commenced the British Magazine, and in the same year he came to Oxford in the summer term, in order to beat up for writers for his publication; on that occasion I became known to him through Mr Palmer. His reputation and position came in aid of his obvious fitness, in point of character and intellect, to become the centre of an ecclesiastical movement, if such a movement were to depend on the action of a party. His delicate health, his premature death, would have frustrated the expectation, even though the new school of opinion had been more exactly thrown into the shape of a party, than in fact was the case. But he zealously backed up the first efforts of those who were principals in it; and, when he went abroad to die, in 1838, he allowed me the solace of expressing my feelings of attachment and gratitude to him by addressing him, in the dedication of a volume of my Sermons, as the man, 'who, when hearts were failing, bade us stir up the gift that was in us, and betake ourselves to our true Mother.'

But there were other reasons, besides Mr Rose's state of health, which hindered those who so much admired him from availing themselves of his close co-operation in the coming fight. United as both he and they were in the general scope of the Movement, they were in discordance with each other from the first in their estimate of the means to be adopted for attaining it. Mr Rose had a position in the Church, a name, and serious responsibilities; he had direct ecclesiastical superiors; he had intimate relations with his own University, and a large clerical connexion through the country. Froude and I were nobodies; with no characters to lose, and no antecedents to fetter us. Rose could not go a-head across country, as Froude had no scruples in doing. Froude was a bold rider, as on horseback, so also in his speculations. After a long conversation with him on the logical bearing of his principles, Mr Rose said of him with quiet humour, that 'he did not seem to be afraid of inferences.' It was simply the truth; Froude had that strong hold of first princples, and that keen perception of their value, that he was comparatively indifferent to the revolutionary action which would attend on their application to a given state of things; whereas in the thoughts of Rose, as a practical man, existing facts had the precedence of every other idea, and the chief test of the soundness of a line of policy lay in the consideration whether it would work. This was one of the first questions, which, as it seemed to me, on every occasion occurred to his mind. With Froude, Erastianism – that is, the union (so he viewed it) of Church and State – was the parent, or if not the parent, the serviceable and sufficient tool, of liberalism. Till that union was snapped, Christian doctrine never could be safe; and, while he well knew how high and unselfish was the temper of Mr Rose, yet he used to apply to him an epithet, reproachful in his own mouth –Rose was a 'conservative'. By bad luck, I brought out this word to Mr Rose in a letter of my own, which I wrote to him in criticism of something he had inserted in his Magazine: I got a vehement rebuke for my pains, for though Rose pursued a conservative line, he had as high a disdain, as Froude could have, of a worldly ambition, and an extreme sensitiveness of such an imputation.

But there was another reason still, and a more elementary one, which severed Mr Rose from the Oxford Movement. Living movements do not come of committees, nor are great ideas worked out through the post, even though it had been the penny post. This principle deeply penetrated both Froude and myself from the first, and recommended to us the course which things soon took spontaneously, and without set purpose of our own. Universities are the natural centres of intellectual movements. How could men act together, whatever was their zeal, unless they were united in a sort of individuality ? Now, first, we had no unity of place. Mr Rose was in Suffolk, Mr Perceval in Surrey, Mr Keble in Gloucestershire; Hurrell Froude had to go for his health to

Barbados. Mr Palmer was indeed in Oxford; this was an important advantage, and told well in the first months of the Movement – but another condition, besides that of place, was required.

A far more essential unity was that of antecedents – a common history, common memories, an intercourse of mind with mind in the past, and a progress and increase in that intercourse in the present. Mr Perceval, to be sure, was a pupil of Mr Keble's; but Keble, Rose, and Palmer, represented distinct parties, or at least tempers, in the Establishment. Mr Palmer had many conditions of authority and influence. He was the only really learned man among us. He understood theology as a science; he was practised in the scholastic mode of controversial writing; and I believe, was as well acquainted, as he was dissatisfied, with the Catholic schools. He was as decided in his religious views, as he was cautious and even subtle in their expression, and gentle in their enforcement. But he was deficient in depth; and besides, coming from a distance, he never had really grown into an Oxford man, nor was he generally received as such; nor had he any insight into the force of personal influence and congeniality of thought in carrying out a religious theory – a condition which Froude and I considered essential to any true success in the stand which had to be made against Liberalism. Mr Palmer had a certain connexion, as it may be called, in the Establishment, consisting of high Church dignitaries, Archdeacons, London Rectors, and the like, who belonged to what was commonly called the high-and-dry school. They were far more opposed than even he was to the irresponsible action of individuals. Of course their *beau ideal* in ecclesiastical action was a board of safe, sound, sensible men. Mr Palmer was their organ and representative; and he wished for a Committee, an Association, with rules and meetings, to protect the interests of the Church in its existing peril. He was in some measure supported by Mr Perceval.

I, on the other hand, had out of my own head begun the Tracts; and these, as representing the antagonist principle of personality, were looked upon by Mr Palmer's friends with considerable alarm. The great point at the time with these good men in London – some of them men of the highest principle, and far from influenced by what we used to call Erastianism – was to put down the Tracts. I, as their editor, and mainly their author, was of course willing to give way. Keble and Froude advocated their continuance strongly, and were angry with me for consenting to stop them. Mr Palmer shared the anxiety of his own friends; and, kind as were his thoughts of us, he still not unnaturally felt, for reasons of his own, some fidget and nervousness at the course which his Oriel friends were taking. Froude, for whom he had a real liking, took a high tone in his project of measures for dealing with bishops and clergy, which must have shocked and scandalized him considerably. As for me, there was matter enough in the early Tracts to give him equal disgust; and doubtless I much tasked his generosity, when he had to defend me, whether against the London dignitaries, or the country clergy. Oriel, from the time of Dr Copleston to Dr Hampden, had had a name far and wide for liberality of thought; it had received a formal recognition from the Edinburgh Review, if my memory serves me truly, as the school of speculative philosophy in England; and on one occasion, in 1833, when I presented myself, with some of the first papers of the Movement, to a country clergyman in Northamptonshire, he paused awhile, and then, eyeing me with significance, asked, 'Whether Whately was at the bottom of them ?'

Mr Perceval wrote to me in support of the judgment of Mr Palmer and the dignitaries. I replied in a letter, which he afterwards published. 'As to the Tracts,' I said to him (I quote my own words from his Pamphlet), 'every one has his own taste. You object to some things, another to others. If we altered to please every one, the effect would be spoiled. They were not intended as symbols *è cathedrâ*, but as the expression of individual minds; and individuals, feeling strongly, while on the one hand, they are incidentally faulty in mode or language, are still peculiarly effective. No great work was done by a system; whereas systems rise out of individual exertions. Luther was an individual. The very faults of an individual excite attention; he loses, but his cause (if good and he powerful-minded) gains. This is the way of things: we promote truth by a self-sacrifice.'

The visit which I made to the Northamptonshire Rector was only one of a series of similar expedients, which I adopted during the year 1833. I called upon clergy in various parts of the country, whether I was acquainted with them or not, and I attended at the houses of friends where several of them were from time to time assembled. I do not think that much came of such attempts, nor were they quite in my way. Also I wrote various letters to clergymen, which fared not much better, except that they advertised the fact, that a rally in favour of the Church was commencing. I did not care whether my visits were made to high Church or low Church; I wished to make a strong pull in union with all who were opposed to the principles of liberalism, whoever they might be. Giving my name to the Editor, I commenced a series of letters in the Record Newspaper: they ran to a considerable length; and were borne by him with great courtesy and patience. The heading given to them was, 'Church Reform'. The first was on the Revival of Church Discipline; the second, on its Scripture proof; the third, on the application of the doctrine; the fourth, was an answer to objections; the fifth, was on the benefits of discipline. And then the series was abruptly brought to a termination. I had said what I really felt, and what was also in keeping with the strong teaching of the Tracts, but I suppose the Editor discovered in me some divergence from his own line of thought; for at length he sent a very civil letter, apologizing for the non-appearance of my sixth communication on the ground that it contained an attack upon 'Temperance Societies', about which he did not wish a controversy in his columns. He added, however, his serious regret at the character of the Tracts. I had subscribed a small sum in 1828 towards the first start of the Record.

Acts of the officious character, which I have been describing, were uncongenial to my natural temper, to the genius of the Movement, and to the historical mode of its success – they were the fruit of that exuberant and joyous energy with which I had returned from abroad, and which I never had before or since. I had the exultation of health restored, and home regained. While I was at Palermo and thought of the breadth of the Mediterranean, and the wearisome journey across France, I could not imagine how I was ever to get to England; but now I was amid familiar scenes and faces once more. And my health and strength came back to me with such a rebound, that some friends at Oxford, on seeing me, did not well know that it was I, and hesitated before they spoke to me. And I had the consciousness that I was employed in that work which I had been dreaming about, and which I felt to be so momentous and inspiring. I had a supreme confidence in our cause; we were upholding that primitive Christianity which was delivered for all time by the early teachers of the Church, and which was registered and attested in the Anglican formularies and by the Anglican divines. That ancient religion had well nigh faded away out of the land, through the political changes of the last 150 years, and it must be restored. It would be in fact a second Reformation – a better reformation, for it would be a return not to the sixteenth century, but to the seventeenth. No time was to be lost, for the Whigs had come to do their worst, and the rescue might come too late. Bishopricks were already in course of suppression; Church property was in course of confiscation; Sees would soon be receiving unsuitable occupants. We knew enough to begin preaching upon, and there was no one else to preach. I felt as on board a vessel, which first gets under weigh, and then clears out the deck, and stores away luggage and live stock into their proper receptacles.

Nor was it only that I had confidence in our cause, both in itself, and in its polemical force, but besides, I despised every rival system of doctrine and its arguments too. As to the high Church and the low Church, I thought that the one had not much more of logical basis than the other; while I had a thorough contempt for the evangelical. I had a real respect for the character of many of the advocates of each party, but that did not give cogency to their arguments; and I thought on the contrary that the Apostolical form of doctrine was essential and imperative, and its grounds of evidence impregnable. Owing to this supreme confidence, it came to pass at that time, that there was a double aspect in my bearing towards others, which it is necessary for me to enlarge upon. My behaviour had a mixture in it both of fierceness and of sport; and on this account, I dare say, it gave offence to many; nor am I here defending it.

I wished men to agree with me, and I walked with them step by step, as far as they would go; this I did sincerely; but if they would stop, I did not much care about it, but walked on, with some satisfaction that I had brought them so far. I liked to make them preach the truth without knowing it, and encouraged them to do so. It was a satisfaction to me that the Record had allowed me to say so much in its columns, without remonstrance. I was amused to hear of one of the Bishops, who, on reading an early Tract on the Apostolical Succession, could not make up his mind whether he held the doctrine or not. I was not distressed at the wonder or anger of dull and self-conceited men, at propositions which they did not understand. When a correspondent, in good faith, wrote to a newspaper, to say that the 'Sacrifice of the Holy Eucharist', spoken of in the Tract, was a false print for 'Sacrament', I thought the mistake too pleasant to be corrected before I was asked about it. I was not unwilling to draw an opponent on step by step, by virtue of his own opinions, to the brink of some intellectual absurdity, and to leave him to get back as he could. I was not unwilling to play with a man, who asked me impertinent questions. I think I had in my mouth the words of the Wise man, 'Answer a fool according to his folly', especially if he was prying or spiteful. I was reckless of the gossip which was circulated about me; and, when I might easily have set it right, did not deign to do so. Also I used irony in conversation, when matter-of-fact men would not see what I meant.

This kind of behaviour was a sort of habit with me. If I have ever trifled with my subject, it was a more serious fault. I never used arguments which I saw clearly to be unsound. The nearest approach which I remember to such conduct, but which I consider was clear of it nevertheless, was in the case of Tract 15. The matter of this Tract was supplied to me by a friend, to whom I had applied for assistance, but who did not wish to be mixed up with the publication. He gave it me, that I might throw it into shape, and I took his arguments as they stood. In the chief portion of the Tract I fully agreed; for instance, as to what it says about the Council of Trent; but there were arguments, or some argument, in it which I did not follow; I do not recollect what it was. Froude, I think, was disgusted with the whole Tract, and accused me of *economy* in publishing it. It is principally through Mr Froude's Remains that this word had got into our language. I think, I defended myself with arguments such as these – that, as every one knew, the Tracts were written by various persons who agreed together in their doctrine, but not always in the arguments by which it was to be proved; that we must be tolerant of difference of opinion among ourselves; that the author of the Tract had a right to his own opinion, and that the argument in question was ordinarily received; that I did not give my own name or authority, nor was asked for my personal belief, but only acted instrument-ally, as one might translate a friend's book into a foreign language. I account these to be good arguments; nevertheless I feel also that such practices admit of easy abuse and are consequently dangerous; but then again, I feel also this – that if all such mistakes were to be severely visited, not many men in public life would be left with a character for honour and honesty.

This absolute confidence in my cause, which led me to the

negligence or wantonness which I have been instancing, also laid me open, not unfairly, to the opposite charge of fierceness in certain steps which I took, or words which I published. In the Lyra Apostolica, I have said that, before learning to love, we must 'learn to hate'; though I had explained my words by adding 'hatred of sin'. In one of my first Sermons I said, 'I do not shrink from uttering my firm conviction that it would be a gain to the country were it vastly more superstitious, more bigoted, more gloomy, more fierce in its religion than at present it shows itself to be.' I added, of course, that it would be an absurdity to suppose such tempers of mind desirable in themselves. The corrector of the press bore these strong epithets till he got to 'more fierce', and then he put in the margin a *query*. In the very first page of the first Tract, I said of the Bishops, that, 'black event though it would be for the country, yet we could not wish them a more blessed termination of their course, than the spoiling of their goods and martyrdom.' In consequence of a passage in my work upon the Arian History, a Northern dignitary wrote to accuse me of wishing to re-establish the blood and torture of the Inquisition. Contrasting heretics and heresiarchs, I had said, 'The latter should meet with no mercy; he assumes the office of the Tempter, and, so far forth as his error goes, must be dealt with by the competent authority, as if he were embodied evil. To spare him is a false and dangerous pity. It is to endanger the souls of thousands, and it is uncharitable towards himself.' I cannot deny that this is a very fierce passage; but Arius was banished, not burned; and it is only fair to myself to say that neither at this, nor any other time of my life, not even when I was fiercest, could I have even cut off a Puritan's ears, and I think the sight of a Spanish *auto-da-fe* would have been the death of me. Again, when one of my friends, of liberal and evangelical opinions, wrote to expostulate with me on the course I was taking, I said that we would ride over him and his, as Othniel prevailed over Chushan-rishathaim, king of Mesopotamia. Again, I would have no dealings with my brother, and I put my conduct upon a syllogism. I said, 'St Paul bids us avoid those who cause divisions; you cause divisions: therefore I must avoid you.' I dissuaded a lady from attending the marriage of a sister who had seceded from the Anglican Church. No wonder that Blanco White, who had known me under such different circumstances, now hearing the general course that I was taking, was amazed at the change which he recognized in me. He speaks bitterly and unfairly of me in his letters contemporaneously with the first years of the Movement; but in 1839, when looking back, he uses terms of me, which it would be hardly modest in me to quote, were it not that what he says of me in praise occurs in the midst of blame. He says: 'In this party [the anti-Peel, in 1829] I found, to my great surprise, my dear friend, Mr Newman of Oriel. As he had been one of the annual Petitioners to Parliament for Catholic Emancipation, his sudden union with the most violent bigots was inexplicable to me. That change was the first manifestation of the mental revolution, which has suddenly made him one of the leading persecutors of Dr Hampden, and the most active and influential member of that association, called the Puseyite party, from which we have those very strange productions, entitled, Tracts for the Times. While stating these public facts, my heart feels a pang at the recollection of the affectionate and mutual friendship between that excellent man and myself; a friendship, which his principles of orthodoxy could not allow him to continue in regard to one, whom he now regards as inevitably doomed to eternal perdition. Such is the venomous character of orthodoxy. What mischief must it create in a bad heart and narrow mind, when it can work so effectually for evil, in one of the most benevolent of bosoms, and one of the ablest of minds, in the amiable, the intellectual, the refined John Henry Newman!' (Vol. iii. p. 131.) He adds that I would have nothing to do with him, a circumstance which I do not recollect, and very much doubt.

I have spoken of my firm confidence in my position; and now let me state more definitely what the position was which I took up, and the propositions about which I was so confident. These were three:

1. First was the principle of dogma: my battle was with liberalism; by liberalism I meant the anti-dogmatic principle and its developments. This was the first point on which I was certain. Here I make a remark: persistence in a given belief is no sufficient test of its truth; but departure from it is at least a slur upon the man who has felt so certain about it. In proportion then as I had in 1832 a strong persuasion of the truth of opinions which I have since given up, so far a sort of guilt attaches to me, not only for that vain confidence, but for all the various proceedings which

were the consequence of it. But here I have the satisfaction of feeling that I have nothing to retract, and nothing to repent of. The main principle of the movement is as dear to me now, as it ever was. I have changed in many things: in this I have not. From the age of fifteen, dogma has been the fundamental principle of my religion: I know no other religion; I cannot enter into the idea of any other sort of religion; religion, as a mere sentiment, is to me a dream and a mockery. As well can there be filial love without the fact of a father, as devotion without the fact of a Supreme Being. What I held in 1816, I held in 1833, and I hold in 1864. Please God, I shall hold it to the end. Even when I was under Dr Whately's influence, I had no temptation to be less zealous for the great dogmas of the faith, and at various times I used to resist such trains of thought on his part, as seemed to me (rightly or wrongly) to obscure them. Such was the fundamental principle of the Movement of 1833.

2. Secondly, I was confident in the truth of a certain definite religious teaching, based upon this foundation of dogma; viz. that there was a visible Church, with sacraments and rites which are the channels of invisible grace. I thought that this was the doctrine of Scripture, of the early Church, and of the Anglican Church. Here again, I have not changed in opinion; I am as certain now on this point as I was in 1833, and have never ceased to be certain. In 1834 and the following years I put this ecclesiastical doctrine on a broader basis, after reading Laud, Bramhall, and Stillingfleet and other Anglican divines on the one hand, and after prosecuting the study of the Fathers on the other; but the doctrine of 1833 was strengthened in me, not changed. When I began the Tracts for the Times I rested the main doctrine, of which I am speaking, upon Scripture, on the Anglican Prayer Book, and on St Ignatius's Epistles. 1 As to the existence of a visible Church, I especially argued out the point from Scripture, in Tract 11, viz. from the Acts of the Apostles and the Epistles. 2 As to the Sacraments and Sacramental rites, I stood on the Prayer Book. I appealed to the Ordination Service, in which the Bishop says, 'Receive the Holy Ghost'; to the Visitation Service, which teaches confession and absolution; to the Baptismal Service, in which the Priest speaks of the child after baptism as regenerate; to the Catechism, in which Sacramental Communion is receiving 'verily and indeed the Body of Blood of Christ'; to the Commination Service, in which we are told to do 'works of penance'; to the Collects, Epistles, and

Gospels, to the calendar and rubricks, portions of the Prayer Book, wherein we find the festivals of the Apostles, notice of certain other Saints, and days of fasting and abstinence.

3. And further, as to the Episcopal system, I founded it upon the Epistles of St Ignatius, which inculcated it in various ways. One passage especially impressed itself upon me: speaking of cases of disobedience to ecclesiastical authority, he says, 'A man does not deceive that Bishop whom he sees, but he practises rather upon the Bishop Invisible, and so the question is not with flesh, but with God, who knows the secret heart.' I wished to act on this principle to the letter, and I may say with confidence that I never consciously transgressed it. I loved to act in the sight of my Bishop, as if I was, as it were, in the sight of God. It was one of my special supports and safeguards against myself; I could not go very wrong while I had reason to believe that I was in no respect displeasing him. It was not a mere formal obedience to rule that I put before me, but I desired to please him personally, as I considered him set over me by the Divine Hand. I was strict in observing my clerical engagements, not only because they *were* engagements, but because I considered myself simply as the servant and instrument of my Bishop. I did not care much for the Bench of Bishops, except as they might be the voice of my Church: nor should I have cared much for a Provincial Council; nor for a Diocesan Synod presided over by my Bishop; all these matters seemed to me to be *jure ecclesiastico*, but what to me was *jure divino* was the voice of my Bishop in his own person. My own Bishop was my Pope; I knew no other; the successor of the Apostles, the Vicar of Christ. This was but a practical exhibition of the Anglican theory of Church Government, as I had already drawn it out myself, after various Anglican Divines. This continued all through my course; when at length in 1845 I wrote to Bishop Wiseman, in whose Vicariate I found myself, to announce my conversion, I could find nothing better to say to him, than that I would obey the Pope as I had obeyed my own Bishop in the Anglican Church. My duty to him was my point of honour; his disapprobation was the one thing which I could not bear. I believe it to have been a generous and honest feeling; and in consequence I was rewarded by having all my time for ecclesiastical superior a man, whom had I had a choice, I should have preferred, out and out, to any other Bishop on the Bench, and for whose memory I have a special affection, Dr Bagot – a man of

noble mind, and as kind-hearted and as considerate as he was noble. He ever sympathized with me in my trials which followed; it was my own fault, that I was not brought into more familiar personal relations with him than it was my happiness to be. May his name be ever blessed!

And now in concluding my remarks on the second point on which my confidence rested, I repeat that here again I have no retractation to announce as to its main outline. While I am now as clear in my acceptance of the principle of dogma, as I was in 1833 and 1816, so again I am now as firm in my belief of a visible Church, of the authority of Bishops, of the grace of the sacraments, of the religious worth of works of penance, as I was in 1833. I have added Articles to my Creed; but the old ones, which I then held with a divine faith, remain.

3. But now, as to the third point on which I stood in 1833, and which I have utterly renounced and trampled upon since – my then view of the Church of Rome – I will speak about it as exactly as I can. When I was young, as I have said already, and after I was grown up, I thought the Pope to be Antichrist. At Christmas 1824–5 I preached a Sermon to that effect. But in 1827 I accepted eagerly the stanza in the Christian Year, which many people thought too charitable, 'Speak *gently* of thy sister's fall.' From the time that I knew Froude I got less and less bitter on the subject. I spoke (successively, but I cannot tell in what order or at what dates) of the Roman Church as being bound up with 'the *cause* of Antichrist', as being *one* of the '*many* antichrists' foretold by St John, as being influenced by 'the *spirit* of Antichrist', and as having something 'very Antichristian' or 'unchristian' about her. From my boyhood and in 1824 I considered, after Protestant authorities, that St Gregory I about AD 600 was the first Pope that was Antichrist, though, in spite of this, he was also a great and holy man; but in 1832–3 I thought the Church of Rome was bound up with the cause of Antichrist by the Council of Trent. When it was that in my deliberate judgment I gave up the notion altogether in any shape, that some special reproach was attached to her name, I cannot tell; but I had a shrinking from renouncing it, even when my reason so ordered me, from a sort of conscience or prejudice, I think up to 1843. Moreover, at least during the Tract Movement, I thought the essence of her offence to consist in the honours which she paid to the Blessed Virgin and the Saints; and the more I grew in devotion, both to the Saints and to Our

Lady, the more impatient was I at the Roman practices, as if those glorified creations of God must be gravely shocked, if pain could be theirs, at the undue veneration of which they were the objects.

On the other hand, Hurrell Froude in his familiar conversations was always tending to rub the idea out of my mind. In a passage of one of his letters from abroad, alluding, I suppose, to what I used to say in opposition to him, he observes: 'I think people are injudicious who talk against the Roman Catholics for worshipping Saints, and honouring the Virgin and images, &c. These things may perhaps be idolatrous; I cannot make up my mind about it; but to my mind it is the Carnival that is real practical idolatry, as it is written, "the people sat down to eat and drink, and rose up to play".' The Carnival, I observe in passing, is, in fact, one of those very excesses, to which, for at least three centuries, religious Catholics have ever opposed themselves, as we see in the life of St Philip, to say nothing of the present day; but this we did not then know. Moreover, from Froude I learned to admire the great medieval Pontiffs; and, of course, when I had come to consider the Council of Trent to be the turning point of the history of Christian Rome, I found myself as free, as I was rejoiced, to speak in their praise. Then, when I was abroad, the sight of so many great places, venerable shrines, and noble churches, much impressed my imagination. And my heart was touched also. Making an expedition on foot across some wild country in Sicily, at six in the morning I came upon a small church; I heard voices, and I looked in. It was crowded, and the congregation was singing. Of course it was the Mass, though I did not know it at the time. And, in my weary days at Palermo, I was not ungrateful for the comfort which I had received in frequenting the Churches, nor did I ever forget it. Then, again, her zealous maintenance of the doctrine and the rule of celibacy, which I recognized as Apostolic, and her faithful agreement with Antiquity in so many other points besides, which were dear to me, was an argument as well as a plea in favour of the great Church of Rome. Thus I learned to have tender feelings towards her; but still my reason was not affected at all. My judgment was against her, when viewed as an institution, as truly as it ever had been.

This conflict between reason and affection I expressed in one of the early Tracts, published July 1834. 'Considering the high gifts and the strong claims of the Church of Rome and its dependencies on our admiration, reverence, love, and gratitude; how could we withstand it, as we do, how could we refrain from being melted into tenderness, and rushing into communion with it, but for the words of Truth itself, which bid us prefer It to the whole world ? "He that loveth father or mother more than Me, is not worthy of me." How could "we learn to be severe, and execute judgment", but for the warning of Moses against even a divinely-gifted teacher, who should preach new gods; and the anathema of St Paul even against Angels and Apostles, who should bring in a new doctrine ?' – *Records*, No. 24. My feeling was something like that of a man, who is obliged in a court of justice to bear witness against a friend; or like my own now, when I have said, and shall say, so many things on which I had rather be silent.

As a matter, then, of simple conscience, though it went against my feelings, I felt it to be a duty to protest against the Church of Rome. But besides this, it was a duty, because the prescription of such a protest was a living principle of my own Church, as expressed not simply in a *catena*, but by a *consensus* of her divines, and by the voice of her people. Moreover, such a protest was necessary as an integral portion of her controversial basis; for I adopted the argument of Bernard Gilpin, that Protestants 'were *not able* to give any *firm and solid* reason of the separation besides this, to wit, that the Pope is Antichrist.' But while I thus thought such a protest to be based upon truth, and to be a religious duty, and a rule of Anglicanism, and a necessity of the case, I did not at all like the work. Hurrell Froude attacked me for doing it; and, besides, I felt that my language had a vulgar and rhetorical look about it. I believed, and really measured, my words, when I used them; but I knew that I had a temptation, on the other hand, to say against Rome as much as ever I could, in order to protect myself against the charge of Popery.

And now I come to the very point, for which I have introduced the subject of my feelings about Rome. I felt such confidence in the substantial justice of the charges which I advanced against her, that I considered them to be a safeguard and an assurance that no harm could ever arise from the freest exposition of what I used to call Anglican principles. All the world was astounded at what Froude and I were saying: men said that it was sheer Popery. I answered, 'True, we seem to be making straight for it; but go on awhile, and you will come to a deep chasm across the path, which makes real approximation impossible.' And I urged in addition, that many Anglican divines had been accused of Popery, yet had died in their Anglicanism – now, the ecclesiastical principles which I professed, they had professed also; and the judgment against Rome which they had formed, I had formed also. Whatever deficiencies then had to be supplied in the existing Anglican system, and however boldly I might point them out, and how that system would not in the process be brought nearer to the special creed of Rome, and might be mended in spite of her. In that very agreement of the two forms of faith, close as it might seem, would really be found, on examination, the elements and principles of an essential discordance.

It was with this absolute persuasion on my mind that I fancied that there could be no rashness in giving to the world in fullest measure the teaching and the writings of the Fathers. I thought that the Church of England was substantially founded upon them. I did not know all that the Fathers had said, but I felt that, even when their tenets happened to differ from the Anglican, no harm could come of reporting them. I said out what I was clear they had said; I spoke vaguely and imperfectly, of what I thought they said, or what some of them had said. Any how, no harm could come of bending the crooked stick the other way, in the process of straightening it; it was impossible to break it. If there was any thing in the Fathers of a startling character, this would be only for a time; it would admit of explanation, or it might suggest something profitable to Anglicans; it could not lead to Rome. I express this view of the matter in a passage of the Preface to the first volume, which I edited, of the Library of the Fathers. Speaking of the strangeness at first sight, presented to the Anglican mind, of some of their principles and opinions, I bid the reader go forward hopefully, and not indulge his criticism till he knows more about them, than he will learn at the outset. 'Since the evil,' I say, 'is in the nature of the case itself, we can do no more than have patience, and recommend patience to others, and, with the racer in the Tragedy, look forward steadily and hopefully to the *event*, τῷ τέλει πίστιν φέρων, when, as we trust, all that is inharmonious and anomalous in the details, will at length be practically smoothed.'

Such was the position, such the defences, such the tactics, by which I thought that it was both incumbent on us, and possible for us, to meet that onset of Liberal principles, of which we were all in immediate anticipation, whether in the Church or in the University. And during the first year of the Tracts, the attack upon the University began. In November 1834 was sent to me by the author, Dr Hampden, the second Edition of a Pamphlet entitled, 'Observations on Religious Dissent, with particular reference to the use of religious tests in the University.' In this Pamphlet it was maintained, that 'Religion is distinct from Theological Opinion', pp. 1, 28, 30, &c.; that it is but a common prejudice to identify theological propositions methodically deduced and stated, with the simple religion of Christ, p. 1; that under Theological Opinion were to be placed the Trinitarian doctrine, p. 27, and the Unitarian, p. 19; that a dogma was theological opinion formally insisted on, pp. 20, 21; that speculation always left an opening for improvement, p. 22; that the Church of England was not dogmatic in its spirit, though the wording of its formularies might often carry the sound of dogmatism, p. 23.

I acknowledged the receipt of this work in the following letter:

The kindness which has led to your presenting me with your late pamphlet, encourages me to hope that you will forgive me, if I take the opportunity it affords of expressing to you my very sincere and deep regret that it has been published. Such an opportunity I could not let slip without being unfaithful to my own serious thoughts on the subject.

While I respect the tone of piety which the Pamphlet displays, I dare not trust myself to put on paper my feelings about the principles contained in it; tending, as they do, in my opinion, altogether to make shipwreck of Christian faith. I also lament, that, by its appearance, the first step has been taken towards interrupting that peace and mutual good understanding which has prevailed so long in this place, and which, if once seriously disturbed, will be succeeded by dissensions the more intractable, because justified in the minds of those who resist innovation by a feeling of imperative duty.

Since that time Phaeton has got into the chariot of the sun; we, alas! can only look on, and watch him down the steep of heaven. Meanwhile, the lands, which he is passing over, suffer from his driving.

Such was the commencement of the assault of Liberalism upon the old orthodoxy of Oxford and England; and it could not have been broken, as it was, for so long a time, had not a great change taken place in the circumstances of that counter-movement which had already started with the view of resisting it. For myself, I was not the person to take the lead of a party; I never was, from first to last, more than a leading author of a school; nor did I ever wish to be any thing else. This is my own account of the matter, and I say it, neither as intending to disown the responsibility of what was done, or as if ungrateful to those who at that time made more of me than I deserved, and did more for my sake and at my bidding than I realized myself. I am giving my history from my own point of sight, and it is as follows – I had lived for ten years among my personal friends; the greater part of the time, I had been influenced, not influencing; and at no time have I acted on others, without their acting upon me. As is the custom of a University, I had lived with my private, nay, with some of my public, pupils, and with the junior fellows of my College, without form or distance, on a footing of equality. Thus it was through friends, younger, for the most part, than myself, that my principles were spreading. They heard what I said in conversation, and told it to others. Undergraduates in due time took their degree, and became private tutors themselves. In this new *status*, in turn, they preached the opinions which they had already learned themselves. Others went down to the country, and became curates of parishes. Then they had down from London parcels of the Tracts, and other publications. They placed them in the shops of local booksellers, got them into newspapers, introduced them to clerical meetings, and converted more or less their Rectors and their brother curates. Thus the Movement, viewed with relation to myself, was but a floating opinion; it was not a power. It never would have been a power, if it had remained in my hands. Years after, a friend, writing to me in remonstrance at the excesses, as he thought them, of my disciples, applied to me my own verse about St Gregory Nazianzen, 'Thou couldst a people raise, but couldst not rule.' At the time that he wrote to me, I had special impediments in the way of such an exercise of power; but at no time could I exercise over others that authority, which under the circumstances was imperatively required. My great principle ever was, Live and let live. I never had the staidness or dignity necessary for a leader. To the last I never recognized the hold I had over young men. Of late years I have read and heard that they even imitated me in various ways. I was quite unconscious of it, and I think my immediate friends knew too well how disgusted I should be at such proceedings, to have the heart to tell me. I felt great impatience at our being called a party, and would not allow that we were such. I had a lounging, free-and-easy way of carrying things on. I exercised no sufficient censorship upon the Tracts. I did not confine them to the writings of such persons as agreed in all things with myself; and, as to my own Tracts, I printed on them a notice to the effect, that any one who pleased, might make what use he would of them, and reprint them with alterations if he chose, under the conviction that their main scope could not be damaged by such a process. It was the same with me afterwards, as regards other publications. For two years I furnished a certain number of sheets for the British Critic from myself and my friends, while a gentleman was editor, a man of splendid talent, who, however, was scarcely an acquaintance of mine, and had no sympathy with the Tracts. When I was Editor myself, from 1838 to 1841, in my very first number, I suffered to appear a critique unfavourable to my work on Justification, which had been published a few months before, from a feeling of propriety, because I had put the book into the hands of the writer who so handled it. Afterwards I suffered an article against the Jesuits to appear in it, of which I did not like the tone. When I had to provide a curate for my new Church at Littlemore, I engaged a friend, by no fault of his, who, before he had entered into his charge, preached a sermon, either in depreciation of baptismal regeneration, or of Dr Pusey's view of it. I showed a similar easiness as to the Editors who helped me in the separate volumes of Fleury's Church History; they were able, learned, and excellent men, but their after history has shown, how little my choice of them was influenced by any notion I could have had of any intimate agreement of opinion between them and myself. I shall have to make the same remark in its place concerning the Lives of the English Saints, which subsequently appeared. All this may seen inconsistent with what I have said of my fierceness. I am not bound to account for it; but there have been men before me, fierce in act, yet tolerant and moderate in their reasonings; at least, so I read history. However, such was the case, and such its effect upon the Tracts. These at first starting were short, hasty, and some of them ineffective; and at the end of the year, when collected into a volume, they had a slovenly appearance.

It was under these circumstances that Dr Pusey joined us. I had known him well since 1827–8, and had felt for him an enthusiastic admiration. I used to call him o^c μέγας. His great learning

his immence diligence, his scholarlike mind, his simple devotion
to the cause of religion, overcame me; and great of course was my
joy, when in the last days of 1833 he showed a disposition to make
common cause with us. His Tract on Fasting appeared as one of
the series with the date of 21 December. He was not, however, I
think fully associated in the Movement till 1835 and 1836, when
he published his Tract on Baptism, and started the Library of the
Fathers. He at once gave to us a position and a name. Without him
we should have had little chance, especially at the early date of
1834, of making any serious resistance to the Liberal aggression.
But Dr Pusey was a Professor and Canon of Christ Church; he had
a vast influence in consequence of his deep religious seriousness,
the munificence of his charities, his Professorship, his family
connexions, and his easy relations with University authorities. He
was to the Movement all that Mr Rose might have been, with that
indispensable addition, which was wanting to Mr Rose, the
intimate friendship and the familiar daily society of the persons
who had commenced it. And he had that special claim on their
attachment, which lies in the living presence of a faithful and loyal
affectionateness. There was henceforth a man who could be the
head and centre of the zealous people in every part of the country,
who were adopting the new opinions; and not only so, but there
was one who furnished the Movement with a front to the world,
and gained for it a recognition from other parties in the
University. In 1829 Mr Froude, or Mr Robert Wilberforce, or Mr
Newman were but individuals; and, when they ranged themselves
in the contest of that year on the side of Sir Robert Inglis, men on
either side only asked with surprise how they got there, and
attached no significancy to the fact; but Dr Pusey was, to use the
common expression, a host in himself; he was able to give a name,
a form, and a personality to what was without him a sort of mob;
and when various parties had to meet together in order to resist
the liberal acts of the Government, we of the Movement took our
place by right among them.

Such was the benefit which he conferred on the Movement
externally; nor were the internal advantages at all inferior to it.
He was a man of large designs; he had a hopeful, sanguine mind;
he had no fear of others; he was haunted by no intellectual
perplexities. People are apt to say that he was once nearer to the
Catholic Church than he is now; I pray God that he may be one
day far nearer to the Catholic Church than he was then; for I

believe that, in his reason and judgment, all the time that I knew him, he never was near to it at all. When I became a Catholic, I was often asked, 'What of Dr Pusey ?' when I said that I did not see symptoms of his doing as I had done, I was sometimes thought uncharitable. If confidence in his position is (as it is) a first essential in the leader of a party, Dr Pusey had it. The most remarkable instance of this, was his statement, in one of his subsequent defences of the Movement, when too it had advanced a considerable way in the direction of Rome, that among its hopeful peculiarities was its 'stationariness'. He made it in good faith; it was his subjective view of it.

Dr Pusey's influence was felt at once. He saw that there ought to be more sobriety, more gravity, more careful pains, more sense of responsibility in the Tracts and in the whole Movement. It was through him that the character of the Tracts was changed. When he gave to us his Tract on Fasting, he put his initials to it. In 1835 he published his elaborate Treatise on Baptism, which was followed by other Tracts from different authors, if not of equal learning, yet of equal power and appositeness. The Catenas of Anglican divines, projected by me, which occur in the Series, were executed with a like aim at greater accuracy and method. In 1836 he advertised his great project for a Translation of the Fathers – but I must return to myself. I am not writing the history either of Dr Pusey or of the Movement; but it is a pleasure to me to have been able to introduce here reminiscences of the place which he held in it, which have so direct a bearing on myself, that they are no digression from my narrative.

I suspect it was Dr Pusey's influence and example which set me, and made me set others, on the larger and more careful works in defence of the principles of the Movement which followed in a course of years – some of them demanding and receiving from their authors, such elaborate treatment that they did not make their appearance till both its temper and its fortunes had changed. I set about a work at once; one in which was brought out with precision the relation in which we stood to the Church of Rome. We could not move a step in comfort, till this was done. It was of absolute necessity and a plain duty from the first, to provide as soon as possible a large statement, which would encourage and re-assure our friends, and repel the attacks of our opponents. A cry was heard on all sides of us, that the Tracts and the writings of the Fathers would lead us to become Catholics, before we were aware of it. This was loudly expressed by members of the Evangelical party, who in 1836 had joined us in making a protest in Convocation against a memorable appointment of the Prime Minister. These clergymen even then avowed their desire, that the next time they were brought up to Oxford to give a vote, it might be in order to put down the Popery of the Movement. There was another reason still, and quite as important. Monsignore Wiseman, with the acuteness and zeal which might be expected from tht great Prelate, had anticipated what was coming, had returned to England by 1836, had delivered Lectures in London on the doctrines of Catholicism, and created an impression through the country, shared in by ourselves, that we had for our opponents in controversy, not only our brethren, but our hereditary foes. These were the circumstances, which led to my publication of 'The Prophetical office of the Church viewed relatively to Romanism and Popular Protestantism.'

Ths work employed me for three years, from the beginning of 1834 to the end of 1836, and was published in 1837. It was composed, after a careful consideration and comparison of the principal Anglican divines of the 17th century. It was first written in the shape of controversial correspondence with a learned French Priest; then it was re-cast, and delivered in Lectures at St Mary's: lastly, with considerable retrenchments and additions, it was re-written for publication.

It attempts to trace out the rudimental lines on which Christian faith and teaching proceed, and to use them as means of determining the relation of the Roman and Anglican systems to each other. In this way it shows that to confuse the two together is impossible, and that the Anglican can be as little said to tend to the Roman, as the Roman to the Anglican. The spirit of the Volume is not so gentle to the Church of Rome, as Tract 71 published the year before; on the contrary, it is very fierce; and this I attribute to the circumstance that the Volume is theological and didactic, whereas the Tract, being controversial, assumes as little and grants as much as possible on the points in dispute, and insists on points of agreement as well as of difference. A further and more direct reason is, that in my Volume I deal with 'Romanism' (as I call it), not so much in its formal decrees and in the substance of its creed, as in its traditional action and its authorized teaching as represented by its prominent writers – whereas the Tract is written as if discussing the differences of the Churches with a view to a reconciliation between them. There is a further reason too, which I will state presently.

But this Volume had a larger scope than that of opposing the Roman system. It was an attempt at commencing a system of theology on the Anglican idea, and based upon Anglican authorities. Mr Palmer, about the same time, was projecting a work of a similar nature in his own way. It was published, I think, under the title, 'A Treatise on the Christian Church'. As was to be expected from the author, it was a most learned, most careful composition; and in its form, I should say, polemical. So happily at least did he follow the logical method of the Roman Schools, that Father Perrone in his Treatise on dogmatic theology, recognized in him a combatant of the true cast, and saluted him as a foe worthy of being vanquished. Other soldiers in that field he seems to have thought little better than the *lanzknechts* of the middle ages, and, I dare say, with very good reason. When I knew that excellent and kind-hearted man at Rome at a later time, he allowed me to put him to ample penance for those light thoughts of me, which he had once had, by encroaching on his valuable time with my theological questions. As to Mr Palmer's book, it was one which no Anglican could write but himself – in no sense, if I recollect aright, a tentative work. The ground of controversy was cut into squares, and then every objection had its answer. This is the proper method to adopt in teaching authoritatively young men; and the work in fact was intended for students in theology. My own book, on the other hand, was of a directly tentative and empirical character. I wished to build up an Anglican theology out of the stores which already lay cut and hewn upon the ground, the past toil of great divines. To do this could not be the work of one man; much less, could it be at once received into Anglican theology, however well it was done. This I fully recognized; and while I trusted that my statements of doctrine would turn out to be true and important; yet I wrote, to use the common phrase, 'under correction'.

There was another motive for my publishing, of a personal nature, which I think I should mention. I felt then, and all along felt, that there was an intellectual cowardice in not finding a basis in reason for my belief, and a moral cowardice in not avowing that basis. I should have felt myself less than a man, if I did not bring it out, whatever it was. This is one principal reason why I wrote and published the 'Prophetical Office'. It was from the same feeling, that in the spring of 1836, at a meeting of residents on the subject of the struggle then proceeding against a Whig appointment, when some one wanted us all merely to act on college and conservative grounds (as I understood him), with as few published statements as possible, I answered, that the person whom we were resisting had committed himself in writing, and that we ought to commit ourselves too. This again was a main reason for the publication of Tract 90. Alas! it was my portion for whole years to remain without any satisfactory basis for my religious profession, in a state of moral sickness, neither able to acquiesce in Anglicanism, nor able to go to Rome. But I bore it, till in course of time my way was made clear to me. If here it be objected to me, that as time went on, I often in my writings hinted at things which I did not fully bring out, I submit for consideration whether this occurred except when I was in great difficulties, how to speak, or how to be silent, with due regard for the position of mind or the feelings of others. However, I may have an opportunity to say more on this subject. But to return to the 'Prophetical Office'.

I thus speak in the Introduction to my Volume:

'It is proposed,' I say,

to offer help towards the formation of a recognized Anglican theology in one of its departments. The present state of our divinity is as follows: the most vigorous, the clearest, the most fertile minds, have through God's mercy been employed in the service of our Church: minds too as reverential and holy, and as fully imbued with Ancient Truth, and as well versed in the writings of the Fathers, as they were intellectually gifted. This is God's great mercy indeed, for which we must ever be thankful. Primitive doctrine has been explored for us in every direction, and the original principles of the Gospel and the Church patiently brought to light. But one thing is still wanting: our champions and teachers have lived in stormy times: political and other influences have acted upon them variously in their day, and have since obstructed a careful consolidation of their judgments. We have a vast inheritance, but no inventory of our treasures. All is given us in profusion; it remains for us to catalogue, sort, distribute, select, harmonize, and complete. We have more than we know how to use; stores of learning, but little that is precise and serviceable; Catholic truth and individual opinion, first principles and the guesses of genius, all mingled in the same works, and requiring to be discriminated. We meet with truths overstated or misdirected, matters of detail variously taken, facts incompletely proved or applied, and rules inconsistently urged or discordantly interpreted. Such indeed is the state of every deep philosophy in its first stages, and therefore of theological knowledge. What we need at present for our Church's well-being, is not invention, nor originality, nor sagacity, nor even learning in our divines, at least in the first place, though all gifts of God are in a measure needed, and never can be unseasonable when used religiously, but we need peculiarly a sound judgment, patient thought, discrimination, a comprehensive mind, an abstinence from all private fancies and caprices and personal tastes – in a word, Divine Wisdom.

The subject of the Volume is the doctrine of the *Via Media*, a name which had already been applied to the Anglican system by writers of name. It is an expressive title, but not altogether satisfactory, because it is at first sight negative. This had been the reason of my dislike to the word 'Protestant'; in the idea which it conveyed, it did not denote the profession of any particular religion at all, and was compatible with infidelity. A *Via Media* was but a receding from extremes – therefore I had to draw it out into a definite shape, and a character; before it could have claims on our respect, it must first be shown to be one, intelligent, and consistent. This was the first condition of any reasonable treatise on the *Via Media*. The second condition, and necessary too, was not in my power. I could only hope that it would one day be fulfilled. Even if the *Via Media* were ever so positive a religious system, it was not as yet objective and real; it had no original anywhere of which it was the representative. It was at present a paper religion. This I confess in my Introduction; I say 'Protestantism and Popery are real religions . . . but the *Via Media*, viewed as an integral system, has scarcely had existence except on paper.' I grant the objection, though I endeavour to lessen it – 'It still remains to be tried, whether what is called Anglo-Catholicism, the religion of Andrewes, Laud, Hammond, Butler, and Wilson, is capable of being professed, acted on, and maintained on a large sphere of action, or whether it be a mere modification or transition-state of either Romanism or popular Protestantism.' I trusted that some day it would prove to be a substantive religion.

Lest I should be misunderstood, let me observe that this hesitation about the validity of the theory of the *Via Media* implied no doubt of the three fundamental points on which it was based, as I have described them above, dogma, the sacramental system, and anti-Romanism.

Other investigations which had to be followed up were of a still more tentative character. The basis of the *Via Media*, consisting of the three elementary points, which I have just mentioned, was clear enough; but, not only had the house itself to be built upon them, but it had also to be furnished, and it is not wonderful if, after building it, both I and others erred in detail in determining what its furniture should be, what was consistent with the style of building, and what was in itself desirable. I will explain what I mean.

I had brought out in the *Prophetical Office* in what the Roman and the Anglican systems differed from each other, but less distinctly in what they agreed. I had indeed enumerated the Fundamentals, common to both in the following passage: 'In both systems the same Creeds are acknowledged. Besides other points in common we both hold, that certain doctrines are necessary to be believed for salvation; we both believe in the doctrines of the Trinity, Incarnation, and Atonement; in original sin; in the necessity of regeneration; in the supernatural grace of the Sacraments; in the Apostolical succession; in the obligation of faith and obedience, and in the eternity of future punishment.' – pp. 55, 56. So much I had said, but I had not said enough. This enumeration implied a great many more points of agreement than were found in those very Articles which were fundamental. If the two Churches were thus the same in fundamentals, they were also one and the same in such plain consequences as were contained in those fundamentals and in such natural observances as outwardly represented them. It was an Anglican principle that 'the abuse of a thing doth not take away the lawful use of it'; and an Anglican Canon in 1603 had declared that the English Church had no purpose to forsake all that was held in the Churches of Italy, France, and Spain, and reverenced those ceremonies and particular points which were Apostolic. Excepting then such exceptional matters, as are implied in this avowal, whether they were many or few, all these Churches were evidently to be considered as one with the Anglican. The Catholic Church in all lands had been one of the first for many centuries; then, various portions had followed their own way to the injury, but not to the destruction, whether of truth or of charity. These portions or branches were mainly three – the Greek, Latin, and Anglican. Each of these inherited the early undivided Church *in solido* as its own possession. Each branch was identical with that early undivided Church, and in the unity of that Church it had unity with the other branches. The three branches agreed together in *all but* their later accidental errors. Some branches had retained in detail portions of Apostolical truth and usage, which the others had not; and these portions might be and should be appropriated again by the others which had let them slip. Thus, the middle age belonged to the Anglican Church, and much more did the middle age of England. The Church of the 12th century was the Church of the 19th. Dr Howley sat in the seat of St Thomas the Martyr; Oxford was a medieval University. Saving our engagements to Prayer Book and Articles, we might breathe and live and act and speak, as in the atmosphere and climate of Henry III's day, or the Confessor's, or of Alfred's. And we ought to be indulgent of all that Rome taught now, as of what Rome taught then, saving our protest. We might boldly welcome, even what we did not ourselves think right to adopt. And, when we were obliged on the contrary boldly to denounce, we should do so with pain, not with exultation. By very reason of our protest, which we had made, and made *ex animo*, we could agree to differ. What the members of the Bible Society did on the basis of Scripture, we could do on the basis of the Church; Trinitarian and Unitarian were further apart than Roman and Anglican. Thus we had a real wish to co-operate with Rome in all lawful things, if she would let us, and if the rules of our own Church let us; and we thought there was no better way towards the restoration of doctrinal purity and unity. And we thought that Rome was not committed by her formal decrees to all that she actually taught; and again, if her disputants had been unfair to us, or her rulers tyrannical, we bore in mind that on our side too there had been rancour and slander in our controversy with her, and violence in our political measures. As to ourselves being instruments in improving the belief or practice of Rome directly, I used to say, 'Look at home; let us first (or at least let us the while) supply our own short-comings, before we attempt to be physicians to any one else.' This is very much the spirit of Tract 71 to which I referred just now. I am well aware that there is a paragraph inconsistent with it in the Prospectus to the Library of the Fathers; but I do not consider myself responsible for it. Indeed, I have no intention whatever of implying that Dr Pusey concurred in the ecclesiastical theory, which I have been drawing out; nor that I took it up myself except by degrees in the course of ten years. It was necessarily the growth of time. In fact, hardly any two persons, who took part in the Movement, agreed in their view of the limit to which our general principles might religiously be carried.

And now I have said enough on what I consider to have been the general objects of the various works which I wrote, edited, or prompted in the years which I am reviewing; I wanted to bring out in a substantive form, a living Church of England in a position proper to herself, and founded on distinct principles; as far as paper could do it, and as earnestly preaching it and influencing others towards it, could tend to make it a fact – a living Church, made of flesh and blood, with voice, complexion, and motion and action, and a will of its own. I believe I had no private motive, and no personal aim. Nor did I ask for more than 'a fair stage and no favour', nor expect the work would be accomplished in my days; but I thought that enough would be secured to continue it in the future under, perhaps, more hopeful circumstances and prospects than the present.

I will mention in illustration some of the principal works, doctrinal and historical, which originated in the object which I have stated.

I wrote my Essay on Justification in 1837; it was aimed at the Lutheran dictum that justification by faith only was the cardinal doctrine of Christianity. I considered that this doctrine was either a paradox or a truism – a paradox in Luther's mouth, a truism in Melanchthon's. I thought that the Anglican Church followed Melanchthon, and that in consequence between Rome and Anglicanism, between high Church and low Church, there was no real intellectual difference on the point. I wished to fill up a ditch, the work of man. In this Volume again, I express my desire to build up a system of theology out of the Anglican divines, and imply that my dissertation was a tentative Inquiry. I speak in the Preface of 'offering suggestions towards a work, which must be uppermost in the mind of every true son of the English Church at this day – the consolidation of a theological system, which, built upon those formularies, to which all clergymen are bound, may tend to inform, persuade, and absorb into itself religious minds, which hitherto have fancied, that, on the peculiar Protestant questions, they were seriously opposed to each other.' – P. vii.

In my University Sermons there is a series of discussions upon the subject of Faith and Reason; these again were the tentative commencement of a grave and necessary work; it was an inquiry into the ultimate basis of religious faith, prior to the distinction into Creeds.

In like manner in a Pamphlet which I published in the summer of 1838 is an attempt at placing the doctrine of the Real Presence on an intellectual basis. The fundamental idea is consonant to that to which I had been so long attached; it is the denial of the existence of space except as a subjective idea of our minds.

The Church of the Fathers is one of the earliest productions of the Movement, and appeared in numbers in the British Magazine, being written with the aim of introducing the religious sentiments, views, and customs of the first ages into the modern Church of England.

The Translation of Fleury's Church History was commenced under these circumstances – I was fond of Fleury for a reason which I express in the Advertisement; because it presented a sort of photograph of ecclesiastical history without any comment upon it. In the event, that simple representation of the early centuries had a good deal to do with unsettling me in my Anglicanism; but how little I could anticipate this, will be seen in the fact that the publication of Fleury was a favourite scheme with Mr Rose. He proposed it to me twice, between the years 1834 and 1837; and I mention it as one out of many particulars curiously illustrating how truly my change of opinion arose, not from foreign influences, but from the working of my own mind, and the accidents around me. The date, from which the portion actually translated began was determined by the Publisher on reasons with which we were not concerned.

Another historical work, but drawn from original sources, was given to the world by my old friend Mr Bowden, being a Life of Pope Gregory VII. I need scarcely recall to those who have read it, the power and the liveliness of the narrative. This composition was the author's relaxation on evenings and in his summer vacations, from his ordinary engagements in London. It had been suggested to him originally by me, at the instance of Hurrell Froude.

The Series of the Lives of the English Saints was projected at a later period, under circumstances which I shall have in the sequel to describe. Those beautiful compositions have nothing in them, as far as I recollect, simply inconsistent with the general objects which I have been assigning to my labours in these years, though the immediate occasion which led to them, and the tone in which they were written, could not in the exercise of the largest indulgence be said to have an Anglican direction.

At a comparatively early date I drew up the Tract on the Roman Breviary. It frightened my own friends on its first appearance, and, several years afterwards, when younger men began to translate for publication the four volumes *in extenso*, they were dissuaded from doing so by advice to which from a sense of duty they listened. It was an apparent accident which introduced me to the knowledge of that most wonderful and most attractive monument of the devotion of saints. On Hurrell Froude's death, in 1836, I was asked to select one of his books as a keepsake. I selected Butler's Analogy; finding that it had been already chosen, I looked with some perplexity along the shelves as they stood before me, when an intimate friend at my elbow said, 'Take that.' It was the Breviary which Hurrell had had with him at Barbados. Accordingly I took it, studied it, wrote my Tract from it, and have it on my table in constant use till this day.

That dear and familiar companion, who thus put the Breviary into my hands, is still in the Anglican Church. So too is that early venerated long-loved friend, together with whom I edited a work which, more perhaps than any other, caused disturbance and annoyance in the Anglican world – Froude's Remains; yet, however judgments might run as to the prudence of publishing it, I never heard any one impute to Mr Keble the very shadow of dishonesty or treachery towards his Church in so acting.

The annotated Translation of the Treatises of St Athanasius was of course in no sense a tentative work; it belongs to another order of thought. This historico-dogmatic work employed me for years. I had made preparations for following it up with a doctrinal history of the heresies which succeeded to the Arian.

I should make mention also of the British Critic. I was Editor of it for three years, from July 1838 to July 1841. My writers belonged to various schools, some to none at all. The subjects are various –classical, academical, political, critical, and artistic, as well as theological, and upon the Movement none are to be found which do not keep quite clear of advocating the cause of Rome.

So I went on for years, up to 1841. It was, in a human point of view, the happiest time of my life. I was truly at home. I had in one of my volumes appropriated to myself the words of Bramhall, 'Bees, by the instinct of nature, do love their hives, and birds their nests.' I did not suppose that such sunshine would last, though I knew not what would be its termination. It was the time of plenty, and, during its seven years, I tried to lay up as much as I could for the dearth which was to follow it. We prospered and spread. I have spoken of the doings of these years, since I was a Catholic, in a passage, part of which I will here quote, though there is a sentence in it that requires some limitation:

'From beginnings so small,' I said,

> from elements of thought so fortuitous, with prospects so unpromising, the Anglo-Catholic party suddenly became a power in the National Church, and an object of alarm to her rulers and friends. Its originators would have found it difficult to say what they aimed at of a practical kind: rather, they put forth views and principles, for their own sake, because they were true, as if they were obliged to say them; and, as they might be themselves surprised at their earnestness in uttering them, they had as great cause to be surprised at the success which attended their propagation. And, in fact, they could only say that those doctrines were in the air; that to assert was to prove, and that to explain was to persuade; and that the Movement in which they were taking part was the birth of a crisis rather than of a place. In a very few years a school of opinion was formed, fixed in its principles, indefinite and progressive in their range; and it extended itself into every part of the country. If we inquire what the world thought of it, we have still more to raise our wonder; for, not to mention the excitement it caused in England, the Movement and its party-names were known to the police of Italy and to the back-woodmen of America. And so it proceeded, getting stronger and stronger every year, till it came into collision with the Nation, and that Church of the Nation, which it began by professing especially to serve.

The greater its success, the nearer was that collision at hand. The first threatenings of what was coming were heard in 1838. At that time, my Bishop in a Charge made some light animadversions, but they *were* animadversions, on the Tracts for the Times. At once I offered to stop them. What took place on the occasion I prefer to state in the words, in which I related it in a Pamphlet addressed to him in a later year, when the blow actually came down upon me.

'In your Lordship's Charge for 1838,' I said,

> an allusion was made to the Tracts for the Times. Some opponents of the Tracts said that you treated them with undue indulgence ... I wrote to the Archdeacon on the subject, submitting the Tract entirely to your Lordship's disposal. What I thought about your Charge will appear from the words I then used to him. I said, 'A Bishop's lightest word *ex cathedrâ* is heavy. His judgment on a book cannot be light. It is a rare occurrence.' And I offered to withdraw any of the Tracts over which I had control, if I were informed which were those to which your Lordship had objections. I afterwards wrote to your Lordship to this effect, that 'I trusted I might say sincerely, that I should feel a more lively pleasure in knowing that I was submitting myself to your Lordship's expressed judgment in a matter of that kind, than I could have even in the widest circulation of the volumes in question.' Your Lordship did not think it necessary to proceed to such a measure, but I felt, and always have felt, that, if ever you determined on it, I was bound to obey.

That day at length came, and I conclude this portion of my narrative, with relating the circumstances of it.

From the time that I had entered upon the duties of Public Tutor at my College, when my doctrinal views were very different from what they were in 1841, I had meditated a comment upon the Articles. Then, when the Movement was in its swing, friends had said to me, 'What will you make of the Articles ?' but I did not share the apprehension which their question implied. Whether, as time went on, I should have been forced, by the necessities of the original theory of the Movement, to put on paper the speculations which I had about them, I am not able to conjecture. The actual cause of my doing so, in the beginning of 1841, was the restlessness, actual and prospective, of those who neither liked the *Via Media*, nor my strong judgment against Rome. I had been enjoined, I think by my Bishop, to keep these men straight, and I wished so to do: but their tangible difficulty was subscription to the Articles; and thus the question of the Articles came before me.

It was thrown in our teeth; 'How can you manage to sign the Articles? they are directly against Rome.' 'Against Rome?' I made answer, 'What do you mean by "Rome"?' and then I proceeded to make distinctions, of which I shall now give an account.

By 'Roman doctrine' might be meant one of three things: 1, the *Catholic teaching* of the early centuries; or 2, the *formal dogmas of Rome* as contained in the later Councils, especially the Council of Trent, and as condensed in the Creed of Pope Pius IV; 3, the *actual popular beliefs and usages* sanctioned by Rome in the countries in communion with it, over and above the dogmas; and these I called 'dominant errors'. Now Protestants commonly thought that in all three senses, 'Roman doctrine' was condemned in the Articles: I thought that the *Catholic teaching* was not condemned; that the *dominant errors* were; and as to the *formal dogmas*, that some were, some were not, and that the line had to be drawn between them. Thus, 1. The use of Prayers for the dead was a Catholic doctrine – not condemned in the Articles; 2. The prison of Purgatory was a Roman dogma – which was condemned in them; but the infallibility of Ecumenical Councils was a Roman dogma – not condemned; and 3. The fire of Purgatory was an authorized and popular error, not a dogma – which was condemned.

Further, I considered that the difficulties, felt by the persons whom I have mentioned, mainly lay in their mistaking, 1, Catholic teaching, which was not condemned in the Articles, for Roman dogma which was condemned; and 2, Roman dogma, which was not condemned in the Articles, for dominant error which was. If they went further than this, I had nothing more to say to them.

A further motive which I had for my attempt, was the desire to ascertain the ultimate points of contrariety between the Roman and Anglican creeds, and to make them as few as possible. I thought that each creed was obscured and misrepresented by a dominant circumambient 'Popery' and 'Protestantism'.

The main thesis then of my Essay was this – the Articles do not oppose Catholic teaching; they but partially oppose Roman dogma; they for the most part oppose the dominant errors of Rome. And the problem was, as I have said, to draw the line as to what they allowed and what they condemned.

Such being the object which I had in view, what were my

prospects of widening and of defining their meaning? The prospect was encouraging; there was no doubt at all of the elasticity of the Articles: to take a palmary instance, the seventeenth was assumed by one party to be Lutheran, by another Calvinistic, though the two interpretations were contradictory to each other; why then should not other Articles be drawn up with a vagueness of an equally intense character? I wanted to ascertain what was the limit of that elasticity in the direction of Roman dogma. But next, I had a way of inquiry of my own, which I state without defending. I instanced it afterwards in my Essay on Doctrinal Development. That work, I believe, I have not read since I published it, and I do not doubt at all that I have made many mistakes in it – partly, from my ignorance of the details of doctrine, as the Church of Rome holds them, but partly from my impatience to clear as large a range for the *principle* of doctrinal Development (waiving the question of historical *fact*) as was consistent with the strict Apostolicity and identity of the Catholic Creed. In like manner, as regards the 39 Articles, my method of inquiry was to leap *in medias res*. I wished to institute an inquiry how far, in critical fairness, the text *could* be opened; I was aiming far more at ascertaining what a man who subscribed it might hold than what he must, so that my conclusions were negative rather than positive. It was but a first essay. And I made it with the full recognition and consciousness, which I had already expressed in my Prophetical Office, as regards the *Via Media*, that I was making only 'a first approximation to the required solution' – 'a series of illustrations supplying hints for the removal' of a difficulty, and with full acknowledgement 'that in minor points, whether in question of fact or of judgment, there was room for difference or error of opinion', and that I 'should not be ashamed to own a mistake, if it were proved against me, nor reluctant to bear the just blame of it.' – *Proph. Off.* p. 31.

In addition, I was embarassed in consequence of my wish to go as far as was possible, in interpreting the Articles in the direction of Roman dogma, without disclosing what I was doing to the parties whose doubts I was meeting, who, if they understood at once the full extent of the licence which the Articles admitted, might be thereby encouraged to proceed still further than at present they found in themselves any call to go.

1. But in the way of such an attempt comes the prompt objection that the Articles were actually drawn up against

'Popery', and therefore it was transcendently absurd and dishonest to suppose that Popery, in any shape – patristic belief, Tridentine dogma, or popular corruption authoritatively sanctioned – would be able to take refuge under their text. This premiss I denied. Not any religious doctrine at all, but a political principle, was the primary English idea of 'Popery' at the date of the Reformation. And what was that political principle, and how could it best be suppressed in England? What was the great question in the days of Henry and Elizabeth? The *Supremacy* – now, was I saying one single word in favour of the Supremacy of the Holy See, in favour of the foreign jurisdiction? No; I did not believe in it myself. Did Henry VIII religiously hold Justification by faith only? did he disbelieve Purgatory? Was Elizabeth zealous for the marriage of the Clergy? or had she a conscience against the Mass? The Supremacy of the Pope was the essence of the 'Popery' to which at the time of the composition of the Articles, the Supreme Head or Governor of the English Church was so violently hostile.

2. But again I said this – let 'Popery' mean what it would in the mouths of the compilers of the Articles, let it even, for argument's sake, include the doctrines of that Tridentine Council, which was not yet over when the Articles were drawn up, and against which they could not be simply directed, yet, consider, what was the religious object of the Government in their imposition? merely to get rid of 'Popery'? No; it had the further object of gaining the 'Papists'. What then was the best way to induce reluctant or wavering minds, and these, I supposed, were the majority, to give in their adhesion to the new symbol? how had the Arians drawn up their Creeds? was it not on the principle of using vague ambiguous language, which to the subscribers would seem to bear a Catholic sense, but which, when worked out in the long run, would prove to be heterodox? Accordingly, there was great antecedent probability, that, fierce as the Articles might look at first sight, their bark would prove worse than their bite. I say antecedent probability, for what extent that surmise might be true, could only be ascertained by investigation.

3. But a consideration came up at once, which threw light on this surmise – what if it should turn out that the very men who drew up the Articles, in the very act of doing so, had avowed, or rather in one of those very Articles themselves had imposed on subscribers, a number of those very 'Papistical' doctrines, which

they were now thought to deny, as part and parcel of that very Protestantism, which they were now thought to consider divine? and this was the fact, and I showed it in my Essay.

Let the reader observe – the 35th Article says: 'The second Book of Homilies doth contain *a godly and wholesome doctrine, and necessary for* these times, as doth the former Book of Homilies.' Here the *doctrine* of the Homilies is recognized as godly and wholesome, and concurrence in that recognition is imposed on all subscribers of the Articles. Let us then turn to the Homilies, and see what this godly doctrine is: I quoted from them to the following effect:

1. They declare that the so-called 'apocryphal' book of Tobit is the teaching of the Holy Ghost, and is Scripture.
2. That the so-called 'apocryphal' book of Wisdom is Scripture, and the infallible and undeceivable word of God.
3. That the Primitive Church, next to the Apostles' time, and, as they imply, for almost 700 years, is no doubt most pure.
4. That the Primitive Church is specially to be followed.
5. That the Four first General Councils belong to the Primitive Church.
6. That there are Six Councils which are allowed and received by all men.
7. Again, they speak of a certain truth which they are enforcing, as declared by God's word, the sentences of the ancient doctors, and judgment of the Primitive Church.
8. Of the learned and holy Bishops and doctors of the Church of the first eight centuries being of great authority and credit with the people.
9. Of the declaration of Christ and His Apostles and all the rest of the Holy Fathers.
10. Of the authority both of Scripture and also of Augustine.
11. Of Augustine, Chrysostom, Ambrose, Jerome, and about thirty other Fathers, to some of whom they give the title of 'Saint', to others of 'ancient Catholic Fathers and doctors, &c.'.
12. They declare that, not only the holy Apostles and disciples of Christ, but the godly Fathers also before and since Christ were endued without doubt with the Holy Ghost.
13. That the ancient Catholic Fathers say that the 'Lord's Supper' is the salve of immortality, the sovereign preservative against death, the food of immortality, the healthful grace.
14. That the Lord's Blessed Body and Blood are received under the form of bread and wine.
15. That the meat in the Sacrament is an invisible meat and a ghostly substance.

16. That the holy Body and Blood of thy God ought to be touched with the mind.

17. That Ordination is a Sacrament.

18. That Matrimony is a Sacrament.

19. That there are other Sacraments besides 'Baptism and the Lord's Supper', though not 'such as' they.

20. That the souls of the Saints are reigning in joy and in heaven with God.

21. That alms-deeds purge the soul from the infection and filthy spots of sin, and are a precious medicine, an inestimable jewel.

22. That mercifulness wipes out and washes away sins, as salves and remedies to heal sores and grievous diseases.

23. That the duty of fasting is a truth more manifest than it should need to be proved.

24. That fasting, used with prayer, is of great efficacy and weigheth much with God; so the Angel Raphael told Tobias.

25. That the puissant and mighty Emperor Theodosius was, in the Primitive Church which was most holy and godly, excommunicated by St Ambrose.

26. That Constantine, Bishop of Rome, did condemn Philippicus, then Emperor, not without a cause indeed, but very justly.

Putting altogether aside the question how far these separate theses came under the matter to which subscription was to be made, it was quite plain, that in the minds of the men who wrote the Homilies, and who thus incorporated them into the Anglican system of doctrine, there was no such nice discrimination between the Catholic and the Protestant faith, no such clear recognition of formal Protestant principles and tenets, no such accurate definition of 'Roman doctrine', as is received at the present day – hence great probability accrued to my presentiment, that the Articles were tolerant, not only of what I called 'Catholic teaching', but of much that was 'Roman'.

4. And here was another reason against the notion that the Articles directly attacked the Roman dogmas as declared at Trent and as promulgated by Pius the Fourth – the Council of Trent was not over, nor its Canons promulgated at the date when the Articles were drawn up,[1] so that those Articles must be aiming at something else. What was that something else ? The Homilies tell

[1] The Pope's Confirmation of the Council, by which its Canons became *de fide*, and his Bull *super confirmatione* by which they were promulgated to the world, are dated 26 January 1564. The Articles are dated 1562.

us: the Homilies are the best comment upon the Articles. Let us turn to the Homilies, and we shall find from first to last that, not only is not the Catholic teaching of the first centuries, but neither again are the dogmas of Rome, the objects of the protect of the compilers of the Articles, but the dominant errors, the popular corruptions, authorized or suffered by the high name of Rome. The eloquent declamation of the Homilies finds its matter almost exclusively in the dominant errors. As to Catholic teaching, nay as to Roman dogma, those Homilies, as I have shown, contained no small portion of it themselves.

5. So much for the writers of the Articles and Homilies – they were witnesses, not authorities, and I used them as such; but in the next place, who were the actual authorities imposing them? I reasonably considered the authority *imponens* to be the Convocation of 1571; but here again, it would be found that the very Convocation, which received and confirmed the 39 Articles, also enjoined by Canon that 'preachers should be *careful*, that they should *never* teach aught in a sermon, to be religiously held and believed by the people, except that which is agreeable to the doctrine of the Old and New Testament, and *which the Catholic Fathers and ancient Bishops have collected* from that very doctrine.' Here, let it be observed, an appeal is made by the convocation *imponens* to the very same ancient authorities, as had been mentioned with such profound veneration by the writers of the Homilies and of the Articles, and thus, if the Homilies contained views of doctrine which now would be called Roman, there seemed to me to be an extreme probability that the Convocation of 1571 also countenanced and received, or at least did not reject, those doctrines.

6. And further, when at length I came actually to look into the text of the Articles, I saw in many cases a patent justification of all that I had surmised as to their vagueness and indecisiveness, and that, not only on questions which lay between Lutherans, Calvinists, and Zuinglians, but on Catholic questions also; and I have noticed them in my Tract. In the conclusion of my Tract I observe: The articles are 'evidently framed on the principle of leaving open large questions on which the controversy hinges. They state broadly extreme truths, and are silent about their adjustment. For instance, they say that all necessary faith must be proved from Scripture; but do not say *who* is to prove it. They say, that the Church has authority in controversies; they do not say

what authority. They say that it may enforce nothing beyond Scripture, but do not say *where* the remedy lies when it does. They say that works *before* grace *and* justification are worthless and worse, and that works *after* grace *and* justification are acceptable, but they do not speak at all of works *with* God's aid *before* justification. They say that men are lawfully called and sent to minister and preach, who are chosen and called by men who have public authority *given* them in the Congregation; but they do not add *by whom* the authority is to be given. They say that Councils called by *princes* may err; they do not determine whether Councils called in the name of Christ may err.'

Such were the considerations which weighed with me in my inquiry how far the Articles were tolerant of a Catholic, or even a Roman interpretation; and such was the defence which I made in my Tract for having attempted it. From what I have already said, it will appear that I have no need or intention at this day to maintain every particular interpretation which I suggested in the course of my Tract, nor indeed had I then. Whether it was prudent or not, whether it was sensible or not, any how I attempted only a first essay of a necessary work, an essay which, as I was quite prepared to find, would require revision and modification by means of the lights which I should gain from the criticism of others. I should have gladly withdrawn any statement, which could be proved to me to be erroneous; I considered my work to be faulty and open to objection in the same sense in which I now consider my Anglican interpretations of Scripture to be erroneous, but in no other sense. I am surprised that men do not apply to the interpreters of Scripture generally the hard names which they apply to the author of Tract 90. He held a large system of theology, and applied it to the Articles: Episcopalians, or Lutherans, or Presbyterians, or Unitarians, hold a large system of theology and apply it to Scripture. Every theology has its difficulties; Protestants hold justification by faith only, though there is no text in St Paul which enunciates it, and though St James expressly denies it; do we therefore call Protestants dishonest? they deny that the Church has a divine mission, though St Paul says that it is 'the Pillar and ground of Truth'; they keep the Sabbath, though St Paul says, 'Let no man judge you in meat or drink or in respect of . . . the sabbath days.' Every creed has texts in its favour, and again texts which run counter to it: and this is generally confessed. And this is what I felt keenly – how had I done worse in Tract 90 than Anglicans, Wesleyans, and Calvinists did daily in their Sermons and their publications ? how had I done worse, than the Evangelical party in their *ex animo* reception of the Services of Baptism and Visitation of the Sick ?[1] Why was I to be dishonest and they immaculate ? There was an occasion on which our Lord gave an answer, which seemed to be appropriate to my own case, when the tumult broke out against my Tract – 'He that is without sin among you, let him first cast a stone at him.' I could have fancied that a sense of their own difficulties of interpretation would have persuaded the great party I have mentioned to some prudence, or at least moderation, in opposing a teacher of an opposite school. But I suppose their alarm and their anger overcame their sense of justice.

In the sudden storm of indignation with which the Tract was received throughout the country on its appearance, I recognize much of real religious feeling, much of honest and true principle, much of straightforward ignorant common sense. In Oxford there was genuine feeling too; but there had been a smouldering stern energetic animosity, not at all unnatural, partly rational, against its author. A false step had been made; now was the time for action. I am told that, even before the publication of the Tract, rumours of its contents had got into the hostile camp in an exaggerated form; and not a moment was lost in proceeding to action, when I was actually fallen into the hands of the Philistines. I was quite unprepared for the outbreak, and was startled at its violence. I do not think I had any fear. Nay, I will add I am not sure that it was not in one point of view a relief to me.

I saw indeed clearly that my place in the Movement was lost;

---

[1] For instance, let candid men consider the form of Absolution contained in that Prayer Book, of which all clergymen, Evangelical and Liberal as well as high Church, and (I think) all persons in University office declare that 'it containeth *nothing contrary to the Word of God.*'

I challenge, in the sight of all England, Evangelical clergymen generally, to put on paper an interpretation of this form of words, consistent with their sentiments, which shall be less forced than the most objectionable of the interpretations which Tract 90 puts upon any passage in the Articles.

'Our Lord Jesus Christ, who hath left *power* to His Church to absolve all sinners who truly repent and believe in Him, of His great mercy forgive thee thine offences; and by *His authority committed to me, I absolve thee from all thy sins,* in the Name of the Father, and of the Son, and of the Holy Ghost. Amen.'

I subjoin the Roman form, as used in England and elsewhere: 'Dominus noster Jesus Christus te absolvat; et ego auctoritate ipsius te absolvo, ab omni vinculo excommunicationis et interdicti, in quantum possum et tu indiges. Deinde ego te absolvo à peccatis tuis, in nomine Patris et Filii et Spiritûs Sancti. Amen.'

public confidence was at an end; my occupation was gone. It was simply an impossibility that I could say any thing henceforth to good effect, when I had been posted up by the marshal on the buttery hatch of every College of my University, after the manner of discommoned pastry-cooks, and when in every part of the country and every class of society, through every organ and opportunity of opinion, in newspapers, in periodicals, at meetings, in pulpits, at dinner-tables, in coffee-rooms, in railway carriages, I was denounced as a traitor who had laid his train and was detected in the very act of firing it against the time-honoured Establishment. There were indeed men, besides my own immediate friends, men of name and position, who gallantly took my part, as Dr Hook, Mr Palmer, and Mr Perceval: it must have been a grievous trial for themselves; yet what after all could they do for me? Confidence in me was lost – but I had already lost full confidence in myself. Thoughts had passed over me a year and a half before in respect to the Anglican claims, which for the time had profoundly troubled me. They had gone: I had not less confidence in the power and the prospects of the Apostolical movement than before; not less confidence than before in the grievousness of what I called the 'dominant errors' of Rome: but how was I any more to have absolute confidence in myself? how was I to have confidence in my present confidence? how was I to be sure that I should always think as I thought now? I felt that by this event a kind Providence had saved me from an impossible position in the future.

First, if I remember right, they wished me to withdraw the Tract. This I refused to do: I would not do so for the sake of those who were unsettled or in danger of unsettlement. I would not do so for my own sake; for how could I acquiesce in a mere Protestant interpretation of the Articles? how could I range myself among the professors of a theology, of which it put my teeth on edge, even to hear the sound?

Next they said, 'Keep silence; do not defend the Tract'; I answered, 'Yes, if you will not condemn it – if you will allow it to continue on sale.' They pressed on me whenever I gave way; they fell back when they saw me obstinate. Their line of action was to get out of me as much as they could; but upon the point of their tolerating the Tract I *was* obstinate. So they let me continue it on sale; and they said they would not condemn it. But they said that this was on condition that I did not defend it, that I stopped the series, and that I myself published my own condemnation in a letter to the Bishop of Oxford. I impute nothing whatever to him, he was ever most kind to me. Also, they said they could not answer for what some individual Bishops might perhaps say about the Tract in their own charges. I agreed to their conditions. My one point was to save the Tract.

Not a line in writing was given me, as a pledge of the observance of the main article on their side of the engagement. Parts of letters from them were read to me, without being put into my hands. It was an 'understanding'. A clever man had warned me against 'understandings' some six years before: I have hated them ever since.

In the last words of my letter to the Bishop of Oxford I thus resigned my place in the Movement:

> 'I have nothing to be sorry for,' I say to him, 'except having made your Lordship anxious, and others whom I am bound to revere. I have nothing to be sorry for, but every thing to rejoice in and be thankful for. I have never taken pleasure in seeming to be able to move a party, and whatever influence I have had, has been found, not sought after. I have acted because others did not act, and have sacrificed a quiet which I prized. May God be with me in time to come, as He has been hitherto! and He will be, if I can but keep my hand clean and my heart pure. I think I can bear, or at least will try to bear, any personal humiliation, so that I am preserved from betraying sacred interests, which the Lord of grace and power has given into my charge.'

PART V

History of my Religious Opinions from 1839 to 1841
Published as a Pamphlet, Thursday, May 19, 1864.

CHAPTER III

And now that I am about to trace, as far as I can, the course of that great revolution of mind, which led me to leave my own home, to which I was bound by so many strong tender ties, I feel overcome with the difficulty of satisfying myself in my account of it, and have recoiled from the attempt, till the near approach of the day, on which these lines must be given to the world, forces me to set about the task. For who can know himself, and the multitude of subtle influences which act upon him ? and who can recollect, at the distance of twenty-five years, all that he once knew about his thoughts and his deeds, and that, during a portion of his life, when even at the time his observation, whether of himself or of the external world, was less than before or after, by very reason of the perplexity and dismay which weighed upon him – when, in spite of the light given to him according to his need amid his darkness, yet a darkness it emphatically was ? And who can suddenly gird himself suddenly to a new and anxious undertaking, which he might be able indeed to perform well, were full and calm leisure allowed him to look through every thing that he had written, whether in published works or private letters ? but, on the other hand, as to that calm contemplation of the past, in itself so desirable, who can afford to be leisurely and deliberate, while he practises on himself a cruel operation, the ripping up of old griefs, and the venturing again upon the 'infandum dolorem' of years, in which the stars of this lower heaven were one by one going out ? I could not in cool blood, nor except upon the imperious call of duty, attempt what I have set myself to do. It is both to head and heart an extreme trial, thus to analyze what has so long gone by, and to bring out the results of that examination. I have done various bold things in my life: this is the boldest: and, were I not sure I should after all succeed in my object, it would be madness to set about it.

In the spring of 1839 my position in the Anglican Church was at its height. I had supreme confidence in my controversial *status*, and I had a great and still growing success, in recommending it to others. I had in the foregoing autumn been somewhat sore at the Bishop's Charge, but I have a letter which shows that all annoyance had passed from my mind. In January, if I recollect aright, in order to meet the popular clamour against myself and others, and to satisfy the Bishop, I had collected into one all the strong things which they, and especially I, had said against the Church of Rome, in order to their insertion among the advertisements appended to our publications. Conscious as I was that my opinions in religion were not gained, as the world said, from Roman sources, but were, on the contrary, the birth of my own mind and of the circumstances in which I had been placed, I had a scorn of the imputations which were heaped upon me. It was true that I held a large bold system of religion, very unlike the Protestantism of the day, but it was the concentration and adjustment of the statements of great Anglican authorities, and I had as much right to do so, as the Evangelical party had, and more right than the Liberal party could show, to hold their own respective doctrines. As I spoke on occasion of Tract 90, I claimed, in behalf of who would in the Anglican Church, the right of holding with Bramhall a comprecation with the Saints and the Mass all but Transubstantiation with Andrewes, or with Hooker that Transubstantiation itself is not a point for Churches to part communion upon, or with Hammond that a General Council, truly such, never did, never shall err in a matter of faith, or with Bull that man had in paradise and lost on the fall, a supernatural habit of grace, or with Thorndike that penance is a propitiation for post-baptismal sin, or with Pearson that the all-powerful name of Jesus is no otherwise given than in the Catholic Church. 'Two can play at that,' was often in my mouth, when men of Protestant sentiments appealed to the Articles, Homilies, or Reformers; in the sense that, if they had a right to speak loud, I had the liberty to speak out as well as they, and had the means, by the same or parallel appeals, of giving them tit for tat. I thought that the Anglican Church was tyrannized over by a mere party, and I aimed at bringing into effect the promise contained in the motto to the Lyra, 'They shall know the difference now.' I only asked to be allowed to show them the difference.

What will best describe my state of mind at the early part of 1839, is an Article in the British Critic for that April. I have looked over it now, for the first time since it was published; and have been struck by it for this reason – it contains the last words which I ever spoke as an Anglican to Anglicans. It may now be read as my parting address and valediction, made to my friends. I little knew it at the time. It reviews the actual state of things, and it ends by looking towards the future. It is not altogether mine; for my memory goes to this – that I had asked a friend to do the work; that then, the thought came on me, that I would do it myself: and that he was good enough to put into my hands what he had with great appositeness written, and that I embodied it in my Article. Every one, I think, will recognize the greater part of it as mine. It was published two years before the affair of Tract 90, and was entitled 'The State of Religious Parties'.

In this Article, I begin by bringing together testimonies from our enemies to the remarkable success of our exertions. One writer said: 'Opinions and views of a theology of a very marked and peculiar kind have been extensively adopted and strenuously upheld, and are daily gaining ground among a considerable and influential portion of the members, as well as ministers of the Established Church.' Another: The Movement has manifested itself 'with the most rapid growth of the hot-bed of these evil days.' Another: 'The *Via Media* is crowded with young en-thusiasts, who never presume to argue, except against the propriety of arguing at all.' Another: 'Were I to give you a full list of the works, which they have produced within the short space of five years, I should surprise you. You would see what a task it would be to make yourself complete master of their system, even in its present probably immature state. The writers have adopted the motto, "In quietness and confidence shall be your strength." With regard to confidence, they have justified their adopting it; but as to quietness, it is not very quiet to pour forth such a succession of controversial publications.' Another: 'The spread of these doctrines is in fact now having the effect of rendering all other distinctions obsolete, and of severing the religious community into two portions, fundamentally and vehemently opposed one to the other. Soon there will be no middle ground left; and every man, and especially every clergyman, will be compelled to make his choice between the two.' Another: 'The time has gone by, when those unfortunate and deeply regretted publications can be passed over without notice, and the hope that their influence would fail is now dead.' Another: 'These doctrines had already made fearful progress. One of the largest churches in Brighton is crowded to hear them; so is the church at Leeds. There are few towns of note, to which they have not extended. They are preached in small towns in Scotland. They obtain in Elginshire, 600 miles north of London. I found them myself in the heart of the highlands of Scotland. They are advocated in the newspaper and periodical press. They have even insinuated themselves into the House of Commons.' And, lastly, a bishop in a Charge – It 'is daily assuming a more serious and alarming aspect. Under the specious pretence of deference to Antiquity and respect for primitive models, the foundations of the Protestant Church are undermined by men, who dwell within her walls, and those who sit in the Reformers' seat are traducing the Reformation.'

After thus stating the phenomenon of the time, as it presented itself to those who did not sympathize in it, the Article proceeds to account for it; and this it does by considering it as a re-action from the dry and superficial character of the religious teaching and the literature of the last generation, or century, and as a result of the need which was felt both by the hearts and the intellects of the nation for a deeper philosophy, and as the evidence and as the partial fulfilment of that need, to which even the chief authors of the then generation, had borne witness. First, I mentioned the literary influence of Walter Scott, who turned men's minds in the direction of the middle ages. 'The general need,' I said, 'of something deeper and more attractive, than what had offered itself elsewhere, may be considered to have led to his popularity; and by means of his popularity he re-acted on his readers, stimulating their mental thirst, feeding their hopes, setting before them visions, which, when once seen, are not easily forgotten, and silently indoctrinating them with nobler ideas, which might afterwards be appealed to as first principles.'

Then I spoke of Coleridge, thus:

While history in prose and verse was thus made the

instrument of Church feelings and opinions, a philosophical basis for the same was laid in England by a very original thinker, who, while he indulged a liberty of speculation, which no Christian can tolerate, and advocated conclusions which were often heathen rather than Christian, yet after all instilled a higher philosophy into inquiring minds, than they had hitherto been accustomed to accept. In this way he made trial of his age, and succeeded in interesting its genius in the cause of Catholic truth.

Then come Southey and Wordsworth, 'two living poets, one of whom in the department of fantastic fiction, the other in that of philosophical meditation, have addressed themselves to the same high principles and feelings, and carried forward their readers in the same direction.'

Then comes the prediction of this re-action hazarded by 'a sagacious observer withdrawn from the world, and surveying its movements from a distance', Mr Alexander Knox. He had said twenty years before the date of my Article: 'No Church on earth has more intrinsic excellence than the English Church, yet no Church probably has less practical influence. . . . The rich provision, made by the grace and providence of God, for habits of a noble kind, is evidence that men shall arise, fitted both by nature and ability, to discover for themselves, and to display to others, whatever yet remains undiscovered, whether in the words or works of God.' Also I referred to 'a much venerated clergyman of the last generation', who said shortly before his death, 'Depend on it, the day will come, when those great doctrines, now buried, will be brought out to the light of day, and then the effect will be fearful.' I remarked upon this, that they who 'now blame the impetuosity of the current, should rather turn their animadversions upon those who have dammed up a majestic river, till it has become a flood.'

These being the circumstances under which the Movement began and progressed, it was absurd to refer it to the act of two or three individuals. It was not so much a movement as a 'spirit afloat'; it was within us, 'rising up in hearts where it was least suspected, and working itself, though not in secret, yet so subtly and impalpably, as hardly to admit of precaution or encounter on any ordinary human rules of opposition. It is,' I continued, 'an adversary in the air, a something one and entire, a whole wherever it is, unapproachable and incapable of being grasped, as being the result of causes far deeper than political or other visible agencies, the spiritual awakening of spiritual wants.'

To make this clear, I proceed to refer to the chief preachers of the revived doctrines at that moment, and to draw attention to the variety of their respective antecedents. Dr Hook and Mr Churton represented the high Church dignitaries of the last century; Mr Perceval, the Tory aristocracy; Mr Keble came from a country parsonage; Mr Palmer from Ireland; Dr Pusey from the Universities of Germany, and the study of Arabic MSS; Mr Dodsworth from the study of Prophecy; Mr Oakeley had gained his views, as he himself expressed it, 'partly by study, partly by reflection, partly by conversation with one or two friends, inquirers like himself': while I speak of myself as being 'much indebted to the friendship of Archbishop Whately.' And thus I am led on to ask, 'What head of a sect is there ? What march of opinions can be traced from mind to mind among preachers such as these ? They are one and all in their degree the organs of one Sentiment, which has risen up simultaneously in many places very mysteriously.'

My train of thought next led me to speak of the disciples of the Movement, and I freely acknowledged and lamented that they needed to be kept in order. It is very much to the purpose to draw attention to this point now, when such extravagances as then occurred, whatever they were, are simply laid to my door, or to the charge of the doctrines which I advocated. A man cannot do more than freely confess what is wrong, say that it need not be, that it ought not to be, and that he is very sorry that it should be. Now I said in the Article, which I am reviewing, that the great truths themselves, which we were preaching, must not be condemned on account of such abuse of them. 'Aberrations there must ever be, whatever the doctrine is, while the human heart is sensitive, capricious and wayward. A mixed multitude went out of Egypt with the Israelites.' 'There will ever be a number of persons,' I continued, 'professing the opinions of a movement party, who talk loudly and strangely, do odd or fierce things, display themselves unnecessarily, and disgust other people; persons, too young to be wise, too generous to be cautious, too warm to be sober, or too intellectual to be humble. Such persons will be very apt to attach themselves to particular persons, to use particular names, to say things merely because others do, and to act in a party-spirited way.'

While I thus republish what I then said about such extravagances as occurred in these years, at the same time I have a very strong conviction that those extravagances furnished quite as much the welcome excuse for those who were jealous or shy of us, as the stumbling-blocks of those who were well inclined to our doctrines. This too we felt at the time; but it was our duty to see that our good should not be evil-spoken of; and accordingly, two or three of the writers of the Tracts for the Times had commenced a Series of what they called 'Plain Sermons' with the avowed purpose of discouraging and correcting whatever was uppish or extreme in our followers: to this Series I contributed a volume myself.

Its conductors say in their Preface:

If therefore as time goes on, there shall be found persons, who admiring the innate beauty and majesty of the fuller system of Primitive Christianity, and seeing the transcendent strength of its principles, *shall become loud and voluble advocates* in their behalf, speaking the more freely, *because they do not feel them deeply as founded* in divine and eternal truth, of such persons *it is our duty to declare plainly*, that, as we should contemplate their condition with serious misgiving, *so would they be the last persons from whom we should* seek support.

But if, on the other hand, there shall be any, who, in the silent humility of their lives, and in their unaffected reverence for holy things, show that they in truth accept these principles as real and substantial, and by habitual purity of heart and serenity of temper, give proof of their deep veneration for sacraments and sacramental ordinances, those persons, *whether our professed adherents or not*, best exemplify the kind of character which the writers of the Tracts for the Times have wished to form.

These clergymen had the best of claims to use these beautiful words, for they were themselves, all of them, important writers in the Tracts, the two Mr Kebles, and Mr Isaac Williams. And this passage, with which they ushered their Series into the world, I quoted in the Article, of which I am giving an account, and I added, 'What more can be required of the preachers of neglected truth, than that they should admit that some, who do not assent to their preaching, are holier and better men than some who do?'.

They were not answerable for the intemperance of those who dishonoured a true doctrine, provided they protested, as they did, against such intemperance. 'They were not answerable for the dust and din which attends any great moral movement. The truer doctrines are, the more liable they are to be perverted.'

The notice of these incidental faults of opinion or temper in adherents of the Movement, led on to a discussion of the secondary causes, by means of which a system of doctrine may be embraced, modified, or developed, of the variety of schools which may all be in the One Church, and of the succession of one phase of doctrine to another, while that doctrine is ever one and the same. Thus I was brought on to the subject of Antiquity, which was the basis of the doctrine of the *Via Media*, and by which was not implied a servile imitation of the past, but such a reproduction of it as is really new, while it is old. 'We have good hope,' I say, 'that a system will be rising up, superior to the age, yet harmonizing with, and carrying out its higher points, which will attract to itself those who are willing to make a venture and to face difficulties, for the sake of something higher in prospect. On this, as on other subjects, the proverb will apply, "Fortes fortuna adjuvat.".'

Lastly, I proceeded to the question of that future of the Anglican Church, which was to be a new birth of the Ancient Religion. And I did not venture to pronounce upon it. 'About the future, we have no prospect before our minds whatever, good or bad. Ever since that great luminary, Augustine, proved to be the last bishop of Hippo, Christians have had a lesson against attempting to foretell, *how* Providence will prosper and' [or ?] 'bring to an end, what it begins.' Perhaps the lately-revived principles would prevail in the Anglican Church; perhaps they would be lost in 'some miserable schism, or some more miserable compromise; but there was nothing rash in venturing to predict that 'neither Puritanism or Liberalism had any permanent inheritance within her.' I suppose I meant to say that in the present age, without the aid of Apostolical principles, the Anglican Church would, in the event, cause to exist.

Then I went on: 'As to Liberalism, we think the formularies of the Church will ever, with the aid of a good Providence, keep it from making any serious inroads upon the Clergy. Besides, it is too cold a principle to prevail with the multitude.' But as regarded what was called Evangelical Religion or Puritanism, there was more to cause alarm. I observed upon its organization; but on the other hand it had no intellectual basis; no internal idea, no principle of unity, no theology. 'Its adherents,' I said, 'are already separating from each other; they will melt away like a snow-drift. It has no straightforward view on any one point, on which it professes to teach, and to hide its poverty, it has dressed itself out in a maze of words. We have no dread of it at all; we only fear what it may lead to. It does not stand on intrenched ground, or make any pretence to a position; it does but occupy the space between contending powers, Catholic Truth and Rationalism. Then indeed will be the stern encounter, when two real and living principles, simple, entire, and consistent, one in the Church, the other out of it, at length rush upon each other, contending not for names and words, or half-views, but for elementary notions and distinctive moral characters.'

Whether the ideas of the coming age upon religion were true or false, at least they would be real. 'In the present day,' I said,

> mistiness is the mother of wisdom. A man who can set down half-a-dozen general propositions, which escape from destroying one another only by being diluted into truisms, who can hold the balance between opposites so skilfully as to do without fulcrum or beam, who never enunciates a truth without guarding himself against being supposed to exclude the contradictory – who holds that Scripture is the only authority, yet that the Church is to be deferred to, that faith only justifies, yet that it does not justify without works, that grace does not depend on the sacraments, yet is not given without them, that bishops are a divine ordinance, yet those who have them not are in the same religious condition as those who have – this is your safe man and the hope of the Church; this is what the Church is said to want, not party men, but sensible, temperate, sober, well-judging persons, to guide it through the channel of no-meaning, between the Scylla and Charybdis of Aye and No.

This state of things, however, I said, could not last, if men were to read and think. They

> will not keep standing in that very attitude which you call sound Church-of-Englandism or orthodox Protestantism. They cannot go on for ever standing on one leg, or sitting without a chair, or walking with their feet tied, or like Tityrus's

stags grazing in the air. They will take one view or another, but it will be a consistent view. It may be Liberalism, or Erastianism, or Popery, or Catholicity; but it will be real.

I concluded the Article by saying, that all who did not wish to be 'democratic, or pantheistic, or popish', must 'look out for *some* Via Media which will preserve us from what threatens, though it cannot restore the dead. The spirit of Luther is dead; but Hildebrand and Loyola are alive. Is it sensible, sober, judicious, to be so very angry with those writers of the day, who point to the fact, that our divines of the seventeenth century have occupied a ground which is the true and intelligible mean between extremes? Is it wise to quarrel with this ground, because it is not exactly what we should choose, had we the power of choice? Is it true moderation, instead of trying to fortify a middle doctrine, to fling stones at those who do? . . . Would you rather have your sons and daughters members of the Church of England or of the Church of Rome?'.

And thus I left the matter. But, while I was thus speaking of the future of the Movement, I was in truth winding up my accounts with it, little dreaming that it was so to be – while I was still, in some way or other, feeling about for an available *Via Media*, I was soon to receive a shock which was to cast out of my imagination all middle courses and compromises for ever. As I have said, this Article appeared in the April number of the British Critic; in the July number, I cannot tell why, there is no Article of mine; before the number for October, the event had happened to which I have alluded.

But before I proceed to describe what happened to me in the summer of 1839, I must detain the reader for a while, in order to describe the *issue* of the controversy between Rome and the Anglican Church, as I viewed it. This will involve some dry discussion; but it is as necessary for my narrative, as plans of buildings and homesteads are often found to be in the proceedings of our law courts.

I have said already that, though the object of the Movement was to withstand the Liberalism of the day, I found and felt this could not be done by mere negatives. It was necessary for us to have a positive Church theory erected on a definite basis. This took me to the great Anglican divines; and then of course I found at once that it was impossible to form any such theory, without cutting across the teaching of the Church of Rome. Thus came in the Roman controversy.

When I first turned myself to it, I had neither doubt on the subject, nor suspicion that doubt would ever come upon me. It was in this state of mind that I began to read up Bellarmine on the one hand, and numberless Anglican writers on the other. But I soon found, as others had found before me, that it was a tangled and manifold controversy, difficult to master, more difficult to put out of hand with neatness and precision. It was easy to make points, not easy to sum up and settle. It was not easy to find a clear issue for the dispute, and still less by a logical process to decide it in favour of Anglicanism. This difficulty, however, had no tendency whatever to harass or perplex me: it was a matter, not of convictions, but of proofs.

First I saw, as all see who study the subject, that a broad distinction had to be drawn between the actual state of belief and of usage in the countries which were in communion with the Roman Church, and her formal dogmas; the latter did not cover the former. Sensible pain, for instance, is not implied in the Tridentine decree upon Purgatory; but it was the tradition of the Latin Church, and I had seen the pictures of souls in flames in the streets of Naples. Bishop Lloyd had brought this distinction out strongly in an Article in the British Critic in 1825; indeed, it was one of the most common objections made to the Church of Rome, that she dared not commit herself by formal decree, to what nevertheless she sanctioned and allowed. Accordingly, in my Prophetical Office, I view as simply separate ideas, Rome quiescent, and Rome in action. I contrasted her creed on the one hand, with her ordinary teaching, her controversial tone, her political and social bearing, and her popular beliefs and practices on the other.

While I made this distinction between the decrees and the traditions of Rome, I drew a parallel distinction between Anglicanism quiescent, and Anglicanism in action. In its formal creed Anglicanism was not at a great distance from Rome: far otherwise, when viewed in its insular spirit, the traditions of its establishment, its historical characteristics, its controversial rancour, and its private judgment. I disavowed and condemned those excesses, and called them 'Protestantism' or 'Ultra-Protestantism': I wished to find a parallel disclaimer, on the part of Roman controversialists, of that popular system of beliefs and usages in their own Church, which I called 'Popery'. When that hope was a dream, I saw that the controversy lay between the book-theology of Anglicanism on the one side, and the living system of what I called Roman corruption on the other. I could not get further than this; with this result I was forced to content myself.

These then were the *parties* in the controversy – the Anglican *Via Media* and the popular religion of Rome. And next, as to the *issue*, to which the controversy between them was to be brought, it was this – the Anglican disputant took his stand upon Antiquity or Apostolicity, the Roman upon Catholicity. The Anglican said to the Roman: 'There is but One Faith, the Ancient, and you have not kept to it'; the Roman retorted: 'There is but One Church, the Catholic, and you are out of it.' The Anglican urged: 'Your special beliefs, practices, modes of action, are nowhere in Antiquity'; the Roman objected: 'You do not communicate with any one Church besides your own and its offshoots, and you have discarded principles, doctrines, sacraments, and usages, which are and ever have been received in the East and the West.' The true Church, as defined in the Creeds, was both Catholic and Apostolic; now, as I viewed the controversy in which I was engaged, England and Rome had divided these notes or prerogatives between them: the cause lay thus, Apostolicity *versus* Catholicity.

However, in thus stating the matter, of course I do not wish it supposed, that I allowed the note of Catholicity really to belong to Rome, to the disparagement of the Anglican Church; but I considered that the special point or plea of Rome in the controversy was Catholicity, as the Anglican plea was Antiquity. Of course I contended that the Roman idea of Catholicity was not ancient and apostolic. It was in my judgment at the utmost only natural, becoming, expedient, that the whole of Christendom should be united in one visible body; while such a unity might, on the other hand, be nothing more than a mere heartless and political combination. For myself, I held with the Anglican divines, that, in the Primitive Church, there was a very real mutual independence between its separate parts, though, from a dictate of charity, there was in fact a close union between them. I considered that each See and Diocese might be compared to a crystal, and that each was similar to the rest, and that the sum total of them all was only a collection of crystals. The unity of the

Church lay, not in its being a polity, but in its being a family, a race, coming down by apostolical descent from its first founders and bishops. And I considered this truth brought out, beyond the possibility of dispute, in the Epistles of St Ignatius, in which the Bishop is represented as the one supreme authority in the Church, that is, in his own place, with no one above him, except as, for the sake of ecclesiastical order and expedience, arrangements had been made by which one was put over or under another. So much for our own claim to Catholicity, which was so perversely appropriated by our opponents to themselves – on the other hand, as to our special strong point, Antiquity, while of course, by means of it, we were able to condemn most emphatically the novel claim of Rome to domineer over other Churches, which were in truth her equals, further than that, we thereby especially con-victed her of the intolerable offence of having added to the Faith. This was the critical head of accusation urged against her by the Anglican disputant, and, as he referred to St Ignatius in proof that he himself was a true Catholic, in spite of being separated from Rome, so he triumphantly referred to the Treatise of Vincentius of Lerins upon the 'Quod semper, quod ubique, quod ab omnibus,' in proof that the controversialists of Rome, in spite of their possession of the Catholic name, were separated in their creed from the Apostolical and primitive faith.

Of course those controversialists had their own answer to him, with which I am not concerned in this place; here I am only concerned with the issue itself, between the one party and the other – Antiquity *versus* Catholicity.

Now I will proceed to illustrate what I have been saying of the *status* of the controversy, as it presented itself to my mind, by extracts from my writings of the dates of 1836, 1840, and 1841. And I introduce them with a remark, which especially applies to the paper, from which I shall quote first, of the date of 1836. That paper appeared in the March and April numbers of the British Magazine of that year, and was entitled 'Home Thoughts Abroad'. Now it will be found, that, in the discussion which it contains, as in various other writings of mine, when I was in the Anglican Church, the argument in behalf of Rome is stated with considerable perspicuity and force. And at the time my friends and supporters cried out 'How imprudent!' and both at the time, and especially at a later date, my enemies have cried out, 'How insidious!'. Friends and foes virtually agreed in their criticism; I had set out the cause which I was combating to the best advantage: this was an offence; it might be from imprudence, it might be with a traitorous design. It was from neither the one nor the other; but for the following reasons. First, I had a great impatience, whatever was the subject, of not bringing out the whole of it, as clearly as I could; next I wished to be as fair to my adversaries as possible; and thirdly I thought that there was a great deal of shallowness among our own friends, and that they undervalued the strength of the argument in behalf of Rome, and that they ought to be roused to a more exact apprehension of the position of the controversy. At a later date (1841) when I really felt the force of the Roman side of the question myself, as a difficulty which had to be met, I had a fourth reason for such frankness in argument, and that was, because a number of persons were unsettled far more than I was, as to the Catholicity of the Anglican Church. It was quite plain, that, unless I was perfectly candid in stating what could be said against it, there was no chance that any representations, which I felt to be in its favour, or at least to be adverse to Rome, would have had any success with the persons in question. At all times I had a deep conviction, to put the matter on the lowest ground, that 'honesty was the best policy'. Accordingly, in July 1841, I expressed myself thus on the Anglican difficulty:

This is an objection which we must honestly say is deeply felt by many people, and not inconsiderable ones; and the more it is openly avowed to be a difficulty, the better; for there is then the chance of its being acknowledged, and in the course of time obviated, as far as may be, by those who have the power. Flagrant evils cure themselves by being flagrant; and we are sanguine that the time is come when so great an evil as this is, cannot stand its ground against the good feeling and common sense of religious persons. It is the very strength of Romanism against us; and, unless the proper persons take it into their serious consideration, they may look for certain to undergo the loss, as time goes on, of some whom they would least like to be lost to our Church.

The measure which I had especially in view in this passage, was the project of a Jerusalem Bishopric, which the then Archbishop of Canterbury was at that time concocting with M Bunsen, and of which I shall speak more in the sequel. And now to return to the Home Thoughts Abroad of the spring of 1836.

The discussion contained in this composition runs in the form of a dialogue. One of the disputants says:

> You say to me that the Church of Rome is corrupt. What then ? to cut off a limb is a strange way of saving it from the influence of some constitutional ailment. Indigestion may cause cramp in the extremities; yet we spare our poor feet notwith-standing. Surely there is such a religious *fact* as the existence of a great Catholic body, union with which is a Christian privilege and duty. Now, we English are separate from it.

The other answers:

> The present is an unsatisfactory, miserable state of things, yet I can grant no more. The Church is founded on a doctrine —on the gospel of Truth; it is a means to an end. Perish the Church (though, blessed be the promise! this cannot be) yet let it perish *rather* than the Truth should fail. Purity of faith is more precious to the Christian than unity itself. If Rome has erred grievously in doctrine, then it is a duty to separate even from Rome.

His friend, who takes the Roman side of the argument, refers to the image of the Vine and its branches, which is found, I think, in St Cyprian, as if a branch cut from the Catholic Vine must necessarily die. Also he quotes a passage from St Augustine in controversy with the Donatists to the same effect; viz. that, as being separated from the body of the Church, they were *ipso facto* cut off from the heritage of Christ. And he quotes St Cyril's argument drawn from the very title Catholic, which no body or communion of men has ever dared or been able to appropriate, besides one. He adds, 'Now, I am only contending for the fact, that the communion of Rome constitutes the main body of the Church Catholic, and that we are split off from it, and in the condition of the Donatists.'

The other replies, by denying the fact that the present Roman communion is like St Augustine's Catholic Church, inasmuch as there must be taken into account the large Anglican and Greek communions. Presently he takes the offensive, naming distinctly the points, in which Rome has departed from Primitive Christianity, viz. 'the practical idolatry, the virtual worship of the Virgin and Saints, which are the offence of the Latin Church, and the degradation of moral truth and duty, which follows from these.' And again: 'We cannot join a Church, did we wish it ever so much, which does not acknowledge our orders, refuses us the Cup, demands our acquiescence in image-worship, and ex-communicates us, if we do not receive it and all other decisions of the Tridentine Council.'

His opponent answers these objections by referring to the doctrine of 'developments of gospel truth'. Besides, 'The Anglican system itself is not found complete in those early centuries; so that the [Anglican] principle [of Antiquity] is self-destructive.' 'When a man takes up this *Via Media*, he is a mere *doctrinaire*'; he is like those, 'who, in some matter of business, start up to suggest their own little crotchet, and are ever measuring mountains with a pocket ruler, or improving the planetary courses.' 'The *Via Media* has slept in libraries; it is a substitute of infancy for manhood.'

It is plain, then, that at the end of 1835 or beginning of 1836, I had the whole state of the question before me, on which, to my mind, the decision between the Churches depended. It is observ-able that the question of the position of the Pope, whether as the centre of unity, or as the source of jurisdiction, did not come into my thoughts at all; nor did it, I think I may say, to the end. I doubt whether I ever distinctly held any of his powers to be *de jure divino*, while I was in the Anglican Church – not that I saw any difficulty in the doctrine; not that, in connection with the history of St Leo, of which I shall speak by and by, the idea of his infallibility did not cross my mind, for it did – but after all, in my view the controversy did not turn upon it; it turned upon the Faith and the Church. This was my issue of the controversy from the beginning to the end. There was a contrariety of claims between the Roman and Anglican religions, and the history of my conversion is simply the process of working it out to a solution. In 1838 I illustrated it by the contrast presented to us between the Madonna and Child, and a Calvary. I said that the peculiarity of the Anglican theology was this – that it 'supposed the Truth to be entirely objective and detached, not' (as in the theology of Rome) 'lying hid in the bosom of the Church as if one with her, clinging to and (as it were) lost in her embrace, but as being sole and unapproachable, as on the Cross or at the Resurrection, with the Church close by, but in the background.'

As I viewed the controversy in 1836 and 1838, so I viewed it in 1840 and 1841. In the British Critic of January 1840, after gradually investigating how the matter lies between the Churches by means of a dialogue, I end thus: 'It would seem, that, in the above discussion, each disputant has a strong point: our strong point is the argument from Primitiveness, that of Romanists from Universality. It is a fact, however it is to be accounted for, that Rome has added to the Creed; and it is a fact, however we justify ourselves, that we are estranged from the great body of Christians over the world. And each of these two facts is at first sight a grave difficulty in the respective systems to which they belong.' Again, 'While Rome, though not deferring to the Fathers, recognizes them, and England, not deferring to the large body of the Church, recognizes it, both Rome and England have a point to clear up.'

And still more strongly, in July 1841:

If the Note of schism, on the one hand, lies against England, an antagonist disgrace lies upon Rome, the Note of idolatry. Let us not be mistaken here; we are neither accusing Rome of idolatry, nor ourselves of schism; we think neither charge tenable; but still the Roman Church practises what is so like idolatry, and the English Church makes much of what is so very like schism, that without deciding what is the duty of a Roman Catholic towards the Church of England in her present state, we do seriously think that members of the English Church have a providential direction given them, how to comport themselves towards the Church of Rome, while she is what she is.

One remark more about Antiquity and the *Via Media*. As time went on, without doubting the strength of the Anglican argument from Antiquity, I felt also that it was not merely our special plea, but our only one. Also I felt that the *Via Media*, which was to represent it, was to be a sort of remodelled and adapted Antiquity. This I advanced both in Home Thoughts Abroad, and in the Article of the British Critic which I have analyzed above. But this circumstance, that after all we must use private judgment upon Antiquity, created a sort of distrust of my theory altogether, which in the conclusion of my Volume on the Prophetical Office (1836–7) I express thus: 'Now that our discussions draw to a close, the thought, with which we entered on the subject, is apt to recur, when the excitement of the inquiry has subsided, and weariness has succeeded, that what has been said is but a dream, the wanton exercise, rather than the practical conclusions of the intellect.' And I conclude the paragraph by anticipating a line of thought into which I was, in the event, almost obliged to take refuge: 'After all,' I say, 'the Church is ever invisible in its day, and faith only apprehends it.' What was this, but to give up the Notes of a visible Church altogether, whether the Catholic Note or the Apostolic?

The Long Vacation of 1839 began early. There had been a great many visitors to Oxford from Easter to Commemoration; and Dr Pusey and myself had attracted attention, more, I think, than in any former year. I had put away from me the controversy with Rome for more than two years. In my Parochial Sermons the subject had at no time been introduced: there had been nothing for two years, either in my Tracts or in the British Critic, of a polemical character. I was returning, for the Vacation, to the course of reading which I had many years before chosen as especially my own. I have no reason to suppose that the thoughts of Rome came across my mind at all. About the middle of June I began to study and master the history of the Monophysites. I was absorbed in the doctrinal question. This was from about June 13th to August 30th. It was during this course of reading that for the first time a doubt came upon me of the tenableness of Anglicanism. I recollect on July 30th mentioning to a friend, whom I had accidentally met, how remarkable the history was; but by the end of August I was seriously alarmed.

I have described in a former work, how the history affected me. My stronghold was Antiquity; now here, in the middle of the fifth century, I found, as it seemed to me, Christendom of the sixteenth and the nineteenth centuries reflected. I saw my face in that mirror, and I was a Monophysite. The Church of the *Via Media* was in the position of the Oriental communion, Rome was, where she now is; and the Protestants were the Eutychians. Of all passages of history, since history has been, who would have thought of going to the sayings and doings of old Eutyches, that *delirus senex*, as (I think) Petavius calls him, and to the enormities of the unprincipled Dioscorus, in order to be converted to Rome!

Now let it be simply understood that I am not writing controversially, but with the one object of relating things as they happened to me in the course of my conversion. With this view I will quote a passage from the account, which I gave in 1850, of my reasonings and feelings in 1839:

It was difficult to make out how the Eutychians or Monophysites were heretics, unless Protestants and Anglicans were heretics also; difficult to find arguments against the Tridentine Fathers, which did not tell against the Fathers of Chalcedon; difficult to condemn the Popes of the sixteenth century, without condemning the Popes of the fifth. The drama of religion, and the combat of truth and error, were ever one and the same. The principles and proceedings of the Church now, were those of the Church then; the principles and proceedings of heretics then, were those of Protestants now. I found it so – almost fearfully; there was an awful similitude, more awful, because so silent and unimpassioned, between the dead records of the past and the feverish chronicle of the present. The shadow of the fifth century was on the sixteenth. It was like a spirit rising from the troubled waters of the old world, with the shape and lineaments of the new. The Church then, as now, might be called peremptory and stern, resolute, overbearing, and relentless; and heretics were shifting, change-able, reserved, and deceitful, ever courting civil power, and never agreeing together, except by its aid; and the civil power was ever aiming at comprehensions, trying to put the invisible out of view, and substituting expediency for faith. What was the use of continuing the controversy, or defending my position, if, after all, I was forging arguments for Arius or Eutyches, and turning devil's advocate against the much-enduring Athanasius and the majestic Leo ? Be my soul with the Saints! and shall I lift up my hand against them ? Sooner may my right hand forget her cunning, and wither outright, as his who once stretched it out against a prophet of God! anathema to a whole tribe of Cranmers, Ridleys, Latimers, and Jewels! perish the names of Bramhall, Ussher, Taylor, Stillingfleet, and Barrow from the face of the earth, ere I should do aught but fall at their feet in love and in worship, whose image was continually before my eyes, and whose musical words were ever in my ears and on my tongue!

Hardly had I brought my course of reading to a close, when the Dublin Review of that same August was put into my hands, by friends who were more favourable to the cause of Rome than I was myself. There was an Article in it on the 'Anglican Claim' by Dr Wiseman. This was about the middle of September. It was on the Donatists, with an application to Anglicanism. I read it, and did not see much in it. The Donatist controversy was known to me for some years, as has appeared already. The case was not parallel to that of the Anglican Church. St Augustine in Africa wrote against the Donatists in Africa. They were a furious party who made a schism within the African Church, and not beyond its limits. It was a case of Altar against Altar, of two occupants of the same See, as that between the Non-jurors in England and the Established Church; not the case of one Church against another, as Rome against the Oriental Monophysites. But my friend, an anxiously religious man, now, as then, very dear to me, a Protestant still, pointed out the palmary words of St Augustine, which were contained in one of the extracts made in the Review, and which had escaped my observation. 'Securus judicat orbis terrarum.' He repeated these words again and again, and, when he was gone, they kept ringing in my ears. 'Securus judicat orbis terrarum'; they were words which went beyond the occasion of the Donatists: they applied to that of the Monophysites. They gave a cogency to the Article, which had escaped me at first. They decided ecclesiastical questions on a simpler rule than that of Antiquity; nay, St Augustine was one of the prime oracles of Antiquity; here then Antiquity was deciding against itself. What a light was hereby thrown upon every controversy in the Church! not that, for the moment, the multitude may not falter in their judgment – not that, in the Arian hurricane, Sees more than can be numbered did not bend before its fury, and fall off from St Athanasius – not that the crowd of Oriental Bishops did not need to be sustained during the contest by the voice and the eye of St Leo; but that the deliberate judgment, in which the whole Church at length rests and acquiesces, is an infallible prescription and a final sentence against such portions of it as protest and secede. Who can account for the impressions which are made on him? For a mere sentence, the words of St Augustine, struck me with a power which I never had felt from any words before. To take a familiar instance, they were like the 'Turn again Whittington' of the chime; or, to take a more serious one, they were like the 'Tolle, lege – Tolle, lege,' of the child, which converted St Augustine himself. 'Securus judicat orbis terrarum!' By those great words of the ancient Father, interpreting and summing up the long and varied course of ecclesiastical history, the theory of the *Via Media* was absolutely pulverized.

I became excited at the view thus opened upon me. I was just starting on a round of visits; and I mentioned my state of mind to two most intimate friends: I think to no others. After a while, I got calm, and at length the vivid impression upon my imagination faded away. What I thought about it on reflection, I will attempt to describe presently. I had to determine its logical value, and its bearing upon my duty. Meanwhile, so far as this was certain – I had seen the shadow of a hand upon the wall. It was clear that I had a good deal to learn on the question of the Churches, and that perhaps some new light was coming upon me. He who has seen a ghost, cannot be as if he had never seen it. The heavens had opened and closed again. The thought for the moment had been, 'The Church of Rome will be found right after all'; and then it had vanished. My old convictions remained as before.

At this time, I wrote my Sermon on Divine Calls, which I published in my volume of Plain Sermons. It ends thus:

> O that we could take that simple view of things, as to feel that the one thing which lies before us is to please God! What gain is it to please the world, to please the great, nay even to please those whom we love, compared with this? What gain is it to be applauded, admired, courted, followed – compared with this one aim, of 'not being disobedient to a heavenly vision'? What can this world offer comparable with that insight into spiritual things, that keen faith, that heavenly peace, that high sanctity, that everlasting righteousness, that hope of glory, which they have, who in sincerity love and follow our Lord Jesus Christ? Let us beg and pray Him day by day to reveal Himself to our souls more fully, to quicken our senses, to give us sight and hearing, taste and touch of the world to come; so to work within us, that we may sincerely say, 'Thou shalt guide me with Thy counsel, and after that receive me with glory. Whom have I in heaven but Thee? and there is none upon earth that I desire in comparison of Thee. My flesh and my heart faileth, but God is the strength of my heart, and my portion for ever.'

Now to trace the succession of thoughts, and the conclusions, and the consequent innovations on my previous belief, and the general conduct, to which I was led, upon this sudden visitation. And first, I will say, whatever comes of saying it, for I leave inferences to others, that for years I must have had something of an habitual notion, though it was latent, and had never led me to distrust my own convictions, that my mind had not found its ultimate rest, and that in some sense or other I was on a journey. During the same passage across the Mediterranean in which I wrote 'Lead kindly light', I also wrote the verses, which are found in the Lyra under the head of 'Providences', beginning, 'When I look back'. This was in 1833; and, since I have begun this narrative, I have found a memorandum under the date of September 7, 1829, in which I speak of myself, as 'now in my rooms in Oriel College, slowly advancing &c. and led on by God's hand blindly, not knowing whither He is taking me'. But, whatever this presentiment be worth, it was no protection against the dismay and disgust, which I felt, in consequence of the dreadful misgiving, of which I have been relating the history. The one question was, what was I to do? I had to make up my mind for myself, and others could not help me. I determined to be guided, not by my imagination, but by my reason. And this I said over and over again in the years which followed, both in conversation and in private letters. Had it not been for this severe resolve, I should have been a Catholic sooner than I was. Moreover, I felt on consideration a positive doubt, on the other hand, whether the suggestion did not come from below. Then I said to myself, Time alone can solve that question. It was my business to go on as usual, to obey those convictions to which I had so long surrendered myself, which still had possession of me, and on which my new thoughts had no direct bearing. That new conception of things should only so far influence me, as it had a logical claim to do so. If it came from above, it would come again – so I trusted – and with more definite outlines and greater cogency and consistency of proof. I thought of Samuel, before 'he knew the word of the Lord'; and therefore I went, and lay down to sleep again. This was my broad view of the matter, and my *prima facie* conclusion.

However, my new historical fact had already to a certain point a logical force. Down had come the *Via Media* as a definite theory or scheme, under the blows of St Leo. My 'Prophetical Office' had come to pieces; not indeed as an argument against 'Roman errors', nor as against Protestantism, but as in behalf of England. I had no longer a distinctive plea for Anglicanism, unless I would be a Monophysite. I had, most painfully, to fall back upon my three original points of belief, which I have spoken so much of in a former passage – the principle of dogma, the sacramental system, and anti-Romanism. Of these three, the first two were better secured in Rome than in the Anglican Church. The Apostolical Succession, the two prominent sacraments, and the primitive Creeds, belonged, indeed, to the latter, but there had been and was far less strictness on matters of dogma and ritual in the Anglican system than in the Roman: in consequence, my main argument for the Anglican claims lay in the positive and special charges, which I could bring against Rome. I had no positive Anglican theory. I was very nearly a pure Protestant. Lutherans had a sort of theology, so had Calvinists; I had none.

However, this pure Protestantism, to which I was gradually left, was really a practical principle. It was a strong, though it was only a negative ground, and it still had great hold on me. As a boy of fifteen, I had so fully imbibed it, that I had actually erased in my *Gradus ad Parnassum*, such titles, under the word 'Papa', as 'Christi Vicarius', 'sacer interpres', and 'sceptra gerens', and substituted epithets so vile that I cannot bring myself to write them down here. The effect of this early persuasion remained as, what I have already called it, a 'stain upon my imagination'. As regards my reason, I began in 1833 to form theories on the subject, which tended to obliterate it. In the first part of Home Thoughts Abroad, written in that year, after speaking of Rome as 'undeniably the most exalted Church in the whole world', and manifesting, 'in all the truth and beauty of the Spirit, that side of high mental excellence, which Pagan Rome attempted but could not realize – high-mindedness, majesty, and the calm conscious-ness of power', – I proceed to say, 'Alas! ... the old spirit has revived, and the monster of Daniel's vision, untamed by its former judgments, has seized upon Christianity as the new instrument of its impieties, and awaits a second and final woe from God's hand. Surely the doctrine of the *Genius Loci* is not without foundation, and explains to us how the blessing or the curse attaches to cities and countries, not to generations. Michael is represented [in the book of Daniel] as opposed to the Prince of the kingdom of Persia. Old Rome is still alive. The Sorceress upon the Seven Hills, in the book of Revelations, is not the Church of Rome, but Rome itself, the bad spirit, which, in its former shape, was the animating spirit of the Fourth Monarchy.' Then I refer to St Malachi's Prophecy which 'makes a like distinction between the City and the Church of Rome. "In the last persecution," it says, "of the Holy Roman Church, Peter of Rome shall be on the throne, who shall feed his flock in many tribulations. When these are past, the City upon the Seven Hills shall be destroyed, and the awful Judge shall judge the people.".' Then I append my moral.

> I deny that the distinction is unmeaning; Is it nothing to be able to look on our Mother, to whom we owe the blessing of Christianity, with affection instead of hatred ? with pity indeed, aye, and fear, but not with horror ? Is it nothing to rescue her from the hard names, which interpreters of prophecy have put upon her, as an idolatress and an enemy of God, when she is deceived rather than a deceiver ? Nothing to be able to account her priests as ordained of God, and anointed for their spiritual functions by the Holy Spirit, instead of considering her communion the bond of Satan ?

This was my first advance in rescuing, on an intelligible, intellectual basis, the Roman Church from the designation of Antichrist; it was not the Church, but the old dethroned Pagan monster, still living in the ruined city, that was Antichrist.

In a Tract in 1838, I profess to give the opinions of the Fathers on the subject, and the conclusions to which I come, are still less violent against the Roman Church, though on the same basis as before. I say that the local Christian Church of Rome has been the means of shielding the pagan city from the fulness of those judgments, which are due to it; and that, in consequence of this, though Babylon has been utterly swept from the earth, Rome remains to this day. The reason seemed to be simply this, that, when the barbarians came down, God had a people in that city. Babylon was a mere prison of the Church; Rome had received her as a guest. 'That vengeance has never fallen: it is still suspended; nor can reasons be given why Rome has not fallen under the rule of God's general dealings with His rebellious creatures, except that a Christian Church is still in that city, sanctifying it, interceding for it, saving it.' I add in a note, 'No opinion, one way or the other, is here expressed as to the question, how far, as the local Church has saved Rome, so Rome has corrupted the local Church; or whether the local Church in consequence, or again whether other Churches elsewhere, may or may not be types of Antichrist.' I quote all this in order to show how Bishop Newton was still upon my mind even in 1838; and how I was feeling after some other interpretation of prophecy instead of his, and not without a good deal of hesitation.

However, I have found notes written in March, 1839, which anticipate my Article in the British Critic of October, 1840, in which I contended that the Churches of Rome and England are both one, and also the one true Church, for the very reason that they had both been stigmatized by the name of Antichrist, proving my point from the text, 'If they have called the Master of the House Beelzebub, how much more them of His household', and quoting largely from Puritans and Independents to show that, in their mouths, the Anglican Church is Antichrist and Antichristian as well as the Roman. I urged in that article that the calumny of being Antichrist is almost 'one of the notes of the true Church'; and that 'there is no medium between a Vice-Christ and Anti-Christ'; for 'it is not the *acts* that make the difference between them, but the *authority* for those acts.' This of course was a new mode of viewing the question; but we cannot unmake ourselves or change our habits in a moment. It is quite clear, that, if I dared not commit myself in 1838, to the belief that the Church of Rome was not a type of Antichrist, I could not have thrown off − the unreasoning prejudice and suspicion, which I cherished about her, for some time after, at least by fits and starts, in spite of this conviction of my reason. I cannot prove this, but I believe it to have been the case from what I recollect of myself. Nor was there any thing in the history of St Leo and the Monophysites to undo the firm belief I had in the existence of what I called the practical abuses and excesses of Rome.

To the inconsistencies then, to the ambition and intrigue, to the sophistries of Rome (as I considered them to be) I now had recourse in my opposition to her, both public and personal. I did so by way of a relief. I had a great and growing dislike, after the summer of 1839, to speak against the Roman Church herself or her formal doctrines. I was very averse to speaking against doctrines, which might possibly turn out to be true, though at the time I had no reason for thinking they were, or against the Church, which had preserved them. I began to have misgivings, that, strong as my own feelings had been against her, yet in some things which I had said, I had taken the statements of Anglican divines for granted without weighing them for myself. I said to a friend in 1840, in a letter, which I shall use presently, 'I am troubled by doubts whether as it is, I have not, in what I have published, spoken too strongly against Rome, though I think I did it in a kind of faith, being determined to put myself into the English system, and say all that our divines said, whether I had fully weighed it or not.' I was sore about the great Anglican divines, as if they had taken me in, and made me say strong things, which facts did not justify. Yet I *did* still hold in substance all that I had said against the Church of Rome in my Prophetical Office. I felt the force of the usual Protestant objections against her; I believed that we had the Apostolical succession in the Anglican Church, and the grace of the sacraments; I was not sure that the difficulty of its isolation might not be overcome, though I was far from sure that it could. I did not see any clear proof that it had committed itself to any heresy, or had taken part against the truth; and I was not sure that it would not revive into full Apostolic purity and strength, and grow into union with Rome herself (Rome explaining her doctrines and guarding against their abuse), that is, if we were but patient and hopeful. I began to wish for union between the Anglican Church and Rome, if, and when, it was possible; and I did what I could to gain weekly prayers for that object. The ground which I felt to be good against her was the moral ground: I felt I could not be wrong in striking at her political and social line of action. The alliance of a dogmatic religion with liberals, high or low, seemed to me a providential direction against moving towards Rome, and a better 'Preservative against Popery', than the three volumes in folio, in which, I think, that prophylactic is to be found. However, on occasions which demanded it, I felt it a duty to give out plainly all that I thought, though I did not like to do so. One such instance occurred, when I had to publish a Letter about Tract 90. In that Letter, I said, 'instead of setting before the soul the Holy Trinity, and heaven and hell, the Church of Rome does seem to me, as a popular system, to preach the Blessed Virgin and the Saints, and purgatory.' On this occasion I recollect expressing to a friend the distress it gave me thus to speak; but, I said, 'How can I help saying it, if I think it? and I *do* think it; my Bishop calls on me to say out what I think; and that is the long and the short of it.' But I recollected Hurrell Froude's words to me, almost his dying words, 'I must enter another protest against your cursing and swearing. What good can it do? and I call it uncharitable to an excess. How mistaken we may ourselves be on many points that are only gradually opening on us!'.

Instead then of speaking of errors in doctrine, I was driven by my state of mind, to insist upon the political conduct, the controversial bearing, and the social methods and manifestations of Rome. And here I found a matter ready to my hand, which affected me the more sensibly for the reason that it lay at our very doors. I can hardly describe too strongly my feeling upon it. I had an unspeakable aversion to the policy and acts of Mr O'Connell, because as I thought, he associated himself with men of all religions and no religion against the Anglican Church, and advanced Catholicism by violence and intrigue. When then I found him taken up by the English Catholics, and, as I supposed, at Rome, I considered I had a fulfilment before my eyes how the Court of Rome played fast and loose, and justified the serious charges which I had seen put down in books against it. Here we saw what Rome was in action, whatever she might be when quiescent. Her conduct was simply secular and political.

This feeling led me into the excess of being very rude to that zealous and most charitable man, Mr Spencer, when he came to Oxford in January, 1840, to get Anglicans to set about praying for Unity. I myself, at that time, or soon after, drew up such prayers; their desirableness was one of the first thoughts which came upon me after my shock; but I was too much annoyed with the political action of the Catholic body in these islands to wish to have anything to do with them personally. So glad in my heart was I to see him, when he came to my rooms with Mr Palmer of Magdalen that I could have laughed for joy; I think I did laugh; but I was very rude to him, I would not meet him at dinner, and that (though I did not say so) because I considered him 'in loco apostatæ' from the Anglican Church, and I hereby beg his pardon for it. I wrote afterwards with a view to apologize, but I dare say he must have thought that I made the matter worse, for these were my words to him:

> The news that you are praying for us is most touching, and raises a variety of indescribable emotions. . . . May their prayers return abundantly into their own bosoms. . . . Why then do I not meet you in a manner comfortable with these first feelings? For this single reason, if I may say it, that your acts are contrary to your words. You invite us to a union of hearts, at the same time that you are doing all you can, not to restore, not to reform, not to re-unite, but to destroy our Church. You go further than your principles require. You are leagued with our enemies. 'The voice is Jacob's voice, but the hands are the hands of Esau.' This is what especially distresses us; this is

what we cannot understand, how Christians, like yourselves, with the clear view you have that a warfare is ever waging in the world between good and evil, should, in the present state of England, ally yourselves with the side of evil against the side of good. . . . Of parties now in the country, you cannot but allow, that next to yourselves we are nearest to revealed truth. We maintain great and holy principles; we profess Catholic doctrines. . . . So near are we as a body to yourselves in modes of thinking, as even to have been taunted with the nicknames which belong to you; and, on the other hand, if there are professed infidels, scoffers, sceptics, unprincipled men, rebels, they are found among our opponents. And yet you take part with them against us . . . You consent to act hand in hand [with these and others] for our overthrow. Alas! all this it is that impresses us irresistibly with the notion that you are a political, not a religious party; that, in order to gain an end on which you set your hearts – an open stage for yourselves in England – you ally yourselves with those who hold nothing against those who hold something. This is what distresses my own mind so greatly, to speak of myself, that, with limitations which need not now be mentioned, I cannot meet familiarly any leading persons of the Roman Communion, and least of all when they come on a religious errand. Break off, I would say, with Mr O'Connell in Ireland and the liberal party in England, or come not to us with overtures for mutual prayer and religious sympathy.

And here came in another feeling, of a personal nature, which had little to do with the argument against Rome, except that, in my prejudice, I viewed what happened to myself in the light of my own ideas of the usual conduct of her advocates and instruments. I was very stern in the case of any interference in our Oxford matters on the part of charitable Catholics, and of any attempt to do me good personally. There was nothing, indeed, at the time more likely to throw me back. 'Why do you meddle? why cannot you let me alone? You can do me no good; you know nothing on earth about me; you may actually do me harm; I am in better hands than yours. I know my own sincerity of purpose; and I am determined upon taking my time.' Since I have been a Catholic, people have sometimes accused me of backwardness in making converts; and Protestants have argued from it that I have no great eagerness to do so. It would be against my nature to act otherwise than I do; but besides, it would be to forget the lessons which I gained in the experience of my own history in the past.

This is the account which I have to give of some savage and ungrateful words in the British Critic of 1840 against the controversialists of Rome:

> By their fruits ye shall know them. . . . We see it attempting to gain converts among us by unreal representations of its doctrines, plausible statements, bold assertions, appeals to the weaknesses of human nature, to our fancies, our eccentricities, our fears, our frivolities, our false philosophies. We see its agents, smiling and nodding and ducking to attract attention, as gipsies make up to truant boys, holding out tales for the nursery, and pretty pictures, and gilt gingerbread, and physic concealed in jam, and sugar-plums for good children. Who can but feel shame when the religion of Ximenes, Borromeo, and Pascal, is so overlaid? Who can but feel sorrow, when its devout and earnest defenders so mistake its genius and its capabilities? We Englishmen like manliness, openness, consistency, truth. Rome will never gain on us, till she learns these virtues, and uses them; and then she *may* gain us, but it will be by ceasing to be what we now mean by Rome, by having a right, not to 'have dominion over our faith', but to gain and possess our affections in the bonds of the gospel. Till she ceases to be what she practically is, a union is impossible between her and England; but, if she does reform (and who can presume to say that so large a part of Christendom never can?) then it will be our Church's duty at once to join in communion with the continental Churches, whatever politicians at home may say to it, and whatever steps the civil power may take in consequence. And though we may not live to see that day, at least we are bound to pray for it; we are bound to pray for our brethren that they and we may be led together into the pure light of the gospel, and be one as we once were one. It was most touching news to be told, as we were lately, that Christians on the Continent were praying together for the spiritual well-being of England. May they gain light, while they aim at unity, and grow in faith while they manifest their love! We too have our duties to them; not of reviling, not of slandering, not of hating, though political interests require it; but the duty of loving brethren still more abundantly in spirit, whose faces, for our sins and their sins, we are not allowed to see in the flesh.

No one ought to indulge in insinuations; it certainly diminishes my right to complain of slanders uttered against myself, when, as in this passage, I had already spoken in disparagement of the controversialists of that religious body, to which I myself now belong.

I have thus put together, as well as I can, what has to be said about my general state of mind from the autumn of 1839 to the summer of 1841; and, having done so, I go on to narrate how my new misgivings affected my conduct, and my relations towards the Anglican Church.

When I got back to Oxford in October, 1839, after the visits which I had been paying, it so happened, there had been, in my absence, occurrences of an awkward character, bringing me into collision both with my Bishop and also with the University authorities; and this drew my attention at once to the state of what would be considered the Movement party there, and made me very anxious for the future. In the spring of the year, as has been seen in the Article analyzed above, I had spoken of the excesses which were to be found among persons commonly included in it; at that time I thought little of such an evil, but the new views, which had come on me during the Long Vacation, on the one hand made me comprehend it, and on the other took away my power of effectually meeting it. A firm and powerful control was necessary to keep men straight; I never had a strong wrist, but at the very time, when it was most needed, the reins had broken in my hands. With an anxious presentiment on my mind of the upshot of the whole inquiry, which it was almost impossible for me to conceal from men who saw me day by day, who heard my familiar conversation, who came perhaps for the express purpose of pumping me, and having a categorical *yes* or *no* to their questions – how could I expect to say anything about my actual, positive, present belief, which would be sustaining or consoling to such persons as were haunted already by doubts of their own? Nay, how could I, with satisfaction to myself, analyze my own mind, and say what I held and what I did not hold? or how could I say with what limitations, shades of difference, or degrees of belief, I still held that body of Anglican opinions which I had openly professed and taught? how could I deny or assert this point or that, without injustice to the new light, in which the whole evidence for those old opinions presented itself to my mind?

However, I had to do what I could, and what was best, under the circumstances; I found a general talk on the subject of the Article in the Dublin Review; and, if it had affected me, it was not wonderful, that it affected others also. As to myself, I felt no kind of certainty that the argument in it was conclusive. Taking it at the worst granting that the Anglican Church had not the Note of Catholicity; yet there were many Notes of the Church. Some belonged to one age or place, some to another. Bellarmine had reckoned Temporal Prosperity among the Notes of the Church; but the Roman Church had not any great popularity, wealth, glory, power, or prospects, in the nineteenth century. It was not at all certain as yet, even that we had not the Note of Catholicity; but, if not this, we had others. My first business then, was to examine this question carefully, and see, whether a great deal could not be said after all for the Anglican Church, in spite of its acknowledged short-comings. This I did in an Article 'on the Catholicity of the English Church', which appeared in the British Critic of January, 1840. As to my personal distress on the point, I think it had gone by February 21st in that year, for I wrote then to Mr Bowden about the important Article in the Dublin, thus: 'It made a great impression here [Oxford]; and, I say what of course I would only say to such as yourself, it made me for a while very uncomfortable in my own mind. The great speciousness of his argument is one of the things which have made me despond so much,' that is, as anticipating its effect upon others.

But, secondly, the great stumbling-block lay in the 39 Articles. It was urged that here was a positive Note *against* Anglicanism – Anglicanism claimed to hold that the Church of England was nothing else than a continuation in this country (as the Church of Rome might be in France or Spain) of that one Church of which in old times Athanasius and Augustine were members. But, if so, the doctrine must be the same; the doctrine of the Old Church must live and speak in Anglican formularies, in the 39 Articles. Did it ? Yes, it did; that is what I maintained; it did in substance, in a true sense. Man had done his worst to disfigure, to mutilate, the old Catholic Truth, but there it was, in spite of them, in the Articles still. It was there – but this must be shown. It was a matter of life and death to us to show it. And I believed that it could be shown; I considered that those grounds of justification, which I gave above, when I was speaking of Tract 90, were sufficient for the purpose; and therefore I set about showing it at once. This was in March,

1840, when I went up to Littlemore. And, as it was a matter of life and death with us, all risks must be run to show it. When the attempt was actually made, I had got reconciled to the prospect of it, and had no apprehensions as to the experiment; but in 1840, while my purpose was honest, and my grounds of reason satisfactory, I did nevertheless recognize that I was engaged in an *experimentum crucis*. I have no doubt that then I acknowledged to myself that it would be a trial of the Anglican Church, which it had never undergone before − not that the Catholic sense of the Articles had not been held or at least suffered by their framers and promulgators, not that it was not implied in the teaching of Andrewes or Beveridge, but that it had never been publicly recognized, while the interpretation of the day was Protestant and exclusive. I observe also, that, though my Tract was an experiment, it was, as I said at the time, 'no *feeler*', the event showed this; for, when my principle was not granted, I did not draw back, but gave up. I would not hold office in a Church which would not allow my sense of the Articles. My tone was, 'This is necessary for us, and have it we must and will, and, if it tends to bring men to look less bitterly on the Church of Rome, so much the better.'

This then was the second work to which I set myself; though when I got to Littlemore, other things interfered to prevent my accomplishing it at the moment. I had in mind to remove all such obstacles as lay in the way of holding the Apostolic and Catholic character of the Anglican teaching; to assert the right of all who chose, to say in the face of day, 'Our Church teaches the Primitive Ancient faith.' I did not conceal this: in Tract 90, it is put forward as the first principle of all, 'It is a duty which we owe both to the Catholic Church, and to our own, to take our reformed confessions in the most Catholic sense they will admit: we have no duties towards their framers.' And still more pointedly in my Letter, explanatory of the Tract, addressed to Dr Jelf, I say:

> The only peculiarity of the view I advocate, if I must so call it, is this − that whereas it is usual at this day to make the *particular belief of their writers* their true interpretation; I would make the *belief of the Catholic Church such*. That is, as it is often said that infants are regenerated in Baptism, not on the faith of their parents, but of the Church, so in like manner I would say that the Articles are received, not in the sense of their

framers, but (as far as the wording will admit or any ambiguity requires it) in the one Catholic sense.

A third measure which I distinctly contemplated, was the resignation of St Mary's, whatever became of the question of the 39 Articles; and as a first step I meditated a retirement to Littlemore. Littlemore was an integral part of St Mary's Parish, and between two and three miles distant from Oxford. I had built a Church there several years before; and I went there to pass the Lent of 1840, and gave myself up to teaching in the Parish school, and practising the choir. At the same time, I had in view a monastic house there. I bought ten acres of ground and began planting; but this great design was never carried out. I mention it, because it shows how little I had really the idea at that time of ever leaving the Anglican Church. That I also contemplated even the further step of giving up St Mary's itself as early as 1839, appears from a letter which I wrote in October, 1840, to Mr Keble, the friend whom it was most natural for me to consult on such a point. It ran as follows:

For a year past a feeling has been growing on me that I ought to give up St Mary's, but I am no fit judge in the matter. I cannot ascertain accurately my own impressions and convictions, which are the basis of the difficulty, and though you cannot of course do this for me, yet you may help me generally, and perhaps supersede the necessity of my going to them at all.

First, it is certain that I do not know my Oxford parishioners; I am not conscious of influencing them, and certainly I have no insight into their spiritual state. I have no personal, no pastoral acquaintance with them. To very few I have any opportunity of saying a religious word. Whatever influence I exert on them is precisely that which I may be exerting on persons out of my parish. In my excuse I am accustomed to say to myself that I am not adapted to get on with them, while others are. On the other hand, I am conscious that by means of my position at St Mary's I do exert a considerable influence on the University, whether on Undergraduates or Graduates. It seems, then, on the whole that I am using St Mary's, to the neglect of its direct duties, for objects not belonging to it; I am converting a parochial charge into a sort of University office.

I think I may say truly that I have begun scarcely any plan

but for the sake of my parish, but every one has turned, independently of me, into the direction of the University. I began Saints'-days Services, daily Services, and Lectures in Adam de Brome's Chapel, for my parishioners; but they have not come to them. In consequence I dropped the last mentioned, having, while it lasted, been naturally led to direct it to the instruction of those who did come, instead of those who did not. The Weekly Communion, I believe, I did begin for the sake of the University.

Added to this the authorities of the University, the appointed guardians of those who form great part of the attendants on my Sermons, have shown a dislike of my preaching. One dissuades men from coming – the late Vice-Chancellor threatens to take his own children away from the Church; and the present, having an opportunity last spring of preaching in my parish pulpit, gets up and preaches against doctrine with which I am in good measure identified. No plainer proof can be given of the feeling in these quarters, than the absurd myth, now a second time put forward, 'that Vice-Chancellors cannot be got to take the office on account of Puseyism'.

But further than this, I cannot disguise from myself that my preaching is not calculated to defend that system of religion which has been received for 300 years, and of which the Heads of Houses are the legitimate maintainers in this place. They exclude me, as far as may be, from the University Pulpit; and, though I never have preached strong doctrine in it, they do so rightly, so far as this, that they understand that my sermons are calculated to undermine things established. I cannot disguise from myself that they are. No one will deny that most of my sermons are on moral subjects, not doctrinal; still I am leading my hearers to the Primitive Church, if you will, but not to the Church of England. Now, ought one to be disgusting the minds of young men with the received religion, in the exercise of a sacred office, yet without a commission, and against the wish of their guides and governors?

But this is not all. I fear I must allow that, whether I will or no, I am disposing them towards Rome. First, because Rome is the only representative of the Primitive Church besides ourselves; in proportion then as they are loosened from the one, they will go to the other. Next, because many doctrines which I have held, have far greater, or their only scope, in the Roman system. And, moreover, if, as is not unlikely, we have in process of time heretical Bishops or teachers among us, an evil which *ipso facto* infects the whole community to which they belong, and if, again (what there are at this moment symptoms of), there be a movement in the English Roman Catholics to break the alliance of O'Connell and of Exeter Hall, strong temptations will be placed in the way of individuals, already imbued with a tone of thought congenial to Rome, to join her Communion.

People tell me, on the other hand, that I am, whether by sermons or otherwise, exerting at St Mary's a beneficial influence on our prospective clergy; but what if I take to myself the credit of seeing further than they, and of having in the course of the last year discovered that what they approve so much is very likely to end in Romanism?

The *arguments* which I have published against Romanism seem to myself as cogent as ever, but men go by their sympathies, not by argument; and if I feel the force of this influence myself, who bow to the arguments, why may not others still more who never have in the same degree admitted the arguments?

Nor can I counteract the danger by preaching or writing against Rome. I seem to myself almost to have shot my last arrow in the Article on English Catholicity. It must be added, that the very circumstance that I have committed myself against Rome has the effect of setting to sleep people suspicious about me, which is painful now that I begin to have suspicions about myself. I mentioned my general difficulty to Rogers a year since, than whom I know no one of a more fine and accurate conscience, and it was his spontaneous idea that I should give up St Mary's, if my feelings continued. I mentioned it again to him lately, and he did not reverse his opinion, only expressed great reluctance to believe it must be so.

Mr Keble's judgment was in favour of my retaining my living; at least for the present; what weighed with me most was his saying, 'You must consider, whether your retiring either from the Pastoral Care only, or from writing and printing and editing in the cause, would not be a sort of scandalous thing, unless it were done very warily. It would be said, "You see he can go on no longer with the Church of England, except in mere Lay Communion"; or people might say you repented of the cause altogether. Till you see [your way to mitigate, if not remove this evil] I certainly should advise you to stay.' I answered as follows:

> Since you think I *may* go on, it seems to follow that, under the circumstances, I *ought* to do so. There are plenty of reasons for it, directly it is allowed to be lawful. The following considerations have much reconciled my feelings to your conclusion.
>
> 1. I do not think that we have yet made fair trial how much the English Church will bear. I know it is a hazardous experiment – like proving cannon. Yet we must not take it for granted, that the metal will burst in the operation. It has borne at various times, not to say at this time, a great infusion of Catholic truth without damage. As to the result, viz. whether this process will not approximate the whole English Church, as a body, to Rome, that is nothing to us. For what we know, it may be the providential means of uniting the whole Church in one, without fresh schismatizing or use of private judgment.

Here I observe, that, what was contemplated was the bursting of the *Catholicity* of the Anglican Church, that is, my *subjective idea* of that Church. Its bursting would not hurt her with the world, but would be a discovery that she was purely and essentially Protestant, and would be really the 'hoisting of the engineer with his own petar.' And this was the result. I continue:

> 2. Say, that I move sympathies for Rome: in the same sense does Hooker, Taylor, Bull, &c. Their *arguments* may be against Rome, but the sympathies they raise must be towards Rome, *so far* as Rome maintains truths which our Church does not teach or enforce. Thus it is a question of *degree* between our divines and me. I may, if so be, go further; I may raise sympathies *more*; but I am but urging minds in the same direction as they do. I am doing just the very thing which all our doctors have ever been doing. In short, would not Hooker, if Vicar of St Mary's, be in my difficulty? – Here it may be objected, that Hooker could preach against Rome, and I could not; but I doubt whether he could have preached effectively against Transubstantiation better than I, though neither he nor I held that doctrine.
>
> 3. Rationalism is the great evil of the day. May not I consider

my post at St Mary's as a place of protest against it ? I am more certain that the Protestant [spirit], which I oppose, leads to infidelity, than that which I recommend, leads to Rome. Who knows what the state of the University may be, as regards Divinity Professors in a few years hence ? And how, a great battle may be coming on, of which Milman's book is a sort of earnest. The whole of *our* day may be a battle with this spirit. May we not leave to another age *its own* evil – to settle the question of Romanism ?

I may add that from this time I had a Curate at St Mary's, who gradually took more and more of my work.

Also, this same year, 1840, I made arrangements for giving up the British Critic, in the following July, which were carried into effect at that date.

Such was about my state of mind, on the publication of Tract 90 in February, 1841. I was indeed in prudence taking steps towards eventually withdrawing from St Mary's, and I was not confident about my permanent adhesion to the Anglican creed; but I was in no actual perplexity or trouble of mind. Nor did the immense commotion consequent upon the publication of the Tract unsettle me again; for I fancied I had weathered the storm, as far as the Bishops were concerned: the Tract had not been condemned: that was the great point, and I made much of it.

To illustrate my feelings during this trial, I will make extracts from my letters addressed severally to Mr Bowden and another friend, which have come into my possession.

1. March 15 – 'The Heads, I believe, have just done a violent act: they have said that my interpretation of the Articles is an *evasion*. Do not think that this will pain me. You see, no *doctrine* is censured, and my shoulders shall manage to bear the charge. If you knew all, or were here, you would see that I have asserted a great principle, and I *ought* to suffer for it – that the Articles are to be interpreted, not according to the meaning of the writers, but (as far as the wording will admit) according to the sense of the Catholic Church.'

2. March 25 – 'I do trust I shall make no false step, and hope my friends will pray for me to this effect. If, as you say, a destiny hangs over us, a single false step may ruin all. I am very well and comfortable; but we are not yet out of the wood.'

3. April 1 – 'The Bishop sent me word on Sunday to write a letter to him '*instanter*'. So I wrote it on Monday: on Tuesday it passed through the press: on Wednesday it was out: and today [Thursday] it is in London.

'I trust that things are smoothing now; and that we have made a *great step* is certain. It is not right to boast, till I am clear out of the wood, i.e. till I know how the letter is received in London. You know, I suppose, that I am to stop the Tracts; but you will see in the Letter, though I speak *quite* what I feel, yet I have managed to take out on *my* side my snubbing's worth. And this makes me anxious how it will be received in London.

'I have not had a misgiving for five minutes from the first: but I do not like to boast, lest some harm come.'

4. April 4 – 'Your letter of this morning was an exceedingly great gratification to me; and it is confirmed, I am thankful to say, by the opinion of others. The Bishop sent me a message that my Letter had his unqualified approbation; and since that, he has sent me a note to the same effect, only going more into detail. It is most pleasant too to my feelings, to have such a testimony to the substantial truth and importance of No. 90, as I have had from so many of my friends, from those who, from their cautious turn of mind, I was least sanguine about. I have not had one misgiving myself about it throughout; and I do trust that what has happened will be overruled to subserve the great cause we all have at heart.'

5. May 9 – 'The Bishops are very desirous of hushing the matter up: and I certainly have done my utmost to co-operate with them, on the understanding that the Tract is not to be withdrawn or condemned.'

And to my friend, Mr Bowden, under date of March 15,

The Heads, I believe, had done a violent act: they have said that my interpretation of the Articles is an *evasion*. Do not think that this will pain me. You see, no *doctrine* is censured, and my shoulders shall manage to bear the charge. If you knew all, or were here, you would see that I have asserted a great principle, and I *ought* to suffer for it – that the Articles are to be interpreted, not according to the meaning of the writers, but (as far as the wording will admit) according to the sense of the Catholic Church.

Upon this occasion of Tract 90 several Catholics wrote to me; I answered one of my correspondents:

> April 8 – You have no cause to be surprised at the discontinuance of the Tracts. We feel no misgivings about it whatever, as if the cause of what we hold to be Catholic truth would suffer thereby. My letter to my Bishop has, I trust, had the effect of bringing the preponderating *authority* of the Church on our side. No stopping of the Tracts can, humanly speaking, stop the spread of the opinions which they have inculcated.
>
> The Tracts are not *suppressed*. No doctrine or principle has been conceded by us, or condemned by authority. The Bishop has but said that a certain Tract is 'objectionable', no reason being stated. I have no intention whatever of yielding any one point which I hold on conviction; and that the authorities of the Church know full well.

In the summer of 1841, I found myself at Littlemore without any harass or anxiety on my mind. I had determined to put aside all controversy, and I set myself down to my translation of St Athanasius; but, between July and November, I received three blows which broke me.

1. I had got but a little way in my work, when my trouble returned on me. The ghost had come a second time. In the Arian History I found the very same phenomenon, in a far bolder shape, which I had found in the Monophysite. I had not observed it in 1832. Wonderful that this should come upon me! I had not sought it out; I was reading and writing in my own line of study, far from the controversies of the day, on what is called a 'metaphysical' subject; but I saw clearly, that in the history of Arianism, the pure Arians were the Protestants, the semi-Arians were the Anglicans, and that Rome now was what it was then. The truth lay, not with the *Via Media*, but with what was called 'the extreme party'. As I am not writing a work of controversy, I need not enlarge upon the argument; I have said something on the subject, in a Volume from which I have already quoted.

2. I was in the misery of this new unsettlement, when a second blow came upon me. The Bishops one after another began to charge against me. It was a formal, determinate movement. This was the real 'understanding'; that, on which I had acted on the first appearance of Tract 90, had come to nought. I think the words,

which had then been used to me, were that 'perhaps two or three of them might think it necessary to say something in their charges'; but by this time they had tided over the difficulty of the Tract, and there was no one to enforce the 'understanding'. They went on in this way, directing charges at me, for three whole years. I recognized it as a condemnation; it was the only one that was in their power. At first I intended to protest; but I gave up the thought in despair.

On 17 October, I wrote thus to a friend:

> I suppose it will be necessary in some shape or other to reassert Tract 90; else, it will seem, after these Bishops' Charges, as if it were silenced, which it has not been, nor do I intend it should be. I wish to keep quiet; but if Bishops speak, I will speak too. If the view were silenced, I could not remain in the Church, nor could many others; and therefore, since it is *not* silenced, I shall take care to show that it isn't.

A day or two after, October 22, a stranger wrote to me to say, that the Tracts for the Times had made a young friend of his a Catholic, and to ask, 'would I be so good as to convert him back'; I made answer:

> If conversions to Rome take place in consequence of the Tracts for the Times, I do not impute blame to them, but to those who, instead of acknowledging such Anglican principles of theology and ecclesiastical polity as they contain, set themselves to oppose them. Whatever be the influence of the Tracts, great or small, they may become just as powerful for Rome, if our Church refuses them, as they would be for our Church if she accepted them. If our rulers speak either against the Tracts, or not at all, if any number of them, not only do not favour, but even do not suffer the principles contained in them, it is plain that our members may easily be persuaded either to give up those principles, or to give up the Church. If this state of things goes on, I mournfully prophesy, not one or two, but many secessions to the Church of Rome.

Two years afterwards, looking back on what had passed, I said, 'There were no converts to Rome, till after the condemnation of No. 90.'

3. As if all this were not enough, there came the affair of the

Jerusalem Bishopric; and, with a brief mention of it, I shall conclude.

I think I am right in saying that it had been long a desire with the Prussian Court to introduce Episcopacy into the new Evangelical Religion, which was intended in that country to embrace both the Lutheran and Calvinistic bodies. I almost think I heard of the project, when I was at Rome in 1833, at the Hotel of the Prussian Minister, M. Bunsen, who was most hospitable and kind, as to other English visitors, so also to my friends and myself. The idea of Episcopacy, as the Prussian king understood it, was, I suppose, very different from that taught in the Tractarian School; but still, I suppose also, that the chief authors of that school would have gladly seen such a measure carried out in Prussia, had it been done without compromising those principles which were necessary to the being of a Church. About the time of the publication of Tract 90, M. Bunsen and the then Archbishop of Canterbury were taking steps for its execution, by appointing and consecrating a Bishop for Jerusalem. Jerusalem, it would seem, was considered a safe place for the experiment; it was too far from Prussia to awaken the susceptibilities of any party at home; if the project failed, it failed without harm to any one; and, if it succeeded, it gave Protestantism a *status* in the East, which, in association with the Monophysite or Jacobite and the Nestorian bodies, formed a political instrument for England, parallel to that which Russia had in the Greek Church, and France in the Latin.

Accordingly, in July 1841, full of the Anglican difficulty on the question of Catholicity, I thus spoke of the Jerusalem scheme in an Article in the British Critic:

> When our thoughts turn to the East, instead of recollecting that there are Christian Churches there, we leave it to the Russians to take care of the Greeks, and the French to take care of the Romans, and we content ourselves with erecting a Protestant Church at Jerusalem, or with helping the Jews to rebuild their Temple there, or with becoming the august protectors of Nestorians, Monophysites, and all the heretics we can hear of, or with forming a league with the Mussulman against Greeks and Romans together.

I do not pretend so long after the time to give a full or exact account of this measure in detail. I will but say that in the Act of Parliament, under date of October 5, 1841 (if the copy, from which I quote, contains the measure as it passed the Houses), provision is made for the consecration of 'British subjects, or the subjects or citizens of any foreign state, to be Bishops in any foreign country, whether such foreign subjects or citizens be or not subjects or citizens of the country in which they are to act, and . . . without requiring such of them as may be subjects or citizens of any foreign kingdom or state to take the oaths of allegiance and supremacy, and the oath of due obedience to the Archbishop for the time being' . . . also 'that such Bishop or Bishops, so consecrated, may exercise within such limits, as may from time to time be assigned for that purpose in such foreign countries by her Majesty, spiritual jurisdiction over the ministers of British congregations of the United Church of England and Ireland, and over *such other Protestant* Congregations, as may be desirous of placing themselves under his or their authority.'

Now here, at the very time that the Anglican Bishops were directing their censure upon me for avowing an approach to the Catholic Church not closer than I believed the Anglican formularies would allow, they were on the other hand fraternizing, by their act or by their sufferance, with Protestant bodies, and allowing them to put themselves under an Anglican Bishop, without any renunciation of their errors or regard to their due reception of baptism and confirmation; while there was great reason to suppose that the said Bishop was intended to make converts from the orthodox Greeks, and the schismatical Oriental bodies, by means of the influence of England. This was the third blow, which finally shattered my faith in the Anglican Church. That Church was not only forbidding any sympathy or concurrence with the Church of Rome, but it actually was courting an intercommunion with Protestant Prussia and the heresy of the Orientals. The Anglican Church might have the Apostolical succession, as had the Monophysites; but such acts as were in progress led me to the gravest suspicion, not that it would soon cease to be a Church, but that, since the 16th century, it had never been a Church all along.

On October 12th I thus wrote to Mr Bowden:

We have not a single Anglican in Jerusalem, so we are sending a Bishop to *make* a communion, not to govern our own people. Next, the excuse is, that there are converted Anglican Jews there who require a Bishop; I am told there are not half-a-dozen. But for *them* the Bishop is sent out, and for them he is a Bishop of the *circumcision* (I think he was a converted Jew, who boasted of his Jewish descent) against the Epistle to the Galatians pretty nearly. Thirdly, for the sake of Prussia, he is to take under him all the foreign Protestants who will come; and the political advantages will be so great, from the influence of England, that there is no doubt they *will* come. They are to sign the Confession of Augsburg, and there is nothing to show that they hold the doctrine of Baptismal Regeneration.

As to myself, I shall do nothing whatever publicly, unless indeed it were to give my signature to a Protest; but I think it would be out of place in *me* to agitate, having been in a way silenced; but the Archbishop is really doing most grave work, of which we cannot see the end.

I did make a solemn Protest, and sent it to the Archbishop of Canterbury, and also sent it to my own Bishop, with the following letter:

It seems as if I were never to write to your Lordship, without giving you pain, and I know that my present subject does not specially concern your Lordship; yet, after a great deal of anxious thought, I lay before you the enclosed Protest.

Your Lordship will observe that I am not asking for any notice of it, unless you think that I ought to receive one. I do this very serious act, in obedience to my sense of duty.

If the English Church is to enter on a new course, and assume a new aspect, it will be more pleasant to me hereafter to think, that I did not suffer so grievous an event to happen, without bearing witness against it.

May I be allowed to say, that I augur nothing but evil, if we in any respect prejudice our title to be a branch of the Apostolic Church? That Article of the Creed, I need hardly observe to your Lordship, is of such constraining power, that, if *we* will not claim it, and use it for ourselves, *others* will use it in their own behalf against us. Men who learn, whether by means of documents or measures, whether from the statements or the acts of persons in authority, that our communion is not a branch of the One Church, I foresee with much grief, will be tempted to look out for that Church elsewhere.

It is to me a subject of great dismay, that, as far as the Church has lately spoken out, on the subject of the opinions which I and others hold, those opinions are, not merely not *sanctioned* (for that I do not ask), but even *suffered*.

I earnestly hope that your Lordship will excuse my freedom in thus speaking to you of some members of your Most Rev. and Right Rev. Body. With every feeling of reverent attachment to your Lordship,

I am, &c.

PROTEST

Whereas the Church of England has a claim on the allegiance of Catholic believers only on the ground of her own claim to be considered a branch of the Catholic Church:

And whereas the recognition of heresy, indirect as well as direct, goes far to destroy such claim in the case of any religious body advancing it:

And whereas to admit maintainers of heresy to communion, without formal renunciation of their errors, goes far towards recognizing the same:

And whereas Lutheranism and Calvinism are heresies, repugnant to Scripture, springing up three centuries since, and anathematized by East as well as West:

And whereas it is reported that the Most Reverend Primate and other Right Reverend Rulers of our Church have consecrated a Bishop with a view to exercising spiritual jurisdiction over Protestant, that is, Lutheran and Calvinist congregations in the East (under the provisions of an Act made in the last session of Parliament to amend an Act made in the 26th year of the reign of his Majesty King George the Third, intituled, 'An Act to empower the Archbishop of Canterbury, or the Archbishop of York for the time being, to consecrate to the office of Bishop persons being subjects or citizens of countries out of his Majesty's dominions'), dispensing at the same time, not in particular cases and accidentally, but as if on principle and universally, with any abjuration of error on the part of such congregations, and with any reconciliation to the Church on the part of the presiding Bishop; thereby giving some sort of formal recognition to the doctrines which such congregations maintain:

And whereas the diocese in England are connected together by so close an intercommunion, that what is done by authority in one, immediately affects the rest:

On these grounds, I in my place, being a priest of the English Church and Vicar of St Mary the Virgin's, Oxford, by way of relieving my conscience, do hereby solemnly protest against the measure aforesaid, and disown it, as removing our Church from her present ground and tending to her disorganization.

JOHN HENRY NEWMAN.

11 NOVEMBER, 1841'

Looking back two years afterwards on the above-mentioned and other acts, on the part of Anglican Ecclesiastical authorities, I observed: 'Many a man might have held an abstract theory about the Catholic Church, to which it was difficult to adjust the Anglican – might have admitted a suspicion, or even painful doubts about the latter – yet never have been impelled onwards, had our Rulers preserved the quiescence of former years; but it is the corroboration of a present, living, and energetic heterodoxy, which realizes and makes them practical; it has been the recent speeches and acts of authorities, who had so long been tolerant of Protestant error, which have given to inquiry and to theory its force and its edge.'

As to the project of a Jerusalem Bishopric, I never heard of any good or harm it has ever done, except what it has done for me; which many think a great misfortune, and I one of the greatest of mercies. It brought me on to the beginning of the end.

PART VI

History of my Religious Opinions from 1841 to 1845
Published as a Pamphlet, Thursday, May 26, 1864.

CHAPTER IV

§ 1.

From the end of 1841, I was on my death-bed, as regards my membership with the Anglican Church, though at the time I became aware of it only by degrees. I introduce what I have to say with this remark, by way of accounting for the character of this remaining portion of my narrative. A death-bed has scarcely a history; it is a tedious decline, with seasons of rallying and seasons of falling back; and since the end is foreseen, or what is called a matter of time, it has little interest for the reader, especially if he has a kind heart. Moreover, it is a season when doors are closed and curtains drawn, and when the sick man neither cares nor is able to record the stages of his malady. I was in these circumstances, except so far as I was not allowed to die in peace – except so far as friends, who had still a full right to come in upon me, and the public world which had not, have given a sort of history to those last four years. But in consequence, my narrative must be in great measure documentary, as I cannot rely on my memory, except for definite particulars, positive or negative. Letters of mine to friends since dead have come into my hands; others have been kindly lent me for the occasion; and I have some drafts of letters, and some notes of my own, though I have no strictly personal or continuous memoranda to consult, and have unluckily mislaid some valuable papers.

And first as to my position in the view of duty; it was this – 1. I

had given up my place in the Movement in my letter to the
Bishop of Oxford in the spring of 1841; but 2. I could not give
up my duties towards the many and various minds who had
more or less been brought into it by me; 3. I expected or
intended gradually to fall back into Lay Communion; 4. I never
contemplated leaving the Church of England; 5. I could not
hold office in its service, if I were not allowed to hold the
Catholic sense of the Articles; 6. I could not go to Rome, while
she suffered honours to be paid to the Blessed Virgin and the
Saints which I thought in my conscience to be incompatible
with the Supreme, Incommunicable Glory of the One Infinite
and Eternal; 7. I desired a union with Rome under conditions,
Church with Church; 8. I called Littlemore my Torres Vedras,
and thought that some day we might advance again within the
Anglican Church, as we had been forced to retire; 9. I kept back
all persons who were disposed to go to Rome with all my might.

And I kept them back for three or four reasons; 1, because
what I could not in conscience do myself, I could not suffer
them to do; 2, because I thought that in various cases they were
acting under excitement; 3, while I held St Mary's, because I
had duties to my Bishop and to the Anglican Church; and 4, in
some cases, because I had received from their Anglican parents
or superiors direct charge of them.

This was my view of my duty from the end of 1841, to my
resignation of St Mary's in the autumn of 1843. And now I shall
relate my view, during that time, of the state of the controversy
between the Churches.

As soon as I saw the hitch in the Anglican argument during
my course of reading in the summer of 1839, I began to look
about, as I have said, for some ground which might supply a
controversial basis for my need. The difficulty in question had
affected my view both of Antiquity and Catholicity; for, while
the history of St Leo showed me that the deliberate and eventual
consent of the great body of the Church ratified a doctrinal
decision as a part of revealed truth, it also showed tht the rule of
Antiquity was not infringed, though a doctrine had not been
publicly recognized as a portion of the dogmatic foundation of
the Church, till centuries after the time of the Apostles. Thus,
whereas the Creeds tell us that the Church is One, Holy,
Catholic, and Apostolic, I could not prove that the Anglican
communion was an integral part of the One Church, on the

ground of its teaching being Apostolic or Catholic, without reasoning in favour of what are commonly called the Roman corruptions; and I could not defend our separation from Rome and her faith without using arguments prejudicial to those great doctrines concerning our Lord, which are the very foundation of the Christian religion. The Via Media was an impossible idea; it was what I had called 'standing on one leg'; and it was necessary, if my old issue of the controversy was to be retained, to go further either one way or the other.

Accordingly, I abandoned that old ground and took another. I deliberately quitted the old Anglican ground as untenable; but I did not do so all at once, though as I became more and more convinced of the state of the case. The Jerusalem Bishopric was the ultimate condemnation of the old theory of the Via Media – if its establishment did nothing else, at least it demolished the sacredness of diocesan rights. If England could be in Palestine, Rome might be in England. But its bearing upon the controversy, as I have shown in the foregoing chapter, was much more serious than this technical ground. From that time the Anglican Church was, in my mind, either not a normal portion of that One Church to which the promises were made, or at least in an abnormal state, and from that time I said boldly (as I did in my Protest, and as indeed I had even intimated in my Letter to the Bishop of Oxford), that the Church in which I found myself had no claim on me, except on condition of its being a portion of the One Catholic Communion, and that that condition must ever be borne in mind as a practical matter, and had to be distinctly proved. All this is not inconsistent with my saying above that, at this time, I had no thought of leaving the Church of England; because I felt some of my old objections against Rome as strongly as ever. I had no right, I had no leave, to act against my conscience. That was a higher rule than any argument about the Notes of the Church.

Under these circumstances I turned for protection to the Note of Sanctity, with a view of showing that we had at least one of the necessary Notes, as fully as the Church of Rome; or, at least, without entering into comparisons, that we had it in such a sufficient sense as to reconcile us to our position, and to supply full evidence, and a clear direction, on the point of practical duty. We had the Note of Life – not any sort of life, not such only as can come of nature, but a supernatural Christian life, which could only come directly from above. Thus, in my Article in the British Critic, to which I have so often referred, in January, 1840 (before the time of Tract 90), I said of the Anglican Church that 'she has the note of possession, a note of freedom from party titles, the note of life – a tough life and a vigorous; she has ancient descent, unbroken continuance, agreement in doctrine with the Ancient Church.' Presently I go on to speak of sanctity: 'Much as Roman Catholics may denounce us at present as schismatical, they could not resist us if the Anglican communion had but that one note of the Church upon it – sanctity. The Church of the day [4th century] could not resist Meletius; his enemies were fairly overcome by him, by his meekness and holiness, which melted the most jealous of them.' And I continue, 'We are almost content to say to Romanists, account us not yet as a branch of the Catholic Church, though we be a branch, till we are like a branch, provided that when we do become like a branch, then you consent to acknowledge us', &c. And so I was led on in the Article to that sharp attack on English Catholics for their shortcomings as regards this Note, a good portion of which I have already quoted in another place. It is there that I speak of the great scandal which I took at their political social, and controversial bearing; and this was a second reason why I fell back upon the Note of Sanctity, because it took me away from the necessity of making any attack upon the doctrines of the Roman Church, nay, from the consideration of her popular beliefs, and brought me upon a ground on which I felt I could not make a mistake; for what is a higher guide for us in speculation and in practice, than that conscience of right and wrong, of truth and falsehood, those sentiments of what is decorous, consistent, and noble, which our Creator has made a part of our original nature? Therefore I felt I could not be wrong in attacking what I fancied was a fact – the unscrupulousness, the deceit, and the intriguing spirit of the agents and representatives of Rome.

This reference to Holiness as the true test of a Church was steadily kept in view in what I wrote in connexion with Tract 90. I say in its Introduction, 'The writer can never be party to forcing the opinions or projects of one school upon another; religious changes should be the act of the whole body. No good can come of a change which is not a development of feelings springing up freely and calmly within the bosom of the whole body itself; every change in religion' must be 'attended by deep repentance; changes' must be 'nurtured in mutual love; we cannot agree without a supernatural influence'; we must come 'together to God to do for us what we cannot do for ourselves.' In my Letter to the Bishop I said,

> I have set myself against suggestions for considering the differences between ourselves and the foreign Churches with a view to their adjustment. (I meant in a way of negotiation, conference, agitation, or the like.) Our business is with ourselves – to make ourselves more holy, more self-denying, more primitive, more worthy of our high calling. To be anxious for a composition of differences is to begin at the end. Political reconciliations are but outward and hollow, and fallacious. And till Roman Catholics renounce political efforts, and manifest in their public measures the light of holiness and truth, perpetual war is our only prospect.

According to this theory, a religious body is part of the One Catholic and Apostolic Church, if it has the succession and the creed of the Apostles, with the note of holiness of life; and there is much in such a view to approve itself to the direct common sense and practical habits of an Englishman. However, with the events consequent upon Tract 90, I sunk my theory to a lower level. For what could be said in apology, when the Bishops and the people of my Church, not only did not suffer, but actually rejected primitive Catholic doctrine, and tried to eject from their communion all who held it? after the Bishops' charges? after the Jerusalem 'abomination'? Well, this could be said; still we were not nothing; we could not be as if we never had been a Church; we were 'Samaria'. This then was that lower level on which I placed myself, and all who felt with me, at the end of 1841.

To bring out this view was the purpose of Four Sermons preached at St Mary's in December of that year. Hitherto I had not introduced the exciting topics of the day into the Pulpit;[1] on this occasion I did. I did so, for the moment was urgent; there was great unsettlement of mind among us, in consequence of those same events which had unsettled me. One special anxiety, very obvious, which was coming on me now, was, that what was 'one

[1] Vide Note C. *Sermon on Wisdom and Innocence.*

man's meat was another man's poison.' I had said even of Tract 90, 'It was addressed to one set of persons, and has been used and commented on by another'; still more was it true now, that whatever I wrote for the service of those whom I knew to be in trouble of mind, would become on the one hand matter of suspicion and slander in the mouths of my opponents, and of distress and surprise to those on the other hand, who had no difficulties of faith at all. Accordingly, when I published these Four Sermons at the end of 1843, I introduced them with a recommendation that none should read them who did not need them. But in truth the virtual condemnation of Tract 90, after that the whole difficulty seemed to have been weathered, was an enormous disappointment and trial. My Protest also against the Jerusalem Bishopric was an unavoidable cause of excitement in the case of many; but it calmed them too, for the very fact of a Protest was a relief to their impatience. And so, in like manner, as regards the Four Sermons, of which I speak, though they acknowledged freely the great scandal which was involved in the recent episcopal doings, yet at the same time they might be said to bestow upon the multiplied disorders and shortcomings of the Anglican Church a sort of place in the Revealed Dispensation, and an intellectual position in the controversy, and the dignity of a great principle, for unsettled minds to take and use – a principle which might teach them to recognize their own consistency, and to be reconciled to themselves, and which might absorb into itself and dry up a multitude of their grudgings, discontents, misgivings, and questionings, and lead the way to humble, thankful, and tranquil thoughts – and this was the effect which certainly it produced on myself.

The point of these Sermons is, that, in spite of the rigid character of the Jewish law, the formal and literal force of its precepts, and the manifest schism, and worse than schism, of the Ten Tribes, yet in fact they were still recognized as a people by the Divine Mercy; that the great prophets Elias and Eliseus were sent to them, and not only so, but were sent to preach to them and reclaim them, without any intimation that they must be reconciled to the line of David and the Aaronic priesthood, or go up to Jerusalem to worship. They were not in the Church, yet they had the means of grace and the hope of acceptance with their Maker. The application of all this to the Anglican Church was immediate – whether, under the circumstances, a man could assume or exercise ministerial functions under the circumstances, or not, might not clearly appear (though it must be remembered that England had the Apostolic Priesthood, whereas Israel had no priesthood at all), but so far was clear, that there was no call at all for an Anglican to leave his Church for Rome, though he did not believe his own to be part of the One Church – and for this reason, because it was a fact that the kingdom of Israel was cut off from the Temple; and yet its subjects, neither in a mass, nor as individuals, neither the multitudes on Mount Carmel, nor the Shunammite and her household, had any command given them, though miracles were displayed before them, to break off from their own people, and to submit themselves to Judah.

It is plain, that a theory such as this – whether the marks of a divine presence and life in the Anglican Church were sufficient to prove that she was actually within the covenant, or only sufficient to prove that she was at least enjoying extraordinary and uncovenanted mercies – not only lowered her level in a religious point of view, but weakened her controversial basis. Its very novelty made it suspicious; and there was no guarantee that the process of subsidence might not continue, and that it might not end in a submersion. Indeed, to many minds, to say that England was wrong was even to say that Rome was right; and no ethical or casuistic reasoning whatever could overcome in their case the argument from prescription and authority. To this objection, as made to my new teaching, I could only answer that I did not make my circumstances. I fully acknowledged the force and effectiveness of the genuine Anglican theory, and that it was all but proof against the disputants of Rome; but still like Achilles, it had a vulnerable point, and that St Leo had found it out for me, and that I could not help it – that, were it not for matter of fact, the theory would be great indeed, it would be irresistible, if it were only true. When I became a Catholic, the Editor of The Christian Observer, Mr Wilkes, who had in former days accused me, to my indignation, of tending towards Rome, wrote to me to ask, which of the two was now right, he or I ? I answered him in a letter, part of which I here insert, as it will serve as a sort of leave-taking of the great theory, which is so specious to look upon, so difficult to prove, and so hopeless to work.

Nov. 8, 1845. I do not think, at all more than I did, that the Anglican principles which I advocated at the date you mention, lead men to the Church of Rome. If I must specify what I mean by 'Anglican principles', I should say, e.g. taking *Antiquity*, not the *existing Church*, as the oracle of truth; and holding that the *Apostolical Succession* is a sufficient guarantee of Sacramental Grace, *without union with the Christian Church throughout the world*. I think these still the firmest, strongest ground against Rome – that is, *if they can be held* [as truths or facts]. They *have* been held by many, and are far more difficult to refute in the Roman controversy, than those of any other religious body.

For myself, I found *I could not* hold them. I left them. From the time I began to suspect their unsoundness, I ceased to put them forward. When I was fairly sure of their unsoundness, I gave up my Living. When I was fully confident that the Church of Rome was the only true Church, I joined her.

I have felt all along that Bp. Bull's theology was the only theology on which the English Church could stand. I have felt, that opposition to the Church of Rome was *part* of that theology; and that he who could not protest against the Church of Rome was no true divine in the English Church. I have never said, nor attempted to say, that any one in office in the English Church, whether Bishop or incumbent, could be otherwise than in hostility to the Church of Rome.

The *Via Media* then disappeared for ever, and a new Theory, made expressly for the occasion, took its place. I was pleased with my new view. I wrote to an intimate friend, Samuel F. Wood, Dec. 13, 1841, 'I think you will give me the credit, Carissime, of not undervaluing the strength of the feelings which draw one [to Rome], and yet I am (I trust) quite clear about my duty to remain where I am; indeed, much clearer than I was some time since. If it is not presumptuous to say, I have . . . a much more definite view of the promised inward Presence of Christ with us in the Sacraments now that the outward notes of it are being removed. And I am content to be with Moses in the desert, or with Elijah excommunicated from the Temple. I say this, putting things at the strongest.'

However, my friends of the moderate Apostolical party, who were my friends for the very reason of my having been so moderate and Anglican myself in general tone in times past, who had stood up for Tract 90 partly from faith in me, and certainly from generous and kind feeling, and had thereby shared an obloquy which was none of theirs, were naturally surprised and offended at a line of argument, novel, and, as it appeared to them, wanton which threw the whole controversy into confusion, stultified my former principles, and substituted, as they would consider, a sort of methodistic self-contemplation, especially abhorrent both to my nature and to my past professions, for the plain and honest tokens, as they were commonly received, of a divine mission in the Anglican Church. They could not tell whither I was going; and were still further annoyed, when I persisted in viewing the reception of Tract 90 by the public and the Bishops as so grave a matter, and when I threw about what they considered mysterious hints of 'eventualities', and would not simply say, 'An Anglican I was born, and an Anglican I will die.' One of my familiar friends, Mr Church, who was in the country at Christmas, 1841–2, reported to me the feeling that prevailed about me; and how I felt towards it will appear in the following letter of mine, written in answer:

Oriel, Dec. 24, 1841. Carissime, you cannot tell how sad your account of Moberly has made me. His view of the sinfulness of the decrees of Trent is as much against union of Churches as against individual conversions. To tell the truth, I never have examined those decrees with this object, and have no view; but that is very different from having a deliberate view against them. Could not he say *which* they are? I suppose Transubstantiation is one. Charles Marriott, though of course he would not like to have it repeated, does not scruple at that. I have not my mind clear. Moberly must recollect that Palmer [of Worcester] thinks they all bear a Catholic interpretation. For myself, this only I see, that there is indefinitely more in the Fathers against our own state of alienation from Christendom than against the Tridentine Decrees.

The only thing I can think of [that I can have said of a startling character], is this, that there were persons who, if our Church committed herself to heresy, *sooner* than think that there was no Church any where, would believe the Roman to be the Church; and therefore would on faith accept what they could not otherwise acquiesce in. I suppose, it would be no relief to him to insist upon the circumstance that there is no immediate danger. Individuals can never be answered for of course; but I should think lightly of that man, who, for some acts of the Bishops, should all at once leave the Church. Now, considering how the Clergy really are improving, considering that this row is even making them read the Tracts, is it not possible we may all be in a better state of mind seven years hence to consider these matters ? and may we not leave them meanwhile to the will of Providence ? I *cannot* believe this work has been of man; God has a right to His own work, to do what He will with it. May we not try to leave it in His hands, and be content ?

If you learn any thing about Barter, which leads you to think that I can relieve him by a letter, let me know. The truth is this — our good friends do not read the Fathers; they assent to us from the common sense of the case: then, when the Fathers, and we, say *more* than their common sense, they are dreadfully shocked.

The Bishop of London has rejected a man, 1. For holding *any* Sacrifice in the Eucharist. 2. The Real Presence. 3. That there is a grace in Ordination.

Are we quite sure that the Bishops will not be drawing up some stringent declarations of faith ? is this what Moberly fears ? Would the Bishop of Oxford accept them ? If so, I should be driven into the Refuge for the Destitute [Littlemore]. But I promise Moberly, I would do my utmost to catch all dangerous persons and clap them into confinement there.

Christmas Day 1841. I have been dreaming of Moberly all night. Should not he and the like see, that it is unwise, unfair, and impatient to ask others, What will you do under circumstances, which have not, which may never come ? Why bring fear, suspicion, and disunion into the camp about things which are merely *in posse* ? Natural, and exceedingly kind as Barter's and another friend's letters were, I think they have done great harm. I speak most sincerely when I say, that there are things which I neither contemplate, nor wish to contemplate; but, when I am asked about them ten times, at length I begin to contemplate them.

He surely does not mean to say, that *nothing* could separate a man from the English Church. e.g. its avowing Socinianism; its holding the Holy Eucharist in a Socinian sense. Yet, he would say, it was not *right* to contemplate such things.

Again, our case is [diverging] from that of Ken's. To say nothing of the last miserable century, which has given us to *start* from a much lower level and with much less to *spare* than a Churchman in the 17th century, questions of *doctrine* are now coming in; with him, it was a question of discipline.

If such dreadful events were realized, I cannot help thinking we should all be vastly more agreed than we think now. Indeed, it is possible (humanly speaking) that those, who have so much the same heart, should widely differ ? But let this be considered, as to alternatives. *What* communion could we join ? Could the Scotch or American sanction the presence of its Bishops and congregations in England, without incurring the imputation of schism, unless indeed (and is that likely ?) they denounced the English as heretical ?

Is not this a time of strange providences ? is it not our safest course, without looking to consequences, to do simply *what* we think right day by day ? shall we not be sure to go wrong if we attempt to trace by anticipation the course of divine Providence ?

Has not all our misery, as a Church, arisen from people being afraid to look difficulties in the face ? They have palliated acts, when they should have denounced them. There is that good fellow, Worcester Palmer, can white-wash the Ecclesiastical Commission and the Jerusalem Bishopric. And what is the consequence ? that our Church has, through centuries, ever been sinking lower and lower, till good part of its pretensions and professions is a mere sham, though it be a duty to make the best of what we have received. Yet, though bound to make the best of other men's shams, let us not incur any of our own. The truest friends of our Church are they, who say boldly when her rulers are going wrong, and the consequences; and (to speak catachrestically) *they* are most likely to die in the Church, who are, under these black circumstances, most prepared to leave it.

And I will add, that, considering the traces of God's grace which surround us, I am very sanguine, or rather confident (if it is right so to speak), that our prayers and our alms will come up as a memorial before God, and that all this miserable confusion tends to good.

Let us not then be anxious, and anticipate differences in prospect, when we agree in the present.

P.S. I think, when friends [i.e. the extreme party] get over their first unsettlement of mind and consequent vague apprehensions, which the new attitude of the Bishops, and our feelings upon it, have brought about, they will get contented and satisfied. They will see that they exaggerated things. . . . Of course it would have been wrong to anticipate what one's feelings would be under such a painful contingency as the Bishops' charging as they have done – so it seems to me nobody's fault. Nor is it wonderful that others' [moderate men] 'are startled' [i.e. at my Protest, &c. &c.]; 'yet they should recollect that the more implicit the reverence one pays to a Bishop, the more keen will be one's perception of heresy in him. The cord is binding and compelling, till it snaps.

Men of reflection would have seen this, if they had looked that way. Last spring, a very high churchman talked to me of resisting my Bishop, of asking him for the Canons under which he acted, and so forth; but those, who have cultivated a loyal feeling towards their superiors, are the most loving servants, or the most zealous protestors. If others became so too, if the clergy of Chester denounced the heresy of their diocesan, they would be doing their duty, and relieving themselves of the share which they otherwise have in any possible defection of their brethren.

St Stephen's [Day December 26]. How I fidget! I now fear that the note I wrote yesterday only makes matters worse by *disclosing* too much. This is always my great difficulty.

In the present state of excitement on both sides, I think of leaving out altogether my reassertion of No. 90 in my Preface to Volume 6 [of Parochial Sermons], and merely saying. 'As many false reports are at this time in circulation about him, he hopes his well-wishers will take this Volume as an indication of his real thoughts and feelings: those who are not, he leaves in God's hands to bring them to a better mind in His own time.' What do you say to the logic, sentiment, and propriety of this?

An old friend, at a distance from Oxford, Archdeacon Robert I. Wilberforce, afterwards a Catholic, now dead some years, who must have said something to me at this time, I do not know what, which challenged a frank reply; for I disclosed to him, I do not know in what words, my frightful suspicion, hitherto only known to two persons, viz. his brother Henry, and Mr (now Sir Frederick) Rogers, that, as regards my Anglicanism, perhaps I might break down in the event – that perhaps we were both out of the Church. I think I recollect expressing my difficulty, as derived from the Arian and Monophysite history, in a form in which it would be most intelligible to him, as being in fact an admission of Bishop Bull's; viz. that in the controversies of the early centuries the Roman Church was ever on the right side, which was of course a *primâ facie* argument in favour of Rome and against Anglicanism now. He answered me thus, under date of 29 January 1842:

> I don't think that I ever was so shocked by any communication, which was ever made to me, as by your letter of this morning. It has quite unnerved me . . . I cannot but write to you, though I am at a loss where to begin . . . I know of no act by which we have dissevered ourselves from the communion of the Church Universal . . . The more I study Scripture, the more am I impressed with the resemblance between the Romish principle in the Church and the Babylon of St John . . . I am ready to grieve that I ever directed my thought to theology, if it is indeed so uncertain, as your doubts seem to indicate.

While my old and true friends were thus in trouble about me, I suppose they felt not only anxiety but pain, to see that I was gradually surrendering myself to the influence of others, who had not their own claims upon me, younger men, and of a cast of mind in no small degree uncongenial to my own. A new school of thought was rising, as is usual in such movements, and was sweeping the original party of the movement aside, and was taking its place. The most prominent person in it, was a man of elegant genius, of classical mind, of rare talent in literary composition – Mr Oakeley. He was not far from my own age; I had long known him, though of late years he had not been in residence at Oxford; and quite lately, he has been taking several signal occasions of renewing that kindness, which he ever showed towards me when we were both in the Anglican Church. His tone of mind was not unlike that which gave a character to the early movement; he was almost a typical Oxford man, and, as far as I recollect, both in political and ecclesiastical views, would have been of one spirit with the Oriel party of 1826–1833. But he had entered late into the Movement; he did not know its first years; and, beginning with a new start, he was naturally thrown together with that body of eager, acute, resolute minds who had begun their Catholic life about the same time as he, who knew nothing about the *Via Media*, but had heard much about Rome. This new party rapidly formed and increased, in and out of Oxford, and, as it so happened, contemporaneously with that very summer, when I received so serious a blow to my ecclesiastical views from the study of the Monophysite controversy. These men cut into the original Movement at an angle, fell across its line of thought, and then set about turning that line in its own direction. They were most of them keenly religious men, with a true concern for their souls as the first matter of all, with a great zeal for me, but giving little certainty at the time as to which way they would ultimately turn. Some in the event have remained firm to Anglicanism, some have become Catholics, and some have found a refuge in Liberalism. Nothing was clearer concerning them, than that they needed to be kept in order; and on me who had had so much to do with the making of them, that duty was as clearly incumbent; and it is equally clear, from what I have already said, that I was just the person, above all others, who could not undertake it. There are no friends like old friends; but of those old friends, few could help me, few could understand me, many were annoyed with me, some were angry, because I was breaking up a compact party, and some, as a matter of conscience, could not listen to me. When I looked round for those whom I might consult in my difficulties, I found the very hypothesis of those difficulties acting as a bar to their giving me their advice. Then I said, bitterly, 'You are throwing me on others, whether I will or no.' Yet still I had good and true friends around me of the old sort, in and out of Oxford too, who were a great help to me. But on the other hand, though I neither was so fond (with a few exceptions) of the persons, nor of the methods of thought, which belonged to this new school, excepting two or three men, as of the old set, though I could not trust in their firmness of purpose, for, like a swarm of flies, they might come and go, and at length be divided and dissipated, yet I had an intense sympathy in their object and in the direction in which their path lay in spite of my old friends, in spite of my old life-long prejudices. In spite of my ingrained fears of Rome, and the decision of my reason and conscience against her usages, in spite of my affection for Oxford and Oriel, yet I had a secret longing love of Rome the Mother of English Christianity, and I had a true devotion to the Blessed Virgin, in whose College I lived, whose Altar I served, and whose Immaculate Purity I had in one of my earliest printed Sermons made much of. And it was the consciousness of this bias in myself, if it is so to be called, which made me preach so earnestly against the danger of being swayed in religious inquiry by our sympathy rather than by our reason. And moreover, the members of this new school looked up to me, as I have said, and did me true kindnesses, and really loved me, and stood by me in trouble, when others went away, and for all this I was grateful; nay, many of them were in trouble themselves, and in the same boat with me, and that was a further cause of sympathy between us; and hence it was, when the new school came on in force, and into collision with the old, I had not the heart, any more than the power, to repel them; I was in great perplexity, and hardly knew where I stood; I took their party; and, when I wanted to be in peace and silence, I had to speak out, and I incurred the charge of weakness from some men, and of mysteriousness, shuffling, and underhand dealing from the majority.

Now I will say here frankly, that this sort of charge is a matter which I cannot properly meet, because I cannot duly realize it. I have never had any suspicion of my own honesty; and, when men say that I was dishonest, I cannot grasp the accusation as a distinct conception, such as it is possible to encounter. If a man said to me, 'On such a day and before such persons you said a thing was white, when it was black', I understand what is meant well enough, and I can set myself to prove an alibi or to explain the mistake; or if a man said to me, 'You tried to gain me over to your party, intending to take me with you to Rome, but you did not succeed', I can give him the lie, and lay down an assertion of my own as firm and as exact as his, that not from the time that I was first unsettled, did I ever attempt to gain any one over to myself or to my Romanizing opinions, and that it is only his own coxcombical fancy which has bred such a thought in him: but my imagination is at a loss in presence of those vague charges, which have commonly been brought against me, charges, which are made up of impressions, and understandings, and inferences, and hearsay, and surmises. Accordingly, I shall not make the attempt, for, in doing so, I should be dealing blows in the air; what I shall attempt is to state what I know of myself and what I recollect, and leave to others its application.

While I had confidence in the *Via Media*, and thought that nothing could overset it, I did not mind laying down large principles, which I saw would go further than was commonly perceived. I considered that to make the *Via Media* concrete and substantive, it must be much more than it was in outline; that the Anglican Church must have a ceremonial, a ritual, and a fulness of doctrine and devotion, which it had not at present, if it were to compete with the Roman Church with any prospect of success. Such additions would not remove it from its proper basis, but would merely strengthen and beautify it: such, for instance, would be confraternities, particular devotions, reverence for the Blessed Virgin, prayers for the dead, beautiful churches, munificent offerings to them and in them, monastic houses, and many other observances and institutions, which I used to say belonged to us as much as to Rome, though Rome had appropriated them, and boasted of them, by reason of our having let them slip from us. The principle, on which all this turned, is brought out in one of the Letters I published on occasion of Tract 90. 'The age is moving,' I said,

'towards something; and most unhappily the one religious communion among us, which has of late years been practically in possession of this something, is the Church of Rome. She alone, amid all the errors and evils of her practical system, has given free scope to the feelings of awe, mystery, tenderness, reverence, devotedness, and other feelings which may be especially called Catholic. The question then is, whether we shall give them up to the Roman Church or claim them for ourselves . . . But if we do give them up, we must give up the men who cherish them. We must consent either to give up the men, or to admit their principles.' With these feelings I frankly admit that, while I was working simply for the sake of the Anglican Church, I did not at all mind, though I found myself laying down principles in its defence, which went beyond that particular kind of defence which high-and-dry men thought perfection, and even though I ended in framing a kind of defence, which they might call a revolution, while I thought it a restoration. Thus, for illustration, I might discourse upon the 'Communion of Saints' in such a manner (though I do not recollect doing so), as might lead the way towards devotion to the Blessed Virgin and the Saints on the one hand, and towards prayers for the dead on the other. In a memorandum of the year 1844 or 1845, I thus speak on this subject: 'If the Church be not defended on establishment grounds, it must be upon principles, which go far beyond their immediate object. Sometimes I saw these further results, sometimes not. Though I saw them, I sometimes did not say that I saw them; so long as I thought they were inconsistent, *not* with our Church, but only with the existing opinions, I was not unwilling to insinuate truths into our Church, which I thought had a right to be there.'

To so much I confess; but I do not confess, I simply deny that I ever said any thing which secrely bore against the Church of England, knowing it myself, in order that others might unwarily accept it. It was indeed one of my great difficulties and causes of reserve, as time went on, that I at length recognized in principles which I had honestly preached as if Anglican, conclusions favourable to the use of Rome. Of course I did not like to confess this; and, when interrogated, was in consequence in perplexity. The prime instance of this was the appeal to Antiquity; St Leo had overset, in my own judgment, its force as the special argument for Anglicanism; yet I was committed to Antiquity, together with the whole Anglican school; what then was I to say, when acute minds urged this or that application of it against the *Via Media* ? it was impossible that, in such circumstances, any answer could be given which was not unsatisfactory, or any behaviour adopted which was not mysterious. Again, sometimes in what I wrote I went just as far as I saw, and could as little say more, as I could see what is below the horizon; and therefore, when asked as to the consequences of what I had said, I had no answer to give. Again, sometimes when I was asked, whether certain conclusions did not follow from a certain principle, I might not be able to tell at the moment, especially if the matter were complicated; and for this reason, if for no other, because there is great difference between a conclusion in the abstract and a conclusion in the concrete, and because a conclusion may be modified in fact by a conclusion from some opposite principle. Or it might so happen that my head got simply confused, by the very strength of the logic which was administered to me, and thus I gave my sanction to conclusions which really were not mine; and when the report of those conclusions came round to me through others, I had to unsay them. And then again, perhaps I did not like to see men scared or scandalized by unfeeling logical inferences, which would not have troubled them to the day of their death, had they not been forced to recognize them. And then I felt altogether the force of the maxim of St Ambrose, 'Non in dialecticâ complacuit Deo salvum facere populum suum' – I had a great dislike of paper logic. For myself, it was not logic that carried me on; as well might one say that the quicksilver in the barometer changes the weather. It is the concrete being that reasons; pass a number of years, and I find my mind in a new place; how ? the whole man moves; paper logic is but the record of it. All the logic in the world would not have made me move faster towards Rome than I did; as well might you say that I have arrived at the end of my journey, because I see the village church before me, as venture to assert that the miles, over which my soul had to pass before it got to Rome, could be annihilated, even though I had been in possession of some far clearer view than I then had, that Rome was my ultimate destination. Great acts take time. At least this is what I felt in my own case; and therefore to come to me with methods of logic, had in it the nature of a provocation, and, though I do not think I ever showed it; made me somewhat indifferent how I met them, and perhaps led me, as a means of relieving my impatience, to be mysterious or irrelevant, or to give in because I could not meet them to my satisfaction. And a greater trouble still than these logical mazes, was the introduction of logic into every subject whatever, so far, that is, as it was done. Before I was at Oriel, I recollect an acquaintance saying to me that 'the Oriel Common Room stank of Logic.' One is not at all pleased when poetry, or eloquence, or devotion is considered as if chiefly intended to feed syllogisms. Now, in saying all this, I am saying nothing against the deep piety and earnestness which were characteristics of this second phase of the Movement, in which I had taken so prominent a part. What I had been observing is, that this phase had a tendency to bewilder and to upset me, and, that instead of saying so, as I ought to have done, perhaps from a sort of laziness, I gave answers at random, which have led to my appearing close or inconsistent.

I have turned up two letters of this period, which in a measure illustrate what I have been saying. The first was written to the Bishop of Oxford on occasion of Tract 90:

March 20, 1841. No one can enter into my situation but myself. I see a great many minds working in various directions and a variety of principles with multiplied bearings; I act for the best. I sincerely think that matters would not have gone better for the Church, had I never written. And if I write I have a choice of difficulties. It is easy for those who do not enter into those difficulties to say, 'He ought to say this and not say that', but things are wonderfully linked together, and I cannot, or rather I would not be dishonest. When persons too interrogate me, I am obliged in many cases to give an opinion, or I seem to be underhand. Keeping silence looks like artifice. And I do not like people to consult or respect me, from thinking differently of my opinions from what I know them to be. And (again to use the proverb) what is one man's food is another man's poison. All these things make my situation very difficult. But that collision must at some time ensue between members of the Church of opposite sentiments, I have long been aware. The time and mode has been in the hand of Providence; I do not mean to exclude my own great imperfections in bringing it about; yet I still feel obliged to think the Tract necessary.

Dr Pusey has shown me your Lordship's letters to him. I am most desirous of saying in print any thing which I can honestly say to remove false impressions created by the Tract.

The second is taken from the notes of a letter which I sent to Dr Pusey in the next year:

October 16, 1842. As to my being entirely with Ward, I do not know the limits of my own opinions. If Ward says that this or that is a development from what I have said, I cannot say Yes or No. It is plausible, it *may* be true. Of course the fact that the Roman Church *has* so developed and maintained, adds great weight to the antecedent plausibility. I cannot assert that it is not true; but I cannot, with that keen perception which some people have, appropriate it. It is a nuisance to me to be *forced* beyond what I can fairly accept.

There was another source of the perplexity with which at this time I was encompassed, and of the reserve and mysteriousness, of which that perplexity gained for me the credit. After Tract 90 the Protestant world would not let me alone; they pursued me in the public journals to Littlemore. Reports of all kinds were circulated about me. 'Imprimis, why did I go up to Littlemore at all? For no good purpose certainly; I dared not tell why.' Why, to be sure, it was hard that I should be obliged to say to the Editors of newspapers that I went up there to say my prayers; it was hard to have to tell the world in confidence, that I had a certain doubt about the Anglican system, and could not at that moment resolve it, or say what would come of it; it was hard to have to confess that I had thought of giving up my Living a year or two before, and that this was a first step to it. It was hard to have to plead, that, for what I knew, my doubts would vanish, if the newspapers would be so good as to give me time and let me alone. Who would ever dream of making the world his confidant? yet I was considered insidious, sly, dishonest, if I would not open my heart to the tender mercies of the world. But they persisted: 'What was I doing at Littlemore?' Doing there! have I not retreated from you? have I not given up my position and my place? am I alone, of Englishmen, not to have the privilege to go where I will, no questions asked? am I alone to be followed about by jealous prying eyes, who note down whether I go in at a back door or at the front, and who the men are who happen to call on me in the afternoon? Cowards! if I advanced one step, you would run away; it is not you that I fear: 'Di me terrent, et Jupiter hostis.' It is because the Bishops still go on charging against me, though I have quite given up: it is that secret misgiving of heart which tells me that they do well, for I have neither lot nor part with them: this it is which weighs me down. I cannot walk into or out of my house, but curious eyes are upon me. Why will you not let me die in peace? Wounded brutes creep into some hole to die in, and no one grudges it them. Let me alone, I shall not trouble you long. This was the keen heavy feeling which pierced me, and, I think, these are the very words in which I expressed it to myself. I asked, in the words of a great motto, 'Ubi lapsus? quid feci?'. One day when I entered my house, I found a flight of Undergraduates inside. Heads of Houses, as mounted patrols, walked their horses round those poor cottages. Doctors of Divinity dived into the hidden recesses of that private tenement uninvited, and drew domestic conclusions from what they saw there. I had thought that an Englishman's house was his castle; but the newspapers thought otherwise, and at last the matter came before my good Bishop. I insert his letter, and a portion of my reply to him:

April 12, 1842. So many of the charges against yourself and your friends which I have seen in the public journals have been, within my own knowledge, false and calumnious, that I am not apt to pay much attention to what is asserted with respect to you in the newspapers.

In [a newspaper] however, of April 9, there appears a paragraph in which it is asserted, as a matter of notoriety, that a 'so-called Anglo-Catholic Monastery is in process of erection at Littlemore, and that the cells of dormitories, the chapel, the refectory, the cloisters all may be seen advancing to perfection, under the eye of a Parish Priest of the Diocese of Oxford'.

Now, as I have understood that you really are possessed of some tenements at Littlemore – as it is generally believed that they are destined for the purposes of study and devotion – and as much suspicion and jealousy are felt about the matter, I am anxious to afford you an opportunity of making me an explanation on the subject.

I know you too well not to be aware that you are the last man living to attempt in my Diocese a revival of the Monastic orders (in any thing approaching to the Romanist sense of the term) without previous communication with me – or indeed that you should take upon yourself to originate any measure of importance without authority from the heads of the Church – and therefore I at once exonerate you from the accusation brought against you by the newspaper I have quoted, but I feel it nevertheless a duty to my Diocese and myself, as well as to you, to ask you to put it in my power to contradict what, if uncontradicted, would appear to imply a glaring invasion of all ecclesiastical discipline on *your* part, or of inexcusable neglect and indifference to my duties on *mine*.

I wrote in answer as follows:

April 14, 1842. I am very much obliged by your Lordship's kindness in allowing me to write to you on the subject of my house at Littlemore; at the same time I feel it hard both on your Lordship and myself that the restlessness of the public mind should oblige you to require an explanation of me.

It is now a whole year that I have been the subject of incessant misrepresentation. A year since I submitted entirely to your Lordship's authority; and with the intention of following out the particular act enjoined upon me, I not only stopped the series of Tracts, on which I was engaged, but withdrew from all public discussion of Church matters of the day, or what may be

called ecclesiastical politics. I turned myself at once to the
preparation for the Press of the translations of St Athanasius to
which I had long wished to devote myself, and I intended and
intend to employ myself in the like theological studies, and in
the concerns of my own parish and in practical works.

With the same view of personal improvement I was led more
seriously to a design which had been long on my mind. For
many years, at least thirteen, I have wished to give myself a life
of greater religious regularity than I have hitherto led; but it is
very unpleasant to confess such a wish even to my Bishop,
because it seems arrogant, and because it is committing me to a
profession which may come to nothing. For what have I done
that I am to be called to account by the world for my private
actions, in a way in which no one else is called ? Why may I not
have that liberty which all others are allowed ? I am often
accused of being underhand and uncandid in respect to the
intentions to which I have been alluding: but no one likes his
own good resolutions noised about, both from mere common
delicacy and from fear lest he should not be able to fulfil them. I
feel it very cruel, though the parties in fault do not know what
they are doing, that very sacred matters between me and my
conscience are made a matter of public talk. May I take a case
parallel though different ? suppose a person in prospect of
marriage; would he like the subject discussed in newspapers,
and parties, circumstances, &c., &c., publicly demanded of
him, at the penalty of being accused of craft and duplicity ?

The resolution I speak of has been taken with reference to
myself alone, and has been contemplated quite independent of
the co-operation of any other human being, and without
reference to success or failure other than personal, and without
regard to the blame or approbation of man. And being a
resolution of years, and one to which I feel God has called me,
and in which I am violating no rule of the Church any more
than if I married, I should have to answer for it, if I did not
pursue it, as a good Providence made openings for it. In
pursuing it then I am thinking of myself alone, not aiming at
any ecclesiastical or external effects. At the same time of course
it would be a great comfort to me to know that God had put it
into the hearts of others to pursue their personal edification in
the same way, and unnatural not to wish to have the benefit of
their presence and encouragement, or not to think it a great

infringement on the rights of conscience if such personal and private resolutions were interfered with. Your Lordship will allow me to add my firm conviction that such religious resolutions are most necessary for keeping a certain class of minds firm in their allegiance to our Church; but still I can as truly say that my own reason for any thing I have done has been a personal one, without which I should not have entered upon it, and which I hope to pursue whether with or without the sympathies of others pursuing a similar course. . . .

As to my intentions, I purpose to live there myself a good deal, as I have a resident curate in Oxford. In doing this, I believe I am consulting for the good of my parish, as my population at Littlemore is at least equal to that of St Mary's in Oxford, and the *whole* of Littlemore is double of it. It has been very much neglected; and in providing a parsonage-house at Littlemore, as this will be, and will be called, I conceive I am doing a very great benefit to my people. At the same time it has appeared to me that a partial or temporary retirement from St Mary's Church might be expedient under the prevailing excitement.

As to the quotation from the [newspaper] which I have not seen, your Lordship will perceive from what I have said, that no 'monastery is in process of erection'; there is no 'chapel'; no 'refectory', hardly a dining-room or parlour. The 'cloisters' are my shed connecting the cottages. I do not understand what 'cells of dormitories' means. Of course I can repeat your Lordship's words that 'I am not attempting a revival of the Monastic Orders, in any thing approaching to the Romanist sense of the term', or 'taking on myself to originate any measure of importance without authority from the Heads of the Church'. I am attempting nothing ecclesiastical, but something personal and private, and which can only be made public, not private, by newspapers and letter-writers, in which sense the most sacred and conscientious resolves and acts may certainly be made the objects of an unmannerly and unfeeling curiosity.

One calumny there was which the Bishop did not believe, and of which of course he had no idea of speaking. It was that I was actually in the service of the enemy. I had forsooth been already received into the Catholic Church, and was rearing at Littlemore a nest of Papists, who, like me, were to take the Anglican oaths which they disbelieved, by virtue of a dispensation from Rome, and thus in due time were to bring over to that unprincipled Church great numbers of the Anglican Clergy and Laity. Bishops gave their countenance to this imputation against me. The case was simply this – as I made Littlemore a place of retirement for myself, so did I offer it to others. There were young men in Oxford, whose testimonials for Orders had been refused by their Colleges; there were young clergymen, who had found themselves unable from conscience to go on with their duties, and had thrown up their parochial engagements. Such men were already going straight to Rome, and I interposed; I interposed for the reasons I have given in the beginning of this portion of my narrative. I interposed from fidelity to my clerical engagements, and from duty to my Bishop; and from the interest which I was bound to take in them, and from belief that they were premature or excited. Their friends besought me to quiet them, if I could. Some of them came to live with me at Littlemore. They were laymen, or in the place of laymen. I kept some of them back for several years from being received into the Catholic Church. Even when I had given up my living, I was still bound by my duty to their parents or friends, and I did not forget still to do what I could for them. The immediate occasion of my resigning St Mary's, was the unexpected conversion of one of them. After that, I felt it was impossible to keep my post there, for I had been unable to keep my word with my Bishop.

The following letters refer, more or less, to these men, whether they were actually with me at Littlemore or not:

1. March 6, 1842. Church doctrines are a powerful weapon; they were not sent into the world for nothing. God's word does not return unto Him void: If I have said, as I have, that the doctrines of the Tracts for the Times would build up our Church and destroy parties, I meant, if they were used, not if they were denounced. Else, they will be as powerful against us, as they might be powerful for us.

If people who have a liking for another, hear him called a Roman Catholic, they will say, 'Then after all Romanism is no such bad thing'. All these persons, who are making the cry, are fulfilling their own prophecy. If all the world agree in telling a man, he has no business in our Church, he will at length begin to think he has none. How easy is it to persuade a man of any thing, when numbers affirm it! so great is the force of imagination. Did every one who met you in the streets look hard at you, you would think you were somehow in fault. I do not know any thing so irritating, so unsettling, especially in the case of young persons, as, when they are going on calmly and unconsciously, obeying their Church and following its divines (I am speaking from facts), as suddenly to their surprise to be conjured not to make a leap, of which they have not a dream and from which they are far removed.

2. 1843 or 1844. I did not explain to you sufficiently the state of mind of those who were in danger. I only spoke of those who were convinced that our Church was external to the Church Catholic, though they felt it unsafe to trust their own private convictions; but there are two other states of mind; 1. that of those who are unconsciously near Rome, and whose *despair* about our Church would at once develop into a state of conscious approximation, or a *quasi*-resolution to go over; 2. those who feel they can with a safe conscience remain with us *while* they are allowed to *testify* in behalf of Catholicism, i.e. as if by such acts they were putting our Church, or at least that portion of it in which they were included, in the position of catechumens.

3. June 20, 1843. I return the very pleasing letter you have permitted me to read. What a sad thing it is, that it should be a plain duty to restrain one's sympathies, and to keep them from boiling over; but I suppose it is a matter of common prudence.

Things are very serious here; but I should not like you to say so, as it might do no good. The Authorities find, that, by the Statutes, they have more than military power; and the general impression seems to be, that they intend to exert it, and put down Catholicism at any risk. I believe that by the Statutes, they can pretty nearly suspend a Preacher, as *seditiosus* or causing dissension, without assigning their grounds in the particular case, nay, banish him, or imprison him. If so, all holders of preferment in the University should make as quiet an *exit* as they can. There is more exasperation on both sides at this moment, as I am told, than ever there was.

4. July 16, 1843.   I assure you that I feel, with only too much sympathy, what you say. You need not be told that the whole subject of our position is a subject of anxiety to others beside yourself. It is no good attempting to offer advice, when perhaps I might raise difficulties instead of removing them. It seems to me quite a case, in which you should, as far as may be, make up your mind for yourself. Come to Littlemore by all means. We shall all rejoice in your company; and, if quiet and retirement are able, as they very likely will be, to reconcile you to things as they are, you shall have your fill of them. How distressed poor Henry Wilberforce must be! Knowing how he values you, I feel for him; but, alas! he has his own position, and every one else has his own, and the misery is that no two of us have exactly the same.

It is very kind of you to be so frank and open with me, as you are; but this is a time which throws together persons who feel alike. May I without taking a liberty sign myself, yours affectionately, &c.

5. August 30, 1843. A. B. has suddenly conformed to the Church of Rome. He was away for three weeks. I suppose I must say in my defence, that he promised me distinctly to remain in our Church three years, before I received him here.

6. June 17, 1845.   I am concerned to find you speak of me in a tone of distrust. If you knew me ever so little, instead of hearing of me from persons who do not know me at all, you would think differently of me, whatever you thought of my opinions. Two years since, I got your son to tell you my intention of resigning St Mary's, before I made it public, thinking you ought to know it. When you expressed some painful feeling upon it, I told him I could not consent to his remaining here, painful as it would be to me to part with him, without your written sanction. And this you did me the favour to give.

I believe you will find that it has been merely a delicacy on your son's part, which has delayed his speaking to you about me for two months past; a delicacy, lest he should say either too much or too little about me. I have urged him several times to speak to you.

Nothing can be done after your letter, but to recommend him to go to A. B. (his home) at once. I am very sorry to part with him.

7. The following letter is addressed to Cardinal Wiseman, then Vicar Apostolic, who accused me of coldness in my conduct towards him:

April 16, 1845.   I was at that time in charge of a ministerial office in the English Church, with persons entrusted to me, and a Bishop to obey; how could I possibly write otherwise than I did without violating sacred obligations and betraying momentous interests which were upon me ? I felt that my immediate, undeniable duty, clear if any thing was clear, was to fulfil that trust. It might be right indeed to give it up, that was another thing; but it never could be right to hold it, and to act as if I did not hold it . . . If you knew me, you would acquit me, I think, of having ever felt towards your Lordship in an unfriendly spirit, or ever having had a shadow on my mind (as far as I dare witness about myself) of what might be called controversial rivalry or desire of getting the better, or fear lest the world should think I had got the worse, or irritation of any kind. You are too kind indeed to imply this, and yet your words lead me to say it. And now in like manner, pray believe, though I cannot explain it to you, that I am encompassed with responsibilities, so great and so various, as utterly to overcome me, unless I have mercy from Him, who all through my life has sustained and guided me, and to whom I can now submit myself, though men of all parties are thinking evil of me.

Such fidelity, however, was taken *in malam partem* by the high Anglican authorities; they thought it insidious. I happen still to have a correspondence which took place in 1843, in which the chief place is filled by one of the most eminent Bishops of the day, a theologian and reader of the Fathers, a moderate man, who at one time was talked of as likely on a vacancy to succeed to the Primacy. A young clergyman in his diocese became a Catholic; the papers at once reported on authority from 'a very high quarter', that, after his reception, 'the Oxford men had been recommending him to retain his living.' I had reasons for thinking that the allusion was made to me, and I authorized the Editor of a Paper, who had inquired of me on the point, to 'give it, as far as I was concerned, an unqualified contradiction' – when from a motive of delicacy he hesitated, I added 'my direct and indignant contradiction.' 'Whoever is the author of it,' I continued to the Editor, 'no correspondence or intercourse of any kind, direct or indirect, has passed between Mr S. and myself, since his conforming to the Church of Rome, except my formally and merely acknowledging the receipt of his letter, in which he informed me of the fact, without, as far as I recollect, my expressing any opinion upon it. You may state this as broadly as I have set it down.' My denial was told to the Bishop; what took place upon it is given in a letter from which I copy. 'My father showed the letter to the Bishop, who, as he laid it down, said, "Ah, those Oxford men are not ingenuous." "How do you mean?" asked my father. "Why," said the Bishop, "they advised Mr B. S. to retain his living after he turned Catholic. I know that to be a fact, because A. B. told me so." ' 'The Bishop,' continues the letter, 'who is perhaps the most influential man in reality on the bench, evidently believes it to be the truth.' Upon this Dr Pusey too wrote in my behalf to the Bishop; and the Bishop instantly beat a retreat. 'I have the honour,' he says in the autograph which I transcribe, 'to acknowledge the receipt of your note, and to say in reply that it has not been stated by me (though such a statement has, I believe, appeared in some of the Public Prints), that Mr Newman had advised Mr B. S. to retain his living, after he had forsaken our Church. But it has been stated to me, that Mr Newman was in close correspondence with Mr B. S., and, being fully aware of his state of opinions and feelings, yet advised him to continue in our communion. Allow me to add,' he says to Dr Pusey, 'that neither your name, nor that of Mr Keble, was mentioned to me in connexion with that of Mr B. S.'

I was not going to let the Bishop off on this evasion, so I wrote to him myself. After quoting his Letter to Dr Pusey, I continued,

I beg to trouble your Lordship with my own account of the two allegations [*close correspondence* and *fully aware*, &c.] which are contained in your statement, and which have led to your speaking of me in terms which I hope never to deserve. 1. Since Mr B. S. has been in your Lordship's diocese, I have seen him in common rooms or private parties in Oxford two or three times, when I never (as far as I can recollect) had any conversation with him. During the same time I have, to the best of my memory, written to him three letters. One was lately, in acknowledgement of his informing me of his change of religion. Another was last summer, when I asked him (to no purpose) to come and stay with me in this place. The earliest of the three letters was written just a year since, as far as I recollect, and it certainly was on the subject of his joining the Church of Rome. I wrote this letter at the earnest wish of a friend of his. I cannot be sure that, on his replying, I did not send him a brief note in explanation of points in my letter which he had misapprehended. I cannot recollect any other correspondence between us.

2. As to my knowledge of his opinions and feelings, as far as I remember, the only point of perplexity which I knew, the only point which to this hour I know, as pressing upon him, was that of the Pope's supremacy. He professed to be searching Antiquity whether the see of Rome had formerly that relation to the whole Church which Roman Catholics now assign to it. My letter was directed to the point, that it was his duty not to perplex himself with arguments on [such] a question . . . and to put it altogether aside. . . . It is hard that I am put upon my memory, without knowing the details of the statement made against me, considering the various correspondence in which I am from time to time unavoidably engaged. . . . Be assured, my Lord, that there are very definite limits, beyond which persons like me would never urge another to retain preferment in the English Church, nor would retain it themselves; and that the censure which has been directed against them by so many of its Rulers has a very grave bearing upon those limits.

The Bishop replied in a civil letter, and sent my own letter to his original informant, who wrote to me the letter of a gentleman. It seems that an anxious lady had said something or other which had been misinterpreted, against her real meaning, into the calumny which was circulated, and so the report vanished into thin air. I closed the correspondence with the following Letter to the Bishop:

I hope your Lordship will believe me when I say, that statements about me, equally incorrect with that which has come to your Lordship's ears, are from time to time reported to me as credited and repeated by the highest authorities in our Church, though it is very seldom that I have the opportunity of denying them. I am obliged by your Lordship's letter to Dr Pusey as giving me such an opportunity.' Then I added, with a purpose, 'Your Lordship will observe that in my Letter I had no occasion to proceed to the question, whether a person holding Roman Catholic opinions can in honesty remain in our Church. Lest then any misconception should arise from my silence, I here take the liberty of adding, that I see nothing wrong in such a person's continuing in communion with us, provided he holds no preferment or office, abstains from the management of ecclesiastical matters, and is bound by no subscription or oath to our doctrines.

This was written on 8 March 1843, and was in anticipation of my own retirement into lay communion. This again leads me to a remark; for two years I was in lay communion, not indeed being a Catholic in my convictions, but in a state of serious doubt, and with the probable prospect of becoming some day, what as yet I was not. Under these circumstances I thought the best thing I could do was to give up duty and to throw myself into lay communion, remaining an Anglican. I could not go to Rome, while I thought what I did of the devotions she sanctioned to the Blessed Virgin and the Saints. I did not give up my fellowship, for I could not be sure that my doubts would not be reduced or overcome, however unlikely I might consider such an event. But I gave up my living; and, for two years before my conversion, I took no clerical duty. My last Sermon was in September, 1843; then I remained at Littlemore in quiet for two years. But it was made a subject of reproach to me at the time, and is at this day, that I did not leave the Anglican Church sooner. To me this seems a wonderful charge; why, even had I been quite sure that Rome was the true Church, the Anglican Bishops would have had no just subject of complaint against me, provided I took no Anglican oath, no clerical duty, no ecclesiastical administration. Do they force all men who go to their Churches to believe in the 39 Articles, or to join in the Athanasian Creed? However, I was to have other measure dealt to me; great authorities ruled it so; and a learned controversialist, Mr Stanley Faber, thought it a shame that I did not leave the Church of England as much as ten years sooner than I did. He said this in print between the years 1847 and 1849. His nephew, an Anglican clergyman, kindly wished to undeceive him on this point. So, in 1850, after some correspondence, I wrote the following letter, which will be of service to this narrative, from its chronological character:

> Dec. 6, 1849. Your uncle says, 'If he (Mr N.) will declare, sans phrase, as the French say, that I have laboured under an entire mistake, and that he was not a concealed Romanist

during the ten years in question,' (I suppose, the last ten years of my membership with the Anglican Church), 'or during any part of the time, my controversial antipathy will be at an end, and I will readily express to him that I am truly sorry that I have made such a mistake.'

So candid an avowal is what I should have expected from a mind like your uncle's. I am extremely glad he has brought it to this issue.

By a 'concealed Romanist' I understand him to mean one, who, professing to belong to the Church of England, in his heart and will intends to benefit the Church of Rome, at the expense of the Church of England. He cannot mean by the expression merely a person who in fact is benefiting the Church of Rome, while he is intending to benefit the Church of England, for that is no discredit to him morally, and he (your uncle) evidently means to impute blame.

In the sense in which I have explained the words, I can simply and honestly say that I was not a concealed Romanist during the whole, or any part of, the years in question.

For the first four years of the ten (up to Michaelmas, 1839), I honestly wished to benefit the Church of England, at the expense of the Church of Rome:

For the second four years I wished to benefit the Church of England without prejudice to the Church of Rome:

At the beginning of the ninth year (Michaelmas, 1843) I began to despair of the Church of England, and gave up all clerical duty; and then, what I wrote and did was influenced by a mere wish not to injure it, and not by the wish to benefit it:

At the beginning of the tenth year I distinctly contemplated leaving it, but I also distinctly told my friends that it was in my contemplation.

Lastly, during the last half of that tenth year I was engaged in writing a book (Essay on Development) in favour of the Roman Church, and indirectly against the English; but even then, till it was finished, I had not absolutely intended to publish it, wishing to reserve to myself the chance of changing my mind when the argumentative views which were actuating me had been distinctly brought out before me in writing.

I wish this statement, which I make from memory, and without consulting any document, severely tested by my writings and doings, as I am confident it will, on the whole, be borne out, whatever real or apparent exceptions (I suspect none) have to be allowed by me in detail.

Your uncle is at liberty to make what use he pleases of this explanation.

I have now reached an important date in my narrative, the year 1843, but before proceeding to the matters which it contains, I will insert portions of my letters from 1841 to 1843, addressed to Catholic acquaintances.

1. April 8, 1841. . . . The unity of the Church Catholic is very near my heart, only I do not see any prospect of it in our time; and I despair of its being effected without great sacrifices on all hands. As to resisting the Bishop's will, I observe that no point of doctrine or principle was in dispute, but a course of action, the publication of certain works. I do not think you sufficiently understood our position. I suppose you would obey the Holy See in such a case; now, when we were separated from the Pope, his authority reverted to our Diocesans. Our Bishop is our Pope. It is our theory, that each diocese is an integral Church, intercommunion being a duty (and the breach of it a sin), but not essential to Catholicity. To have resisted my Bishop, would have been to place myself in an utterly false position, which I never could have recovered. Depend upon it, the strength of any party lies in its being *true to its theory*. Consistency is the life of a movement.

I have no misgivings whatever that the line I have taken can be other than a prosperous one: that is, in itself, for of course Providence may refuse to us its legitimate issues for our sins.

I am afraid, that in one respect you may be disappointed. It is my trust, though I must not be too sanguine, that we shall not have individual members of our communion going over to yours. What one's duty would be under other circumstances, what our duty ten or twenty years ago, I cannot say; but I do think that there is less of private judgment in going with one's Church, than in leaving it. I can earnestly desire a union between my Church and yours. I cannot listen to the thought of your being joined by individuals among us.

2. April 26, 1841. My only anxiety is lest your branch of the Church should not meet us by those reforms which surely are *necessary*. It never could be, that so large a portion of

Christendom should have split off from the communion of Rome, and kept up a protest for 300 years for nothing. I think I never shall believe that so much piety and earnestness would be found among Protestants, if there were not some very grave errors on the side of Rome. To suppose the contrary is most unreal, and violates all one's notions of moral probabilities. All aberrations are founded on, and have their life in, some truth or other – and Protestantism, so widely spread and so long enduring, must have in it, and must be witness for, a great truth or much truth. That I am an advocate for Protestantism, you cannot suppose – but I am forced into a *Via Media*, short of Rome, as it is at present.

3. May 5, 1841.   While I most sincerely hold that there is in the Roman Church a traditionary system which is not necessarily connected with her essential formularies, yet, were I ever so much to change my mind on this point, this would not tend to bring me from my present position, providentially appointed in the English Church. That your communion was unassailable, would not prove that mine was indefensible. Nor would it at all affect the sense in which I receive our Articles; they would still speak against certain definite errors, though you had reformed them.

I say this lest any lurking suspicion should be left in the mind of your friends that persons who think with me are likely, by the growth of their present views, to find it imperative on them to pass over to your communion. Allow me to state strongly, that if you have any such thoughts, and proceed to act upon them, your friends will be committing a fatal mistake. We have (I trust) the principle and temper of obedience too intimately wrought into us to allow of our separating ourselves from our ecclesiastical superiors because in many points we may sympathize with others. We have too great a horror of the principle of private judgment to trust it in so immense a matter as that of changing from one communion to another. We may be cast out of our communion, or it may decree heresy to be truth – you shall say whether such contingencies are likely; but I do not see other conceivable causes of our leaving the Church in which we were baptized.

For myself, persons must be well acquainted with what I have written before they venture to say whether I have much

changed my main opinions and cardinal views in the course of
the last eight years. That my *sympathies* have grown towards
the religion of Rome I do not deny; that my *reasons* for
shunning her communion have lessened or altered it would be
difficult perhaps to prove. And I wish to go by reason, not by
feeling.

4. June 18, 1841. You urge persons whose views agree
with mine to commence a movement in behalf of a union
between the Churches. Now in the letters I have written, I have
uniformly said that I did not expect that union in our time, and
have discouraged the notion of all sudden proceedings with a
view to it. I must ask your leave to repeat on this occasion most
distinctly, that I cannot be party to any agitation, but mean to
remain quiet in my own place, and to do all I can to make others
take the same course. This I conceive to be my simple duty; but,
over and above this, I will not set my teeth on edge with sour
grapes. I know it is quite within the range of possibilities that
one or another of our people should go over to your communion; however, it would be a greater misfortune to you than
grief to us. If your friends wish to put a gulf between themselves
and us, let them make converts, but not else. Some months ago,
I ventured to say that I felt it a painful duty to keep aloof from
all Roman Catholics who came with the intention of opening
negotiations for the union of the Churches: when you now urge
us to petition our Bishops for a union, this, I conceive, is very
like an act of negotiation.

5. I have the first sketch or draft of a letter, which I wrote to a
zealous Catholic layman: it runs as follows, as far as I have
preserved it, but I think there were various changes and additions:

September 12, 1841. It would rejoice all Catholic minds
among us, more than words can say, if you could persuade
members of the Church of Rome to take the line in politics
which you so earnestly advocate. Suspicion and distrust are the
main causes at present of the separation between us, and the
nearest approaches in doctrine will but increase the hostility,
which, alas, our people feel towards yours, while these causes
continue. Depend upon it, you must not rely upon our Catholic
tendencies till they are removed. I am not speaking of myself, or
of any friends of mine; but of our Church generally. Whatever

our personal feelings may be, we shall but tend to raise and spread a *rival* Church to yours in the four quarters of the world, unless *you* do what none but you *can* do. Sympathies, which would flow over to the Church of Rome, as a matter of course, did she admit them, will but be developed in the consolidation of our own system, if she continues to be the object of our suspicions and fears. I wish, of course I do, that our own Church may be built up and extended, but still, not at the cost of the Church of Rome, not in opposition to it. I am sure, that, while you suffer, we suffer too from the separation; *but we cannot remove the obstacles*; it is with you to do so. You do not fear us; we fear you. Till we cease to fear you, we cannot love you.

While you are in your present position, the friends of Catholic unity in our Church are but fulfilling the prediction of those of your body who are averse to them, viz. that they will be merely stengthening a rival communion to yours. Many of you say that *we* are your greatest enemies; we have said so ourselves: so we are, so we shall be, as things stand at present. We are keeping people from you, by supplying their wants in our own Church. We *are* keeping persons from you: do you wish us to keep them from you for a time or for ever ? It rests with you to determine. I do not fear that you will succeed among us; you will not supplant our Church in the affections of the English nation; only through the English Church can you act upon the English nation. I wish of course our Church should be consolidated, with and through and in your communion, for its sake, and your sake, and for the sake of unity.

Are you aware that the more serious thinkers among us are used, as far as they dare form an opinion, to regard the spirit of Liberalism as the characteristic of the destined Antichrist ? In vain does any one clear the Church of Rome from the badges of Antichrist, in which Protestants would invest her, if she deliberately takes up her position in the very quarter, whither we have cast them, when we took them off from her. Antichrist is described as the *ἄνομος*, as exalting himself above the yoke of religion and law. The spirit of lawlessness came in with the Reformation, and Liberalism is its offspring.

And now I fear I am going to pain you by telling you, that you consider the approaches in doctrine on our part towards you, closer than they really are. I cannot help repeating what I have many times said in print, that your services and devotions to St Mary in matter of fact do most deeply pain me. I am only stating it as a fact.

Again, I have nowhere said that I can accept the decrees of Trent throughout, not implied it. The doctrine of Transubstantiation is a great difficulty with me, as being, as I think, not primitive. Nor have I said that our Articles in all respects admit of a Roman interpretation; the very word 'Transubstantiation' is disowned in them.

Thus, you see, it is not merely on grounds of expedience that we do not join you. There are positive difficulties in the way of it. And, even if there were not, we shall have no divine warrant for doing so, while we think that the Church of England is a branch of the true Church, and that intercommunion with the rest of Christendom is necessary, not for the life of a particular Church, but for its health only. I have never disguised that there are actual circumstances in the Church of Rome, which pain me much; of the removal of these I see no chance, while we join you one by one; but if our Church were prepared for a union, she might make her terms; she might gain the Cup; she might protest against the extreme honours paid to St Mary; she might make some explanation of the doctrine of Transubstantiation. I am not prepared to say that a reform in other branches of the Roman Church would be necessary for our uniting with them, however desirable in itself, so that we were allowed to make a reform in our own country. We do not look towards Rome as believing that its communion is infallible, but that union is a duty.

6. The following letter was occasioned by the present made to me of a book, by the friend to whom it is written; more will be said on the subject of it presently:

Nov. 22, 1842.   I only wish that your Church were more known among us by such writings. You will not interest us in her, till we see her, not in politics, but in her true functions of exhorting, teaching, and guiding. I wish there were a chance of making the leading men among you understand, what I believe is no novel thought to yourself. It is not by learned discussions, or acute arguments, or reports of miracles, that the heart of England can be gained. It is by men 'approving themselves', like the Apostle, 'ministers of Christ'.

As to your question, whether the Volume you have sent is not calculated to remove my apprehensions that another gospel is substituted for the true one in your practical instructions, before I can answer it in any way, I ought to know how far the Sermons which it comprises are *selected* from a number, or whether they are the whole, or such as the whole, which have been published of the author's. I assure you, or at least I trust, that, if it is ever clearly brought home to me that I have been wrong in what I have said on this subject, my public avowal of that conviction will only be a question of time with me.

If, however, you saw our Church as we see it, you would easily understand that such a change of feeling, did it take place, would have no necessary tendency, which you seem to expect, to draw a person from the Church of England to that of Rome. There is a divine life among us, clearly manifested, in spite of all our disorders, which is as great a note of the Church, as any can be. Why should we seek our Lord's presence elsewhere, when He vouchsafes it to us where we are? What *call* have we to change our communion?

Roman Catholics will find this to be the state of things in time to come, whatever promise they may fancy there is of a large secession to their Church. This man or that may leave us, but there will be no general movement. There is, indeed, an incipient movement of our *Church* towards yours, and this your leading men are doing all they can to frustrate by their unwearied efforts at all risks to carry off individuals. When will they know their position, and embrace a larger and wiser policy?

§ 2.

The letter which I have last inserted is addressed to my dear friend, Dr Russell, the present President of Maynooth. He had, perhaps, more to do with my conversion than any one else. He called upon me, in passing through Oxford in the summer of 1841, and I think I took him over some of the buildings of the University. He called again another summer, on his way from Dublin to London. I do not recollect that he said a word on the subject of religion on either occasion. He sent me at different times several letters; he was always gentle, mild, unobtrusive, uncontroversial. He let me alone. He also gave me one or two books. Veron's Rule of Faith and some Treatises of the Wallenburghs was one; a volume of St Alfonso Liguori's Sermons was another; and it is to those Sermons that my letter to Dr Russell relates.

Now it must be observed that the writings of St Alfonso, as I knew them by the extracts commonly made from them, prejudiced me as much against the Roman Church as any thing else, on account of what was called their 'Mariolatry'; but there was nothing of the kind in this book. I wrote to ask Dr Russell whether any thing had been left out in the translation; he answered that there certainly were omissions in one sermon about the Blessed Virgin. This omission, in the case of a book intended for Catholics, at least showed that such passages as are found in the works of Italian Authors were not acceptable to every part of the Catholic world. Such devotional manifestations in honour of our Lady had been my great *crux* as regards Catholicism; I say frankly, I do not fully enter into them now; I trust I do not love her the less, because I cannot enter into them. They may be fully explained and defended; but sentiment and taste do not run with logic: they are suitable for Italy, but they are not suitable for England. But, over and above England, my own case was special; from a boy I had been led to consider that my Maker and I, His creature, were the two beings, luminously such, *in rerum naturâ*. I will not here speculate, however about my own feelings. Only this I know full well now, and did not know then, that the Catholic Church allows no image of any sort, material or immaterial, no dogmatic symbol, no rite, no sacrament, no Saint, not even the Blessed Virgin herself, to come between the soul and its Creator. It is face to face, 'solus cum solo', in all matters between man and his God. He alone creates; He alone has redeemed; before His awful eyes we go in death; in the vision of Him is our eternal beatitude.

1. Solus cum solo – I recollect but indistinctly what I gained from the Volume of which I have been speaking; but it must have been something considerable. At least I had got a key to a difficulty; in these Sermons (or rather heads of sermons, as they seem to be, taken down by a hearer), there is much of what would be called legendary illustration; but the substance of them is plain, practical, awful preaching upon the great truths of salvation. What I can speak of with greater confidence is the effect produced on me a little later by studying the Exercises of St Ignatius. For here again, in a matter consisting in the purest and most direct acts

of religion – in the intercourse between God and the soul, during a season of recollection, of repentance, of good resolution, of inquiry into vocation – the soul was 'sola cum solo'; there was no cloud interposed between the creature and the Object of his faith and love. The command practically enforced was, 'My son, give Me thy Heart.' The devotions then to Angels and Saints as little interfered with the incommunicable glory of the Eternal, as the love which we bear our friends and relations, our tender human sympathies, are inconsistent with that supreme homage of the heart to the Unseen, which really does but sanctify and exalt, not jealously destroy, what is of earth. At a later date Dr Russell sent me a large bundle of penny or half-penny books of devotion, of all sorts, as they are found in the booksellers' shops at Rome; and, on looking them over, I was quite astonished to find how different they were from what I had fancied, how little there was in them to which I could really object. I have given an account of them in my Essay on the Development of Doctrine. Dr Russell sent me St Alfonso's book at the end of 1842; however, it was still a long time before I got over my difficulty, on the score of the devotions paid to the Saints; perhaps, as I judge, from a letter I have turned up, it was some way into 1844, before I could be said fully to have got over it.

2. I am not sure that I did not also at this time feel the force of another consideration did not also weigh with me then. The idea of the Blessed Virgin was as it were *magnified* in the Church of Rome, as time went on – but so were all the Christian ideas; as that of the Blessed Eucharist. The whole scene of pale, faint, distant Apostolic Christianity is seen in Rome, as through a telescope or magnifier. The harmony of the whole, however, is of course what it was. It is unfair then to take one Roman idea, that of the Blessed Virgin, out of what may be called its context.

3. Thus I am brought to the principle of development of doctrine in the Christian Church, to which I gave my mind at the end of 1842. I had made mention of it in the passage, which I quoted many pages back (vide p. 218), in Home Thoughts Abroad, published in 1836; and even at an earlier date I had introduced it into my History of the Arians in 1832; nor had I ever lost sight of it in my speculations. And it is certainly recognized in that celebrated Treatise of Vincent of Lerins, which has so often been taken as the basis of Anglicanism. In 1843 I began to consider it attentively; I made it the subject of my last University

Sermon on February 2; and the general view to which I came is stated thus in a letter to a friend of the date of July 14, 1844 – it will be observed that, now as before, my *issue* is still Creed *versus* Church:

> The kinds of consideration which weigh with me are such as the following – 1. I am far more certain (according to the Fathers) that we *are* in a state of culpable separation, *than* that developments do *not* exist under the Gospel, and that the Roman developments are not the true ones. 2. I am far more certain, that *our* (modern) doctrines are wrong, *than* that the *Roman* (modern) doctrines are wrong. 3. Granting that the Roman (special) doctrines are not found drawn out in the early Church, yet I think there is sufficient trace of them in it, to recommend and prove them, *on the hypothesis* of the Church having a divine guidance, though not sufficient to prove them by itself. So that the question simply turns on the nature of the promise of the Spirit, made to the Church. 4. The proof of the Roman (modern) doctrine is as strong (or stronger) in Antiquity, as that of certain doctrines which both we and Romans hold: e.g. there is more of evidence in Antiquity for the necessity of Unity, than for the Apostolical Succession; for the Supremacy of the See of Rome, than for the Presence in the Eucharist; for the practice of Invocation, than for certain books in the present Canon of Scripture, &c. &c. 5. The analogy of the Old Testament, and also of the New, leads to the acknowledgment of doctrinal developments.

4. And thus I was led on to a further consideration. I saw that the principle of development not only accounted for certain facts, but was in itself a remarkable philosophical phenomenon, giving a character to the whole course of Christian thought. It was discernible from the first years of the Catholic teaching up to the present day, and gave to that teaching a unity and individuality. It served as a sort of test, which the Anglican could not exhibit, that modern Rome was in truth ancient Antioch, Alexandria, and Constantinople, just as a mathematical curve has its own law and expression.

5. And thus again I was led on to examine more attentively what I doubt not was in my thoughts long before, viz. the concatenation of argument by which the mind ascends from its first to its final religious idea; and I came to the conclusion that

there was no medium, in true philosophy, between Atheism and Catholicity, and that a perfectly consistent mind, under those circumstances in which it finds itself here below, must embrace either the one or the other. And I hope this still: I am a Catholic by virtue of my believing in a God; and if I am asked why I believe in a God, I answer that it is because I believe in myself, for I feel it impossible to believe in my own existence (and of that fact I am quite sure) without believing also in the existence of Him, who lives as a Personal, All-seeing, All-judging Being in my conscience. Now, I dare say, I have not expressed myself with philosophical correctness, because I have not given myself to the study of what metaphysicians have said on the subject; but I think I have a strong true meaning in what I say which will stand examination.

6. Moreover, I found a corroboration of the fact of the logical connexion of Theism with Catholicism in a consideration parallel to that which I had adopted on the subject of development of doctrine. The fact of the operation from first to last of that principle of development in the truths of Revelation, is an argument in favour of the identity of Roman and Primitive Christianity; but as there is a law which acts upon the subject-matter of dogmatic theology, so is there a law in the matter of religious faith. In the third part of this narrative I spoke of certitude as the consequence, divinely intended and enjoined upon us, of the accumulative force of certain given reasons which, taken one by one, were only probabilities. Let it be recollected that I am historically relating my state of mind, at the period of my life which I am surveying. I am not speaking theologically, nor have I any intention of going into controversy, or of defending myself; but speaking historically of what I held in 1843–4, I say, that I believed in a God on a ground of probability, that I believed in Christianity on a probability, and that I believed in Catholicism on a probability, and that these three grounds of probability, distinct from each other of course in subject matter, were still all of them one and the same in nature of proof, as being probabilities – probabilities of a special kind, a cumulative, a transcendent probability but still probability; inasmuch as He who made us has so willed, that in mathematics indeed we should arrive at certitude by rigid demonstration, but in religious inquiry we should arrive at certitude by accumulated probabilities – He has willed, I say, that we should so act, and, as willing it, He co-operates with us in our acting, and thereby enables us to do that which He wills us to

do, and carries us on, if our will does but co-operate with His, to a certitude which rises higher than the logical force of our conclusions. And thus I came to see clearly, and to have a satisfaction in seeing, that, in being led on into the Church of Rome, I was not proceeding on any secondary or isolated grounds of reason, or by controversial points in detail, but was protected and justified, even in the use of those secondary or particular arguments, by a great and broad principle. But, let it be observed, that I am stating a matter of fact, not defending it; and if any Catholic says in consequence that I have been converted in a wrong way, I cannot help that now.

I have nothing more to say on the subject of the change in my religious opinions. On the one hand I came gradually to see that the Anglican Church was formally in the wrong, on the other that the Church of Rome was formally in the right; then, that no valid reasons could be assigned for continuing in the Anglican, and again that no valid objections could be taken to joining the Roman. Then, I had nothing more to learn; what still remained for my conversion, was, not further change of opinion, but to change opinion itself into the clearness and firmness of intellectual conviction.

Now I proceed to detail the acts, to which I committed myself during this last stage of my inquiry.

In 1843, I took two very significant steps – 1. In February, I made a formal Retractation of all the hard things which I had said against the Church of Rome. 2. In September, I resigned the Living of St Mary's, Littlemore included – I will speak of these two acts separately.

1. The words, in which I made my Retractation, have given rise to much criticism. After quoting a number of passages from my writings against the Church of Rome, which I withdrew, I ended thus:

> If you ask me how an individual could venture, not simply to hold, but to publish such views of a communion so ancient, so wide-spreading, so fruitful in Saints, I answer that I said to myself, 'I am not speaking my own words, I am but following almost a *consensus* of the divines of my own Church. They have ever used the strongest language against Rome, even the most able and learned of them. I wish to throw myself into their

system. While I say what they say, I am safe. Such views, too, are necessary for our position.' Yet I have reason to fear still, that such language is to be ascribed, in no small measure, to an impetuous temper, a hope of approving myself to persons I respect, and a wish to repel the charge of Romanism.

These words have been, and are, again and again cited against me, as if a confession that, when in the Anglican Church, I said things against Rome which I did not really believe.

For myself, I cannot understand how any impartial man can so take them; and I have explained them in print several times. I trust that by this time their plain meaning has been satisfactorily brought out by what I have said in former portions of this Narrative; still I have a word or two to say in addition to my former remarks upon them.

In the passage in question I apologize for *saying out* in controversy charges against the Church of Rome, which withal I affirm that I fully *believed* at the time when I made them. What is wonderful in such an apology ? There are surely many things a man may hold, which at the same time he may feel that he has no right to say publicly, and which it may annoy him that he has said publicly. The law recognizes this principle. In our own time, men have been imprisoned and fined for saying true things of a bad king. The maxim has been held, that, 'The greater the truth, the greater is the libel.' And so as to the judgment of society, a just indignation would be felt against a writer who brought forward wantonly the weaknesses of a great man, though the whole world knew that they existed. No one is at liberty to speak ill of another without a justifiable reason, even though he knows he is speaking truth, and the public knows it too. Therefore, though I believed what I said against the Roman Church, nevertheless I could not religiously speak it out, unless I was really justified, not only in believing ill, but in speaking ill. I did believe what I said on what I thought to be good reasons; but had I also a just cause for saying out what I believed ? I thought I had, and it was this, viz. that to say out what I believed was simply necessary in the controversy for self-defence. It was impossible to let it alone: the Anglican position could not be defended without assailing the Roman. In this, as in most cases of conflict, one party was right or the other, not both; and the best defence was to attack. Is not this almost a truism in the Roman controversy ? Is it not what every one says, who speaks on the subject at all ? does any serious man abuse the Church of Rome, for the sake of abusing her, or because that abuse justifies his own religious position ? What is the meaning of the very word 'Protestantism', but that there is a call to speak out ? This then is what I said; 'I know I spoke strongly against the Church of Rome; but it was no mere abuse, for I had a serious reason for doing so.'

But, not only did I think such language necessary for my Church's religious position, but I recollected that all the great Anglican divines had thought so before me. They had thought so, and they had acted accordingly. And therefore I observe in the passage in question, with much propriety, that I had not used strong language simply out of my own head, but that in doing so I was following the tract, or rather reproducing the teaching, of those who had preceded me.

I was pleading guilty to using violent language, but I was pleading also that there were extenuating circumstances in the case. We all know the story of the convict, who on the scaffold bit off his mother's ear. By doing so he did not deny the fact of his own crime, for which he was to hang; but he said that his mother's indulgence when he was a boy, had a good deal to do with it. In like manner I had made a charge, and I had made it *ex animo*; but I accused others of having, by their own example, led me into believing it and publishing it.

I was in a humour, certainly, to bite off their ears. I will freely confess, indeed I said it some pages back, that I was angry with the Anglican divines. I thought they had taken me in; I had read the Fathers with their eyes; I had sometimes trusted their quotations or their reasonings; and from reliance on them, I had used words or made statements, which by right I ought rigidly to have examined myself. I had thought myself safe, while I had their warrant for what I said. I had exercised more faith than criticism in the matter. This did not imply any broad misstatements on my part, arising from reliance on their authority, but it implied carelessness in matters of detail. And this of course was a fault.

But there was a far deeper reason for my saying what I said in this matter, on which I have not hitherto touched; and it was this— The most oppressive thought, in the whole process of my change of opinion, was the clear anticipation, verified by the event, that it would issue in the triumph of Liberalism. Against the Anti-dogmatic principle I had thrown my whole mind; yet now I was doing more than any one else could do, to promote it. I was one of those who had kept it at bay in Oxford for so many years; and thus my very retirement was its triumph. The men who had driven me from Oxford were distinctly the Liberals; it was they who had opened the attack upon Tract 90, and it was they who would gain a second benefit, if I went on to abandon the Anglican Church. But this was not all. As I have already said, there are but two alternatives, the way to Rome, and the way to Atheism: Anglicanism is the halfway house on the one side, and Liberalism is the halfway house on the other. How many men were there, as I knew full well, who would not follow me now in my advance from Anglicanism to Rome, but would at once leave Anglicanism and me for the Liberal camp. It is not at all easy (humanly speaking) to wind up an Englishman to a dogmatic level. I had done so in good measure, in the case both of young men and of laymen, the Anglican *Via Media* being the representative of dogma. The dogmatic and the Anglican principle were one, as I had taught them: but I was breaking the *Via Media* to pieces, and would not dogmatic faith altogether be broken up, in the minds of a great number, by the demolition of the *Via Media*? Oh! how unhappy this made me! I heard once from an eye-witness the account of a poor sailor whose legs were shattered by a ball, in the action off Algiers in 1816, and who was taken below for an operation. The surgeon and the chaplain persuaded him to have a leg off; it was done and the tourniquet applied to the wound. Then, they broke it to him that he must have the other off too. The poor fellow said, 'You should have told me that, gentlemen', and deliberately unscrewed the instrument and bled to death. Would not that be the case with many friends of my own? How could I ever hope to make them believe in a second theology, when I had cheated them in the first? with what face could I publish a new edition of a dogmatic creed, and ask them to receive it as gospel? Would it not be plain to them that no certainty was to be found any where? Well, in my defence I could but make a lame apology; however, it was the true one, viz. that I had not read the Fathers cautiously enough; that in such nice points, as those which determine the angle of divergence between the two Churches, I had made considerable miscalculations. But how came this about? Why, the fact was, unpleasant as it was to avow, that I had leaned too much upon the assertions of Ussher, Jeremy Taylor, or Barrow, and had been deceived by them. Valeat quantum – it was all that *could* be said. This then was a chief reason of that wording of the Retractation, which has given so much offence, because the bitterness, with which it was written, was not understood – and the following letter will illustrate it:

April 3, 1844.   I wish to remark on William's chief distress, that my changing my opinion seemed to unsettle one's confidence in truth and falsehood as external things, and led one to be suspicious of the new opinion as one became distrustful of the old. Now in what I shall say, I am not going to speak in favour of my second thoughts in comparison of my first, but against such scepticism and unsettlement about truth and falsehood generally, the idea of which is very painful.

The case with me, then, was this, and not surely an unnatural one – as a matter of feeling and of duty I threw myself into the system which I found myself in. I saw that the English Church had a theological idea or theory as such, and I took it up. I read Laud on Tradition, and thought it (as I still think it) very masterly. The Anglican Theory was very distinctive. I admired it and took it on faith. It did not (I think) occur to me to doubt it; I saw that it was able, and supported by learning, and I felt it was a duty to maintain it. Further, on looking into Antiquity and reading the Fathers, I saw such portions of it as I examined, fully confirmed (e.g. the supremacy of Scripture). There was only one question about which I had a doubt, viz. whether it would *work*, for it has never been more than a paper system. . . .

So far from my change of opinion having any fair tendency to unsettle persons as to truth and falsehood viewed as objective realities, it should be considered whether such change is not *necessary*, if truth be a real objective thing, and be made to confront a person who has been brought up in a system *short* of truth. Surely the *continuance* of a person, who wishes to go right, in a wrong system, and not his *giving it up*, would be that which militated against the objectiveness of Truth, leading, as it would, to the suspicion, that one thing and another were equally pleasing to our Maker, where men were sincere.

Nor surely is it a thing I need be sorry for, that I defended the system in which I found myself, and thus have had to unsay my words. For is it not one's duty, instead of beginning with criticism, to throw oneself generously into that form of religion which is providentially put before one? Is it right, or is it wrong, to begin with private judgment? May we not, on the other hand, look for a blessing *through* obedience even to an erroneous system, and a guidance even by means of it out of it? Were those who were strict and conscientious in their Judaism, or those who were lukewarm and sceptical, more likely to be led into Christianity, when Christ came? Yet in proportion to their previous zeal, would be their appearance of inconsistency. Certainly, I have always contended that obedience even to an erring conscience was the way to gain light, and that it mattered not where a man began, so that he began on what came to hand, and in faith; and that any thing might become a divine method of Truth; that to the pure all things are pure, and have a self-correcting virtue and a power of germinating. And though I have no right at all to assume that this mercy is granted to me, yet the fact, that a person in my situation *may* have it granted to him, seems to me to remove the perplexity which my change of opinion may occasion.

It may be said – I have said it to myself – 'Why, however, did you *publish*? had you waited quietly, you would have changed your opinion without any of the misery, which now is involved in the change, of disappointing and distressing people.' I answer, that things are so bound up together, as to form a whole, and one cannot tell what is or is not a condition of what. I do not see how possibly I could have published the Tracts, or other works professing to defend our Church, without accompanying them with a strong protest or argument against Rome. The one obvious objection against the whole Anglican line is, that it is Roman; so that I really think there was no alternative between silence altogether, and forming a theory and attacking the Roman system.

2. And now, in the next place, as to my Resignation of St Mary's, which was the second of the steps which I took in 1843. The ostensible, direct, and sufficient reason for my doing so was the persevering attack of the Bishops on Tract 90. I alluded to it in the letter which I have inserted above, addressed to one of the most influential among them. A series of their *ex cathedrâ* judgments, lasting through three years, and including a notice of no little severity in a Charge of my own Bishop, came as near to a condemnation of my Tract, and, so far, to a repudiation of the

ancient Catholic doctrine, which was the scope of the Tract, as was possible in the Church of England. It was in order to shield the Tract from such a condemnation, that I had at the time of its publication in 1841 so simply put myself at the disposal of the higher powers in London. At that time, all that was distinctly contemplated in the way of censure, was contained in the message which my Bishop sent me, that it was 'objectionable'. That I thought was the end of the matter. I had refused to suppress it, and they had yielded that point. Since I published the former portions of this narrative, I have found what I wrote to Dr Pusey on March 24, while the matter was in progress. 'The more I think of it,' I said, 'the more reluctant I am to suppress Tract 90, though *of course* I will do it if the Bishop wishes it; I cannot, however, deny that I shall feel it a severe act.' According to the notes which I took of the letters or messages which I sent to him in the course of that day, I presently wrote to him, 'My first feeling was to obey without a word; I will obey still; but my judgment has steadily risen against it ever since.' Then in the Postscript, 'If I have done any good to the Church, I do ask the Bishop this favour, as my reward for it, that he would not insist on a measure, from which I think good will not come. However, I will submit to him.' Afterwards, I got stronger still and wrote: 'I have almost come to the resolution, if the Bishop publicly intimates that I must suppress the Tract, or speaks strongly in his charge against it, to suppress it indeed, but to resign my living also. I could not in conscience act otherwise. You may show this in any quarter you please.'

All my then hopes, all my satisfaction at the apparent fulfilment of those hopes, was at an end in 1843. It is not wonderful then, that in May of that year, when two out of the three years were gone, I wrote on the subject of my retiring from St Mary's to the same friend, who I had consulted upon it in 1840. But I did more now; I told him my great unsettlement of mind on the question of the Churches. I will insert portions of two of my letters:

> May 4, 1843. . . . At present I fear, as far as I can analyze my own convictions, I consider the Roman Catholic Communion to be the Church of the Apostles, and that what grace is among us (which, through God's mercy, is not little) is extraordinary, and from the overflowings of His dispensation. I am very far more sure that England is in schism, than that the Roman

additions to the Primitive Creed may not be developments, arising out of a keen and vivid realizing of the Divine Depositum of Faith.

You will now understand what gives edge to the Bishops' Charges, without any undue sensitiveness on my part. They distress me in two ways – first, as being in some sense protests and witnesses to my conscience against my own unfaithfulness to the English Church, and next, as being samples of her teaching, and tokens how very far she is from even aspiring to Catholicity.

Of course my being unfaithful to a trust is my great subject of dread – as it has long been, as you know.

When he wrote to make natural objections to my purpose, such as the apprehension that the removal of clerical obligations might have the indirect effect of propelling me towards Rome, I answered:

May 18, 1843. . . . My office or charge at St Mary's is not a mere *state*, but a continual *energy*. People assume and assert certain things of me in consequence. With what sort of sincerity can I obey the Bishop ? how am I to act in the frequent cases, in which one way or another the Church of Rome comes into consideration ? I have to the utmost of my power tried to keep persons from Rome, and with some success; but even a year and a half since, my arguments, though more efficacious with the persons I aimed at than any others could be, were of a nature to infuse great suspicion of me into the minds of lookers-on.

By retaining St Mary's, I am an offence and a stumbling-block. Persons are keen-sighted enough to make out what I think on certain points, and then they infer that such opinions are compatible with holding situations of trust in our Church. A number of younger men take the validity of their interpreta-tion of the Articles, &c., from me on *faith*. Is not my present position a cruelty, as well as a treachery towards the Church ?

I do not see how I can either preach or publish again, while I hold St Mary's – but consider again the following difficulty in such a resolution, which I must state at some length.

Last Long Vacation the idea suggested itself to me of publishing the Lives of the English Saints; and I had a conversation with [a publisher] upon it. I thought it would be useful, as employing the minds of men who were in danger of running wild, bringing them from doctrine to history, and from speculation to fact – again, as giving them an interest in the English soil, and the English Church, and keeping them from seeking sympathy in Rome, as she is; and further, as tending to promote the spread of right views.

But, within the last month, it has come upon me, that, if the scheme goes on, it will be a practical carrying out of No. 90; from the character of the usages and opinions of ante-reformation times.

It is easy to say, 'Why *will* you do *any* thing? why won't you keep quiet? what business had you to think of such plan at all?' But I cannot leave a number of poor fellows in the lurch. I am bound to do my best for a great number of people both in Oxford and elsewhere. If *I* did not act, others would find means to do so.

Well, the plan has been taken up with great eagerness and interest. Many men are setting to work. I set down the names of men, most of them engaged, the rest half engaged and probable, some actually writing.

About thirty names follow, some of them at that time of the school of Dr Arnold, others of Dr Pusey's, some my personal friends and of my own standing, others whom I hardly knew, while of course the majority were of the party of the new Movement. I continue:

The plan has gone so far, that it would create surprise and talk, were it now suddenly given over. Yet how is it compatible with my holding St Mary's, being what I am?

Such was the object and the origin of the projected Series of the English Saints; and, since the publication was connected, as has been seen, with my resignation of St Mary's, I may be allowed to conclude what I have to say on the subject here, though it may read like a digression. As soon then as the first of the Series got into print, the whole project broke down. I had already anticipated that some portions of the Series would be written in a style inconsistent with the professions of a beneficed clergyman, and therefore I had given up my Living; but men of great weight went further in their misgivings than I, when they saw the Life of St Stephen Harding, and decided that it was of such a character as to be inconsistent even with its proceeding from an Anglican publisher: and so the scheme was given up at once. After the two first parts, I retired from the Editorship, and those Lives only were published in addition, which were then already finished, or in advanced preparation. The following passages from what I or others wrote at the time will illustrate what I have been saying:

In November 1844, I wrote thus to the author of one of them:

I am not Editor, I have no direct control over the Series. It is T.'s work; he may admit what he pleases; and exclude what he pleases. I was responsible for them, in the way in which an Editor is responsible. Had I continued Editor, I should have exercised a control over all. I laid down in the Preface that doctrinal subjects were, if possible, to be excluded. But, even then, I also set down that no writer was to be held answerable for any of the Lives but his own. When I gave up the Editorship, I had various engagements with friends for separate Lives remaining on my hands. I should have liked to have broken from them all, but there were some from which I could not break, and I let them take their course. Some have come to nothing; others like yours have gone on. I have seen such, either in MS or Proof. As time goes on, I shall have less and less to do with the Series. I think the engagement between you and me should come to an end. I have any how abundant responsibility on me, and too much. I shall write to T. that if he wants the advantage of your assistance, he must write to you direct.

In accordance with this letter, I had already advertised in January 1844, ten months before it, that 'other Lives', after St Stephen Harding, would 'be published by their respective authors on their own responsibility.' This notice was repeated in February, in the advertisement to the second volume entitled 'The Family of St Richard', though to this volume, for some reason which I cannot now recollect, I also put my initials. In the Life of St Augustine, the author, a man of nearly my own age, says in like manner, 'No one but himself is responsible for the way in which these materials have been used.' I have in MS another advertisement to the same effect, but I cannot tell whether it ever appeared in print.

I will add, since the authors have been considered 'hot-headed fanatic young men', whom I was in charge of and whom I suffered to do intemperate things, that, while the writer of St Augustine was in 1844 past forty, the author of the proposed Life of St Boniface, Mr Bowden, was forty-six; Mr Johnson, who was to write St Aldhelm, forty-three; and most of the others were on one side or other of thirty. Three, I think, were under twenty-five.

Moreover of these writers some became Catholics, some remained Anglicans, and others have professed what are called free or liberal opinions.

The immediate cause of the resignation of my Living is stated in the following letter, which I wrote to my Bishop:

> August 29. 1843. It is with much concern that I inform your Lordship, that Mr A. B., who has been for the last year an inmate of my house here, has just conformed to the Church of Rome. As I have ever been desirous, not only of faithfully discharging the trust, which is involved in holding a living in your Lordship's diocese, but of approving myself to your Lordship, I will for your information state one or two circumstances connected with this unfortunate event. . . . I received him on condition of his promising me, which he distinctly did, that he would remain quietly in our Church for three years. A year has passed since that time, and, though I saw nothing in him which promised that he would eventually be contented with his present position, yet for the time his mind became as settled as one could wish, and he frequently expressed his satisfaction at being under the promise which I had exacted of him.

I felt it impossible to remain any longer in the service of the Anglican Church, when such a breach of trust, however little I had to do with it, would be laid at my door. I wrote in a few days to a friend:

> September 7, 1843. I this day ask the Bishop leave to resign St Mary's. Men whom you little think, or at least whom I little thought, are in almost a hopeless way. Really we may expect any thing. I am going to publish a Volume of Sermons, including those Four against moving.

I resigned my living on September 18th. I had not the means of doing it legally at Oxford. The late Mr Goldsmid was kind enough to aid me in resigning it in London. I found no fault with the Liberals; they had beaten me in a fair field. As to the act of the Bishops, I thought, to borrow a scriptural image from Walter Scott that they had 'seethed the kid in his mother's milk'.

I said to a friend:

> Victrix causa diis placuit, sed victa Catoni.

And now I may be almost said to have brought almost to an end, as far as is necessary for a sketch such as this is, the history both of my changes of religious opinions, and of the public acts which they involved. I had only one final advance of mind to accomplish, and one final step to take. That further advance of mind was to be able honestly to say that I was *certain* of the conclusions at which I had already arrived. That further step, imperative when such certitude was attained, was my *submission* to the Catholic Church. And I had only one more act to perform, and that was the act of submission itself.

This submission did not take place till two full years after the resignation of my living in September 1843; nor could I have made it at an earlier day, without doubt and apprehension, that is, with any true conviction of mind or certitude.

In the interval, of which it remains to speak, viz. between the autumns of 1843 and 1845, I was in lay communion with the Church of England, attending its services as usual, and abstaining altogether from intercourse with Catholics, from their places of worship, and from those religious rites and usages, such as the Invocation of Saints, which are characteristics of their creed. I did all this on principle; for I never could understand how a man could be of two religions at once.

What then I now have to add is of a private nature, being my preparation for the great event, for which I was waiting. And I shall almost confine what I have to say about myself between these two autumns to this one point – the difficulty I was in, as to the best mode of revealing the state of my mind to my friends and others, and how I managed to reveal it.

Up to January 1842, I had not disclosed my state of unsettlement to more than three persons, as has been mentioned above, and as is repeated in the course of the letters which I am now about to give to the reader. To two of them, intimate and familiar companions, in the Autumn of 1839: to the third, an old friend too, whom I have also named above, I suppose, when I was in great distress of mind upon the affair of the Jerusalem Bishopric. In May 1843, I made it known, as has been seen, to the friend, by whose advice I wished, as far as possible, to be guided. To mention it on set purpose to any one, unless indeed I was asking advice, I should have felt to be a crime. If there is any thing that was abhorrent to me, it was the scattering doubts, and unsettling consciences without necessity. A strong presentiment that my existing opinions would ultimately give way, and that the grounds of them were unsound, was not a sufficient warrant for disclosing the state of my mind. I had no guarantee yet, that that presentiment would be realized. Supposing I were crossing ice, which came right in my way, which I had good reasons for considering sound, and which I saw numbers before me crossing in safety, and supposing a stranger from the bank, in a voice of authority, and in an earnest tone, warned me that it was dangerous, and then was silent, I think I should be startled, and should look about me anxiously, but I think too that I should go on, till I had better grounds for doubt; and such was my state, I believe, till the end of 1842. Then again, when my dissatisfaction became greater, it was hard at first to determine the point of time, when it was too strong to suppress with propriety. Certitude of course is a point, but doubt is a progress; I was not near certitude yet. Certitude is a reflex action; it is to know that one knows. Of that I believe I was not possessed, till close upon my reception into the Catholic Church. Again, a practical, effective doubt is a point too, but who can easily ascertain it for himself? Who can determine when it is, that the scales in the balance of opinion begin to turn, and what was a greater probability in behalf of a belief becomes a positive doubt against it?

In considering this question in its bearing upon my conduct in 1843, my own simple answer to my great difficulty had been, *Do* what your present state of opinion requires in the light of duty, and let that *doing* tell: speak by *acts*. This I had done; my first *act* of the year had been in February. After three months' deliberation I had published my retractation of the violent charges which I had made against Rome: I could not be wrong in doing so much as this; but I did no more at the time: I did not retract my Anglican teaching. My second *act* had been in September in the same year; after much sorrowful lingering and hesitation, I had resigned my Living. I tried indeed, before I did so, to keep Littlemore for myself, even though it was still to remain an integral part of St Mary's. I had given to it a Church and a sort of Parsonage; I had made it a Parish, and I loved it; I thought in 1843 that perhaps I need not forfeit my existing relations towards it. I could indeed submit to become the curate at will of another, but I hoped still that an arrangement was possible, by which, while I had the curacy, I might have been my own master in serving it. I had hoped an exception might have been made in my favour, under the circumstances; but I did not gain my request. Perhaps I was asking what was impracticable, and it is well for me that it was so.

These had been my two acts of the year, and I said, 'I cannot be wrong in making them; let that follow which must follow in the thoughts of the world about me, when they see what I do.' And, as time went on, they fully answered my purpose. What I felt it a simple duty to do, did create a general suspicion about me, without such responsibility as would be involved in my initiating any direct act for the sake of creating it. Then, when friends wrote me on the subject, I either did not deny or I confessed my state of mind, according to the character and need of their letters. Sometimes in the case of intimate friends, whom I should otherwise have been leaving in ignorance of what others knew on every side of them, I invited the question.

And here comes in another point for explanation. While I was fighting in Oxford for the Anglican Church, then indeed I was very glad to make converts, and, though I never broke away from that rule of my mind (as I may call it), of which I have already spoken, of finding disciples rather than seeking them, yet, that I made advances to others in a special way, I have no doubt; this came to an end, however, as soon as I fell into misgivings as to the true ground to be taken in the controversy. For then, when I gave up my place in the Movement, I ceased from any such proceedings: and my utmost endeavour was to tranquillize such persons, especially those who belonged to the new school, as were unsettled in their religious views, and, as I judged, hasty in their conclusions. This went on till 1843; but, at that date, as soon as I turned my face Romeward, I gave up, as far as ever was possible, the thought of in any respect and in any shape acting upon others. Then I myself was simply my own concern. How could I in any sense direct others, who had to be guided in so momentous a matter myself? How could I be considered in a position, even to say a word to them one way or the other? How could I presume to unsettle them, as I was unsettled, when I had no means of bringing them out of such unsettlement? And, if they were unsettled already, how could I point to them a place of refuge, when I was not sure that I should choose it for myself? My only line, my only duty, was to keep simply to my own case. I recollected Pascal's words, 'Je mourrai seul.' I deliberately put out of my thoughts all other works and claims, and said nothing to any one, unless I was obliged.

But this brought upon me a great trouble. In the newspapers there were continual reports about my intentions; I did not answer them; presently strangers or friends wrote, begging to be allowed to answer them; and, if I still kept to my resolution and said nothing, then I was thought to be mysterious, and a prejudice was excited against me. But, what was far worse, there were a number of tender, eager hearts, of whom I knew nothing at all, who were watching me, wishing to think as I thought, and to do as I did, if they could but find it out; who in consequence were distressed, that, in so solemn a matter, they could not see what was coming, and who heard reports about me this way or that, on a first day and on a second; and felt the weariness of waiting, and the sickness of delayed hope, and did not understand that I was as perplexed as they were and, being of more sensitive complexion of mind than myself, were made ill by the suspense. And they too of course for the time thought me mysterious and inexplicable. I ask their pardon as far as I was really unkind to them. There was a gifted and deeply earnest lady, who in a parabolical account of that time, has described both my conduct as she felt it, and that of such as herself. In a singularly graphic, amusing vision of pilgrims, who were making their way across a bleak common in great discomfort, and who were ever warned against, yet continually nearing, 'the king's highway' on the right, she says, 'All my fears and disquiets were speedily renewed by seeing the most daring of our leaders (the same who had first forced his way through the palisade, and in whose courage and sagacity we all put implicit trust) suddenly stop short, and declare that he would go on no further. He did not, however, take the leap at once, but quietly sat down on the top of the fence with his feet hanging towards the road, as if he meant to take his time about it, and let himself down easily.' I do not wonder at all that I thus seemed so unkind to a lady, who at that time had never seen me. We were both in trial in our different ways. I am far from denying that I was acting selfishly both in her case and in that of others; but it was a religious selfishness. Certainly to myself my own duty seemed clear. That they are whole can heal others; but in my case it was, 'Physician heal thyself'. My own soul was my first concern, and it seemed an absurdity to my reason to be converted in partnership. I wished to go to my Lord by myself, and in my own way, or rather His way. I had neither wish, nor, I may say, thought of taking a number with me. Moreover, it is but the truth to say, that it had ever been an annoyance to me to seem to be the head of a party; and that even from fastidiousness of mind, I could not bear to find a thing done elsewhere, simply or mainly because I did it myself, and that, from distrust of myself, I shrank from the thought, whenever it was brought home to me, that I was influencing others. But nothing of this could be known to the world.

The following three letters are written to a friend who had every claim upon me to be frank with him, Archdeacon Manning – it will be seen that I disclose the real state of my mind to him, in proportion as he presses me.

1. October 14, 1843. I would tell you in a few words why I have resigned St Mary's, as you seem to wish, were it possible to do so. But it is most difficult to bring out in brief, or even *in extenso*, any just view of my feelings and reasons.

The nearest approach I can give to a general account of them is to say, that it has been caused by the general repudiation of the view, contained in No. 90, on the part of the Church. I could not stand against such an unanimous expression of opinion from the Bishops, supported, as it has been, by the concurrence, or at least silence, of all classes in the Church, lay and clerical. If there ever was a case, in which an individual teacher has been put aside and virtually put away by a community, mine is one. No decency has been observed in the attacks upon me from authority; no protests have been offered against them. It is felt – I am far from denying, justly felt – that I am a foreign material, and cannot assimilate with the Church of England.

Even my own Bishop has said that my mode of interpreting the Articles makes them mean *any thing or nothing*. When I heard this delivered, I did not believe my ears. I denied to others that it was said . . . Out came the charge, and the words could not be mistaken. This astonished me the more, because I published that Letter to him (how unwillingly you know), on the understanding that *I* was to deliver his judgment on No. 90 *instead* of him. A year elapses, and a second, and heavier judgment came forth. I did not bargain for this – nor did he, but the tide was too strong for him.

I fear that I must confess, that, in proportion as I think the English Church is showing herself intrinsically and radically alien from Catholic principles, so do I feel the difficulties of defending her claims to be a branch of the Catholic Church. It seems a dream to call a communion Catholic, when one can neither appeal to any clear statement of Catholic doctrine in its formularies, nor interpret ambiguous formularies by the received and living Catholic sense, whether past or present. Men of Catholic views are too truly but a party in our Church. I cannot deny that many other independent circumstances, which it is not worth while entering into, have led me to the same conclusion.

I do not say all this to every body, as you may suppose; but I do not like to make a secret of it to you.

2. Oct. 25, 1843. You have engaged in a dangerous correspondence; I am deeply sorry for the pain I shall give you.

I must tell you then frankly (but I combat arguments which to me, alas, are shadows), that it is not from disappointment, irritation, or impatience, that I have, whether rightly or wrongly, resigned St Mary's; but because I think the Church of Rome the Catholic Church, and ours not part of the Catholic Church, because not in communion with Rome; and because I feel that I could not honestly be a teacher in it any longer.

This thought came to me last summer four years . . . I mentioned it to two friends in the autumn . . . It arose in the first instance from the Monophysite and Donatist controversies, the former of which I was engaged with in the course of theological study to which I had given myself. This was at a time when no Bishop, I believe, had declared against us, and when all was progress and hope. I do not think I have ever felt disappointment or impatience, certainly not then; for I never looked forward to the future, nor do I realize it now.

My first effort was to write that article on the Catholicity of the English Church; for two years it quieted me. Since the summer of 1839 I have written little or nothing on modern controversy . . . You know how unwillingly I wrote my letter to the Bishop in which I committed myself again, as the safest course under circumstances. The article I speak of quieted me till the end of 1841, over the affair of No. 90, when that wretched Jerusalem Bishopric (no personal matter) revived all my alarms. They have increased up to this moment. At that time I told my secret to another person in addition.

You see then that the various ecclesiastical and quasi-ecclesiastical acts, which have taken place in the course of the last two years and a half, are not the *cause* of my state of opinion, but are keen stimulants and weighty confirmations of a conviction forced upon me, while engaged in the *course of duty*, viz. that theological reading to which I had given myself. And this last-mentioned circumstance is a fact, which has never, I think, come before me till now that I write to you.

It is three years since, on account of my state of opinion, I urged the Provost in vain to let St Mary's be separated from Littlemore; thinking I might with a safe conscience serve the latter, though I could not comfortably continue in so public a place as a University. This was before No. 90.

Finally, I have acted under advice, and that, not of my own choosing, but what came to me in the way of duty, nor the advice of those only who agree with me, but of near friends who differ from me.

I have nothing to reproach myself with, as far as I see, in the matter of impatience; i.e. practically or in conduct. And I trust that He, who has kept me in the slow course of change hitherto, will keep me still from hasty acts, or resolves with a doubtful conscience.

This I am sure of, that such interposition as yours, kind as it is, only does what *you* would consider harm. It makes me realize my own views to myself; it makes me see their consistency; it assures me of my own deliberateness; it suggests to me the traces of a Providential Hand; it takes away the pain of disclosures; it relieves me of a heavy secret.

You may make what use of my letters you think right.

3. My correspondent wrote to me once more, and I replied thus:

October 31, 1843.   Your letter has made my heart ache more, and caused me more and deeper sighs than any I have had a long while, though I assure you there is much on all sides of me to cause sighing and heart-ache. On all sides — I am quite haunted by the one dreadful whisper repeated from so many quarters, and causing the keenest distress to friends. You know but a part of my present trial, in knowing that I am unsettled myself.

Since the beginning of this year I have been obliged to tell the state of my mind to some others; but never, I think, without being in a way obliged, as from friends writing to me as you did, or guessing how matters stood. No one in Oxford knows it or here [Littlemore], but one near friend whom I felt I could not help telling the other day. But, I suppose, many more suspect it.

On receiving these letters, my correspondent, if I recollect rightly, at once communicated the matter of them to Dr Pusey, and this will enable me to describe as nearly as I can, the way in which he first became aware of my changed state of opinion.

I had from the first a great difficulty in making Dr Pusey understand such differences of opinion as existed between himself and me. When there was a proposal about the end of 1838 for a subscription for a Cranmer Memorial, he wished us both to subscribe together to it. I could not, of course, and wished him to subscribe by himself. That he would not do; he could not bear the thought of our appearing to the world in separate positions, in a matter of importance. And, as time went on, he would not take any hints, which I gave him, on the subject of my growing inclination to Rome. When I found him so determined, I often had not the heart to go on. And then I knew, that, from affection to me, he so often took up and threw himself into what I said, that I felt the great responsibility I should incur, if I put things before him just as I might view them myself. And, not knowing him so well as I did afterwards, I feared lest I should unsettle him. And moreover, I recollected well, how prostrated he had been with illness in 1832, and I used always to think that the start of the Movement had given him a fresh life. I fancied that his physical energies even depended on the presence of a vigorous hope and bright prospects for his imagination to feed upon; so much so, that when he was so unworthily treated by the authorities of the place in 1843, I recollect writing to the late Mr Dodsworth to state my anxiety, lest, if his mind became dejected in consequence, his health should suffer seriously also. These were difficulties in my way; and then again, another difficulty was, that, as we were not together under the same roof, we only saw each other at set times; others indeed, who were coming in or out of my rooms freely, and according to the need of the moment, knew all my thoughts easily; but for him to know them well, formal efforts were necessary. A common friend of ours broke it all to him in 1841, as far as matters had gone at that time, and showed him clearly the logical conclusions which must lie in propositions to which I had committed myself; but somehow or other in a little while, his mind fell back into its former happy state, and he could not bring himself to believe that he and I should not go on pleasantly together to the end. But that affectionate dream needs must have been broken at last; and two years afterwards, that friend to whom I wrote the letters which I have just now inserted, set himself, as I have said, to break it. Upon that, I too begged Dr Pusey to tell in private to any one he would, that I thought in the event I should leave the Church of England. However, he would not do so; and at the end of 1844 had almost relapsed into his former thoughts about me, if I may judge from a letter of his which I have found. Nay, at the Commemoration of 1845, a few months before I left the Anglican Church, I think he said about me to a friend, 'I trust after all we shall keep him.'

In that autumn of 1843, at the time that I spoke to Dr Pusey, I asked another friend also to communicate in confidence, to whom he would, the prospect which lay before me.

To another friend, Mr James Hope, now Mr Hope Scott, I gave the opportunity of knowing it, if he would, in the following Postscript to a letter:

> While I write, I will add a word about myself. You may come near a person or two who, owing to circumstances, know more exactly my state of feeling than you do, though they would not tell you. Now I do not like that you should not be aware of this, though I see no *reason* why you should know what they happen to know. Your wishing it would *be* a reason.

I had a dear and old friend, near his death; I never told him my state of mind. Why should I unsettle that sweet calm tranquillity, when I had nothing to offer him instead ? I could not say, 'Go to Rome'; else I should have shown him the way. Yet I offered myself for his examination. One day he led the way to my speaking out; but, rightly or wrongly, I could not respond. My reason was, 'I have no certainty on the matter myself. To say "I think" is to tease and to distress, not to persuade.'

I wrote to him on Michaelmas Day, 1843:

> As you may suppose, I have nothing to write to you about, pleasant. I *could* tell you some very painful things; but it is best not to anticipate trouble, which after all can but happen, and, for what one knows, may be averted. You are always so kind, that sometimes, when I part with you, I am nearly moved to tears, and it would be a relief to be so, at your kindness and at my hardness. I think no one ever had such kind friends as I have.

The next year, 22 January, I wrote to him: 'Pusey has quite

enough on him, and generously takes on himself more than enough, for me to add burdens when I am not obliged; particularly too, when I am very conscious, that there *are* burdens, which I am or shall be obliged to lay upon him some time or other, whether I will or no.'

And on February 21:

> Half-past ten. I am just up, having a bad cold: the like has not happened to me (except twice in January) in my memory. You may think you have been in my thoughts, long before my rising. Of course you are so continually, as you well know. I could not come to see you; I am not worthy of friends. With my opinions, to the full of which I dare not confess, I feel like a guilty person with others, though I trust I am not so. People kindly think that I have much to bear externally, disappointment, slander, &c. No, I have nothing to bear, but the anxiety which I feel for my friends' anxiety for me, and their perplexity. This [letter] is a better Ash-Wednesday than birthday present; [his birthday was the same day as mine; it was Ash-Wednesday that year]; but I cannot help writing about what is uppermost. And now, my dear A., all kindness and best wishes to you, my oldest friend, whom I must not speak more about, and with reference to myself, lest you should be angry.

It was not in his nature to have doubts: he used to look at me with anxiety, and wonder what had come over me.

On Easter Monday:

> All that is good and gracious descend upon you and yours from the influences of this Blessed Season; and it will be so (so be it!) for what is the life of you all, as day passes after day, but a simple endeavour to serve Him, from whom all blessing comes ? Though we are separated in place, yet this we have in common, that you are living a calm and cheerful time, and I am enjoying the thought of you. It is your blessing to have a clear heaven, and peace around, according to the blessing pronounced on Benjamin. So it is, my dear A., and so may it ever be.

He was in simple good faith. He died in September that year. I had expected that his last illness would have brought light to my mind, as to what I ought to do. It brought none. I made a note, which runs thus: 'I sobbed bitterly over his coffin, to think that he left me still dark as to what the way of truth was, and what I ought to do in order to please God and fulfil His will.' I think I wrote to Charles Marriott to say, that at that moment, with the thought of my friend before me, my strong view in favour of Rome remained just what it was. On the other hand, my firm belief that grace was to be found within the Anglican Church remained too.[1] I wrote to another friend thus:

> Sept. 16, 1844. I am full of wrong and miserable feelings, which it is useless to detail, so grudging and sullen, when I should be thankful. Of course, when one sees so blessed an end, and that, the termination of so blameless a life, of one who really fed on our ordinances and got strength from them, and see the same continued in a whole family, the little children finding quite a solace of their pain in the Daily Prayer, it is impossible not to feel more at ease in our Church, as at least a sort of Zoar, a place of refuge and temporary rest, because of the steepness of the way. Only, may we be kept from unlawful security, lest we have Moab and Ammon for our progeny, the enemies of Israel.

I could not continue in this state, either in the light of duty or of reason. My difficulty was this: I had been deceived greatly once; how could I be sure that I was not deceived a second time? I thought myself right then; how was I to be certain that I was right now? How many years had I thought myself sure of what I now rejected? how could I ever again have confidence in myself? As in 1840 I listened to the rising doubt in favour of Rome, now I listened to the waning doubt in favour of the Anglican Church. To be certain is to know that one knows; what inward test had I, that I should not change again, after that I had become a Catholic? I had still apprehension of this, though I thought a time would come, when it would depart. However, some limit ought to be put to these vague misgivings; I must do my best and then leave it to a higher Power to prosper it. So, at the end of 1844. I came to the resolution of writing an Essay on Doctrinal Development; and then, if, at the end of it, my convictions in favour of the Roman Church were not weaker, of taking the necessary steps for admission into her fold. I acted upon this resolution in the

---

[1] On this subject, vid. my Third Lecture on 'Anglican Difficulties', also Note E, *Anglican Church*. (*This footnote did not appear in the original pamphlet.*)

beginning of 1845, and worked at my Essay steadily into the autumn.

I told my resolution to various friends at the beginning of the year; indeed, by this time the state of my mind was generally known, and I made no great secret of it. I will illustrate it by letters of mine which have been put into my hands.

November 16, 1844. I am going through what must be gone through; and my trust only is that every day of pain is so much taken from the necessary draught which must be exhausted. There is no fear (humanly speaking) of my moving for a long time yet. This has got out without my intending it; but it is all well. As far as I know myself, my one great distress is the perplexity, unsettlement, alarm, scepticism, which I am causing to so many; and the loss of kind feeling and good opinion on the part of so many, known and unknown, who have wished well to me. And of these two sources of pain it is the former that is the constant, urgent, unmitigated one. I had for days a literal ache all about my heart; and from time to time all the complaints of the Psalmist seemed to belong to me.

And as far as I know myself, my one paramount reason for contemplating a change is my deep, unvarying conviction that our Church is in schism, and that my salvation depends on my joining the Church of Rome. I may use *argumenta ad hominem* to this person or that; but I am not conscious of resentment, or disgust, at any thing that has happened to me. I have no visions whatever of hope, no schemes of action, in any other sphere more suited to me. I have no existing sympathies with Roman Catholics; I hardly ever, even abroad, was at one of their services; I know none of them, I do not like what I hear of them.

And then, how much I am giving up in so many ways! and to me sacrifices irreparable, not only from my age, when people hate changing, but from my especial love of old associations and the pleasures of memory. Nor am I conscious of any feeling, enthusiastic or heroic, of pleasure in the sacrifice; I have nothing to support me here.

What keeps me yet is what has kept me long; a fear that I am under a delusion; but the conviction remains firm under all circumstances, in all frames of mind. And this most serious feeling is growing on me; viz. that the reasons for which I believe as much as our system teaches, *must* lead me to believe more, and that not to believe more is to fall back into scepticism.

A thousand thanks for your most kind and consoling letter; though I have not yet spoken of it, it was a great gift.

Shortly after I wrote to the same friend thus:

My intention is, if nothing comes upon me, which I cannot foresee, to remain quietly *in statu quo* for a considerable time, trusting that my friends will kindly remember me and my trial in their prayers. And I should give up my fellowship some time before any thing further took place.

One very dear friend, now no more, Charles Marriott, sent me a letter at the beginning of the next year, from which, from love of him, I quote some sentences:

January 15, 1845. You know me well enough to be aware, that I never see through any thing at first. Your letter to B. casts a gloom over the future, which you can understand, if you have understood me, as I believe you have. But I may speak out at once, of what I see and feel at once, and doubt not that I shall ever feel: that your whole conduct towards the Church of England and towards us, who have striven and are still striving to seek after God for ourselves, and to revive true religion among others, under her authority and guidance, has been generous and considerate, and, were that word appropriate, dutiful, to a degree that I could scarcely have conceived possible, more unsparing of self than I should have thought nature could sustain. I have felt with pain every link that you have severed, and I have asked no questions, because I felt that you ought to measure the disclosure of your thoughts according to the occasion, and the capacity of those to whom you spoke. I write in haste, in the midst of engagements engrossing in themselves, but partly made tasteless, partly embittered by what I have heard; but I am willing to trust even you, whom I love best on earth, in God's Hand, in the earnest prayer that you may be so employed as is best for the Holy Catholic Church.

There was a lady, who was very anxious on the subject, and I wrote to her the following letters:

1. October, 1844. What can I say more to your purpose? If

you will ask me any specific questions, I will answer them, as far as I am able.

2. November 7, 1844.   I am still where I was; I am not moving. Two things, however, seem plain, that every one is prepared for such an event, next, that every one expects it of me. Few indeed, who do not think it suitable, fewer still, who do not think it likely. However, I do not think it either suitable or likely. I have very little reason to doubt about the issue of things, but the when and the how are known to Him, from whom, I trust, both the course of things and the issue come. The expression of opinion, and the latent and habitual feeling about me, which is on every side and among all parties, has great force. I insist upon it, because I have a great dread of going by my own feelings, lest they should mislead me. By one's sense of duty one must go; but external facts support one in doing so.

3. January 8, 1845.   What am I say in answer to your letter ? I know perfectly well, I ought to let you know more of my feelings and state of mind than you do know. But how is that possible in a few words ? Any thing I say must be abrupt; nothing can I say which will not leave a bewildering feeling, as needing so much to explain it, and being isolated, and (as it were) unlocated, and not having any thing with it to show its bearings upon other parts of the subject.

   At present, My full belief is, in accordance with your letter, that, if there is a move in our Church, very few persons indeed will be partners to it. I doubt whether one or two at the most among residents at Oxford. And I don't know whether I can wish it. The state of the Roman Catholics is at present so unsatisfactory. This I am sure of, that nothing but a simple, direct call of duty is a warrant for any one leaving our Church; no preference of another Church, no delight in its services, no hope of greater religious advancement in it, no indignation, no disgust, at the persons and things, among which we may find ourselves in the Church of England. The simple question is, Can *I* (it is personal, not whether another, but can *I*) be saved in the English Church ? am *I* in safety, were I to die tonight ? Is it a mortal sin in *me*, not joining another communion ? P.S. I hardly see my way to concur in attendance, though occasional, in the Roman Catholic chapel, unless a man has made up his mind pretty well to join it eventually. Invocations are not *required* in the Church of Rome; somehow, I do not like using them except under the sanction of the Church, and this makes me unwilling to admit them in members of our Church.

4. March 30.   Now I will tell you more than any one knows except two friends. My own convictions are as strong, as I suppose they can become: only it is so difficult to know whether it is a call of *reason* or of conscience. I cannot make out, if I am impelled by what seems *clear*, or by a sense of *duty*. You can understand how painful this doubt is; so I have waited, hoping for light, and using the words of the Psalmist, 'Show some token upon me.' But I suppose I have no right to wait for ever for this. Then I am waiting, because friends are most considerately bearing me in mind, and asking guidance for me; and, I trust, I should attend to any new feelings which came upon me, should that be the effect of their kindness. And then this waiting subserves the purpose of preparing men's minds. I dread shocking, unsettling people. Any how, I can't avoid giving incalculable pain. So, if I had my will, I should like to wait till the summer of 1846, which would be a full seven years from the time that my convictions first began to fall on me. But I don't think I shall last so long.

My present intention is to give up my Fellowship in October, and to publish some work or treatise between that and Christmas. I wish people to know *why* I am acting, as well as *what* I am doing; it takes off that vague and distressing surprise, 'What *can* have made him?'.

5. June 1.   What you tell me of yourself makes it plain that it is your duty to remain quietly and patiently, till you see more clearly where you are; else you are leaping in the dark.

In the early part of this year, if not before, there was an idea afloat that my retirement from the Anglican Church was owing to the feeling that I had so been thrust aside, without any one's taking my part. Various measures were, I believe, talked of in consequence of this surmise. Coincidentally with it appeared an exceedingly kind article about me in a Quarterly, in its April number. The writer praised me in feeling and beautiful language far above my deserts. In the course of his remarks, he said, speaking of me as Vicar of St Mary's: 'He had the future race of clergy hearing him. Did he value and feel tender about, and cling to his position ? . . . Not at all . . . No sacrifice to him perhaps, he did not care about such things.'

There was a censure implied, however covertly, in these words; and it is alluded to in the following letter, addressed to a very intimate friend:

> April 3, 1845. . . . Accept this apology, my dear Church, and forgive me. As I say so, tears come into my eyes – that arises from the accident of this time, when I am giving up so much I love. Just now I have been overset by James Mozley's article in the *Christian Rememberancer*; yet really, my dear Church, I have never for an instant had even the temptation of repenting my leaving Oxford. The feeling of repentance has not even come into my mind. How could it ? How could I remain at St Mary's a hypocrite ? how could I be answerable for souls (and life so uncertain), with the convictions, or at least persuasions, which I had upon me ? It is indeed a responsibility to act as I am doing; and I feel His hand heavy on me without intermission, who is all Wisdom and Love, so that my heart and mind are tired out, just as the limbs might be from a load on one's back. That sort of dull aching pain is mine; but my responsibility really is nothing to what it would be, to be answerable for souls, for confiding loving souls, in the English Church, with my convictions. My love to Marriott, and save me the pain of sending him a line.

In July a Bishop thought it worth while to give out to the world that 'the adherents of Mr Newman are few in number. A short time will now probably suffice to prove this fact. It is well known that he is preparing for secession; and, when that event takes place, it will be seen how few will go with him.'

I am now close upon the date of my reception into the Catholic Church; and have reserved for this place some sentences from a letter addressed to me at the beginning of the year by a very dear friend, now no more, Charles Marriott. I quote them for the love which I bear him, and the value that I set on his good word.

> January 15, 1845.   You know me well enough to be aware, that I never see through any thing at first. Your letter to Badeley casts a gloom over the future, which you can understand, if you

have understood me, as I believe you have. But I may speak out at once, of what I see and feel at once, and doubt not that I shall ever feel: that your whole conduct towards the Church of England and towards us, who have striven and are still striving to seek after God for ourselves, and to revive true religion among others, under her authority and guidance, has been generous and considerate, and, were that word appropriate, dutiful, to a degree that I could scarcely have conceived possible, more unsparing of self than I should have thought nature could sustain. I have felt with pain every link that you have severed, and I have asked no questions, because I felt that you ought to measure the disclosure of your thoughts according to the occasion, and the capacity of those to whom you spoke. I write in haste, in the midst of engagements engrossing in themselves, but partly made tasteless, partly embittered by what I have heard; but I am willing to trust even you, whom I love best on earth, in God's Hand, in the earnest prayer that you may be so employed as is best for the Holy Catholic Church.

I had begun my Essay on the Development of Doctrine in the first months of 1845, and I was hard at it all through the year till October. As I advanced, my view so cleared that instead of speaking any more of 'the Roman Catholics', I boldly called them Catholics. Before I got to the end, I resolved to be received, and the book remains in the state in which it was then, unfinished.

One of my friends at Littlemore had been received into the Church on Michaelmas Day, at the Passionist House at Aston, near Stone, by Father Dominic, the Superior. At the beginning of October the latter was passing through London to Belgium; and, as I was in some perplexity what steps to take for being received myself, I assented to the proposition made to me that the good priest should take Littlemore in his way, with a view to his doing for me the same charitable service as he had done to my friend.

On October the 8th I wrote to a number of friends the following letter:

Littlemore, October 8th, 1845. I am this night expecting Father Dominic, the Passionist, who, from his youth, has been led to have distinct and direct thoughts, first of the countries of the North, then of England. After thirty years' (almost) waiting, he was without his own act sent here. But he has had little to do with conversions. I saw him here for a few minutes on St John

Baptist's day last year. He is a simple, holy man; and withal gifted with remarkable powers. He does not know of my intention; but I mean to ask of him admission into the One Fold of Christ. . . .

I have so many letters to write, that this must do for all who choose to ask about me. With my best love to dear Charles Marriott, who is over your head, &c., &c.

P.S. This will not go till all is over. Of course it requires no answer.

For a while after my reception, I proposed to betake myself to some secular calling. I wrote thus in answer to a very gracious letter of congratulation sent me by Cardinal Acton:

Nov. 25, 1845.   I hope you will have anticipated, before I express it, the great gratification which I received from your Eminence's letter. That gratification, however, was tempered by the apprehension, that kind and anxious well-wishers at a distance attach more importance to my step than really belongs to it. To me indeed personally it is of course an inestimable gain; but persons and things look great at a distance, which are not so when seen close; and, did your Eminence know me, you would see that I was one, about whom there has been far more talk for good and bad than he deserves, and about whose movements far more expectation has been raised than the event will justify.

As I never, I do trust, aimed at any thing else than obedience to my own sense of right, and have been magnified into the leader of a party without my wishing it or acting as such, so now, much as I may wish to the contrary, and earnestly as I may labour (as is my duty) to minister in a humble way to the Catholic Church, yet my powers will, I fear, disappoint the expectations of both my own friends, and of those who pray for the peace of Jerusalem.

If I might ask of your Eminence a favour, it is that you would kindly moderate those anticipations. Would it were in my power to do, what I do not aspire to do! At present certainly I cannot look forward to the future, and, though it would be a good work if I could persuade others to do as I have done, yet it seems as if I had quite enough to do in thinking of myself.

Soon, Dr Wiseman, in whose Vicariate Oxford lay, called me to

Oscott; and I went there with others; afterwards he sent me to Rome, and finally placed me in Birmingham.

I wrote to a friend:

January 20, 1846. You may think how lonely I am. 'Obliviscere populum tuum et domum patris tui,' has been in my ears for the last twelve hours. I realize more that we are leaving Littlemore, and it is like going on the open sea.

I left Oxford for good on Monday, February 23, 1846. On the Saturday and Sunday before, I was in my House at Littlemore simply by myself, as I had been for the first day or two when I had originally taken possession of it. I slept on Sunday night at my dear friend's, Mr Johnson's, at the Observatory. Various friends came to see the last of me; Mr Copeland, Mr Church, Mr Buckle, Mr Pattison, and Mr Lewis. Dr Pusey too came up to take leave of me; and I called on Dr Ogle, one of my very oldest friends, for he was my private Tutor, when I was an Undergraduate. In him I took leave of my first College, Trinity, which was so dear to me, and which held on its foundation so many who have been kind to me both when I was a boy, and all through my Oxford life. Trinity had never been unkind to me. There used to be much snap-dragon growing on the walls opposite my freshman's rooms there, and I had for years taken it as the emblem of my own perpetual residence even unto death in my University.

On the morning of the 23rd I left the Observatory. I have never seen Oxford since, excepting its spires, as they are seen from the railway.

PART VII

General Answer to Mr Kingsley:
The Position of My Mind Since 1845
Published as a Pamphlet, Thursday, 2 June 1864

CHAPTER V

From the time that I became a Catholic of course I have no further history of my religious opinions to narrate. In saying this, I do not mean to say that my mind has been idle, or that I have given up thinking on theological subjects; but that I have had no variations to record, and have had no anxiety of heart whatever. I have been in perfect peace and contentment; I never have had one doubt. I was not conscious to myself, on my conversion, of any change, intellectual or moral, wrought in my mind. I was not conscious of firmer faith in the fundamental truths of Revelation, or of more self-command; I had not more fervour; but it was like coming into port after a rough sea; and my happiness on that score remains to this day without interruption.

Nor had I any trouble about receiving those additional articles, which are not found in the Anglican Creed. Some of them I believed already, but not any one of them was a trial to me. I made a profession of them upon my reception with the greatest ease, and I have the same ease in believing them now. I am far of course from denying that every article of the Christian Creed, whether as held by Catholics or by Protestants, is beset with intellectual difficulties; and it is simple fact, that, for myself, I cannot answer those difficulties. Many persons are very sensitive of the difficulties of Religion; I am as sensitive of them as any one; but I have never been able to see a connexion between apprehending those difficulties, however keenly, and multiplying them to any extent, and on the other hand doubting the doctrines to which they are attached. Ten thousand difficulties do not make one doubt, as I understand the subject; difficulty and doubt are incommensurate. There of course may be difficulties in the evidence; but I am speaking of difficulties intrinsic to the doctrines themselves, or to their relations with each other. A man may be annoyed that he cannot work out a mathematical problem, of which the answer is or is not given to him, without doubting that it admits of an answer, or that a certain particular answer is the true one. Of all points of faith, the being of a God is, to my own apprehension, encompassed with most difficulty, and yet borne in upon our minds with most power.

People say that the doctrine of Transubstantiation is difficult to believe; I did not believe the doctrine till I was a Catholic. I had no difficulty in believing it, as soon as I believed that the Catholic Roman Church was the oracle of God, and that she had declared this doctrine to be part of the original revelation. It is difficult, impossible, to imagine, I grant – but how is it difficult to believe? Yet Macaulay thought it so difficult to believe, that he had need of a believer in it of talents as eminent as Sir Thomas More, before he could bring himself to conceive that the Catholics of an en-lightened age could resist 'the overwhelming force of the argu-ment against it.' 'Sir Thomas More,' he says, 'is one of the choice specimens of wisdom and virtue; and the doctrine of transubstan-tiation is a kind of proof charge. A faith which stands that test, will stand any test.' But for myself, I cannot indeed prove it, I cannot tell *how* it is; but I say, 'Why should it not be? What's to hinder it? What do I know of substance or matter? just as much as the greatest philosophers, and that is nothing at all' – so much is this the case, that there is a rising school of philosophy now, which considers phenomena to constitute the whole of our knowledge in physics. The Catholic doctrine leaves phenomena alone. It does not say that the phenomena go; on the contrary, it says that they remain: nor does it say that the same phenomena are in several places at once. It deals with what no one on earth knows any thing about, the material substances themselves. And, in like manner, of that majestic Article of the Anglican as well as of the Catholic Creed – the doctrine of the Trinity in Unity. What do I know of the Essence of the Divine Being? I know that my abstract idea of three is simply incompatible with my idea of one; but when I come to the question of concrete fact, I have no means of proving that there is not a sense in which one and three can equally be predicated of the Incommunicable God.

But I am going to take upon myself the responsibility of more than the mere Creed of the Church; as the parties accusing me are determined I shall do. They say, that now, in that I am a Catholic, though I may not have offences of my own against honesty to answer for, yet, at least, I am answerable for the offences of others, of my co-religionists, of my brother priests, of the Church herself. I am quite willing to accept the responsibility; and, as I have been able, as I trust, by means of a few words, to dissipate, in the minds of all those who do not begin with disbelieving me, the suspicion with which so many Protestants start, in forming their judgment of Catholics, viz. that our Creed is actually set up in inevitable superstition and hypocrisy, as the original sin of Catholicism; so now I will proceed, as before, identifying myself with the Church and vindicating it − not of course denying the enormous mass of sin and error which exists of necessity in that world-wide multiform Communion − but going to the proof of this one point, that its system is in no sense dishonest, and that therefore the upholders and teachers of that system, as such, have a claim to be acquitted in their own persons of that odious imputation.

Starting then with the being of a God (which, as I have said, is as certain to me as the certainty of my own existence, though when I try to put the grounds of that certainty into logical shape I find a difficulty in doing so in mood and figure to my satisfaction), I look out of myself into the world of men, and there I see a sight which fills me with unspeakable distress. The world seems simply to give the lie to that great truth, of which my whole being is so full; and the effect upon me is, in consequence, as a matter of necessity, as confusing as if it denied that I am in existence myself. If I looked into a mirror, and did not see my face, I should have the sort of feeling which actually comes upon me, when I look into this living busy world, and see no reflexion of its Creator. This is, to me, one of those great difficulties of this absolute primary truth, to which I referred just now. Were it not for this voice, speaking so clearly in my conscience and my heart, I should be an atheist, or a pantheist, or a polytheist when I looked into the world. I am speaking for myself only; and I am far from denying the real force of the arguments in proof of a God, drawn from the general facts of human society and the course of history, but these do not warm me or enlighten me; they do not take away the winter of my desolation, or make the buds unfold and the leaves grow within me, and my moral being rejoice. The sight of the world is nothing else than the prophet's scroll, full of 'lamentations, and mourning, and woe.'

To consider the world in its length and breadth, its various history, the many races of man, their starts, their fortunes, their mutual alienation, their conflicts; and then their ways, habits, governments, forms of worship; their enterprises, their aimless courses, their random achievements and acquirements, the impotent conclusion of long-standing facts, the tokens so faint and broken, of a superintending design, the blind evolution of what turn out to be great powers or truths, the progress of things, as if from unreasoning elements, not towards final causes, the greatness and littleness of man, his far-reaching aims, his short duration, the curtain hung over his futurity, the disappointments of life, the defeat of good, the success of evil, physical pain, mental anguish, the prevalence and intensity of sin, the pervading idolatries, the corruptions, the dreary hopeless irreligion, that condition of the whole race, so fearfully yet exactly described in the Apostle's words, 'having no hope and without God in the world' – all this is a vision to dizzy and appal; and inflicts upon the mind the sense of a profound mystery, which is absolutely beyond human solution.

What shall be said to this heart-piercing, reason-bewildering fact ? I can only answer, that either there is no Creator, or this living society of men is in a true sense discarded from His presence. Did I see a boy of good make and mind, with the tokens on him of a refined nature, cast upon the world without provision, unable to say whence he came, his birth-place or his family connexions, I should conclude that there was some mystery connected with his history, and that he was one, of whom, from one cause or other, his parents were ashamed. Thus only should I be able to account for the contrast between the promise and the condition of his being. And so I argue about the world – *if* there be a God, *since* there is a God, the human race is implicated in some terrible aboriginal calamity. It is out of joint with the purposes of its Creator. This is a fact, a fact as true as the fact of its existence; and thus the doctrine of what is theologically called original sin becomes to me almost as certain as that the world exists, and as the existence of God.

And now, supposing it were the blessed and loving will of the

Creator to interfere in this anarchical condition of things, what are we to suppose would be the methods which might be necessarily or naturally involved in His purpose of mercy? Since the world is in so abnormal a state, surely it would be no surprise to me, if the interposition were of necessity equally extraordinary – or what is called miraculous. But that subject does not directly come into the scope of my present remarks. Miracles as evidence, involve a process of reason, or an argument; and of course I am thinking of some mode of inference which does not immediately run into argument. I am rather asking what must be the face-to-face antagonist, by which to withstand and baffle the fierce energy of passion and the all-corroding, all-dissolving scepticism of the intellect in religious inquiries? I have no intention at all of denying that truth is the real object of our reason, and that, if it does not attain to truth, either the premiss or the process is in fault; but I am not speaking here of right reason, but of reason as it acts in fact and concretely in fallen man. I know that even the unaided reason, when correctly exercised, leads to a belief in God, in the immortality of the soul, and in a future retribution; but I am considering the faculty of reason actually and historically; and in this point of view, I do not think I am wrong in saying that its tendency is towards a simple unbelief in matters of religion. No truth, however sacred, can stand against it, in the long run; and hence it is that in the pagan world, when our Lord came, the last traces of the religious knowledge of former times were all but disappearing from those portions of the world in which the intellect had been active and had had a career.

And in these latter days, in like manner, outside the Catholic Church things are tending – with far greater rapidity than in that old time from the circumstance of the age – to atheism in one shape or other. What a scene, what a prospect, does the whole of Europe present at this day! and not only Europe, but every government and every civilization through the world, which is under the influence of the European mind! Especially, for it most concerns us, how sorrowful, in the view of religion, even taken in its most elementary, most attenuated form, is the spectacle presented to us by the educated intellect of England, France, and Germany! Lovers of their country and of their race, religious men, external to the Catholic Church, have attempted various expedients to arrest fierce wilful human nature in its onward course, and to bring it into subjection. The necessity of some form

of religion for the interests of humanity, has been generally
acknowledged: but where was the concrete representative of
things invisible, which would have the force and the toughness
necessary to be a breakwater against the deluge ? Three centuries
ago the establishment of religion, material, legal, and social, was
generally adopted as the best expedient for the purpose, in those
countries which separated from the Catholic Church; and for a
long time it was successful; but now the crevices of those
establishments are admitting the enemy. Thirty years ago,
education was relied upon: ten years ago there was a hope that
wars would cease for ever, under the influence of commercial
enterprise and the reign of the useful and fine arts; but will any one
venture to say that there is any thing any where on this earth,
which will afford a fulcrum for us, whereby to keep the earth from
moving onwards ?

The judgment, which experience passes whether on establishments or on education, as a means of maintaining religious truth
in this anarchical world, must be extended even to the Scripture,
though Scripture be divine. Experience proves surely that the
Bible does not answer a purpose for which it was never intended.
It may be accidentally the means of the conversion of individuals;
but a book, after all, cannot make a stand against the wild living
intellect of man, and in this day it begins to testify, as regards its
own structure and contents, to the power of that universal
solvent, which is so successfully acting upon religious establishments.

Supposing then it to be the Will of the Creator to interfere in
human affairs, and to make provisions for retaining in the world a
knowledge of Himself, so definite and distinct as to be proof
against the energy of human scepticism, in such a case – I am far
from saying that there was no other way – but there is nothing to
surprise the mind, if He should think fit to introduce a power into
the world, invested with the prerogative of infallibility in religious
matters. Such a provision would be a direct, immediate, active,
and prompt means of withstanding the difficulty; it would be an
instrument suited to the need; and, when I find that this is the very
claim of the Catholic Church, not only do I feel no difficulty in
admitting the idea, but there is a fitness in it, which recommends it
to my mind. And thus I am brought to speak of the Church's
infallibility, as a provision, adapted by the mercy of the Creator,
to preserve religion in the world, and to restrain that freedom of

thought, which of course in itself is one of the greatest of our natural gifts, and to rescue it from its own suicidal excesses. And let it be observed that, neither here nor in what follows, shall I have occasion to speak directly of Revelation in its subject matter, but in reference to the sanction which it gives to truths which may be known independently of it – as it bears upon the defence of natural religion. I say, that a power, possessed of infallibility in religious teaching, is happily adapted to be a working instrument, in the course of human affairs, for smiting hard and throwing back the immense energy of the aggressive, capricious, untrustworthy intellect – and in saying this, as in the other things that I have to say, it must still be recollected that I am all along bearing in mind my main purpose, which is a defence of myself.

I am defending myself here from a plausible charge brought against Catholics, as will be seen better as I proceed. The charge is this – that I, as a Catholic, not only make profession to hold doctrines which I cannot possibly believe in my heart, but that I also believe in the existence of a power on earth, which at its own will imposes upon men any new set of *credenda*, when it pleases, by a claim to infallibility; in consequence, that my own thoughts are not my own property; that I cannot tell that tomorrow I may not have to give up what I hold today, and that the necessary effect of such a condition of mind must be a degrading bondage, or a bitter inward rebellion relieving itself in secret infidelity, or the necessity of ignoring the whole subject of religion in a sort of disgust, and of mechanically saying every thing that the Church says, and leaving to others the defence of it. As then I have above spoken of the relation of my mind towards the Catholic Creed, so now I shall speak of the attitude which it takes up in the view of the Church's infallibility.

And first, the initial doctrine of the infallible teacher must be an emphatic protest against the existing state of mankind. Man had rebelled against his Maker. It was this that caused the divine interposition: and the first act of the divinely accredited messenger must be to proclaim it. The Church must denounce rebellion as of all possible evils the greatest. She must have no terms with it; if she would be true to her Master, she must ban and anathematize it. This is the meaning of a statement of mine, which has furnished matter for one of those special accusations to which I am at present replying: I have, however, no fault at all to confess in regard to it; I have nothing to withdraw, and in consequence I here deliberately repeat it. I said, 'The Catholic Church holds it better for the sun and moon to drop from heaven, for the earth to fail, and for all the many millions on it to die of starvation in extremest agony, as far as temporal affliction goes, than that one soul, I will not say, should be lost, but should commit one single venial sin, should tell one wilful untruth, or should steal one poor farthing without excuse.' I think the principle here enunciated to be the mere preamble in the formal credentials of the Catholic Church, as an Act of Parliament might begin with a '*Whereas*'. It is because of the intensity of the evil which has possession of mankind, that a suitable antagonist has been provided against it; and the initial act of that divinely-commissioned power is of course to deliver her challenge and to defy the enemy. Such a preamble then gives a meaning to her position in the world, and an interpretation to her whole course of teaching and action.

In like manner she has ever put forth, with most energetic distinctness, those other great elementary truths, which either are an explanation of her mission or give a character to her work. She does not teach that human nature is irreclaimable, else wherefore should she be sent ? not, that it is to be shattered and reversed, but to be extricated, purified, and restored; not, that it is a mere mass of hopeless evil, but that it has the promise upon it of great things, and even now, in its present state of disorder and excess, has a virtue and a praise proper to itself. But in the next place she knows and she preaches that such a restoration, as she aims at effecting in it, must be brought about, not simply through certain outward provisions of preaching and teaching, even though they be her own, but from an inward spiritual power or grace imparted directly from above, and of which she is the channel. She has it in charge to rescue human nature from its misery, but not simply by restoring it on its own level, but by lifting it up to a higher level than its own. She recognizes in it real moral excellence though degraded, but she cannot set it free from earth except by exalting it towards heaven. It was for this end that a renovating grace was put into her hands, and therefore from the nature of the gift, as well as from the reasonableness of the case, she goes on, as a further point, to insist, that all true conversion must begin with the first springs of thought, and to teach that each individual man must be in his own person one whole and perfect temple of God, while he is also one of the living stones which build up a visible religious community. And thus the distinctions between nature and grace, and between outward and inward religion, become two further articles in what I have called the preamble of her divine commission.

Such truths as these she vigorously reiterates, and pertinaciously inflicts upon mankind; as to such she observes no half-measures, no economical reserve, no delicacy or prudence. 'Ye must be born again,' is the simple, direct form of words which she uses after her Divine Master; 'your whole nature must be reborn, your passions, and your affections, and your aims, and your conscience, and your will, must all be bathed in a new element, and reconsecrated to your Maker – and, the last not the least, your intellect.' It was for repeating these points of her teaching in my own way, that certain passages of one of my Volumes have been brought into the general accusation which has been made against my religious opinions. The writer has said that I was demented if I believed, and unprincipled if I did not believe, in my own statement that a lazy, ragged, filthy, story-telling beggar-woman, if chaste, sober, cheerful, and religious, had a prospect of heaven, such as was absolutely closed to an accomplished statesman, or lawyer, or noble, be he ever so just, upright, generous, honourable, and conscientious, unless he had also some portion of the divine Christian graces – yet I should have thought myself defended from criticism by the words which our Lord used to the chief priests, 'The publicans and harlots go into the kingdom of God before you.' And I was subjected again to the same alternative of imputations, for having ventured to say that consent to an unchaste wish was indefinitely more heinous than any lie viewed apart from its causes, its motives, and its consequences: though a lie, viewed under the limitation of these conditions, is a random utterance, an almost outward act, not directly from the heart, however disgraceful and despicable it may be, however prejudicial to the social contract, however deserving of public reprobation; whereas we have the express words of our Lord to the doctrine that 'whoso looketh on a woman to lust after her, hath committed adultery with her already in his heart.' On the strength of these texts, I have surely as much right to believe in these doctrines which have have caused so much surprise, as to believe in the doctrine of original sin, or that there is a supernatural revelation, or that a Divine Person suffered, or that punishment is eternal.

Passing now from what I have called the preamble of that grant of power, with which the Church is invested, to that power itself, Infallibility, I make two brief remarks – 1. on the one hand, I am not here determining any thing about the essential seat of that power, because that is a question doctrinal, not historical and practical; 2. nor, on the other hand, am I extending the direct subject-matter, over which that power of Infallibility has jurisdiction, beyond religious opinion – and now as to the power itself.

This power, viewed in its fulness, is as tremendous as the giant evil which has called for it. It claims, when brought into exercise but in the legitimate manner, for otherwise of course it is but quiescent to know for certain the very meaning of every portion of that Divine Message in detail, which was committed by our Lord to His Apostles. It claims to know its own limits, and to decide what it can determine absolutely and what it cannot. It claims, moreover, to have a hold upon statements not directly religious, so far as this – to determine whether they indirectly relate to religion, and, according to its own definitive judgment, to pronounce whether or not, in a particular case, they are simply consistent with revealed truth. It claims to decide magisterially, whether or not, that such and such statements are or are not prejudicial to the Apostolic *depositum* of faith, in their spirit or in their consequences, and to allow them, or condemn and forbid them, accordingly. It claims to impose silence at will on any matters, or controversies, of doctrine, which on its own *ipse dixit*, it pronounces to be dangerous, or inexpedient, or inopportune. It claims that, whatever may be the judgment of Catholics upon such acts, these acts should be received by them with those outward marks of reverence, submission, and loyalty, which Englishmen, for instance, pay to the presence of their sovereign, without expressing any criticism on them, on the ground that in their matter they are inexpedient, or in their manner violent or harsh. And lastly, it claims to have the right of inflicting spiritual punishment, of cutting off from the ordinary channels of the divine life, and of simply excommunicating, those who refuse to submit themselves to its formal declarations. Such is the infallibility lodged in the Catholic Church, viewed in the concrete, as clothed and surrounded by the appendages of its high sovereignty: it is, to repeat what I said above, a supereminent prodigious power sent upon earth to encounter and master a giant evil.

And now, having thus described it, I profess my own absolute submission to its claim. I believe the whole revealed dogma as taught by the Apostles, as committed by the Apostles to the Church, and as declared by the Church to me. I receive it, as it is infallibly interpreted by the authority to whom it is thus committed, and (implicitly) as it shall be, in like manner, further interpreted by that same authority till the end of time. I submit, moreover, to the universally received traditions of the Church, in which lies the matter of those new dogmatic definitions which are from time to time made, and which in all times are the clothing and the illustration of the Catholic dogma as already defined. And I submit myself to those other decisions of the Holy See, theological or not, through the organs which it has itself appointed, which, waiving the question of their infallibility, on the lowest ground come to me with a claim to be accepted and obeyed. Also, I consider that, gradually and in the course of ages, Catholic inquiry has taken certain definite shapes, and has thrown itself into the form of a science, with a method and a phraseology of its own, under the intellectual handling of great minds, such as St Athanasius, St Augustine, and St Thomas; and I feel no temptation at all to break in pieces the great legacy of thought thus committed to us for these latter days.

All this being considered as the profession which I make *ex animo*, as for myself, so also on the part of the Catholic body, as far as I know it, it will at first sight be said that the restless intellect of our common humanity is utterly weighed down, to the repression of all independent effort and action whatever, so that, if this is to be the mode of bringing it into order, it is brought into order only to be destroyed. But this is far from the result, far from what I conceive to be the intention of that high Providence who has provided a great remedy for a great evil — far from borne out by the history of the conflict between Infallibility and Reason in the past, and the prospect of it in the future. The energy of the human intellect 'does from opposition grow'; it thrives and is joyous, with a tough elastic strength, under the terrible blows of the divinely-fashioned weapon, and is never so much itself as when it has lately been overthrown. It is the custom with Protestant writers to consider that, whereas there are two great principles in action in the history of religion, Authority and Private Judgment, they have all the Private Judgment to themselves, and we have the full inheritance and the superincumbent oppression of Authority. But this is not so; it is the vast Catholic body itself, and it only, which affords an arena for both combatants in that awful, never-dying duel. It is necessary for the very life of religion, viewed in its large operations and its history, that the warfare should be incessantly carried on. Every exercise of Infallibility is brought out into act by an intense and varied operation of the Reason, both as its ally and as its opponent, and provokes again, when it has done its work, a reaction of Reason against it; and, as in a civil polity the State exists and endures by means of the rivalry and collision, the encroachments and defeats of its constituent parts, so in like manner Catholic Christendom is no simple exhibition of religious absolutism, but presents a continuous picture of Authority and Private Judgment alternately advancing and retreating as the ebb and flow of the tide – it is a vast assemblage of human beings with wilful intellects and wild passions, brought together into one by the beauty and the Majesty of a Superhuman Power – into what may be called a large reformatory or training-school, not as if into a hospital or into a prison, not in order to be sent to bed, not to be buried alive, but (if I may change my metaphor) brought together as if into some moral factory, for the melting, refining, and moulding, by an incessant noisy process, the raw material of human nature, so excellent, so dangerous, so capable of divine purposes.

St Paul says in one place that his Apostolical power is given him to edification, and not to destruction. There can be no better account of the Infallibility of the Church. It is a supply for a need, and it does not go beyond that need. Its object is, and its effect also, not to enfeeble the freedom or vigour of human thought in religious speculation, but to resist and control its extravagance. What have been its great works ? All of them in the distinct province of theology – to put down Arianism, Eutychianism, Pelagianism, Manichæism, Lutheranism, Jansenism. Such is the broad result of its action in the past – and now as to the securities which are given us that so it ever will act in time to come.

First, Infallibility cannot act outside of a definite circle of thought, and it must in all its decisions, or *definitions*, as they are called, profess to be keeping within it. The great truths of the moral law, of natural religion, and of Apostolical faith, are both its boundary and its foundation. It must not go beyond them, and it must ever appeal to them. Both its subject-matter, and its articles in that subject-matter, are fixed. And it must ever profess to be guided by Scripture and by tradition. It must refer to the particular Apostolic truth which it is enforcing, or (what is called) *defining*. Nothing, then, can be presented to me, in time to come, as part of the faith, but what I ought already to have received, and hitherto have been kept from receiving (if so), merely because it has not been brought home to me. Nothing can be imposed upon me different in kind from what I hold already – much less contrary to it. The new truth which is promulgated, if it is to called new, must be at least homogeneous, cognate, implicit, viewed relatively to the old truth. It must be what I may even have guessed, or wished, to be included in the Apostolic revelation; and at least it will be of such a character, that my thoughts readily concur in it or coalesce with it, as soon as I hear it. Perhaps I and others actually have always believed it, and the only question which is now decided in my behalf, is that I have henceforth the satisfaction of having to believe, that I have only been holding all along what the Apostles held before me.

Let me take the doctrine which Protestants consider our greatest difficulty, that of the Immaculate Conception. Here I entreat the reader to recollect my main drift, which is this. I have no difficult in receiving the doctrine; and that, because it so intimately harmonizes with that circle of recognized dogmatic truths, into which it has been recently received – but if *I* have no difficulty, why may not another have no difficulty also ? why may not a hundred ? a thousand ? Now I am sure that Catholics in general have not any intellectual difficulty at all on the subject of the Immaculate Conception; and that there is no reason why they should. Priests have no difficulty. You tell me that they *ought* to have a difficulty – but they have not. Be large-minded enough to believe, that men may reason and feel very differently from yourselves; how is it that men, when left to themselves, fall into such various forms of religion, except that there are various types of mind among them, very distinct from each other ? From my testimony then about myself, if you believe it, judge of others also who are Catholics: we do not find the difficulties which you do in the doctrines which we hold; we have no intellectual difficulty in that doctrine in particular, which you call a novelty of this day. We priests need not be hypocrites, though we be called upon to believe in the Immaculate Conception. To that large class of minds, who believe in Christianity, after our manner – in the particular temper, spirit, and light, (whatever word is used,) in which Catholics believe it – there is no burden at all in holding that the Blessed Virgin was conceived without original sin; indeed, it is a simple fact to say, that Catholics have not come to believe it because it is defined, but that it was defined because they believed it.

So far from the definition in 1854 being a tyrannical infliction on the Catholic world, it was received every where on its promulgation with the greatest enthusiasm. It was in consequence of the unanimous petition, presented from all parts of the Church to the Holy See, in behalf of an *ex cathedrâ* declaration that the doctrine was Apostolic, that it was declared so to be. I never heard of one Catholic having difficulties in receiving the doctrine, whose faith on other grounds was not already suspicious. Of course there were grave and good men, who were made anxious by the doubt whether it could be formally proved to be Apostolical either by Scripture or tradition, and who accordingly, though believing it themselves, did not see how it could be defined by authority and imposed upon all Catholics as a matter of faith; but this is another matter. The point in question is, whether the doctrine is a burden. I believe it to be none. So far from it being so, I sincerely think that St Bernard and St Thomas, who scrupled at it in their day, had they lived into this, would have rejoiced to accept it for its own sake. Their difficulty, as I view it, consisted in matters of words, ideas, and arguments. They thought the doctrine inconsistent with other doctrines; and those who defended it in that age had not that precision in their view of it, which has been given to it by means of the long disputes of the centuries which followed. And in this want of precision lay the difference of opinion, and the controversy.

Now the instance which I have been taking suggests another remark; the number of those (so called) new doctrines will not oppress us, if it takes eight centuries to promulgate even one of them. Such is about the length of time through which the preparation has been carried on for the definition of the Immaculate Conception. This of course is an extraordinary case; but it is difficult to say what is ordinary, considering how few are the formal occasions on which the voice of Infallibility has been solemnly lifted up. It is to the Pope in Ecumenical Council that we look, as to the normal seat of Infallibility: now there have been only eighteen such Councils since Christianity was – an average of one to a century – and of these Councils some passed no doctrinal decree at all, others were employed on only one, and many of them were concerned with only elementary points of the Creed. The Council of Trent embraced a large field of doctrine certainly; but I should apply to its Canons a remark contained in that University Sermon of mine, which has been so ignorantly criticized in the Pamphlet which has been the occasion of this Volume – I there have said that the various verses of the Athanasian Creed are only repetitions in various shapes of one and the same idea; and in like manner, the Tridentine Decrees are not isolated from each other, but are occupied in bringing out in detail, by a number of separate declarations, as if into bodily form, a few necessary Theses condemned by Popes, and on their dogmatic decisions generally. I acknowledge that at first sight they seem from their number to be a greater burden on the faith of individuals than are the Canons of Councils; still I do not believe in matter of fact that they are so at all, and I give this reason for it – it is not that a Catholic, layman or priest, is indifferent to the subject, or, from a sort of recklessness, will accept any thing that is placed before him, or is willing, like a lawyer, to speak according to his brief, but that in such condemnations the Holy See is engaged, for the most part, in repudiating one or two great lines of error, such as Lutheranism or Jansenism, principally ethical not doctrinal, which are foreign to the Catholic mind, and that it is but expressing what any good Catholic, of fair abilities, though unlearned, would say himself, from common and sound sense, if the matter could be put before him.

Now I will go on in fairness to say what I think *is* the great trial to the Reason, when confronted with that august prerogative of the Catholic Church, of which I have been speaking. I enlarged just now upon the concrete shape and circumstances, under which pure infallible authority presents itself to the Catholic. That authority has the prerogative of an indirect jurisdiction on subject-matters which lie beyond its own proper limits, and it most reasonably has such a jurisdiction. It could not act in its own province, unless it had a right to act out of it. It could not properly defend religious truth, without claiming for that truth what may be called its *pomœria*; or, to take another illustration, without acting as we act, as a nation, in claiming as our own, not only the land on which we live, but what are called British waters. The Catholic Church claims, not only to judge infallibly on religious questions, but to animadvert on opinions in secular matters which bear upon religion, on matters of philosophy, of science, of literature, of history, and it demands our submission to her claim. It claims to censure books, to silence authors, and to forbid discussions. In all this it does not so much speak doctrinally, as enforce measures of discipline. It must of course be obeyed without a word, and perhaps in process of time it will tacitly recede from its own injunctions. In such cases the question of faith does not come in at all; for what is matter of faith is true for all times, and never can be unsaid. Nor does it at all follow, because there is a gift of infallibility in the Catholic Church, that therefore the parties who are in possession of it are in all their proceedings infallible. 'O, it is excellent,' says the poet, 'to have a giant's strength, but tyrannous, to use it like a giant.' I think history supplies us with instances in the Church, where legitimate power has been harshly used. To make such admission is no more than saying that the divine treasure, in the words of the Apostle, is 'in earthen vessels'; nor does it follow that the substance of the acts of the ruling power is not right and expedient, because its manner may have been faulty. Such high authorities act by means of instruments; we know how such instruments claim for themselves the name of their principals, who thus get the credit of faults which really are not theirs. But granting all this to an extent greater than can with any show of reason be imputed to ruling power in the Church, what difficulty is there in the fact of this want of prudence or moderation more than can be urged, with far greater justice, against Protestant communities and institutions ? What is there in it to make hypocrites, if it has not that effect upon Protestants ? We are called upon, not to profess any thing, but to submit and be silent, as Protestant Churchmen have before now obeyed the royal command to abstain from certain theological questions. Such injunctions, as I have been contemplating, are laid merely upon our actions, not upon our thoughts. How, for instance, does it tend to make a man a hypocrite, to be forbidden to publish libel ? his thoughts are as free as before: authoritative prohibitions may tease and irritate, but they have no bearing whatever upon the exercise of reason.

So much at first sight; but I will go on to say further, that, in spite of all that the most hostile critic may urge about the encroachments or severities of high ecclesiastics, in times past, in the use of their power, I think that the event has shown after all, that they were mainly in the right, and that those whom they were hard upon were mainly in the wrong. I love, for instance, the name of Origen: I will not listen to the notion that so great a soul was lost; but I am quite sure that, in the contest between his doctrine and followers and the ecclesiastical power, his opponents were right, and he was wrong. Yet who can speak with patience of his enemy and the enemy of St John Chrysostom, that Theophilus, bishop of Alexandria? who can admire or revere Pope Vigilius? And here another consideration presents itself to my thoughts. In reading ecclesiastical history, when I was an Anglican, it used to be forcibly brought home to me, how the initial error of what afterwards became heresy was the urging forward some truth against the prohibition of authority at an unseasonable time. There is a time for every thing, and many a man desires a reformation of an abuse, or the fuller development of a doctrine, or the adoption of a particular policy, but forgets to ask himself whether the right time for it is come; and, knowing that there is no one who will be doing any thing towards its accomplishment in his own lifetime unless he does it himself, he will not listen to the voice of authority, and he spoils a good work in his own century, in order that another man, as yet unborn, may not have the opportunity of bringing it happily to perfection in the next. He may seem to the world to be nothing else than a bold champion for the truth and a martyr to free opinion, when he is just one of those persons whom the competent authority ought to silence, and, though the case may not fall within that subject matter in which that authority is infallible, or the formal conditions of the exercise of that gift may be wanting, it is clearly the duty of authority to act vigorously in the case. Yet its act will go down to posterity as an instance of a tyrannical interference with private judgment, and of the silencing of a reformer, and of a base love of corruption or error; and it will show still less to advantage, if the ruling power happens in its proceedings to act with any defect of prudence or consideration. And all those who take the part of that ruling authority will be considered as time-servers, or indifferent to the cause of uprightness and truth; while, on the other hand, the said authority may be accidentally supported by a violent ultra party, which exalts opinions into dogmas, and has it principally at heart to destroy every school of thought but its own.

Such a state of things may be provoking and discouraging at the time, in the case of two classes of persons; of moderate men who wish to make differences in religious opinion as little as they fairly can be made; and of such as keenly perceive, and are honestly eager to remedy, existing evils – evils, of which divines in this or that foreign country know nothing at all, and which even at home, where they exist, it is not every one who has the means of estimating. This is a state of things both of past time and of the present. We live in a wonderful age; the enlargement of the circle of secular knowledge just now is simply a bewilderment, and the more so, because it has the promise of continuing, and that with greater rapidity, and more signal results. Now these discoveries, certain or probable, have in matter of fact an indirect bearing upon religious opinions, and the question rises how are the respective claims of revelation and of natural science to be adjusted. Few minds in earnest can remain at ease without some sort of rational grounds for their religious belief; to reconcile theory and fact is almost an instinct of the mind. When then a flood of facts, ascertained or suspected, comes pouring in upon us, with a multitude of others in prospect, all believers in Revelation, be they Catholic or not, are roused to consider their bearing upon themselves, both for the honour of God, and from tenderness for those many souls who, in consequence of the confident tone of the schools of secular knowledge, are in danger of being led away into a bottomless liberalism of thought.

I am not going to criticize here that vast body of men, in the mass, who at this time would profess to be liberals in religion; and who look towards the discoveries of the age, certain or in progress, as their informants, direct or indirect, as to what they shall think about the unseen and the future. The Liberalism which gives a colour to society now, is very different from that character of thought which bore the name thirty or forty years ago. Now it is scarcely a party; it is the educated lay world. When I was young, I knew the word first as giving name to a periodical, set up by Lord Byron and others. Now, as then, I have no sympathy with the philosophy of Byron. Afterwards, Liberalism was the badge of a theological school, of a dry and repulsive character, not very dangerous in itself, though dangerous as opening the door to evils which it did not itself either anticipate or comprehend. At present it is nothing else than that deep, plausible scepticism, of which I spoke above, as being the development of human reason, as practically exercised by the natural man.

The Liberal religionists of this day are a very mixed body, and therefore I am not intending to speak against them. There may be, and doubtless is, in the hearts of some or many of them a real antipathy or anger against revealed truth, which it is distressing to think of. Again; in many men of science or literature there may be an animosity arising from almost a personal feeling; it being a matter of party, a point of honour, the excitement of a game, or a satisfaction to the soreness or annoyance occasioned by the acrimony or narrowness of apologists for religion, to prove that Christianity or that Scripture is untrustworthy. Many scientific and literary men, on the other hand, go on, I am confident, in a straightforward impartial way, in their own province and on their own line of thought, without any disturbance from religious difficulties in themselves, or any wish at all to give pain to others by the result of their investigations. It would ill become me, as if I were afraid of truth of any kind, to blame those who pursue secular facts, by means of the reason which God has given them, to their logical conclusions: or to be angry with science, because religion is bound in duty to take cognizance of its teaching. But putting these particular classes of men aside, as having no special call on the sympathy of the Catholic, of course he does most deeply enter into the feelings of a fourth and large class of men, in the educated portions of society, of religious and sincere minds, who are simply perplexed – frightened or rendered desperate, as the case may be –by the utter confusion into which late discoveries or speculations have thrown their most elementary ideas of religion. Who does not feel for such men ? who can have one unkind thought of them ? I take up in their behalf St Augustine's beautiful words, 'Illi in vos sæviant', &c. Let them be fierce with you who have no experience of the difficulty with which error is discriminated from truth, and the way of life is found amid the illusions of the world. How many a Catholic has in his thoughts followed such men, many of them so good, so true, so noble! how often has the wish risen in his heart that some one from among his own people should come forward as the champion of revealed truth against its opponents! Various persons, Catholic and Protestant, have asked me to do so myself; but I had several strong difficulties in the way. One of the greatest is this, that at the moment it is so difficult to say precisely what it is that is to be encountered and overthrown. I am far from denying that scientific knowledge is really growing, but it is by fits and starts; hypotheses rise and fall; it is difficult to anticipate which of them will keep their ground and what the state of knowledge in relation to them will be from year to year. In this condition of things, it has seemed to me to be very undignified for a Catholic to commit himself to the work of chasing what might turn out to be phantoms, and in behalf of some special objections, to be ingenious in devising a theory, which, before it was completed, might have to give place to some theory newer still, from the fact that those former objections had already come to nought under the uprising of others. It seemed to be specially a time in which Christians had a call to be patient, in which they had no other way of helping those who were alarmed, than that of exhorting them to have a little faith and fortitude, and to 'beware', as the poet says, 'of dangerous steps.' This seemed so clear to me, as I thought, more of the matter, as to make me surmise, that, if I attempted what had so little promise in it, I should find that the highest Catholic Authority was against the attempt, and that I should have spent my time and my thought, in doing what either it would be imprudent to bring before the public at all, or what, did I do so, would only complicate matters further which were already complicated, without my interference, more than enough. And I interpret recent acts of that authority as fulfilling my expectation; I interpret them as tying the hands of a controversialist, such as I should be, and teaching us that true wisdom, which Moses inculcated on his people, when the Egyptians were pursuing them, 'Fear ye not, stand still; the Lord shall fight for you, and ye shall hold your peace.' And so far from finding a difficulty in obeying in this case, I have cause to be thankful and to rejoice to have so clear a direction in a matter of difficulty.

But if we would ascertain with correctness the real course of a principle, we must look at it at a certain distance, and as history represents it to us. Nothing carried on by human instruments, but has its irregularities, and affords ground for criticism, when minutely scrutinized in matters of detail. I have been speaking of that aspect of the action of an infallible authority, which is most open to invidious criticism from those who view it from without; I have tried to be fair, in estimating what can be said to its disadvantage, as witnessed at a particular time in the Catholic Church, and now I wish its adversaries to be equally fair in their judgment upon its historical character. Can, then, the infallible authority, with any show of reason, be said in fact to have destroyed the energy of the Catholic intellect ? Let it be observed, I have not here to speak of any conflict which ecclesiastical authority has had with science, for this simple reason, that conflict there has been none, and that, because the secular sciences, as they now exist, are a novelty in the world, and there has been no time yet for a history of relations between theology and these new methods of knowledge, and indeed the Church may be said to have kept clear of them, as is proved by the constantly cited case of Galileo. Here 'exceptio probat regulam': for it is the one stock argument. Again, I have not to speak of any relations of the Church to the new sciences, because my simple question all along has been whether the assumption of infallibility by the proper authority is adapted to make me a hypocrite, and till that authority passes decrees on pure physical subjects and calls on me to subscribe them (which it never will do, because it has not the power), it has no tendency by its acts to interfere with my private judgment on those points. The simple question is whether authority has so acted upon the reason of individuals, that they can have no opinion of their own, and have but an alternative of slavish superstition or secret rebellion of heart; and I think the whole history of theology puts an absolute negative upon such a supposition.

It is hardly necessary to argue out so plain a point. It is individuals, and not the Holy See, that have taken the initiative, and given the lead to the Catholic mind, in theological inquiry. Indeed, it is one of the reproaches urged against the Roman Church, that it has originated nothing, and has only served as a sort of *remora* or break in the development of doctrine. And it is an objection, which I really embrace as a truth; for such I conceive to be the main purpose of its extraordinary gift. It is said, and truly, that the Church of Rome possessed no great mind in the whole period of persecution. Afterwards for a long while, it has not a single doctor to show; St Leo, its first, is the teacher of one point of doctrine; St Gregory, who stands at the very extremity of the first age of the Church, has no dogma or philosophy. The great luminary of the western world is, as we know, St Augustine; he, no infallible teacher, has formed the intellect of Christian Europe; indeed to the African Church generally we must look for the best early exposition of Latin ideas. Moreover, of the African divines, the first in order of time, and not the least influential, is the strong-minded and heterodox Tertullian. Nor is the Eastern intellect, as such, without its share in the formation of the Latin teaching. The free thought of Origen is visible in the writings of the Western Doctors, Hilary and Ambrose; and the independent mind of Jerome has enriched his own vigorous commentaries on Scripture, from the stores of the scarcely orthodox Eusebius. Heretical questions have been transmuted by the living power of the Church into salutary truths. The case is the same as regards the Ecumenical Councils. Authority in its most imposing exhibition, grave Bishops, laden with the traditions and rivalries of particular nations or places, have been guided in their decisions by the commanding genius of individuals, sometimes young and of inferior rank. Not that uninspired intellect overruled the super-human gift which was committed to the Council, which would be a self-contradictory assertion, but that in that process of inquiry and deliberation, which ended in an infallible enunciation, individual reason was paramount. Thus Malchion, a mere presbyter, was the instrument of the great Council of Antioch in the third century in meeting and refuting, for the assembled Fathers, the heretical Patriarch of that see. Parallel to this instance is the influence, so well known, of a young deacon, St Athanasius, with the 318 Fathers at Nicæa. In medieval times we read of St Anselm at Bari, as the champion of the Council there held, against the Greeks. At Trent, the writings of St Bonaventura, and, what is more to the point, the address of a Priest and theologian, Salmeron, had a critical effect on some of the definitions of dogma. In some of these cases the influence might be partly moral, but in others it was that of a discursive knowledge of ecclesiastical writers, a scientific acquaintance with theology, and a force of thought in the treatment of doctrine.

There are of course intellectual habits which theology does not tend to form, as for instance the experimental, and again the philosophical; but that is because it *is* theology, not because of the gift of infallibility. But, as far as this goes, I think it could be shown that physical science on the other hand, or again mathe-matical, affords but an imperfect training for the intellect. I do not see then how any objection about the narrowness of theology comes into our question, which simply is, whether the belief in an infallible authority destroys the independence of the mind; and I consider that the whole history of the Church, and especially the history of the theological schools, gives a negative to the accusation. There never was a time when the intellect of the educated class was more active, or rather more restless, than in the middle ages. And then again all through Church history from the first, how slow is authority in interfering! Perhaps a local teacher, or a doctor in some local school, hazards a proposition, and a controversy ensues. It smoulders or burns in one place, no one interposing; Rome simply lets it alone. Then it comes before a Bishop; or some priest, or some professor in some other seat of learning takes it up; and then there is a second stage of it. Then it comes before a University, and it may be condemned by the theological faculty. So the controversy proceeds year after year, and Rome is still silent. An appeal perhaps is next made to a seat of authority inferior to Rome; and then at last after a long while it comes before the supreme power. Meanwhile, the question has been ventilated and turned over again, and viewed on every side of it, and authority is called upon to pronounce a decision, which has already been arrived at by reason. But even then, perhaps the supreme authority hesitates to do so, and nothing is determined on the point for years; or so generally and vaguely, that the whole controversy has to be gone through again, before it is ultimately determined. It is manifest how a mode of proceeding, such as this, tends not only to the liberty, but to the courage, of the individual theologian or controversialist. Many a man has ideas, which he hopes are true, and useful for his day, but he is not confident about them, and wishes to have them discussed. He is willing or rather would be thankful to give them up, if they can be proved to be erroneous or dangerous, and by means of controversy he obtains his end. He is answered, and he yields; or on the contrary he finds that he is considered safe. He would not dare to do this, if he knew an authority, which was supreme and final, was watching every word he said, and made signs of assent or dissent to each sentence, as he uttered it. Then indeed he would be fighting, as the Persian soldiers, under the lash, and the freedom of his intellect might truly be said to be beaten out of him. But this has not been so – I do not mean to say that, when controversies run high, in schools or even in small portions of the Church, an interposition may not advisably take place; and again, questions may be of that urgent nature, that an appeal must, as a matter of duty, be made at once to the highest authority in the Church; but, if we look into the history of controversy, we shall find, I think, the general run of things to be such as I have represented it. Zosimus treated Pelagius and Cœlestius with extreme forbearance; St Gregory VII was equally indulgent with Berengarius; by reason of the very power of the Popes they have commonly been slow and moderate in their use of it.

And here again is a further shelter for the legitimate exercise of the individual reason – the multitude of nations which are within the fold of the Church will be found to have acted for its protection, against any narrowness, on the supposition of narrowness, in the various authorities at Rome, with whom lies the practical decision of controverted questions. How have the Greek traditions been respected and provided for in the later Ecumenical Councils, in spite of the countries that held them being in a state of schism! There are important points of doctrine which have been (humanly speaking) exempted from the infallible sentence, by the tenderness with which its instruments, in framing it, have treated the opinions of particular places. Then, again, such national influences have a providential effect in moderating the bias which the local influences of Italy may exert upon the See of St Peter. It stands to reason that, as the Gallican Church has in it a French element, so Rome must have in it an element of Italy; and it is no prejudice to the zeal and devotion with which we submit ourselves to the Holy See to admit this plainly. It seems to me, as I have been saying, that Catholicity is not only one of the notes of the Church, but, according to the divine purposes, one of its securities. I think it would be a very serious evil, which Divine Mercy avert! that the Church should be contracted in Europe within the range of particular nationalities. It is a great idea to introduce Latin civilization into America, and to improve the Catholics there by the energy of French devotedness; but I trust that all European races will ever have a place in the Church, and assuredly I think that the loss of the English, not to say the German element, in its composition has been a most serious misfortune. And certainly, if there is one consideration more than another which should make us English grateful to Pius the Ninth, it is that, by giving us a Church of our own, he has prepared the way for our own habits of mind, our own manner of reasoning, our own tastes, and our own virtues, finding a place and thereby a sanctification, in the Catholic Church.

There is only one other subject, which I think it is necessary to introduce here, as bearing upon the vague suspicions which are attached in this country to the Catholic Priesthood. It is one of which my accuser says much – the charge of reserve and economy. He founds it in no slight degree on what I have said on the subject in my History of the Arians, and in a note upon one of my

Sermons in which I refer to it. The principle of Reserve is also advocated by an admirable writer in two numbers of the Tracts for the Times, and of these I was the Editor.

Now, as to the Economy itself, it is founded upon the words of our Lord, 'Cast not your pearls before swine'; and it was observed by the early Christians, more or less, in their intercourse with the heathen populations among whom they lived. In the midst of the abominable idolatries and impurities of that fearful time, the Rule of the Economy was an imperative duty. But that rule, at least as I have explained and recommended it, in anything that I have written, did not go beyond (1) the concealing the truth when we could do so without deceit, (2) stating it only partially, and (3) representing it under the nearest form possible to a learner or inquirer, when he could not possibly understand it exactly. I conceive that to draw Angels with wings is an instance of the third of these economical modes; and to avoid the question, 'Do Christians believe in a Trinity ?' by answering, 'They believe in only one God', would be an instance of the second. As to the first, it is hardly an Economy, but comes under what is called the *Disciplina Arcani*. The second and third economical modes Clement calls *lying*; meaning that a partial truth is in some sense a lie, as is also a representative truth. And this, I think, is about the long and the short of the ground of the accusation which has been so violently urged against me, as being a patron of the Economy.

Of late years I have come to think, as I believe most writers do, that Clement meant more than I have said. I used to think he used the word 'lie' as an hyperbole, but I now believe that he, as other early Fathers, thought that, under certain circumstances, it was lawful to tell a lie. This doctrine I never maintained, though I used to think, as I do now, that the theory of the subject is surrounded with considerable difficulty; and it is not strange that I should say so, considering that great English writers declare without hesitation that in certain extreme cases, as to save life, honour, or even property, a lie is allowable. And thus I am brought to the direct question of truth, and of the truthfulness of Catholic priests generally in their dealings with the world, as bearing on the general question of their honesty, and of their internal belief in their religious professions.

It would answer no purpose, and it would be departing from the line of writing which I have been observing all along, if I entered into any formal discussion on this question; what I shall do here, as I have done in the foregoing pages, is to give my own testimony on the matter in question, and there to leave it. Now first I will say, that, when I became a Catholic, nothing struck me more at once than the English out-spoken manner of the Priests. It was the same at Oscott, at Old Hall Green, at Ushaw; there was nothing of that smoothness, or mannerism, which is commonly imputed to them, and they were more natural and unaffected than many an Anglican clergyman. The many years, which have passed since, have only confirmed my first impression. I have ever found it in the priests of this Diocese; did I wish to point out a straight-forward Englishman, I should instance the Bishop, who has, to our great benefit, for so many years presided over it.

And next, I was struck, when I had more opportunity of judging of the Priests, by the simple faith in the Catholic Creed and system of which they always gave evidence, and which they never seemed to feel, in any sense at all, to be a burden. And now that I have been in the Church nineteen years, I cannot recollect hearing of a single instance in England of an infidel priest. Of course there are men from time to time, who leave the Catholic Church for another religion, but I am speaking of cases, when a man keeps a fair outside to the world and is a hollow hypocrite in his heart.

I wonder that the self-devotion of our priests does not strike Protestants in this point of view. What do they gain by professing a Creed, in which, if my assailant is to be believed, they really do not believe? What is their reward for committing themselves to a life of self-restraint and toil, and perhaps to a premature and miserable death? The Irish fever cut off between Liverpool and Leeds thirty priests and more, young men in the flower of their days, old men who seemed entitled to some quiet time after their long toil. There was a bishop cut off in the North; but what had a man of his ecclesiastical rank to do with the drudgery and danger of sick calls, except that Christian faith and charity constrained him? Priests volunteered for the dangerous service. It was the same with them on the first coming of the cholera, that mysterious awe-inspiring infliction. If they did not heartily believe in the Creed of the Church, then I will say that the remark of the Apostle had its fullest illustration — 'If in this life only we have hope in Christ, we are of all men most miserable.' What could support a set of hypocrites in the presence of a deadly disorder, one of them following another in long order up the forlorn hope, and one after another perishing? And such, I may say, in its substance, is every Mission-Priest's life. He is ever ready to sacrifice himself for his people. Night and day, sick or well himself, in all weathers, off he is, on the news of a sick call. The fact of a parishioner dying without the Sacraments through his fault is terrible to him; why terrible, if he has not a deep absolute faith, which he acts upon with a free service? Protestants admire this, when they see it; but they do not seem to see as clearly, that it excludes the very notion of hypocrisy.

Sometimes, when they reflect upon it, it leads them to remark on the wonderful discipline of the Catholic priesthood; they say that no Church has so well ordered a clergy, and that in that respect it surpasses their own; they wish they could have such exact discipline among themselves. But is it an excellence which can be purchased? is it a phenomenon which depends on nothing else than itself, or is it an effect which has a cause? You cannot buy devotion at a price. 'It hath never been heard of in the land of Chanaan, neither hath it been seen in Theman. The children of Agar, the merchants of Meran, none of these have known its way.' What then is that wonderful charm, which makes a thousand men act all in one way, and infuses a prompt obedience to rule, as if they were under some stern military compulsion? How difficult to find an answer, unless you will allow the obvious one, that they believe intensely what they profess!

I cannot think what it can be, in a day like this, which keeps up the prejudice of this Protestant country against us, unless it be the vague charges which are drawn from our books of Moral Theology; and with a short notice of the work in particular which my accuser especially throws in our teeth, I shall in a very few words bring these observations to a close.

St Alfonso Liguori, then, it cannot be denied, lays down that an equivocation, (that is, a play upon words, in which one sense is taken by the speaker, and another sense intended by him for the hearer), is allowable, if there is a just cause, that is, in an extraordinary case, and may even be confirmed by an oath. I shall give my opinion on this point as plainly as any Protestant can wish; and therefore I avow at once that in this department of morality, much as I admire the high points of the Italian character, I like the English rule of conduct better; but, in saying so, I am not, as will shortly be seen, saying any thing disrespectful to St

Alfonso, who was a lover of truth, and whose intercession I trust I shall not lose, though, on the matter under consideration, I follow other guidance in preference to his.

Now I make this remark first – great English authors, Jeremy Taylor, Milton, Paley, Johnson, men of very different schools of thought, distinctly say, that under certain extraordinary circumstances it is allowable to tell a lie. Taylor says:

> To tell a lie for charity, to save a man's life, the life of a friend, of a husband, of a prince, of a useful and a public person, hath not only been done at all times, but commended by great and wise and good men. Who would not save his father's life, at the charge of a harmless lie, from persecutors or tyrants?

Again, Milton says:

> What man in his senses would deny, that there are those whom we have the best grounds for considering that we ought to deceive – as boys, madmen, the sick, the intoxicated, enemies, men in error, thieves? I would ask, by which of the commandments is a lie forbidden? You will say, by the ninth. If then my lie does not injure my neighbour, certainly it is not forbidden by this commandment.

Paley says: 'There are falsehoods, which are not lies, that is, which are not criminal.' Johnson: 'The general rule is, that truth should never be violated; there must, however, be some exceptions. If, for instance, a murderer should ask you which way a man is gone.'

Now, I am not using these instances as an *argumentum ad hominem*; but the purpose to which I put them is this:

1. First, I have set down the distinct statements of Taylor, Milton, Paley, and Johnson; now, would any one give ever so little weight to these statements, in forming a real estimate of the veracity of the writers, if they now were alive? Were a man, who is so fierce with St Alfonso, to meet Paley or Johnson tomorrow in society, would he look upon him as a liar, a knave, as dishonest and untrustworthy? I am sure he would not. Why then does he not deal out the same measure to Catholic priests? If a copy of Scavini, which speaks of equivocation as being in a just cause allowable, be found in a student's room at Oscott, not Scavini himself, but even the unhappy student, who has what a Protestant calls a bad book in his possession, is judged to be for life unworthy of credit. Are all Protestant textbooks, which are used at the

University, immaculate? Is it necessary to take for gospel every word of Aristotle's Ethics, or every assertion of Hey or Burnett on the Articles? Are textbooks the ultimate authority, or rather are they not manuals in the hands of a lecturer, and the groundwork of his remarks? But, again, let us suppose, not the case of a student, or of a professor, but of Scavini himself, or of St Alfonso; now here again I ask, since you would not scruple in holding Paley for an honest man, in spite of his defence of lying, why do you scruple at holding St Alfonso honest? I am perfectly sure that you would not scruple at Paley personally; you might not agree with him, but you would not go further than to call him a bold thinker: then why should St Alfonso's person be odious to you, as well as his doctrine?

Now I wish to tell you why you are not afraid of Paley; because, you would say, when he advocated lying, he was taking *extreme* or *special cases*. You would have no fear of a man who you knew had shot a burglar dead in his own house, because you know you are *not* a burglar: so you would not think that Paley had a habit of telling lies in society, because in the case of a cruel alternative he thought it the lesser evil to tell a lie. Then why do you show such suspicion of a Catholic theologian, who speaks of certain extraordinary cases in which an equivocation in a penitent cannot be visited by his confessor as if it were a sin? for this is the exact point of the question.

But again, why does Paley, why does Jeremy Taylor, when no practical matter is actually before him, lay lay down a maxim about the lawfulness of lying, which will startle most readers? The reason is plain. He is forming a theory of morals, and he must treat every question in turn as it comes. And this is just what St Alfonso or Scavini is doing. You only try your hand yourself at a treatise on the rules of morality, and you will see how difficult the work is. What is the *definition* of a lie? Can you give a better than that it is a sin against justice, as Taylor and Paley consider it? but, if so, how can it be a sin at all, if your neighbour is not injured? If you do not like this definition, take another; and then, by means of that, perhaps you will be defending St Alfonso's equivocation. However, this is what I insist upon; that St Alfonso, as Paley, is considering the different portions of a large subject, and he must, on the subject of lying, give his judgment, though on that subject it is difficult to form any judgment which is satisfactory.

But further still: you must not suppose that a philosopher or moralist uses in his own case the licence which his theory itself would allow him. A man in his own person is guided by his own conscience; but in drawing out a system of rules he is obliged to go by logic, and follow the exact deduction of conclusion from conclusion, and must be sure that the whole system is coherent and one. You hear of even immoral or irreligious books being written by men of decent character; there is a late writer who says that David Hume's sceptical works are not at all the picture of the man. A priest might write a treatise which was really lax on the subject of lying, which might come under the condemnation of the Holy See, as some treatises on that score have already been condemned, and yet in his own person be a rigorist. And, in fact, it is notorious from St Alfonso's Life, that he, who has the repute of being so lax a moralist, had one of the most scrupulous and anxious of consciences himself. Nay, further than this, he was originally in the Law, and on one occasion he was betrayed into the commission of what seemed like a deceit, though it was an accident; and that was the very occasion of his leaving the profession and embracing the religious life.

The account of this remarkable occurrence is told us in his Life:

Notwithstanding he had carefully examined over and over the details of the process, he was completely mistaken regarding the sense of one document, which constituted the right of the adverse party. The advocate of the Grand Duke perceived the mistake, but he allowed Alfonso to continue his eloquent address to the end without interruption; as soon, however, as he had finished, he rose, and said with cutting coolness, 'Sir, the case is not exactly what you suppose it to be; if you will review the process, and examine this paper attentively, you will find there precisely the contrary of all you have advanced.' 'Willingly,' replied Alfonso, without hesitating; 'the decision depends on this question – whether the fief were granted under the law of Lombardy, or under the French Law.' The paper being examined, it was found that the Grand Duke's advocate was in the right. 'Yes,' said Alfonso, holding the paper in his hand, 'I am wrong, I have been mistaken.' A discovery so unexpected, and the fear of being accused of unfair dealing, filled him with consternation, and covered him with confusion, so much so, that every one saw his emotion. It was in vain that the President Caravita, who loved him, and knew his integrity, tried to console him, by telling him that such mistakes were not uncommon, even among the first men at the bar. Alfonso would listen to nothing, but, overwhelmed with confusion, his head sunk on his breast, he said to himself, 'World, I know you now; courts of law, never shall you see me again!' And turning his back on the assembly, he withdrew to his own house, incessantly repeating to himself, 'World, I know you now.' What annoyed him most was, that having studied and re-studied the process during a whole month, without having discovered this important flaw, he could not understand how it had escaped his observation.

And this is the man, so easily scared at the very shadow of trickery, who is so flippantly pronounced to be a patron of lying.

But, in truth, a Catholic theologian has objects in view which men in general little compass; he is not thinking of himself, but of a multitude of souls, sick souls, sinful souls, carried away by sin, full of evil, and he is trying with all his might to rescue them from their miserable state; and, in order to save them from more heinous sins, he tries, to the full extent that his conscience will allow him to go, to shut his eyes to such sins, as are, though sins, yet lighter in character or degree. He knows perfectly well that, if he is as strict as he would wish to be, he shall be able to do nothing at all with the run of men; so he is as indulgent with them as ever he can be. Let it not be for an instant supposed, that I allow of the maxim of doing evil that good may come; but, keeping clear of this, there is a way of winning men from greater sins by winking for the time at the less, or at mere improprieties or faults; and this is the key to the difficulty which Catholic books of moral theology so often cause to the Protestant. They are intended for the Preacher.

2. And I observe upon Taylor, Milton, and Paley thus: What would a Protestant clergyman say to me, if I accused him of teaching that a lie was allowable; and if, when he asked for my proof, I said in reply that such was the doctrine of Taylor and Milton ? Why, he would sharply retort, '*I* am not bound by Taylor or Milton'; and if I went on urging that 'Taylor was one of his authorities', he would answer that Taylor was a great writer, but great writers were not therefore infallible. This is pretty much the answer which I make, when I am considered in this matter a disciple of St Alfonso.

I plainly and positively state, and without any reserve, that I do not at all follow this holy and charitable man in this portion of his teaching. There are various schools of opinion allowed in the Church: and on this point I follow others. I follow Cardinal Gerdil, and Natalis Alexander, nay, St Augustine. I will quote one passage from Natalis Alexander:

> They certainly lie, who utter the words of an oath, without the will to swear or bind themselves: or who make use of mental reservations and *equivocations* in swearing, since they signify by words what they have not in mind, contrary to the end for which language was instituted, viz. as signs of ideas. Or they mean something else than the words signify in themselves and the common custom of speech.

And, to take an instance: I do not believe any priest in England would dream of saying, 'My friend is not here'; meaning, 'He is not in my pocket or under my shoe.' Nor should any consideration make me say so myself. I do not think St Alfonso would in his own case have said so; and he would have been as much shocked at Taylor and Paley, as Protestants are at him.

And now, if Protestants wish to know what our real teaching is, as on other subjects, so on that of lying, let them look, not at our books of casuistry, but at our catechisms. Works on pathology do not give the best insight into the form and the harmony of the human frame; and, as it is with the body, so is it with the mind. The Catechism of the Council of Trent was drawn up for the express purpose of providing preachers with subjects for their Sermons; and, as my whole work has been a defence of myself, I may here say that I rarely preach a Sermon, but I go to this beautiful and complete Catechism to get both my matter and my doctrine. There we find the following notices about the duty of Veracity:

> 'Thou shalt not bear false witness,' &c.: let attention be drawn to two laws contained in this commandment – the one, forbidding false witness; the other bidding, that removing all pretence and deceits, we should measure our words and deeds by simple truth, as the Apostle admonished the Ephesians of that duty in these words: 'Doing truth in charity, let us grow in Him through all things.'

To deceive by a lie in joke or for the sake of compliment, though to no one there accrues loss or gain in consequence, nevertheless is altogether unworthy: for thus the Apostle admonishes, 'Putting aside lying, speak ye truth'. For therein is great danger of lapsing into frequent and more serious lying, and from lies in joke men gain the habit of lying, whence they gain the character of not being truthful. And thence again, in order to gain credence to their words, they find it necessary to make a practice of swearing.

Nothing is more necessary for us than truth of testimony, in those things, which we neither know ourselves, nor can allowably be ignorant of, on which point there is extant that maxim of St Augustine's; Whoso conceals the truth, and whoso puts forth a lie, each is guilty; the one because he is not willing to do a service, the other because he has a wish to do a mischief.

It is lawful at times to be silent about the truth, but out of a court of law; for in court, when a witness is interrogated by the judge according to law, the truth is wholly to be brought out.

Witnesses, however, must beware, lest, from over-confidence in their memory, they affirm for certain, what they have not verified.

In order that the faithful may with more good will avoid the sin of lying, the Parish Priest shall set before them the extreme misery and turpitude of this wickedness. For, in holy writ, the devil is called the father of a lie; for, in that he did not remain in Truth, he is a liar, and the father of a lie. He will add, with the view of ridding men of so great a crime, the evils which follow upon lying; and, whereas they are innumerable, he will point out [at least] the sources and the general heads of these mischiefs and calamities, viz. 1. How great is God's displeasure and how great His hatred of a man who is insincere and a liar. 2. What little security there is that a man who is specially hated by God may not be visited by the heaviest punishments. 3. What more unclean and foul, as St James says, than ... that a fountain by the same jet should send out sweet water and bitter? 4. For that tongue, which just now praised God, next, as far as in it lies, dishonours Him by lying. 5. In consequence, liars are shut out from the possession of heavenly beatitude. 6. That too is the worst evil of lying, that that disease of the mind is generally incurable.

Moreover, there is this harm too, and one of vast extent, and touching men generally, that by insincerity and lying faith and truth are lost, which are the firmest bonds of human society, and, when they are lost, supreme confusion follows in life, so that men seem in nothing to differ from devils.

Lastly, the Parish Priest will set those right who excuse their insincerity and allege the example of wise men, who, they say, are used to lie for an occasion. He will tell them, what is most true, that the wisdom of the flesh is death. He will exhort his hearers to trust in God, when they are in difficulties and straits, nor to have recourse to the expedient of a lie.

They who throw the blame of their own lie on those who have already by a lie deceived them, are to be taught that men must not revenge themselves, nor make up for one evil by another. . . .

There is much more in the Catechism to the same effect, and it is of universal obligation; whereas the decision of a particular author in morals need not be accepted by any one.

To one other authority I appeal on this subject, which commands from me attention of a special kind, for it is the teaching of a Father. It will serve to bring my work to a conclusion.

'St Philip,' says the Roman Oratorian who wrote his Life, 'had a particular dislike of affectation both in himself and others, in speaking, in dressing, or in any thing else.'

He avoided all ceremony which savoured of worldly compliment, and always showed himself a great stickler for Christian simplicity in every thing; so that, when he had to deal with men of worldly prudence, he did not very readily accommodate himself to them.

And he avoided, as much as possible, having any thing to do with *two-faced persons*, who did not go simply and straightforwardly to work in their transactions.

As for liars, he could not endure them, and he was *continually reminding* his spiritual children, *to avoid them as they would a pestilence.*

These are the principles on which I have acted before I was a Catholic; these are the principles which, I trust, will be my stay and guidance to the end.

I have closed this history of myself with St Philip's name upon St Philip's feast-day; and, having done so, to whom can I more suitably offer it, as a memorial of affection and gratitude, than to St Philip's sons, my dearest brothers of this House, the Priests of the Birmingham Oratory, AMBROSE ST JOHN, HENRY AUSTIN MILLS, HENRY BITTLESTON, EDWARD CASWALL, WILLIAM PAINE NEVILLE, and HENRY IGNATIUS DUDLEY RYDER ? who have been so faithful to me; who have been so sensitive of my needs; who have been so indulgent to my failings; who have carried me through so many trials; who have grudged no sacrifice, if I asked for it; who have been cheerful under discouragements of my causing; who have done so many good works, and let me have the credit of them – with whom I have lived so long, with whom I hope to die.

And to you especially, dear AMBROSE ST JOHN; whom God gave me, when He took every one else away; who are the link between my old life and my new; who have now for twenty-one years been so devoted to me, so patient, so zealous, so tender; who have let me lean so hard upon you; who have watched me so narrowly; who have never thought of yourself, if I was in question.

And in you I gather up and bear in memory those familiar affectionate companions and counsellors, who in Oxford were given to me, one after another, to be my daily solace and relief; and all those others, of great name and high example, who were my thorough friends, and showed me true attachment in times long past; and also those many younger men, whether I knew them or not, who have never been disloyal to me by word or deed; and of all these, thus various in their relations to me, those more especially who have since joined the Catholic Church.

And I earnestly pray for this whole company, with a hope against hope, that all of us, who once were so united, and so happy in our union, may even now be brought at length, by the Power of the Divine Will, into One Fold and under One Shepherd.

May 26, 1864.
In Festo Corp. Christ.

APPENDIX A (1864)

First published as a Pamphlet, June 16 1864

Answer in Detail to Mr Kingsley's Accusations.

In proceeding now, according to the engagement with which I entered upon my undertaking, to examine in detail the Pamphlet which has been written against me, I am very sorry to be obliged to say, that it is as slovenly and random and futile in its definite charges, as it is iniquitous in its method of disputation. And now I proceed to show this without any delay; and shall consider in order,

1 My Sermon on the Apostolical Christian.
2 My Sermon on Wisdom and Innocence.
3 The Anglican Church.
4 The Lives of the English Saints.
5 Ecclesiastical Miracles.
6 Popular Religion.
7 The Economy.
8 Lying and Equivocation.

1

My Sermon on 'The Apostolical Christian' being the 19th of 'Sermons on Subjects of the Day'

This writer says, 'What Dr Newman means by Christians . . . he has not left in doubt'; and then, quoting a passage from this Sermon which speaks of 'the humble monk and the holy nun' being 'Christians after the very pattern given us in Scripture', he observes, 'This is his *definition* of Christians.' – p. 24.

This is not the case. I have neither given a definition, nor implied one, nor intended one; nor could I, either now or in 1843–4, or at any time, allow of the particular definition he ascribes to me. As if all Christians must be monks or nuns!

What I have said is, that monks and nuns are patterns of Christian perfection; and that Scripture itself supplies us with this pattern. Who can deny this? Who is bold enough to say that St John Baptist, who, I suppose, is a Scripture Character, is not a pattern-monk; and that Mary, who 'sat at our Lord's feet', was not a pattern-nun ? and 'Anna too, who served God with fastings and prayers night and day ?'. Again, what is meant but this by St Paul's saying, 'It is good for a man not to touch a woman ?' and, when speaking of the father or guardian of a young girl, 'He that giveth her in marriage doeth well; but he that giveth her not in marriage doeth better?'. And what does St John mean but to praise virginity, when he says of the hundred forty and four thousand on Mount Sion, 'These are they which were not defiled with women, for they are virgins'? And what else did our Lord mean, when He said, 'There be eunuchs who have made themselves eunuchs for the kingdom of heaven's sake. He that is able to receive it, let him receive it ?'

He ought to know his logic better: I have said that 'monks and nuns find their pattern in Scripture': he adds, *Therefore* I hold all Christians are monks and nuns.

This is Blot *one*.

Now then for Blot *two*.

'Monks and nuns the *only* perfect Christians . . . what more ?' — p. 24.

A second fault in logic. I said no more than that monks and nuns were perfect Christians: he adds, *Therefore* 'monks and nuns are the *only* perfect Christians.' Monks and nuns are *not* the only perfect Christians; I never thought so or said so, now or at any other time.

P. 50. 'In the Sermon . . . monks and nuns are spoken of as the *only true* Bible Christians.' This, again, is not the case. What I said is, that 'monks and nuns are Bible Christians': it does not follow, nor did I mean, that 'all Bible Christians are monks and nuns.' Bad logic again. Blot *three*.

My Sermon on 'Wisdom and Innocence', being the 20th of 'Sermons on Subjects of the Day'

This writer says, p. 24, about my Sermon 20, 'By the world appears to be signified, especially, the Protestant public of these realms.'

He also asks, p. 28 'Why was it preached? . . . to insinuate, that the admiring young gentlemen, who listened to him, stood to their fellow-countrymen in the relation of the early Christians to the heathen Romans? or that Queen Victoria's Government was to the Church of England, what Nero's or Diocletian's was to the Church of Rome? It may have been so.'

May or may not, it wasn't. He insinuates, what not even with his little finger does he attempt to prove. Blot *four*.

He asserts, p. 24, that I said in the Sermon in question, that 'Sacramental Confession and the celibacy of the clergy are "notes" of the Church.' And, just before, he puts the word 'notes' in inverted commas, as if it was mine. That is, he garbles. It is *not* mine. Blot *five*.

He says that I '*define* what I mean by the Church in two "notes" of her character.' I do not define, or dream of defining.

1. He says that I teach that the celibacy of the clergy enters into the *definition* of the Church. I do no such thing; that is the blunt truth. Define the Church by the celibacy of the clergy! why, let him read 1 Tim. iii; there he will find that bishops and deacons are spoken of as married. How, then, could I be the dolt to say or imply that the celibacy of the clergy was a part of the definition of the Church? Blot *six*.

And again in p. 50. 'In the Sermon a celibate clergy is made a note of the Church.' Thus the untruth is repeated. Blot *seven*.

2. And now for Blot *eight*. Neither did I say that 'Sacramental confession' was 'a note of the Church.' Nor is it. Nor could I with

any cogency have brought this as an argument against the Church of England, for the Church of England has retained Confession, nay, Sacramental Confession. No fair man can read the form of Absolution in the Anglican Prayer in the Visitation of the Sick, without seeing that that Church *does* sanction and provide for Confession and Absolution. If that form does not contain the profession of a grave Sacramental act, words have no meaning. The form is almost in the words of the Roman form; and, by the time that this Clergyman has succeeded in explaining it away, he will have also got skill enough to explain away the Roman form; and if he did but handle my words with that latitude with which he interprets his own formularies, he would prove that, instead of my being superstitious and frantic, I was the most Protestant of preachers and the most latitudinarian of thinkers. It would be charity in him, in his reading of my words, to use some of that power of evasion, of which he shows himself such a master in his dealing with his own Prayer Book. Yet he has the assurance at p. 28 to ask, 'Why was the Sermon preached ? to insinuate that a Church which had sacramental confession and a celibate clergy was the only true Church ?'.

'Why ?' I will tell the reader, *why*; and with this view will speak, first of the contents of the Sermon, then of its subject, then of its circumstances.

1. It was one of the last six Sermons which I wrote when I was an Anglican. It was one of the five Sermons I preached in St Mary's between Christmas and Easter, 1843, the year when I gave up my Living. The MS. of the Sermon is destroyed; but I believe, and my memory too bears me out, as far as it goes, that the sentence in question about Celibacy and Confession *was not preached at all*. The Volume, in which this Sermon is found, was published *after* that I had given up St Mary's, when I had no call on me to restrain the expression of anything which I might hold: and I state an important fact about it in the Advertisement, which this truth-loving writer *suppresses*. Blot *nine*.

My words, which stared him in the face, are as follows:

In preparing these Sermons for publication, *a few words and sentences* have in several places been *added*, which will be found to express more *of private or personal opinion*, than it was expedient to introduce into the *instruction* delivered in Church to a parochial Congregation. Such introduction, however, seems unobjectionable in the case of compositions, which are *detached* from the sacred place and service to which they once belonged, and *submitted to the reason* and judgment of the general reader.

This Volume of Sermons then cannot be criticized at all as *preachments*; they are *essays*; of a man who, at the time of publishing them, was *not* a preacher. Such passages, as that in question, are just the very ones which I added *upon* my publishing them. I always was on my guard in the pulpit of saying anything which looked towards Rome; and therefore all his rhetoric about my 'disciples', 'admiring young gentlemen who listened to me', 'fanatic and hot-headed young men, who hung upon my every word', becomes simple rubbish.

I have more to say on this point. The writer says, p. 28, 'I know that men used to suspect Dr Newman – I have been inclined to do so myself – of *writing a whole Sermon, not for the sake of the text or of the matter*, but for the sake of one simple passing hint – one phrase, one epithet.' Can there be a plainer testimony borne to the practical character of my Sermons at St Mary's than this gratuitous insinuation ? Many a preacher of Tractarian doctrine has been accused of not letting his parishioners alone, and of teasing them with his private theological notions. You would gather from the general tone of this Writer that that was my way. Every one who was in the habit of hearing me, knows that it wasn't. This Writer either knows nothing about it, and then he ought to be silent; or he does know, and then he ought to speak the truth. Others spread the same report twenty years ago as he does now, and the world believed that my Sermons at St Mary's were full of red-hot Tractarianism. Then strangers came to hear me preach, and were astonished at their own disappointment. I recollect the wife of a great prelate from a distance coming to hear me, and then expressing her surprise to find that I preached nothing but a plain humdrum Sermon. I recollect how, when on the Sunday before Commemoration one year, a number of strangers came to hear me, and I preached in my usual way, residents in Oxford, of high position, were loud in their satisfaction that on a great occasion, I had made a simple failure, for after all there was nothing in the Sermon to hear. Well, but they were not going to let me off, for all my common-sense view of duty. Accordingly, they got up the charitable theory which this Writer revives. They said that there was a double purpose in those plain addresses of mine, and that my Sermons were never so artful as when they seemed common-place; that there were sentences which redeemed their apparent simplicity and quietness. So they watched during the delivery of a Sermon, which to them was too practical to be useful, for the concealed point of it, which they could at least imagine, if they could not discover. 'Men used to suspect Dr Newman,' he says, 'of writing a *whole* Sermon, *not* for the sake of *the text or of the matter*, but for the sake of . . . *one* phrase, *one* epithet, *one* little barbed arrow, which, as he *swept magnificently* past on the stream of his calm eloquence, *seemingly* unconscious of all presences, save those unseen, he delivered unheeded,' &c. pp. 28, 29. To all appearance, he says, I was 'unconscious of all presences'; so this kind Writer supplies the true interpretation of this unconsciousness. He is not able to deny that 'the *whole* Sermon' had the *appearance* of being '*for the sake* of the text and matter'; therefore he suggests that perhaps it wasn't. And then he emptily talks of the 'magnificent sweep of my eloquence', and my 'oratoric power'. Did he forget that the Sermon of which he thus speaks can be read by others as well as him ? Now, the sentences are as short as Aristotle's, and as grave as Bishop Butler's. It is written almost in the condensed style of Tract 90. Eloquence there is none. I put this down as Blot *ten*.

2. And now as to the subject of the Sermon. The series of which the Volume consists are such Sermons as are, more or less, exceptions to the rule which I ordinarily observed, as to the subjects which I introduced into the pulpit of St Mary's. They are not purely ethical or doctrinal. They were for the most part caused by circumstances of the day or of the time, and they belong to various years. One was written in 1832, two in 1836, two in 1838, five in 1840, five in 1841, four in 1842, seven in 1843. Many of them are engaged on one subject, viz. in viewing the Church in its relation to the world. By the world was meant, not simply those multitudes which were not in the Church, but the existing body of human society, whether in the Church or not, whether Catholics, Protestants, Greeks, or Mahometans, theists or idolaters, as being ruled by principles, maxims, and instincts of their own, that is, of an unregenerate nature, whatever their supernatural privileges might be, greater or less, according to their form of religion. This view of the relation of the Church to the world as taken apart from questions of ecclesiastical politics,

as they may be called, is often brought out in my Sermons. Two occur to me at once; No. 3 of my Plain Sermons, which was written in 1829, and No. 15 of my Third Volume, written in 1835. Then, on the other hand, by Church I meant – in common with all writers connected with the Tract Movement, whatever their shades of opinion, and with the whole body of English divines, except those of the Puritan or Evangelical School – the whole of Christendom, from the Apostles' time till now, whatever their later divisions into Latin, Greek, and Anglican. I have explained this view of the subject above at pp. 148–150 of this Volume. When then I speak, in the particular Sermon before us, of the members, or the rulers, or the action of 'the Church', I mean neither the Latin, nor the Greek, nor the English, taken by itself, but of the whole Church as one body: of Italy as one with England, of the Saxon or Norman as one with the Caroline Church. *This* was specially the one Church, and the points in which one branch or one period differed from another were not and could not be Notes of the Church, because Notes necessarily belonged to the whole of the Church everywhere and always.

This being my doctrine as to the relation of the Church to the world, I laid down in the Sermon three principles concerning it, and there left the matter. The first is, that Divine Wisdom had framed for its action, laws which man, if left to himself, would have antecedently pronounced to be the worst possible for its success, and which in all ages have been called by the world, as they were in the Apostles' days, 'foolishness'; that man ever relies on physical and material force, and on carnal inducements – as Mahomet with his sword and his houris, or indeed almost as that theory of religion, called, since the Sermon was written, 'muscular Christianity'; but that our Lord, on the contrary, has substituted meekness for haughtiness, passiveness for violence, and innocence for craft: and that the event has shown the high wisdom of such an economy, for it has brought to light a set of natural laws, unknown before, by which the seeming paradox that weakness should be stronger than might, and simplicity than worldly policy, is readily explained.

Secondly, I said that men of the world, judging by the event, and not recognizing the secret causes of the success, viz. a higher order of natural laws – natural, though their source and action were supernatural (for 'the meek inherit the earth', by means of a meekness which comes from above) – these men, I say, concluded, that the success which they witnessed must arise from some evil secret which the world had not mastered – by means of magic, as they said in the first ages, by cunning as they say now. And accordingly they thought that the humility and inoffensiveness of Christians, or of Churchmen, was a mere pretence and blind to cover the real causes of that success, which Christians could explain and would not; and that they were simply hypocrites.

Thirdly, I suggested that shrewd ecclesiastics, who knew very well that there was neither magic nor craft in the matter, and, from their intimate acquaintance with what actually went on within the Church, discerned what were the real causes of its success, were of course under the temptation of substituting reason for conscience, and, instead of simply obeying the command, were led to do good that good might come, that is, to act *in order* to their success, and not from a motive of faith. Some, I said, did yield to the temptation more or less, and their motives became mixed; and in this way the world in a more subtle shape has got into the Church; and hence it has come to pass, that, looking at its history from first to last, we cannot possibly draw the line between good and evil there, and say either that every thing is to be defended, or some things to be condemned. I expressed the difficulty, which I supposed to be inherent in the Church, in the following words. I said, '*Priestcraft has ever been considered the badge*, and its imputation is a kind of Note of the Church; and *in part indeed truly*, because the presence of powerful enemies, and the sense of their own weakness, *has sometimes tempted Christians to the abuse, instead of the use of Christian wisdom, to be wise without being harmless*; but partly, nay, for the most part, not truly, but slanderously, and merely because the world called this wisdom craft, when it was found to be a match for its own numbers and power.' This passage he has partly garbled, partly omitted. Blot *eleven*.

Such is the substance of the Sermon: and as to the main drift of it, it was this; that I was, there and elsewhere, scrutinizing the course of the Church as a whole, as if philosophically, as an historical phenomenon, and observing the laws on which it was conducted. Hence the Sermon, or Essay as it more truly is, is written in a dry and unimpassioned way: it shows as little of human warmth of feeling, I repeat, as a Sermon of Bishop Butler's. Yet, under that calm exterior there was a deep and keen sensitiveness, as I shall now proceed to show.

3. If I mistake not, it was written with a secret thought about myself. Every one preaches according to his frame of mind, at the time of preaching. One heaviness especially oppressed me at that season, which this Writer, twenty years afterwards, has set himself with a good will to renew: it arose from the sense of the base calumnies which were thrown upon me on all sides. In this trouble of mind I gained, while I reviewed the history of the Church, at once an argument and a consolation. My argument was this: if I, who knew my own innocence, was so blackened by party prejudice, perhaps those high rulers and those servants of the Church, in the many ages which intervened between the early Nicene times and the present, who were laden with such grievous accusations, were innocent also; and this reflection served to make me tender towards those great names of the past, to whom weaknesses or crimes were imputed, and reconciled me to difficulties in ecclesiastical proceedings, which there were no means now of properly explaining. And the sympathy thus excited for them, re-acted on myself, and I found comfort in being able to put myself under the shadow of those who had suffered as I was suffering, and who seemed to promise me their recompense, since I had a fellowship in their trial. In a letter to my Bishop at the time of Tract 90, part of which I have quoted, I said that I had ever tried to 'keep innocency'; and now two years had passed since them, and men were louder and louder in heaping on me the very charges, which this Writer repeats out of my Sermon, of 'fraud and cunning', 'craftiness and deceitfulness', 'double-dealing', 'priestcraft', of being 'mysterious, dark, subtle, designing', when I was all the time conscious to myself, in my degree, and after my measure, of 'sobriety, self-restraint, and control of word and feeling'. I had had experience how my past success had been imputed to 'secret management'; and how, when I had shown surprise at that success, that surprise again was imputed to 'deceit'; and how my honest heartfelt submission to authority had been called, as it was called in a colonial Bishop's charge, 'mystic humility'; and how my silence was called an 'hypocrisy'; and my faithfulness to my clerical engagements a secret correspondence with the enemy. And I found a way of destroying my sensitiveness about these things which jarred upon my sense of justice, and otherwise would have been too much for me, by the contemplation of a large law of the Divine Dispensation, and found myself more and more able to

bear in my own person a present trial, of which in my past writings I had expressed an anticipation.

For thus feeling and thus speaking this Writer has the charitableness and the decency to call me 'Mawworm'. 'I found him telling Christians,' he says, 'that they will always seem "artificial", and "wanting in openness and manliness"; that they will always be "a mystery" to the world; and that the world will always think them rogues; and bidding them glory in what the world (that is, the rest of their fellow-countrymen) disown, and say with Mawworm, "I like to be despised." . . . How was I to know that the preacher . . . was utterly blind to the broad meaning and the plain practical result of a Sermon like this delivered before fanatic and hot-headed young men, who hung upon his every word?' – p. 29. Hot-headed young men! why, man, you are writing a Romance. You think the scene is Alexandria or the Spanish main, where you may let your imagination play revel to the extent of inveracity. It is good luck for me that the scene of my labours was not at Moscow or Damascus. Then I might be one of your ecclesiastical Saints, of which I sometimes hear in conversation, but with whom, I am glad to say, I have no personal acquaintance. Then you might ascribe to me a more deadly craft than mere quibbling and lying; in Spain I should have been an Inquisitor, with my rack in the background; I should have had a concealed dagger in Sicily; at Venice I should have brewed poison; in Turkey I should have been the Sheik-el-Islam with my bowstring; in Khorassan I should have been a veiled Prophet. 'Fanatic young men!' Why he is writing out a list of a Dramatic Personæ; 'guards, conspirators, populace', and the like. He thinks I was ever moving about with a train of Capulets at my heels. 'Hot-headed fanatics, who hung on my every word'! If he had taken to write a history, and not a play, he would have easily found out, as I have said, that from 1841 I had severed myself from the younger generation of Oxford, that Dr Pusey and I had then closed our theological meetings at his house, that I had brought my own weekly evening parties to an end, that I preached only by fits and starts at St Mary's, so that the attendance of young men was broken up, that in those very weeks from Christmas till over Easter, during which this Sermon was preached, I was but five times in the pulpit there. He would have known, that it was written at a time when I was shunned rather than sought, when I had great sacrifices in anticipation, when I was thinking much of myself; that I was ruthlessly tearing myself away from my own followers, and that, in the musings of that Sermon, I was at the very utmost only delivering a testimony in my behalf for time to come, not sowing my rhetoric broadcast for the chance of present sympathy. Blot *twelve*.

I proceed: he says at p. 29, 'I found him actually using of such prelates (and, as I thought, of himself and his party likewise), the words "They yield outwardly; to assent inwardly were to betray the faith. Yet they are called deceitful and double-dealing, because they do as much as they can, not more than they may." ' This too is a proof of my duplicity! Let this writer go with some one else, just a little further than he has gone with me; and let him get into a court of law for libel; and let him be convicted; and let him still fancy that his libel, though a libel, was true, and let us then see whether he will not in such a case 'yield outwardly', without assenting internally; and then again whether we should please him, if we called him 'deceitful and double-dealing', because 'he did as much as he could, not more than he ought to do.' But Tract 90 will supply a real illustration of what I meant. I yielded to the Bishops in outward act, viz. in not defending the Tract, and in closing the Series; but, not only did I not assent inwardly to any condemnation of it, but I opposed myself to the proposition of a condemnation on the part of authority. Yet I was then by the public called 'deceitful and double-dealing', as this Writer calls me now, 'because I did as much as I felt I could do, and not more than I felt I could honestly do.' Many were the publications of the day and the private letters which accused me of shuffling, because I closed the Series of Tracts, yet kept the Tracts on sale, as if I ought to comply not only with what my Bishop asked, but with what he did not ask, and perhaps did not wish. However, such teaching, according to this Writer, was likely to make young men suspect, that truth was not a virtue for its own sake, but only for the sake of 'the spread of Catholic opinions', and the 'salvation of their own souls'; and that 'cunning was the weapon which heaven had allowed to them to defend themselves against the persecuting Protestant public.' – p. 30. Blot *thirteen*.

And now I draw attention to another point. He says at p. 29, 'How was I to know that the preacher . . . did not foresee, that fanatic and hot-headed young men would think that they obeyed him, by becoming affected, artificial, sly, shifty, ready for concealments and *equivocations*?' How should he know! What!

I suppose that we are to think every man a knave till he is proved not to be such. Know! had he no friend to tell him whether I was 'affected' or 'artificial' myself? Could he not have done better than impute *equivocations* to me, at a time when I was in no sense answerable for the *amphibologia* of the Roman casuists? Has he a single fact which belongs to me personally or by profession to couple my name with equivocation in 1843? How should he know that I was not sly, smooth, artificial, non-natural! he should know by that common manly frankness, if he had it, by which we put confidence in others, till they are proved to have forfeited it; he should know it by my own words in that very Sermon, in which I say it is best to be natural, and that reserve is at best but an unpleasant necessity. I say, 'I do not deny that there is something very engaging in a frank and unpretending manner; some persons have it more than others; in *some persons it is a great grace*. But it must be recollected that I am speaking of *times of persecution and oppression* to Christians, such as the text foretells; and then surely frankness will become nothing else than indignation at the oppressor, and vehement speech, if it is permitted. Accordingly, as persons have deep *feelings*, so they will find the necessity of self-control, lest they should say what they ought not.' He omits these words. I call, then, this base insinuation that I taught equivocation. Blot the *fourteenth*.

Lastly, he sums up thus: 'If Dr Newman would . . . persist (as in this Sermon) in dealing with matters dark, offensive, doubtful, sometimes actually forbidden, at least according to the notions of the great majority of English Churchmen; if he would always do so in a tentative, paltering way, seldom or never letting the world know how much he believed, how far he intended to go; if, in a word, his method of teaching was a suspicious one, what wonder if the minds of men were filled with suspicions of him?' – p. 30.

Now first he is speaking of my Sermons; where, then, is his proof that in my Sermons I dealt in matters dark, offensive, doubtful, actually forbidden? he has said nothing in proof that I have not been able flatly to deny.

'Forbidden according to the notions of the great majority of English Churchmen.' I should like to know what opinions, beyond those which relate to the Creed, *are* held by the 'majority of English Churchmen' – are his own? is it not perfectly well known, that 'the great majority' think of him and his views with a feeling which I will not describe, because it is not necessary for my argument ? So far is certain, that he has not the majority with him.

'In a tentative, paltering way.' The word 'paltering' I reject, as vague; as to 'tentative', he must show that I was tentative in my Sermons; and he has eight volumes to look through. As to the ninth, my University Sermons, of course I was 'tentative'; but not because 'I would seldom or never let the world know how much I believed, or how far I intended to go'; but because in deep subjects, which had not been fully investigated, I said as much as I believed, and about as far as I saw I could go; and a man cannot do more; and I account no man to be a philosopher who attempts to do more. How long am I to have the office of merely negative assertions which are but supported by former assertions, in which John is ever helping Tom, and the elephant stands upon the tortoise ? This is Blot *fifteen*.

The Anglican Church

This Writer says – 'If there is, as there is, a strong distrust of certain Catholics, it is restricted to the proselytizing priests among them; and especially to those, who, like Dr Newman, have turned round upon their mother Church (I had almost said their mother country), with contumely and slander.' – p. 32.

No one has a right to make a charge, without at least an attempt to prove what he says; but this Writer is consistent with himself. From the time that he first spoke of me in the Magazine, *when* has he ever even professed to give evidence of any sort for any one of his charges, from his own sense of propriety, and without being challenged on the point? After the sentence which I have been quoting, and another like it, he coolly passes on to Tract 90! Blot *sixteen*; but I shall dwell on it awhile, for its own sake.

Now I have been bringing out my mind in this Volume on every subject which has come before me; and therefore I am bound to state plainly what I feel and have felt, since I was a Catholic, about the Anglican Church. I said, in a former page, that, on my conversion, I was not conscious of any change in me of thought or feeling, as regards matters of doctrine; this, however, was not the case as regards some matters of fact, and, unwilling as I am to give offence to religious Anglicans, I am bound to confess that I felt a great change in my view of the Church of England. I cannot tell how soon there came on me – but very soon – an extreme astonishment that I had ever imagined it to be a portion of the Catholic Church. For the first time, I looked at it from without, and (as I should myself say) saw it as it was. Forthwith I could not get myself to see in it anything else than what I had so long fearfully suspected, from as far back as 1836 – a mere national institution. As if my eyes were suddenly opened, so I saw it – spontaneously, apart from any definite act of reason or any argument; and so I have seen it ever since. I suppose, the main cause of this lay in the contrast which was presented to me by the Catholic Church. I then recognized at once a reality which was quite a new thing with me. Then I was sensible that I was not making for myself a Church by an effort of thought; I needed not to make an act of faith in her; I had not painfully to force myself into a position, but my mind fell back upon itself in relaxation and in peace, and I gazed at her almost passively as a great objective fact. I looked at her – at her rites, her ceremonial, and her precepts; and I said, 'This *is* a religion'; and then, when I looked back upon the poor Anglican Church, for which I had laboured so hard, and upon all that appertained to it, and thought of our various attempts to dress it up doctrinally and esthetically, it seemed to me to be the veriest of nonentities. Vanity of vanities, all is vanity! How can I make a record of what passed within me, without seeming to be satirical ? But I speak plain, serious words. As people call me credulous for acknowledging Catholic claims, so they call me satirical for disowning Anglican pretensions; to them it *is* credulity, to them it *is* satire; but it is not so in me. What they think exaggeration, I think truth. I am not speaking of the Anglican Church in any disdain, though to them I seem contemptuous. To them of course it is 'Aut Cæsar aut nullus', but not to me. It may be a great creation, though it be not divine, and this is how I judge of it. Men, who abjure the divine right of kings, would be very indignant, if on that account they were considered disloyal. And so I recognize in the Anglican Church a time-honoured institution, of noble historical memories, a monument of ancient wisdom, a momentous arm of political strength, a great national organ, a source of vast popular advantage, and, to a certain point, a witness and teacher of religious truth. I do not think that, if what I have written about it since I have been a Catholic, be equitably considered as a whole, I shall be found to have taken any other view than this; but that it is something sacred, that it is an oracle of revealed doctrine, that it can claim a share in St Ignatius or St Cyprian, that it can take the rank, contest the teaching, and stop the path of the Church of St Peter, that it can call itself 'the Bride of the Lamb', this is the view of it which simply disappeared from my mind on my conversion, and which it would be almost a miracle to reproduce. 'I went by, and lo! it was gone; I sought it, but its place could nowhere be found;' and nothing can bring it back to me. And, as to its possession of an episcopal succession from the time of the Apostles, well, it may have it, and, if the Holy See ever so decided, I will believe it, as being the decision of a higher judgment than my own; but, for myself, I must have St Philip's gift, who saw the sacerdotal character on the forehead of a gaily-attired youngster, before I can by my own wit acquiesce in it, for antiquarian arguments are altogether unequal to the urgency of visible facts. Why is it that I must pain dear friends by saying so, and kindle a sort of resentment against me in the kindest of hearts ? but I must, though to do it be not only a grief to me, but most impolitic at the moment. Anyhow, this is my mind; and, if to have it, if to have betrayed it, before now, involuntarily by my words or my deeds, if on a fitting occasion, as now, to have avowed it, if all this be a proof of the justice of the charge brought against me of having 'turned round upon my Mother-Church with contumely and slander', in this sense, but in no other sense, do I plead guilty to it without a word in extenuation.

In no other sense surely; the Church of England has been the instrument of Providence in conferring great benefits on those who have been baptized; had I been born an English Presbyterian, me; had I been born in Dissent, perhaps I should never have known our Lord's divintiyt; and I not come to to Oxford, perhaps I never should have heard of the visible Church, or of Tradition, or other Catholic doctrines. And as I have received so much good from the Anglican Establishment itself, can I have the heart, or rather the want of charity, considering that it does for so many others, what it has done for me, to wish to see it overthrown ? I have no such wish while it is what it is, and while we are so small a body. Nor for its own sake, but for the sake of the many congregations to which it ministers, I will do nothing against it. While Catholics are so weak in England, it is doing our work; and, though it does us harm in a measure, at present the balance is in our favour. What our duty would be at another time and in other circumstances, supposing, for instance, the Establishment lost its dogmatic faith, or at least did not preach it, is another matter altogether. In secular history we read of hostile nations having long truces, and renewing them from time to time, and that seems to be the position the Catholic Church may fairly take up at present in relation to the Anglican Establishment.

Doubtless the National Church has hitherto been a serviceable breakwater against doctrinal errors, more fundamental than its own. How long this will last in the years now before us, it is impossible to say, for the Nation drags down its Church to its own level; but still the National Church has the same sort of influence over the Nation that a periodical has upon the party which it represents, and my own idea of a Catholic's fitting attitude towards the National Church in this its supreme hour, is that of assisting and sustaining it, if it be in our power, in the interest of dogmatic truth. I should wish to avoid every thing, except under the direct call of duty, which went to weaken its hold upon the public mind, or to unsettle its establishment, or to embarrass and lessen its maintenance of those great Christian and Catholic principles and doctrines which it has up to this time successfully preached.

I say, 'except under the call of duty'; and this exception, I am obliged to admit, is not a slight one; it is one which necessarily places a bar to any closer relation between it and ourselves, than that of an armed truce. For, in the first place, it stands to reason that even a volume, such as this has been, exerts an influence adverse to the Establishment – at least in the case of many minds; and this I cannot avoid, though I have sincerely attempted to keep as wide of controversy in the course of it, as ever I could. And next I cannot deny, what must be ever a very sore point with Anglicans, that, if any Anglican comes to me after careful thought and prayer, and with deliberate purpose, and says, 'I believe in the Holy Catholic Church, and that your Church and yours alone is it, and I demand admittance into it', it would be the greatest of sins in me to reject such a man, as being a distinct contravention of our Lord's maxim, 'Freely ye have received, freely give.'

I have written three volumes which may be considered controversial; Loss and Gain in 1847; Lectures on Difficulties felt by Anglicans in submitting to the Catholic Church in 1850; and Lectures on the present Position of Catholics in England in 1851. And though I have neither time nor need to go into the matter minutely, a few words will suffice for some general account of what has been my object and my tone in these works severally.

Of these three, the Lectures on the 'Position of Catholics' have nothing to do with the Church of England, as such; they are directed against the Protestant or Ultra-Protestant Tradition on the subject of Catholicism since the time of Queen Elizabeth, in which parties indeed in the Church of England have largely participated, but which cannot be confused with Anglican teaching itself. Much less can that Tradition be confused with the doctrine of the Laudian or of the Tractarian School. I owe nothing to Protestantism; and I spoke against it even when I was an Anglican, as well as in these Catholic Lectures. If I spoke in them against the Church Established, it was because, and so far as, at the time when they were delivered, the Establishment took a violent part against the Catholic Church, on the basis of the Protestant Tradition. Moreover, I had never as an Anglican been a lover of the actual Establishment; Hurrell Froude's Remains, in which it is called an 'incubus' and 'Upas Tree', will stand in evidence, as for him, so for me; for I was one of the Editors. What I said even as an Anglican, it is not strange that I said when I was not. Indeed I have been milder in my thoughts of the Establishment ever since I have been a Catholic than before, and for an obvious reason – when I was an Anglican, I viewed it as repressing a higher doctrine than its own; and now I view it as keeping out a lower and more dangerous.

Then as to my Lectures on Anglican Difficulties. Neither were these formally directed against the National Church. They were addressed to the 'Children of the Movement of 1833', to impress upon them, that, whatever was the case with others, their duty at least was to become Catholics, since Catholicism was the real scope and issue of that Movement. 'There is but one thing,' I say, 'that forces me to speak. . . . It will be a miserable thing for you and for me, if I have been instrumental in bringing you but half-way, if I have co-operated in removing your invincible ignorance, but am able to do no more.' – p. 5. Such being the drift of the Volume, the reasoning directed against the Church of England goes no further than this, that it had no claims whatever on such of its members as were proceeding onwards with the Movement into the Catholic Church.

Lastly, as to Loss and Gain: it is the story, simply ideal, of the conversion of an Oxford man. Its drift is to show how little there is in Anglicanism to satisfy and retain a young and earnest heart. In this Tale, all the best characters are sober Church-of-England people. No Tractarians proper are introduced: and this is noted in the Advertisement: 'No *proper* representative is intended in this Tale, of the religious opinions, which had lately so much influence in the University of Oxford.' There *could* not be such in the Tale, without the introduction of friends, which was impossible in its very notion. But, since the scene was to be laid during the very years, and at the head-quarters, of Tractarianism, some expedient was necessary in order to meet what was a great difficulty. My expedient was the introduction of what may be called Tractarians *improper*; and I took them the more readily, because, though I knew that such there were, I knew none of them personally. I mean such men as I used to consider of 'the gilt-gingerbread school', from whom I expected little good, persons whose religion lay in ritualism or architecture, and who 'played at Popery' or at Anglicanism. I repeat I knew no such men, because it is one thing to desire fine churches and ceremonies (which of course I did myself), and quite another thing to desire these and nothing else; but at that day there was in some quarters, though not in those where I had influence, a strong movement in the esthetic direction. Doubtless I went too far in my apprehension of such a movement: for one of the best, and most devoted and hard-working Priests I ever knew was the late Father Hutchison, of the London Oratory, and I believe it was architecture that directed his thoughts towards the Catholic Church. However, I had in my mind an external religion which was inordinate; and, as the men who were considered instances of it, were personally unknown to me, even by name, I introduced them, under imaginary representatives, in Loss and Gain, and that, in order to get clear of Tractarians proper; and of the three men, whom I have introduced, the Anglican is the best. In like manner I introduced two 'gilt-gingerbread' young ladies, who were ideal, absolutely, utterly, without a shred of concrete existence about them; and I introduced them with the remark that they were 'really kind charitable persons', and '*by no means* put forth as *a type* of a class', that 'among such persons were to be found the gentlest spirits and the tenderest hearts', and that 'these sisters had open hands, if they had not wise heads', but that 'they did not know much of matters ecclesiastical, and they knew less of themselves.'

It has been said, indeed, I know not to what extent, that I introduced my friends or partisans into the Tale; this is utterly untrue. Only two cases of this misconception have come to my knowledge, and I at once denied each of them outright; and I take this opportunity of denying generally the truth of all other similar changes. No friend of mine, no one connected in any way with the Movement, entered into the composition of any one of the characters. Indeed, putting aside the two instances which have been distinctly brought before me, I have not even any sort of suspicion who the persons are, whom I am thus accused of introducing.

Next, this writer goes on to speak of Tract 90; a subject of which I have treated at great length in a former passage of this narrative, and, in consequence, need not take up again now.

Series of Lives of the English Saints

I have given the history of this publication above at pp. 33–34. It was to have consisted of almost 300 Lives, and I was to have been the Editor. It was brought to an end, before it was well begun, by the act of friends who were frightened at the first Life printed, the Life of St Stephen Harding. Thus I was not responsible except for the first two numbers; and the Advertisements distinctly declared this. I had just the same responsibility about the other Lives, that my assailant had, and not a bit more. However, it answers his purpose to consider me responsible.

Next, I observe, that his delusion about 'hot-headed fanatic young men' continues: here again I figure with my strolling company. 'They said,' he observed, 'what they believed; at least, what they had been taught to believe that they ought to believe. And who had taught them? Dr Newman can best answer that question,' p. 33. Well, I will do what I can to solve the mystery.

Now as to the juvenile writers in the proposed series. One was my friend Mr Bowden, who in 1843 was a man of 46 years old; he was to have written St Boniface. Another was Mr Johnson, a man of 42; he was to have written St Aldelm. Another was the author of St Augustine: let us hear something about him from this writer:

'Dr Newman,' he says, 'might have said to the Author of the Life of St Augustine, when he found him, in *the heat and haste of youthful fanaticism*, outraging historic truth and the law of evidence, "This must not be." ' – p. 33.

Good. This juvenile was past 40 – well, say 39. Blot *seventeen*. 'This must not be.' This is what I ought to have said, it seems! And then, you see, I have not the talent, and never had, of some people, for lecturing my equals, much less men twenty years older than myself.

But again, the author of St Augustine's Life distinctly says in his

Advertisement, '*No one but himself* is responsible for the way in which these materials have been used.' Blot *eighteen*.

Thirty-three Lives were actually published. Out of the whole number this writer notices *three*. Of these one is 'charming'; therefore I am not to have the benefit of it. Another 'outrages historic truth and the law of evidence'; therefore 'it was notoriously sanctioned by Dr Newman.' And the third was 'one of the most offensive', and Dr Newman must have formally connected himself with it in 'a moment of amiable weakness.' – p. 33. What even-handed justice is here! Blot *nineteen*.

But to return to the juvenile author of St Augustine – 'I found,' says this writer, 'the Life of St Augustine saying, that, though the pretended visit of St Peter to England wanted *historic evidence*, "yet it has undoubtedly been received as a *pious opinion* by the Church at large, as we learn from the often-quoted words of St Innocent I (who wrote AD 416) that St Peter was instrumental in the conversion of the West generally." ' – p. 34. He brings this passage against me (with which, however, I have nothing more to do than he has) as a great misdemeanour; but let us see what his criticism is worth. 'And this sort of argument,' continues the passage, 'though it ought to be kept *quite distinct from* documentary and historic proof, will *not be without its effect* on devout minds,' &c. I should have thought this a very sober doctrine, viz. that we must not confuse together two things quite distinct from each other, criticism and devotion, proof and opinion – that a *devout* mind will hold *opinions* which it cannot demonstrate by 'historic *proof*'. What, I ask, is the harm of saying this ? Is *this* my Assailant's definition of opinion, 'a thing which *can* be proved ?' I cannot answer for him, but I can answer for men in general. Let him read Sir David Brewster's 'More Worlds than One' – this principle, which is so shocking to my assailant, is precisely the argument of Sir David's book; he tells us that the plurality of worlds *cannot* be *proved*, but *will* be *received* by religious men. He asks, p. 229, '*If* the stars are *not* suns, for what conceivable *purpose* were they created ?' and then he lays down dogmatically, p. 254, 'There is no *opinion, out of* the region of *pure demonstration*, more universally *cherished* than the doctrine of the Plurality of worlds.' And in his Title-page he styles his 'opinion' 'the *creed* of the philosopher and the *hope* of the Christian.' If Brewster may bring devotion into Astronomy, why may not my friend bring it into History ? and that the more, when he actually declares that it ought to be kept *quite distinct* from history, and by no means assumes that he is an historian because he is a hagiographer; whereas, somehow or other, Sir David does seem to me to show a zeal greater than becomes a *savant*, and to assume that he himself is a theologian because he is an astronomer. This writer owes Sir David as well as me an apology. Blot *twenty*.

He ought to wish his original charge against me in the Magazine dead and buried; but he has the good sense and good taste to revive it again and again. This is one of the places which he has chosen for it. Let him then, just for a change, substitute Sir David Brewster for me in his sentence; Sir David has quite as much right to the compliment as I have, as far as this Life of St Augustine is concerned. Then he will be saying, that, because Sir David teaches that the belief in more worlds than one is a pious opinion, and not a demonstrated fact, he 'does not care for truth for its own sake, or teach men to regard it as a virtue,' p. 34. Blot *twenty-one*.

However, he goes on to give in this same page one other evidence of my disregard of truth. The author of St Augustine's Life also asks the following question: '*On what evidence* do we put faith in the existence of St George, the patron of England? Upon such, assuredly, as an acute *critic or skilful pleader* might easily scatter to the winds; the belief of prejudiced or credulous witnesses, the unwritten record of empty pageants and bauble decorations. On the side of scepticism might be exhibited a powerful array of suspicious legends and exploded acts. Yet, *after all, what Catholic is there but would count it a profaneness to question the existence of St George?*' On which my assailant observes, 'When I found Dr Newman allowing his disciples . . . in page after page, in Life after Life, to talk nonsense of this kind which is not only sheer Popery, *but saps the very foundation of historic truth*, was it so wonderful that I conceived him to have taught and thought like them?' p. 34, that is, to have taught lying.

Well and good; here again take a parallel; not St George, but Lycurgus.

Mr Grote says: 'Plutarch begins his biography of Lycurgus with the following ominous words: "Concerning the lawgiver Lycurgus, we can assert *absolutely nothing*, which is not controverted. There are different stories in respect to his birth, his travels, his death, and also his mode of proceeding, political as well as legislative: least of all is the time in which he lived agreed on." And this exordium *is but too well borne out* by the unsatisfactory nature of the accounts which we read, not only in Plutarch himself, but in those other authors, out of whom we are obliged to make up our idea of the memorable Lycurgian system.' – Greece, vol. ii. p. 455. But Bishop Thirlwall says, 'Experience proves that *scarcely any amount of variation*, as to the time or circumstances of a fact, in the authors who record it, *can be a sufficient ground* for doubting its reality.' – Greece, vol. i. p. 332.

Accordingly, my assailant is virtually saying of the latter of these two historians, 'When I found the Bishop of St David's talking nonsense of this kind, which saps the very foundation of historic truth,' was it 'hasty or far-fetched' to conclude 'that he did not care for truth for its own sake, or teach his disciples to regard it as a virtue?' p. 34. Nay, further, the Author of St Augustine is no more a disciple of mine, than the Bishop of St David's is of my Assailant's, and therefore the parallel will be more exact if I accuse this Professor of History of *teaching* Dr Thirlwall not to care for truth, as a virtue, for its own sake. Blot *twenty-two*.

It is hard on me to have this dull, profitless work, but I have pledged myself – so now for St Walburga.

Now will it be believed that this Writer suppresses the fact that the miracles of St Walburga are treated by the author of her Life as mythical? yet that is the tone of the whole composition. This Writer can notice it in the Life of St Neot, the first of the three Lives which he criticizes; these are his words: 'Some of them, the writers, for instance, of Volume 4, which contains, among others, a charming life of St Neot, treat the stories openly as legends and myths, and tell them as they stand, without asking the reader, or themselves, to believe them altogether. The method is harmless enough, if the legends had stood alone; but dangerous enough, when they stand side by side with stories told in earnest, like that of St Walburga.' – pp. 34–35.

Now, first, that the miraculous stories *are* treated, in the Life of St Walburga, as legends and myths. Throughout, the miracles and extraordinary occurrences are spoken of as 'said' or 'reported'; and the suggestion is made that, even though they occurred, they might have been after all natural. Thus, in one of the very passages which my Assailant quotes, the author says 'Illuminated men feel the privileges of Christianity, and to them the evil influence of

Satanic power is horribly discernible, like the Egyptian darkness which could be felt; and *the only way to express* their keen perception of it is *to say*, that they *see* upon the countenances of the slaves of sin, the marks, and lineaments, and stamp of the evil one; and [that] they *smell* with their nostrils the horrible fumes that arise from their *vices* and uncleansed *heart*,' &c., p. 38. This introduces St Sturme and the gambolling Germans; what does it mean but that 'the intolerable scent' was nothing physical, or strictly miraculous, but the horror, parallel to physical distress, with which the Saint was affected, from his knowledge of the state of their souls ? My assailant is a lucky man, if mental pain has never come upon him with a substance and a volume, as forcible as if it were bodily.

And so in like manner, the Author of the Life says, as this writer actually has quoted him, 'a story *was told and believed*,' p. 94. 'One evening, *says her history*,' p. 87. 'Another incident *is thus related*,' p. 88. 'Immediately, *says* Wülfhard,' p. 91. 'A vast number of other cases are *recorded*,' p. 92. And there is a distinct intimation that they may be myths, in a passage which this Assailant himself quotes, 'All these have the *character* of a gentle mother correcting the idleness and faults of careless and thoughtless children with tenderness.' – p. 95. I think the criticism which he makes upon this Life is one of the most wanton passages in his Pamphlet. The Life is beautifully written, full of poetry, and, as I have said, bears on its very surface the profession of a legendary and mythical character. Blot *twenty-three*.

In saying all this, I have no intention whatever of implying that miracles did not illustrate the Life of St Walburga; but neither the Author nor I have bound ourselves to the belief of certain instances in particular. My Assailant, in the passage which I just now quoted from him, made some distinction, which was apparently intended to save St Neot, while it condemned St Walburga. He said that legends are 'dangerous enough, when they stand side by side with stories told in earnest like St Walburga.' He will find he has here Dr Milman against him, as he has already had Sir David Brewster, and the Bishop of St David's. He accuses me of having 'outraged historic truth and the law of evidence', because friends of mine have considered that, though opinions need not be convictions, nevertheless that legends may be connected with history: now, on the contrary, let us hear the Dean of St Paul's:

'*History*, to be *true*, must condescend to speak the language of *legend*; the *belief* of the times is *part* of the *record* of the times; and, though there may occur what may baffle its more calm and searching philosophy, *it must not disdain* that which was the primal, almost universal, motive of human life.' – Latin. Christ., vol. i. p. 388. Dr Milman's decision justifies me in putting this down as Blot *twenty-four*.

However, there is one miraculous account for which this writer makes me directly answerable, and with reason; and with it I shall conclude my reply to his criticisms on the 'Lives of the English Saints.' It is the medicinal oil which flows from the relics of St Walburga.

Now, as I shall have occasion to remark under my next Head, these two questions among others occur, in judging of a miraculous story; viz. whether the matter of it is extravagant, and whether it is a fact. And first, it is plain there is nothing extravagant in this report of the relics having a supernatural virtue; and for this reason, because there are such instances in Scripture, and Scripture cannot be extravagant. For instance, a man was restored to life by touching the relics of the Prophet Eliseus. The sacred text runs thus: 'And Elisha died, and they buried him. And the bands of the Moabites invaded the land at the coming in of the year. And it came to pass, as they were burying a man, that, behold, they spied a band of men; and they cast the man into the sepulchre of Elisha. And, when the man was let down, *and touched the bones of Elisha, he revived*, and stood upon his feet.' Again, in the case of an inanimate substance, which had touched a living Saint: 'And God wrought *special miracles* by the hands of Paul; so that *from his body* were brought unto the sick *handkerchiefs or aprons*, and *the diseases departed from them*.' And again in the case of a pool: 'An *Angel went down* at a certain season into the pool, and troubled the water; whosoever then first, after the troubling of the water, stepped in, *was made whole of whatsoever disease* he had.' 2 Kings [4 Kings] xiii. 20, 21. Acts xix. 11, 12. John v. 4. Therefore there is nothing *extravagant* in the *character* of the miracle.

The main question then (I do not say the only remaining question, but the main question) is the *matter of fact* – *is* there an oil flowing from St Walburga's tomb, which is medicinal ? To this question I confined myself in the Preface to the Volume. Of the accounts of medieval miracles, I said that there was no *extrava-*

gance in their *general character*, but I could not affirm that there was always *evidence* for them. I could not simply accept them as *facts*, but I could not reject them in their *nature* – they *might* be true, for they were not impossible: but they were *not proved* to be true, because there was not trustworthy testimony. However, as to St Walburga, I made *one* exception, the fact of the medicinal oil, since for that miracle there was distinct and successive testimony. And then I went on to give a chain of witnesses. It was my duty to state what those witnesses said in their very words; and I did so; they were in Latin, and I gave them in Latin. One of them speaks of the 'sacrum oleum' flowing 'de membris ejus virgineis, maximè tamen pectoralibus'; and I so printed it – if I had left it out, this sweet-tempered Writer would have accused me of an 'economy'. I gave the testimonies in full, tracing them from the Saint's death. I said, 'She is one of the principal Saints of her age and country.' Then I quoted Basnage, a Protestant, who says, 'Six writers are extant, who have employed themselves in relating the deeds or miracles of Walburga.' Then I said that her 'renown was not the mere natural *growth* of ages, but begins with the very century of the Saint's death.' Then I observed that only two miracles seem to have been 'distinctly reported of her as occurring in her lifetime; and they were handed down apparently by tradition.' Also, that they are said to have commenced about AD 777. Then I spoke of the medicinal oil as having testimony to it in 893, in 1306, after 1450, in 1615, and in 1620. Also, I said that Mabillon seems not to have believed some of her miracles; and that the earliest witness had got into trouble with his Bishop. And so I left it, as a question to be decided by evidence, not deciding any thing myself.

What was the harm of all this? but my Critic has muddled it together in a most extraordinary manner, and I am far from sure that he knows himself the definite categorical charge which he intends it to convey against me. One of his remarks is, 'What has become of the holy oil for the last 240 years, Dr Newman does not say,' p. 37. Of course I did not, because I did not know; I gave the evidence as I found it; he assumes that I had a point to prove, and then asks why I did not make the evidence larger than it was. I put this down as Blot *twenty-five*.

I can tell him more about it now; the oil still flows; I have had some of it in my possession; it is medicinal; some think it is so by a natural quality, others by a divine gift. Perhaps it is on the confines of both.

5

Ecclesiastical Miracles

What is the use of going on with this Writer's criticism upon me, when I am confined to the dull monotony of exposing and oversetting him again and again, with a persistence, which many will think merciless, and few will have the interest to read ? Yet I am obliged to do so, lest I should seem to be evading difficulties.

Now as to Miracles. Catholics believe that they happen in any age of the Church, though not for the same purpose, in the same number, or with the same evidence, as in Apostolic times. The Apostles wrought them in evidence of their divine mission; and with this object they have been sometimes wrought by Evangelists of countries since, as even Protestants allow. Hence we hear of them in the history of St Gregory in Pontus, and St Martin in Gaul; and in their case, as in that of the Apostles, they were both numerous and clear. As they are granted to Evangelists, so are they granted, though in less measure and evidence, to other holy men; and as holy men are not found equally at all times and in all places, therefore miracles are in some places and times more than in others. And since, generally, they are granted to faith and prayer, therefore in a country in which faith and prayer abound, they will be more likely to occur, than where and when faith and prayer are not; so that their occurrence is irregular. And further, as faith and prayer obtain miracles, so still more commonly do they gain from above the ordinary interventions of Providence; and, as it is often very difficult to distinguish between a providence and a miracle, and there will be more providences than miracles, hence it will happen that many occurrences will be called miraculous, which, strictly speaking, are not such, and not more than providential mercies, or what are sometimes called 'graces' or 'favours'.

Persons, who believe all this, in accordance with Catholic

teaching, as I did and do, they, on the report of a miracle, will of necessity, the necessity of good logic, be led to say, first, 'It *may* be', and secondly, 'But I must have *good evidence* in order to believe it.' It *may* be, because miracles take place in all ages; it must be clearly *proved*, because perhaps after all it may be only a providential mercy, or an exaggeration, or a mistake, or an imposture. Well, this is precisely what I have said, which this Writer considers so irrational. I have said, as he quotes me, p. 36, 'In this day, and under our present circumstances, we can only reply, that there is no reason why they should not be.' Surely this is good logic, *provided* that miracles *do* occur in all ages; and so again is it logical to say, 'There is nothing, *prima facie*, in the miraculous accounts in question, to repel a *properly taught* or religiously disposed mind.' What is the matter with this statement ? My assailant does not pretend to say *what* the matter is, and he cannot; but he expresses a rude, unmeaning astonishment. Next, I stated *what* evidence there is for the miracles of which I was speaking; what is the harm of that ? He observes, 'What evidence Dr Newman requires, he makes evident at once. He at least will fear for himself, and swallow the whole as it comes.' – p. 36. What random abuse is this, or to use *his own words* of me just before, what 'stuff and nonsense!'. What is it I am 'swallowing' ? 'the whole' what ? the evidence ? or the miracles ? I have swallowed neither, nor implied any such thing. Blot *twenty-six*.

But to return: I have just said that a Catholic's state of mind, of logical necessity, will be, 'It *may* be a miracle, but it has to be *proved*.' *What* has to be proved ? 1. That the event occurred as stated, and is not a false report or an exaggeration. 2. That it is clearly miraculous, and not a mere providence or answer to prayer within the order of nature. What is the fault of saying this ? The inquiry is parallel to that which is made about some extraordinary fact in secular history. Supposing I hear that King Charles II died a Catholic, I should say, 1. It *may* be. 2. What is your *proof* ? Accordingly, in the passage which this writer quotes, I observe, 'Miracles are the kind of facts proper to ecclesiastical history, just as instances of sagacity or daring, personal prowess, or crime, are the facts proper to secular history.' What is the harm of this ? But this writer says, 'Verily his [Dr Newman's] idea of secular history is almost as degraded as his idea of ecclesiastical', p. 36, and he ends with this muddle of an *Ipse dixit*! Blot *twenty-seven*.

In like manner about the Holy Coat at Trèves, he says of me, 'Dr Newman . . . seems *hardly sure* of the authenticity of the holy coat.' Why *need* I be, more than I am sure that Richard III murdered the little princes ? If I have not *means* of making up my mind one way or the other, surely my most logical course is '*not* to be sure.' He continues, 'Dr Newman "does not see *why it may not have been* what it professes to be.".' Well, is not that just what this Writer would say of a great number of the facts recorded in secular history ? is it not what he would be obliged to say of much that is told us about the armour and other antiquities in the Tower of London ? To this I alluded in the passage from which he quotes; but he has *garbled* that passage, and I must show it. He quotes me to this effect:

> Is the Tower of London shut again sightseers because the coats of mail or pikes there may have half-legendary tales connected with them ? why then may not the country people come up in joyous companies, singing and piping to see the holy coat at Trèves ?

On this he remarks, 'To *see*, forsooth! to *worship*, Dr Newman would have said, had he known (as I take for granted he does not) the facts of that imposture.' Here, if I understand him, he implies that the people came up, not only to see, but to worship, and that I have slurred over the fact that their coming was an act of religious homage, that is, what *he* would call 'worship'. Now, will it be believed that, so far from concealing this, I had carefully stated it in the sentence immediately preceding, and *he suppresses it* ? I say, 'The world pays civil honour to a jewel said to be Alfred's on the probability; we pay *religious honour* to relics, if so be, on the probability. Is the Tower of London,' I proceed, 'shut', &c. Blot *twenty-eight*.

These words of mine, however, are but one sentence in a long argument, conveying the Catholic view on the subject of ecclesiastical miracles; and, as it is carefully worked out, and very much to the present point, and will save me doing over again what I could not do better or more fully now, if I set about it, I shall make a very long extract from the Lecture in which it occurs, and so bring this Head to an end.

The argument, I should first observe, which is worked out, is this, that Catholics set out with a definite religious tenet as a first principle, and Protestants with a contrary one, and that on this account it comes to pass that miracles are credible to Catholics and incredible to Protestants.

We affirm that the Supreme Being has wrought miracles on earth ever since the time of the Apostles; Protestants deny it. Why do we affirm, why do they deny? We affirm it on a first principle, they deny it on a first principle; and on either side the first principle is made to be decisive of the question . . . Both they and we start with the miracles of the Apostles; and then their first principle or presumption against our miracles is this, 'What God did once, He is *not* likely to do again'; while our first principle or presumption for our miracles is this; 'What God did once, He *is* likely to do again.' They say, It cannot be supposed He will work *many* miracles; we, It cannot be supposed He will work *few*.

The Protestant, I say, laughs at the very idea of miracles or supernatural powers as occurring at this day; his first principle is rooted in him; he repels from him the idea of miracles; he laughs at the notion of evidence; one is just as likely as another; they are all false. Why? because of his first principle, There are no miracles since the Apostles. Here, indeed, is a short and easy way of getting rid of the whole subject, not by reason, but by a first principle which he calls reason, supposing his first principle is false.

There is in the Church a vast tradition and testimony about miracles; how is it to be accounted for? If miracles *can* take place, then the *fact* of the miracle will be a natural explanation of the *report*, just as the fact of a man dying accounts satisfactorily for the news that he is dead; but the Protestant cannot so explain it, because he thinks miracles cannot take place; so he is necessarily driven, by way of accounting for the report of them, to impute that report to fraud. He cannot help himself. I repeat it; the whole mass of accusations which Protestants bring against us under this head, Catholic credulity, imposture, pious frauds, hypocrisy, priestcraft, this vast and varied superstructure of imputation, you see, all rests on an assumption, on an opinion of theirs, for which they offer no kind of proof. What then, in fact, do they say more than this, *If* Protestantism be true, you Catholics are a most awful set of knaves? Here, at least, is a most sensible and undeniable position.

Now, on the other hand, let me take our own side of the question, and consider how we ourselves stand relatively to the charge made against us. Catholics, then, hold the mystery of the Incarnation; and the Incarnation is the most stupendous event which ever can take place on earth; and after it and henceforth, I do not see how we can scruple at any miracle on the mere ground of its being unlikely to happen. . . . When we start with assuming that miracles are not unlikely, we are putting forth a position which lies embedded, as it were, and involved in the great revealed fact of the Incarnation. So much is plain on starting; but more is plain too. Miracles are not only not unlikely, but they are positively likely; and for this simple reason, because for the most part, when God begins, He goes on. We conceive, that when He first did a miracle, He began a series; what He commenced, He continued: what has been, will be. Surely this is good and clear reasoning. To my own mind, certainly, it is incomparably more difficult to believe that the Divine Being should do one miracle and no more, than that He should do a thousand; that He should do one great miracle only, than that He should do a multitude of lesser besides. . . . If the Divine Being does a thing once, He is, judging by human reason, likely to do it again. This surely is common sense. If a beggar gets food at a gentleman's house once, does he not send others thither after him ? If you are attacked by thieves once, do you forthwith leave your windows open at night? . . . Nay, suppose you yourselves were once to see a miracle, would you not feel the occurrence to be like passing a line ? would you, in consequence of it, declare, 'I never will believe another if I hear of one?' would it not, on the contrary, predispose you to listen to a new report ? . . .

When I hear the report of a miracle, my first feeling would be of the same kind as if it were a report of any natural exploit or event. Supposing, for instance, I heard a report of the death of some public man; it would not startle me, even if I did not at once credit it, for all men must die. Did I read of any great feat of valour, I should believe it, if imputed to Alexander or Cœur-de-Lion. Did I hear of any act of baseness, I should disbelieve it, if imputed to a friend whom I knew and loved. And so in like manner were a miracle reported to me as wrought by a Member of Parliament, or a Bishop of the Establishment, or a Wesleyan preacher, I should repudiate the notion: were it referred to a saint, or the relic of a saint, or the intercession of a saint, I should not be startled at it, though I might not at once believe it. And I certainly should be right in this conduct, supposing my First Principle be true. Miracles to the Catholic are historical facts, and nothing short of this; and they are to be regarded and dealt with as other facts; and as natural facts, under circumstances, do not startle Protestants, so supernatural, under circumstances, do not startle the Catholic. They may or may not have taken place in particular cases; he may be unable to determine which; he may have no distinct evidence; he may suspend his judgment, but he will say 'It is very possible'; he never will say 'I cannot believe it'.

Take the history of Alfred; you know his wise, mild, beneficent, yet daring character, and his romantic vicissitudes of fortune. This great king has a number of stories, or, as you may call them, legends told of him. Do you believe them all? no. Do you, on the other hand, think them incredible? no. Do you call a man a dupe or blockhead for believing them? no. Do you call an author a knave or a cheat who records them? no. You go into neither extreme, whether of implicit faith or of violent reprobation. You are not so extravagant; you see that they suit his character, they may have happened: yet this is so romantic, that has so little evidence, a third is so confused in dates or in geography, that you are in matter of fact indisposed towards them. Others are probably true, others certainly. Nor do you force everyone to take your view of particular stories; you and your neighbour think differently about this or that in detail, and agree to differ. There is in the museum at Oxford, a jewel or trinket said to be Alfred's; it is shown to all comers; I never heard the keeper of the museum accused of hypocrisy or fraud for showing, with Alfred's name appended, what he might or might not himself believe to have belonged to that great king; nor did I ever see any party of strangers who were looking at it with awe, regarded by any self-complacent bystander with scornful compassion. Yet the curiosity is not to a certainty Alfred's. The world pays civil honour to it on the probability; we pay religious honour to relics, if so be, on the probability. Is the Tower of London shut against sightseers, because the coats of mail and pikes there may have half-legendary tales connected with them? why then may not the country people come up, in joyous companies, singing and piping, to see the Holy Coat at Trèves? There is our Queen again, who is so truly and justly popular; she roves about in the midst of tradition and romance; she scatters myths and legends from her as she goes along; she is a being of poetry, and you might fairly be sceptical whether she had any personal existence. She is always at some beautiful, noble, bounteous work or other, if you trust the papers. She is doing alms-deeds in the Highlands; she meets beggars in her rides at Windsor; she writes verses in albums, or draws sketches, or is mistaken for the housekeeper by some blind old woman, or she runs up a hill as if she were a child. Who finds fault with these things? he would be a cynic, he would be white-livered, and would have gall for blood, who was not struck with this graceful, touching evidence of the love her subjects bear her. Who could have the head, even if he had the heart, who could be so cross and peevish, who could be so solemn and perverse, as to say that some of these stories *may* be simple lies, and all of them might have stronger evidence than they carry with them? Do you think she is displeased at them? Why then should He, the Great Father, who once walked the earth, look sternly on the unavoidable mistakes of His own subjects and children in their devotion to Him and His? Even granting they mistake some cases in particular, from the infirmity of human nature and the contingencies of evidence, and fancy there is or has been a miracle here and there when there is not, though a tradition, attached to a picture, or to a shrine, or a well, be very doubtful, though one relic be sometimes mistaken for another, and St Theodore stands for St Eugenius or St Agathocles, still, once take into account our First Principle, that He is likely to continue mircles among us, which is as good as the Protestant's, and I do not see why He should feel much displeasure with us on account of this, or should cease to work wonders in our behalf. In the Protestant's view, indeed, who assumes that miracles never are, our thaumatology is one great falsehood; but this is *his* First Principle, as I have said so often, which he does not prove but assume. If *he*, indeed, upheld *our* system, or *we* held *his* principle, in either case he or we should be impostors; but though we should be partners to a fraud if we thought like Protestants, we surely are not if we think like Catholics.

Such then is the answer I make to those who would urge

against us the multitude of miracles recorded in our Saints' Lives and devotional works, for many of which there is little evidence, and for some next to none. We think them true in the same sense in which Protestants think the history of England true. When they say *that*, they do not mean to say that there are no mistakes, but no mistakes of consequence, none which alter the general course of history. Nor do they mean they are equally sure of every part; for evidence is fuller and better for some things than for others. They do not stake their credit on the truth of Froissart or Sully, they do not pledge themselves for the accuracy of Doddington or Walpole, they do not embrace as an Evangelist Hume, Sharon Turner, or Macaulay. And yet they do not think it necessary, on the other hand, to commence a religious war against all our historical catechisms, and abstracts, and dictionaries, and tales, and biographies, through the country; they have no call on them to amend and expurgate books of archaeology, antiquities, heraldry, architecture, geography, and statistics, to re-write our inscriptions, and to establish a censorship on all new publications for the time to come. And so as regards the miracles of the Catholic Church; if, indeed, miracles never can occur, then, indeed, impute the narratives to fraud; but till you prove they are not likely, we shall consider the histories which have come down to us true on the whole, though in particular cases they may be exaggerated or unfounded. Where, indeed, they can certainly be proved to be false, there we shall be bound to do our best to get rid of them; but till that is clear, we shall be liberal enough to allow others to use their private judgment in their favour, as we use ours in their disparagement. For myself, lest I appear in any way to be shrinking from a determinate judgment on the claims of some of those miracles and relics, which Protestants are so startled at, and to be hiding particular questions in what is vague and general, I will avow distinctly, that, *putting out of the question* the *hypothesis of unknown laws of nature* (which is an evasion from the force of any proof), I think it impossible to *withstand the evidence* which is brought for the liquefaction of the blood of St Januarius at Naples, and for the motion of the eyes of the pictures of the Madonna in the Roman States. I *see no reason to doubt* the material of the Lombard crown at Monza; and I *do not see why* the Holy Coat of Trèves may not have been what it professes to be. I *firmly believe* that portions of the True Cross are at Rome and elsewhere, that the Crib of Bethlehem is at Rome, and the bodies of St Peter and St Paul also. . . . Many men when they hear an educated man so speak, will at once impute the avowal to insanity, or to an idio-syncrasy, or to imbecility of mind, or to decrepitude of powers, or to fanaticism, or to hypocrisy. They have a right to say so, if they will; and we have a right to ask them why they do not say it of those who bow down before the Mystery of mysteries, the Divine Incarnation?

In my Essay on Miracles of the year 1826, I proposed three questions about a professed miraculous occurrence, 1, is it antecedently *probable*? 2, is it in its *nature* certainly miraculous? 3, has it sufficient *evidence*? These are the three heads under which I still wish to conduct the inquiry into the miracles of Ecclesiastical History.

Popular Religion

This Writer uses much rhetoric against a Lecture of mine, in which I bring out, as honestly as I can, the state of countries which have long received the Catholic Faith, and hold it by the force of tradition, universal custom, and legal establishment; a Lecture in which I give pictures, drawn principally from the middle ages, of what, considering the corruption of the human race generally, that state is sure to be – pictures of its special sins and offences, *sui generis*, which are the result of that Faith when it is separated from Love or Charity, or of what Scripture calls a 'dead faith', of the Light shining in darkness, and the truth held in unrighteousness. The nearest approach which this Writer is able to make towards stating what I have said in this Lecture, is to state the very reverse. Observe: we have already had some instances of the haziness of his ideas concerning the 'Notes of the Church.' These Notes are, as any one knows who has looked into the subject, certain great and simple characteristics, which He who founded the Church has stamped upon her in order to draw both the reason and the imagination of men to her, as being really a divine work, and a religion distinct from all other religious communities; the principal of these Notes being that she is Holy, One, Catholic, and Apostolic, as the Creed says. Now, to use his own word, he has the incredible 'audacity' to say, that I have declared, not the divine characteristics of the Church, but the sins and scandals in her, to be her Notes – as if I made God the Author of evil. He says distinctly, 'Dr Newman, with a kind of desperate audacity, *will* dig forth such *scandals* as *Notes* of the Catholic Church.' This is what I get at his hands for my honesty. Blot *twenty-nine*.

Again, he says, 'Dr Newman uses the blasphemy and profanity which he confesses to be so common in Catholic countries, as an argument *for*, and not *against* the "Catholic Faith".' – p. 44. That is, because I admit that profaneness exists in the Church, therefore I consider it a token of the Church. Yes, certainly, just as our national form of cursing is an evidence of the being of a God, and as a gallows is the glorious sign of a civilized country – but in no other way. Blot *thirty*.

What is it that I really say ? I say as follows: Protestants object that the communion of Rome does not fulfil satisfactorily the expectations which we may justly form concerning the True Church, as it is delineated in the four Notes, enumerated in the Creed; and among others, e.g. in the Note of sanctity; and they point, in proof of what they assert, to the state of Catholic countries. Now, in answer to this objection, it is plain what I might have done, if I had not had a conscience. I might have denied the fact. I might have said, for instance, that the middle ages were as virtuous, as they were believing. I might have denied that there was any violence, any superstition, any immorality, any blasphemy during them. And so as to the state of countries which have long had the light of Catholic truth, and have degenerated. I might have admitted nothing against them, and explained away everything which plausibly told to their disadvantage. I did nothing of the kind; and what effect has this had upon this estimable critic ? 'Dr Newman takes a seeming pleasure,' he says, 'in detailing instances of dishonesty on the part of Catholics.' – p. 44. Blot *thirty-one*. Any one who knows me well, would testify that my 'seeming pleasure', as he calls it, at such things, is just the impatient sensitiveness, which relieves itself by means of a definite delineation of what is so hateful to it.

However, to pass on. All the miserable scandals of Catholic countries, taken at the worst, are, as I view the matter, no argument against the Church itself; and the reason which I give in the Lecture is, that, according to the proverb, *Corruptio optimi est pessima*. The Jews could sin in a way no other contemporary race could sin, for theirs was a sin against light; and Catholics can sin with a depth and intensity with which Protestants cannot sin. There will be more blasphemy, more hatred of God, more of diabolical rebellion, more of awful sacrilege, more of vile hypocrisy in a Catholic country than anywhere else, because there is in it more of sin against light. Surely, this is just what Scripture says, 'Woe unto thee, Chorazin! woe unto thee Bethsaida!'. And, again, surely what is told us by religious men, say by Father Bresciani, about the present unbelieving party in Italy, fully bears out the divine text: 'If, after they have escaped the pollutions of the world . . . they are again entangled therein and overcome, the latter end is worse with them than the beginning. For it had been better for them not to have known the way of righteousness, than, after they have known it, to turn from the holy commandments delivered unto them.'

And what is true of those who thus openly oppose themselves to the truth, as it was true of the Evil One in the beginning, will in an analogous way be true in the case of all sin, be it of a heavier or lighter character, which is found in a Catholic country – sin will be strangely tinged or dyed by religious associations or beliefs, and will exhibit the tragic inconsistencies of the excess of knowledge over love, or of much faith with little obedience. The mysterious battle between good and evil will assume in a Catholic country its most frightful shape, when it is not the collision of two distinct and far-separated hosts, but when it is carried on in hearts and souls, taken one by one, and when the eternal foes are so intermingled and interfused that to human eyes they seem to coalesce into a multitude of individualities. This is in course of years, the real, the hidden condition of a nation, which has been bathed in Christian ideas, whether it be a young vigorous race, or an old and degenerate; and it will manifest itself socially and historically in those characteristics, sometimes grotesque, some-times hideous, sometimes despicable, of which we have so many instances, medieval and modern, both in this hemisphere and in the western. It is, I say, the necessary result of the intercommunion of divine faith and human corruption.

But it has a light side as well as a dark. First, much which seems profane, is not in itself profane, but in the subjective view of the Protestant beholder. Scenic representations of our Lord's Passion are not profane to a Catholic population; in like manner, there are usages, customs, institutions, actions, often of an indifferent nature, which will be necessarily mixed up with religion in a Catholic country, because all things whatever are so mixed up. Protestants have been sometimes shocked, most absurdly as a Catholic rightly decides, at hearing that Mass is sometimes said for a good haul of fish. There is no sin here, but only a difference from Protestant customs. Other phenomena of a Catholic nation are at most mere extravagances. And then as to what is really sinful, if there be in it fearful instances of blasphemy or superstition, there are also special and singular fruits and exhibitions of sanctity; and, if the many do not seem to lead better lives for all their religious knowledge, at least they learn, as they can learn nowhere else, how to repent thoroughly and to die well.

The visible state of a country, which professes Catholicism, need not be the measure of the spiritual result of that Catholicism, at the Eternal Judgment Seat; but no one could say that that visible state was a Note that Catholicism was divine.

All this I attempted to bring out in the Lecture of which I am speaking; and that I had some success, I am glad to infer from the message of congratulation upon it, which I received at the time, from a foreign Catholic layman, of high English reputation, with whom I had not the honour of a personal acquaintance. And having given the key to the Lecture, which the Writer so wonderfully misrepresents, I pass on to another head.

7

The Economy

For the subject of the Economy, I shall refer to my discussion upon
it in my History of the Arians, after one word about this Writer.
He puts into his title-page these words from a Sermon of mine: 'It
is not more than an hyperbole to say, that, in certain cases, a lie is
the nearest approach to truth.' This Sermon he attacks; but I do
not think it necessary to defend it here, because any one who reads
it, will see that he is simply incapable of forming a notion of what
it is about. It treats of subjects which are entirely out of his depth;
and, as I have already shown in other instances, and observed in
the beginning of this Volume, he illustrates in his own person the
very thing that shocks him, viz. that the nearest approach to truth,
in given cases, is a lie. He does his best to make something of it, I
believe; but he gets simply perplexed. He finds that it annihilates
space, robs him of locomotion, almost scoffs at the existence of
the earth, and he is simply frightened and cowed. He can but say
'the man who wrote that sermon was already past the possibility
of conscious dishonesty,' p. 49. Perhaps it is hardly fair, after such
a confession on his part of being fairly beat, to mark down a blot;
however, let it be Blot *thirty-two*.

Then again, he quotes from me thus: 'Many a theory or view of
things, on which an institution is founded, or a party held
together, is of the same kind (economical). Many an argument,
used by zealous and earnest men, has this economical character,
being not the very ground on which they act (for they continue in
the same course, though it be refuted), yet in a certain sense, a
representation of it, a proximate description of their feelings, in
the shape of argument, on which they can rest, to which they can
recur when perplexed, and appeal when they are questioned.' He
calls these 'startling words', p. 48. Yet here again he illustrates
their truth; for in his own case, he has acted on them in this very

controversy with the most happy exactness. Surely he referred to my Sermon on Wisdom and Innocence, when called on to prove me a liar, as 'a proximate description of his feelings about me, in the shape of argument', and he has 'continued in the same course, though it has been refuted.' Blot *thirty-three*.

Then, as to 'a party being held together by a mythical representation', or economy. Surely 'Church and King', 'Reform', 'Non-intervention', are such symbols; or let this Writer answer Mr Kinglake's question in his 'Crimean War'. 'Is it true that . . . great armies were gathering, and that for the sake of the *Key* and the *Star* the peace of the nations was brought into danger ?' Blot *thirty-four*.

In the beginning of this work, pp. 84–90, I refuted his gratuitous accusation against me at pp. 60–61, founded on my calling one of my Anglican Sermons a Protestant one: so I have nothing to do but to register it here as Blot *thirty-five*.

Then he says that I committed an economy in placing in my original title-page, that the question between him and me, was whether 'Dr Newman teaches that Truth is no virtue.' It was a 'wisdom of the serpentine type', since I did not add, 'for its own sake'. Now observe: First, as to that matter of fact, in the course of my Letters, which bore that title-page, I printed the words 'for its own sake', *five* times over. Next, pray, what kind of a virtue is that, which is *not* done for its own sake ? So that, after all, is this Writer's idea of virtue! a something that is done for the sake of something *else*; a sort of expedience! He is honest, it seems, simply *because* honesty is 'the best policy', and on that score it is that he thinks himself virtuous. Why, 'for its own sake' enters into the very idea or definition of a virtue. Defend me from such virtuous men, as this Writer would inflict upon us! Blot *thirty-six*.

These Blots are enough just now; so I proceed to a brief sketch of what I held in 1833 upon the Economy, as a rule of practice. I wrote this two months ago; perhaps the composition is not quite in keeping with the run of this Appendix; and it is short; but I think it will be sufficient for my purpose:

The doctrine of the *Economia*, had, as I have shown, pp. 116–18, a large signification which applied to the divine ordinances; it also had a definite application to the duties of Christians, whether clergy or laity, in preaching, in instructing or catechizing, or in ordinary intercourse with the world around them.

As Almighty God did not all at once introduce the Gospel to the world, and thereby gradually prepared men for its profitable reception, so, according to the doctrine of the early Church, it was a duty, for the sake of the heathen among whom they lived, to observe a great reserve and caution in communicating to them the knowledge of 'the whole counsel of God'. This cautious dispensation of the truth, after the manner of a discreet and vigilant steward, is denoted by the word 'economy'. It is a mode of acting which comes under the head of Prudence, one of the four Cardinal Virtues.

The principle of the Economy is this; that out of various courses, in religious conduct or statement, all and each *allowable antecedently and in themselves*, that ought to be taken which is most expedient and most suitable at the time for the object in hand.

Instances of its application and exercise in Scripture are such as the following – 1. Divine Providence did but gradually impart to the world in general, and to the Jews in particular, the knowledge of His will – He is said to have 'winked at the times of ignorance among the heathen'; and He suffered in the Jews divorce Because of the hardness of their hearts.' 2. He has allowed Himself to be represented as having eyes, ears, and hands, as having wrath, jealousy, grief, and repentance. 3. In like manner, our Lord spoke harshly to the Syro-Phœnician woman, whose daughter He was about to heal, and made as if He would go further, when the two disciples had come to their journey's end. 4. Thus too Joseph 'made himself strange to his brethren', and Elisha kept silence on request of Naaman to bow in the house of Rimmon. 5. Thus St Paul circumcised Timothy, while he cried out 'Circumcision availeth not.'

It may be said that this principle, true in itself, yet is dangerous, because it admits of an easy abuse, and carries men away into what becomes insincerity and cunning. This is undeniable; to do evil that good may come, to consider that the means, whatever they are, justify the end, to sacrifice truth to expedience, unscrupulousness, recklessness, are grave offences. These are abuses of the Economy. But to call them *economical* is to give a fine name to what occurs every day, independent of any knowledge of the *doctrine* of the Economy. It is the abuse of a rule which nature suggests to every one. Every one looks out for the 'mollia tempora fandi', and 'mollia verba' too.

Having thus explained what is meant by the Economy as a rule of social intercourse between men of different religious, or, again, political, or social views, next I go on to state what I said in the Arians.

I say in that Volume first, that our Lord has given us the *principle* in His own words – 'Cast not your pearls before swine'; and that He exemplified it in His teaching by parables; that St Paul expressly distinguishes between the milk which is necessary to one set of men, and the strong meat which is allowed to others, and that, in two Epistles. I say, that the Apostles in the Acts observe the same rule in their speeches, for it is a fact, that they do not preach the high doctrines of Christianity, but only 'Jesus and the resurrection' or 'repentance and faith'. I also say, that this is the very reason that the Fathers assign for the silence of various writers in the first centuries on the subject of our Lord's divinity. I also speak of the catechetical system practised in the early Church, and the *disciplina arcani* as regards the doctrine of the Holy Trinity, to which Bingham bears witness; also of the defence of this rule by Basil, Cyril of Jerusalem, Chrysostom, and Theodoret.

And next the question may be asked, whether I have said any thing in my Volume *to guard* the doctrine, thus laid down, from the abuse to which it is obviously exposed: and my answer is easy. Of course, had I had any idea that I should have been exposed to such hostile misrepresentations, as it has been my lot to undergo on the subject, I should have made more direct avowals than I have done of my sense of the gravity and the danger of that abuse. Since I could not foresee when I wrote, that I should have been wantonly slandered, I only wonder that I have anticipated the charge as fully as will be seen in the following extracts.

For instance, speaking of the Disciplina Arcani, I say – (1) 'The elementary information given to the heathen or catechumen was *in no sense undone* by the subsequent secret teaching, which was in fact but the *filling up of a bare but correct outline*', p. 58, and I contrast this with the conduct of the Manichæans 'who represented the initiatory discipline as founded on a *fiction* or hypothesis, which was to be forgotten by the learner as he made progress in the *real* doctrine of the Gospel.' (2) As to allegorising, I say that the Alexandrians erred, whenever and as far as they proceeded '*to obscure* the primary meaning of Scripture, and to *weaken the force of historical facts* and express declarations', p. 69. (3) And that they were 'more open to *censure*', when, on being '*urged by objections* to various passages in the history of the Old Testament, as derogatory to the divine perfections or to the Jewish Saints, they had *recourse to an allegorical explanation by way of answer*', p. 61. (4) I add, '*It is impossible to defend such a procedure*, which seems to imply *a want of faith* in those who had recourse to it'; for 'God has given us *rules of right and wrong*', *ibid*. (5) Again, I say – 'The *abuse of the Economy* in *the hands of unscrupulous reasoners*, is obvious. *Even the honest* controversialist or teacher will find it very difficult to represent, *without misrepresenting*, what it is yet his duty to present to his hearers with caution or reserve. Here the obvious rule to guide our practice is, to be careful ever to maintain *substantial truth* in our use of the economical method,' pp. 69, 70. (6) And so far from concurring at all hazards with Justin, Gregory, or Athanasius, I say, 'It *is plain* they *were justified or not* in their Economy, *according* as they did or did not *practically mislead their opponents*,' p. 70. (7) I proceed, 'It is so difficult to hit the mark in these perplexing cases, that it is not wonderful, should these or other Fathers have failed at times, and said more or less than was proper', *ibid*.

The Principle of the Economy is familiarly acted on among us every day. When we would persuade others, we do not begin by treading on their toes. Men would be thought rude who introduced their own religious notions into mixed society and were devotional in a drawing-room. Have we never thought lawyers tiresome who came down for the assizes and talked law all through dinner? Does the same argument tell in the House of Commons, on the hustings, and at Exeter Hall? Is an educated gentleman never worsted at an election by the tone and arguments of some clever fellow, who, whatever his shortcomings in other respects, understands the common people?

As to the Catholic Religion in England at the present day, this only will I observe – that the truest expedience is to answer right out, when you are asked; that the wisest economy is to have no management; that the best prudence is not to be a coward; that the most damaging folly is to be found out shuffling; and that the first of virtues is to 'tell truth, and shame the devil.'

Lying and Equivocation

This Writer says, 'Though a lie be a sin, the fact of its being a venial one seems to have gained for it as yet a very slight penance.' – p. 53. Yet he says also that Dr Newman takes 'a perverse pleasure in eccentricities', because I say that 'it is better for sun and moon to drop from heaven than that one soul should tell one wilful untruth' – p. 40. That is, he first accuses us without foundation of making light of a lie; and, when he finds that we don't, then he calls us inconsistent. I have noticed these words of mine, and two passages besides, which he quotes, above at pp. 280–1. Here I will but observe on the subject of venial sin generally, that he altogether forgets our doctrine of Purgatory. This punishment may last till the day of judgement; so much for duration; then as to intensity, let the image of fire, by which we denote it, show what we think of it. Here is the expiation of venial sins. Yet Protestants, after the manner of this Writer, are too apt to play fast and loose; to blame us because we hold that sin may be venial, and to blame us again when we tell them what we think will be its punishment. Blot *thirty-seven*.

At the end of his Pamphlet he makes a distinction between the Catholic clergy and gentry in England, which I know the latter consider to be very impertinent; and he makes it apropos of a passage in one of my original letters in January. He quotes me as saying that 'Catholics differ from Protestants, as to whether this or that act in particular is conformable to the rule of truth', p. 54; and then he goes on to observe, that I have 'calumniated the Catholic gentry', because 'there is no difference whatever, of detail or other, between their truthfulness and honour, and the truthfulness and honour of the Protestant gentry among whom they live'. But again he has garbled my words; they run thus:

Truth is the same in itself and in substance, to Catholic and Protestant; so is purity; both virtues are to be referred to that moral sense which is the natural possession of us all. But, when we come to the question in detail, whether this or that act in particular is conformable to the rule of truth, or again to the rule of purity, then *sometimes* there is a difference of opinion *between individuals, sometimes between schools*, and *sometimes* between religious communions.

I knew indeed perfectly well, and I confessed that 'Protestants think that the Catholic system, as such, leads to a lax observance of the rule of truth'; but I added, 'I am very sorry that they should think so', and I never meant myself to grant that all Protestants were on the strict side, and all Catholics on the lax. Far from it; there is a stricter party as well as a laxer party among Protestants. I have already spoken of Protestant writers who in certain cases allow of lying, I have also spoken of Catholic writers who do not allow of equivocation; when I wrote 'a difference of opinion between individuals', and 'between schools', I meant between Protestant and Protestant, and particular instances were in my mind. I did not say then, or dream of saying, that Catholics, priests and laity, were lax on the point of lying, and that Protestants were strict, any more than I meant to say that all Catholics were pure, and all Protestants impure; but I meant to say that, whereas the rule of Truth is one and the same both to Catholic and Protestant, nevertheless some Catholics were lax, some strict, and again some Protestants were strict, some lax; and I have already had opportunities of recording my own judgment on which side the Writer is *himself*, and therefore he may keep his forward vindication of 'honest gentlemen and noble ladies', who, in spite of their priests, are still so truthful, till such time as he can find a worse assailant of them than I am, and they no better champion of them than himself. And as to the Priests of England, those who know them, as he does *not*, will pronounce them no whit inferior in this great virtue to the gentry, whom he says that he *does*; and I cannot say more. Blot *thirty-eight*.

Lastly, this Writer uses the following words, which I have more than once quoted, and with a reference to them I shall end my remarks upon him. 'I am henceforth,' he says, 'in doubt and fear, as much *as an honest man can be*, concerning every word Dr Newman may write. How can I tell that I shall not be the dupe of some cunning equivocation, of one of the three kinds, laid down as permissible by the blessed St Alfonso da Liguori and his pupils, even when confirmed with an oath. . . ?'

I will tell him why he need not fear; because he has *left out* one very important condition in the statement of St Alfonso – and very applicable to my own case, even if I followed St Alfonso's view of the subject. St Alfonso says '*ex justâ causâ*'; but our 'honest man', as he styles himself, has *omitted these words*; which are a key to the whole question. Blot *thirty-nine*. Here endeth our 'honest man'. Now for the subject of Lying.

Almost all authors, Catholic and Protestant, admit, that *when a just cause is present*, there is some kind or other of verbal misleading, which is not sin. Even silence is in certain cases virtually such a misleading, according to the Proverb, 'Silence gives consent'. Again, silence is absolutely forbidden to a Catholic, as a mortal sin, under certain circumstances, e.g. to keep silence, instead of making a profession of faith.

Another mode of verbal misleading, and the most direct, is actually saying the thing that is not; and it is defended on the principle that such words are not a lie, when there is a 'justa causa', as killing is not murder in the case of an executioner.

Another ground of certain authors for saying that an untruth is not a lie where there is a just cause, is, that veracity is a kind of justice, and therefore, when we have no duty of justice to tell truth to another, it is no sin not to do so. Hence we may say the thing that is not, to children, to madmen, to men who ask impertinent questions, to those whom we hope to benefit by misleading.

Another ground, taken in defending certain untruths, *ex justâ causâ*, as if not lies, is that veracity is for the sake of society, and, if in no case we might lawfully mislead others, we should actually be doing society great harm.

Another mode of verbal misleading is equivocation or a play upon words; and it is defended on the view that to lie is to use words in a sense which they will not bear. But an equivocator uses them in a received sense, though there is another received sense, and therefore, according to this definition, he does not lie.

Others say that all equivocations are, after all, a kind of lying, faint lies or awkward lies, but still lies; and some of these disputants infer, that therefore we must not equivocate, and others that equivocation is but a half-measure, and that it is better to say at once that in certain cases untruths are not lies.

Others will try to distinguish between evasions and equivocations; but they will be answered, that, though there are evasions which are clearly not equivocations, yet that it is difficult scientifically to draw the line between them.

To these must be added the unscientific way of dealing with lies, viz. that on a great or cruel occasion a man cannot help telling a lie, and he would not be a man, did he not tell it, but still it is wrong and he ought not to do it, and he must trust that the sin will be forgiven him, though he goes about to commit it. It is a frailty, and had better not be anticipated, and not thought of again, after it is once over. This view cannot for a moment be defended, but, I suppose, it is very common.

And now I think the historical course of thought upon the matter has been this: the Greek Fathers thought that, when there was a *justâ causâ*, an untruth need not be a lie. St Augustine took another view, though with great misgiving; and, whether he is rightly interpreted or not, is the doctor of the great and common view that all untruths are lies, and that there can be *no* just cause of untruth. In these later times, this doctrine has been found difficult to work, and it has been largely taught that, though all untruths are lies, yet that certain equivocations, when there is a just cause, are not untruths.

Further, there have been and all along through these later ages, other schools, running parallel with the above mentioned, one of which says that equivocations, &c. after all *are* lies, and another which says that there are untruths which are not lies.

And now as to the 'just cause', which is the condition, *sine quâ non*. The Greek Fathers make them such as these, self-defence, charity, zeal for God's honour, and the like.

St Augustine seems to deal with the same 'just causes' as the Greek Fathers, even though he does not allow of their availableness as depriving untruths, spoken with such objects, of their sinfulness. He mentions defence of life and of honour, and the safe custody of a secret. Also the Anglican writers, who have followed the Greek Fathers, in defending untruths when there is the 'just cause', consider that just cause to be such as the preservation of life and property, defence of law, the good of others. Moreover, their moral rights, e.g. defence against the inquisitive, &c.

St Alfonso, I consider, would take the same view of the 'justa causa' as the Anglican divines; he speaks of it as 'quicunque finis *honestus*, ad servanda bona spiritui vel corpori utilia'; which is very much the view which they take of it, judging by the instances which they give.

In all cases, however, and as contemplated by all authors, Clement of Alexandria, or Milton, or St Alfonso, such a causa is, in fact, extreme, rare, great, or at least special. Thus the writer in the *Mélanges Théologiques* (Liège, 1852–3, p. 453) quotes Lessius: 'Si absque justa causa fiat, est abusio orationis contra virtutem veritatis, et civilem consuetudinem, etsi proprie non sit mendacium.' That is, the virtue of truth, and the civil custom, are the *measure* of the just cause. And so Voit, 'If a man has used a reservation (restrictione non purè mentali) without a *grave* cause, he has sinned gravely.' And so the author himself, from whom I quote, and who defends the Patristic and Anglican doctrine that there *are* untruths which are not lies, says, 'Under the name of mental reservation theologians authorize many lies, *when there is for them a grave reason* and proportionate' i.e. to their character –p. 459. And so St Alfonso, in another Treatise, quotes St Thomas to the effect, that, if from one cause two immediate effects follow, and, if the good effect of that cause is *equal in value* to the bad effect (bonus *æquivalet* malo), then nothing hinders that the good may be intended and the evil permitted. From which it will follow that, since the evil to society from lying is very great, the just cause which is to make it allowable, must be very great also. And so Kenrick: 'It is confessed by all Catholics that, in the common intercourse of life, all ambiguity of language is to be avoided; but it is debated whether such ambiguity is ever lawful. Most theologians answer in the affirmative, supposing a *grave cause* urges, and the true mind of the speaker can be collected from the adjunct, though in fact it be not collected.'

However, there are cases, I have already said, of another kind, in which Anglican authors would think a lie allowable; such as when a question is *impertinent*. Accordingly, I think the best word for embracing all the cases which would come under the 'justa causa', is, not 'extreme', but 'special', and I say the same as regards St Alfonso; and therefore, above in pp. 301 and 302, whether I speak of St Alfonso or Paley, I should have used the word 'special' or 'extraordinary', not 'extreme'.

What I have been saying shows what different schools of opinion there are in the Church in the treatment of this difficult doctrine; and, by consequence, that a given individual, such as I am, *cannot* agree with all, and has a full right to follow which he will. The freedom of the Schools, indeed, is one of those rights of reason, which the Church is too wise really to interfere with. And this applies not to moral questions only, but to dogmatic also.

It is supposed by Protestants that, because St Alfonso's writings have had such high commendation bestowed upon them by authority, therefore they have been invested with a quasi-infallibility. This has arisen in good measure from Protestants not knowing the force of theological terms. The words to which they refer are the authoritative decision that 'nothing in his works has been found *worthy of censure*, "censurâ dignum" '; but this does not lead to the conclusions which have been drawn from it. Those words occur in a legal document, and cannot be interpreted except in a legal sense. In the first place, the sentence is negative; nothing in St Alfonso's writings is positively approved; and secondly it is not said that there are no faults in what he has written, but nothing which comes under the ecclesiastical *censura*, which is something very definite. To take and interpret them, in the way commonly adopted in England, is the same mistake, as if one were to take the word 'Apologia' in the English sense of apology, or 'Infant' in law to mean a little child.

1. Now first as to the meaning of the form of words viewed as a proposition. When they were brought before the fitting authorities at Rome by the Archbishop of Besançon, the answer returned to him contained the condition that those words were to be interpreted, 'with due regard to the mind of the Holy See concerning the approbation of writings of the servants of God, ad effectum Canonizationis.' This is intended to prevent any Catholic taking the words about St Alfonso's works in too large a sense. Before a Saint is canonized, his works are examined and a judgment pronounced upon them. Pope Benedict XIV says, 'The *end* or *scope* of this judgment is, that it may appear, whether the doctrine of the servant of God, which he has brought out in his writings, is free from any soever *theological censure*.' And he remarks in addition, 'It never can be said that the doctrine of a servant of God is *approved* by the Holy See, but at most it can only be said that it is not disapproved (non reprobatam) in case that the Revisers had reported that there is nothing found by them in his works, which is adverse to the decrees of Urban VIII, and that the judgment of the Revisers has been approved by the sacred Congregation, and confirmed by the Supreme Pontiff.' The Decree of Urban VIII here referred to is, 'Let works be examined,

whether they contain errors against faith or good morals (*bonos mores*), or any new doctrine, or a doctrine foreign and alien to the common sense and custom of the Church.' The author from whom I quote this (M. Vandenbroeck, of the diocese of Malines) observes, 'It is therefore clear, that the approbation of the works of the Holy Bishop touches not the truth of every proposition, adds nothing to them, nor even gives them by consequence a degree of intrinsic probability.' He adds that it gives St Alfonso's theology an extrinsic probability, from the fact that, in the judgment of the Holy See, no proposition deserves to receive a censure; but that 'that probability will cease nevertheless in a particular case, for any one who should be convinced, whether by evident arguments, or by a decree of the Holy See, or otherwise, that the doctrine of the Saint deviates from the truth.' He adds, 'From the fact that the approbation of the works of St Alfonso does not decide the truth of each proposition, it follows, as Benedict XIV has remarked, that we may combat the doctrine which they contain; only, since a canonised saint is in question, who is honoured by a solemn *culte* in the Church, we ought not to speak except with respect, nor to attack his opinions except with temper and modesty.'

2. Then, as to the meaning of the word *censura*: Benedict XIV enumerates a number of 'Notes' which come under that name; he says, 'Our of propositions which are to be noted with theological censure, some are heretical, some erroneous, some close upon error, some savouring of heresy', and so on; and each of these terms has its own definite meaning. Thus by 'erroneous' is meant, according to Viva, a proposition which is not *immediately* opposed to a revealed proposition, but only to a theological *conclusion* drawn from premises which are *de fide*; 'savouring of heresy', when a proposition is opposed to a theological conclusion not evidently drawn from premises which are *de fide*, but most probably and according to the common mode of theologising, and so with the rest. Therefore when it was said by the Revisers of St Alfonso's works that they were not 'worthy of censure', it was only meant that they did not fall under these particular Notes.

But the answer from Rome to the Archbishop of Besançon went further than this; it actually took pains to declare that any one who pleased might follow other theologians instead of St Alfonso. After saying that no Priest was to be interfered with who followed

St Alfonso in the Confessional, it added, 'This is said, however, without on that account judging that they are reprehended who follow opinions handed down by other approved authors.'

And this too, I will observe, that St Alfonso made many changes of opinion himself in the course of his writings; and it could not for an instant be supposed that we were bound to every one of his opinions, when he did not feel himself bound to them in his own person. And, what is more to the purpose still, there are opinions, or some opinion, of his which actually has been proscribed by the Church since, and cannot now be put forward or used. I do not pretend to be a well-read theologian myself, but I say this on the authority of a theological professor of Breda, quoted in the *Mélanges Théol.* for 1850–1. He says: 'It may happen, that, in the course of time, errors may be found in the works of St Alfonso and be proscribed by the Church, *a thing which in fact has already occurred.*'

In not ranging myself then with those who consider that it is justifiable to use words in a double sense, that is, to equivocate, I put myself, first, under the protection of Cardinal Gerdil, who, in a work lately published at Rome, has the following passage, which I owe to the kindness of a friend:

Gerdil

In an oath one ought to have respect to the intention of the party swearing, and the intention of the party to whom the oath is taken. Whoso swears binds himself in virtue of the words, not according to the sense he retains in his own mind, but in *the sense according to which he perceives that they are understood by him to whom the oath is made.* When the mind of the one is discordant with the mind of the other, if this happens by deceit or cheat of the party swearing, he is bound to observe the oath according to the right sense (*sana mente*) of the party receiving it; but, when the discrepancy in the sense comes of misunderstanding, without deceit of the party swearing, in that case he is not bound, except to that to which he had in mind to wish to be bound. It follows hence, that *whoso uses mental reservation or equivocation in the oath*, in order to deceive the party to whom he offers it, *sins most grievously*, and is always bound to observe the oath *in the sense in which he knew that his words were* taken by the other party, according to the decision of St

Augustine, 'They are perjured, who, having kept the words, have deceived the expectations of those to whom the oath was taken'. He who swears externally, without the inward intention of swearing, commits a most grave sin, and remains all the same under the obligation to fulfil it. . . . In a word, all that is contrary to good faith, is iniquitous, and by introducing the name of God the iniquity is aggravated by the guilt of sacrilege.

Natalis Alexander

They certainly lie, who utter the words of an oath, and without the will to swear or bind themselves; or who *make use of mental reservations and equivocations* in swearing, since they signify by words what they have not in mind, contrary to the end for which language was instituted, viz. as signs of ideas. Or they mean something else than the words signify in themselves, and the common custom of speech, and the circumstances of persons and business-matters; and thus they abuse words which were instituted for the cherishing of society.

Contenson

Hence is apparent how worthy of condemnation is the temerity of those half-taught men, who give a colour to lies and *equivocations* by the words and instances of Christ. Than whose doctrine, which is an art of deceiving, nothing can be pestilent. And that, both because what you do not wish done to yourself, you should not do to another; now the patrons of equivocations and mental reservations would not like to be themselves deceived by others, &c. . . . and also because St Augustine, &c. . . . In truth, as there is no pleasant living with those whose language we do not understand, and, as St Augustine teaches, a man would more readily live with his dog than with a foreigner, less pleasant certainly is our converse with those who make use of frauds artificially covered, overreach their hearers by deceits, address them insidiously, observe the right moment, and catch at words to their purpose, by which truth is hidden under a covering; and so on the other hand nothing is sweeter than the society of those, who both love and speak the naked truth . . . without their mouth professing one thing and their mind hiding another, or spreading before it the cover of double words. Nor does it matter that they colour their lies with the name of *equivocations or mental reservations*. For Hilary says, 'The sense, not the speech, makes the crime'.

Concina allows of what I shall presently call *evasions*, but nothing beyond, if I understand him; but he is most vehement against mental reservation of every kind, so I quote him.

Concina

That mode of speech, which some theologians call pure mental reservation, others call reservation not simply mental; that language which to me is lying, to the greater part of recent authors is only amphibological . . . I have discovered that nothing is adduced by more recent theologians for the lawful use of *amphibologies* which has not been made use of already by the ancients, whether philosophers or some Fathers, in defence of lies. Nor does there seem to me other difference when I consider their respective grounds, except that the ancients frankly called those modes of speech lies, and the more recent writers, not a few of them, call them amphibological, equivocal, and *material*.

In another place he quotes Caramuel, so I suppose I may do so too, for the very reason that his theological reputation does not place him on the side of strictness. Concina says, 'Caramuel himself, who bore away the palm from all others in relaxing the evangelical and natural law, says,

Caramuel

I have an innate aversion to mental reservations. If they are contained within the bounds of piety and sincerity, then they are not necessary; . . . but if otherwise they are the destruction of human society and sincerity, and are to be condemned as pestilent. Once admitted, they open the way to all lying, all perjury. And the whole difference in the matter is, that what yesterday was called a lie, changing, not its nature and malice, but its name, is today entitled 'mental reservation'; and this is to sweeten poison with sugar, and to colour guilt with the appearance of virtue.

St Thomas

When the sense of the party swearing, and of the party to whom he swears, is not the same, if this proceeds from the deceit of the former, the oath ought to be kept according to the right sense of the party to whom it is made. But if the party swearing does not make use of deceit, then he is bound according to his own sense.

St Isidore

With whatever artifice of words a man swears, nevertheless God who is the witness of his conscience, so takes the oath as he understands it, to whom it is sworn. And he becomes twice guilty, who both takes the name of God in vain, and deceives his neighbour.

St Augustine

I do not question that this is most justly laid down, that the promise of an oath must be fulfilled, not according to the words of the party taking it, but according to the expectation of the party to whom it is taken, of which he who takes it is aware.

And now, under the protection of these authorities, I say as follows:

Casuistry is a noble science, but it is one to which I am led, neither by my abilities nor my turn of mind. Independently, then, of the difficulties of the subject, and the necessity, before forming an opinion, of knowing more of the arguments of theologians upon it than I do, I am very unwilling to say a word here on the subject of Lying and Equivocation. But I consider myself bound to speak; and therefore, in this strait, I can do nothing better, even for my own relief, than submit myself and what I shall say to the judgment of the Church, and to the consent, so far as in this matter there be a consent, of the *Schola Theologorum*.

Now, in the case of one of those special and rare exigencies or emergencies, which constitute the *justa causa* of dissembling or misleading, whether it be extreme as the defence of life, or a duty as the custody of a secret, or of a personal nature as to repel an impertinent inquirer, or a matter too trivial to provoke question, as in dealing with children or madmen, there seem to be four courses:

1. *To say the thing that is not.* Here I draw the reader's attention to the words *material* and *formal*. 'Thou shalt not kill'; *murder* is the *formal* transgression of this commandment, but *accidental homicide* is the *material* transgression. The *matter* of the act is the same in both cases; but in the *homicide*, there is nothing more than the act, whereas in *murder* there must be the intention, &c. which constitutes the formal sin. So, again, an executioner commits the material act, but not that formal killing which is a breach of the commandment. So a man, who, simply to save himself from starving, takes a loaf which is not his own, commits only the material, not the formal act of stealing, that is, he does not commit a sin. And so a baptized Christian, external to the Church, who is in invincible ignorance, is a material heretic, and not a formal. And in like manner, if to say the thing which is not be in special cases lawful, it may be called a *material lie*.

The first mode then which has been suggested of meeting those special cases, in which to mislead by words has a sufficient object, or has a *just causa*, is by a material lie.

The second mode is by an *œquivocatio*, which is not equivalent to the English word 'equivocation', but means sometimes a *play upon words*, sometimes an *evasion*.

2. *A play upon words.* St Alfonso certainly says that a play upon words is allowable; and, speaking under correction, I should say that he does so on the ground that lying is *not* a sin against justice, that is, against our neighbour, but a sin against God; because words are the signs of ideas, and therefore if a word denotes two ideas, we are at liberty to use it in either of its senses; but I think I must be incorrect here in some respect, because the Catechism of the Council, as I have quoted it at p. 306, says, 'Vanitate et mendacio fides ac veritas tolluntur, arctissima vincula *societatis humanæ*; quibus sublatis, sequitur summa vitæ *confusio*, ut *homines nihil a dæmonibus differre videantur*'.

3. *Evasion* – when, for instance, the speaker diverts the attention of the hearer to another subject; suggests an irrelevant fact or makes a remark, which confuses him and gives him something to think about; throws dust into his eyes; states some

truth, from which he is quite sure his hearer will draw an illogical and untrue conclusion, and the like. Bishop Butler seems distinctly to sanction such a proceeding, in a passage which I shall extract below.

The greatest school of evasion, I speak seriously, is the House of Commons; and necessarily so, from the nature of the case. And the hustings is another.

An instance is supplied in the history of St Athanasius: he was in a boat on the Nile, flying persecution; and he found himself pursued. On this he ordered his men to turn his boat round, and ran right to meet the satellites of Julian. They asked him, 'Have you seen Athanasius ?' and he told his followers to answer, 'Yes, he is close to you.' *They* went on their course, and *he* ran into Alexandria, and there lay hid till the end of the persecution.

I gave another instance above, in reference to a doctrine of religion. The early Christians did their best to conceal their Creed on account of the misconceptions of the heathen about it. Were the question asked of him, 'Do you worship a Trinity ?' and did they answer, 'We worship one God, and none else'; the inquirer might, or would, infer that they did not acknowledge the Trinity of Divine Persons.

It is very difficult to draw the line between these evasions, and what are commonly called in English *equivocations*; and of this difficulty, again, I think, the scenes in the House of Commons supply us with illustrations.

4. The fourth method is *silence*. For instance, not giving the *whole* truth in a court of law. If St Alban, after dressing himself in the Priest's clothes, and being taken before the persecutor, had been able to pass off for his friend, and so gone to martyrdom without being discovered; and had he in the course of examination answered all questions truly, but not given the whole truth, the most important truth, that he was the wrong person, he would have come very near to telling a lie, for a half-truth is often a falsehood. And his defence must have been the *justa causa*, viz. either that he might in charity or for religion's sake save a priest, or again that the judge had no right to interrogate him on the subject.

Now, of these four modes of misleading others by the tongue, when there is a *justa causa* (supposing there can be such) – a material lie, that is an untruth which is not a lie, an equivocation, an evasion, and silence – First, I have no difficulty whatever in recognizing as allowable the method of *silence*.

Secondly, but, if I allow of *silence*, why not of the method of *material lying*, since half of a truth *is* often a lie ? And, again, if all killing be not murder, nor all taking from another stealing, why must all untruths be lies ? Now I will say freely that I think it difficult to answer this question, whether it be urged by St Clement or by Milton; at the same time, I never have acted, and I think, when it came to the point, I never should act upon such a theory myself, except in one case, stated below. This I say for the benefit of those who speak hardly of Catholic theologians, on the ground that they admit text-books which allow of equivocation. They are asked, how can we trust you, when such are your views ? but such views, as I already have said, need not have any thing to do with their own practice, merely from the circumstance that they are contained in their text-books. A theologian draws out a system; he does it partly as a scientific speculation; but much more for the sake of others. He is lax for the sake of others, not of himself. His own standard of action is much higher than that which he imposes upon men in general. One special reason why religious men, after drawing out a theory, are unwilling to act upon it themselves, is this: that they practically acknowledge a broad distinction between their reason and their conscience; and that they feel the latter to be the safer guide, though the former may be the clearer, nay even though it be the truer. They would rather be wrong with their conscience, than right with their reason. And again here is this more tangible difficulty in the case of exceptions to the rule of Veracity, that so very little external help is given us in drawing the line, as to when untruths are allowable and when not; whereas that sort of killing which is not murder, is most definitely marked off by legal enactments, so that it cannot possibly be mistaken for such killing as *is* murder. On the other hand the cases of exemption from the rule of Veracity are left to the private judgment of the individual, and he may easily be led on from acts which are allowable to acts which are not. Now this remark does *not* apply to such acts as are related in Scripture, as being done by a particular inspiration, for in such cases there *is* a command. If I had my own way, I would oblige society, that is, its great men, its lawyers, its divines, its literature, publicly to acknowledge, as such, those instances of untruth which are not lies, as for instance, untruths in war; and then there could be no danger in them to the individual Catholic, for he would be acting under a rule.

Thirdly, as to playing upon words, or equivocation, I suppose it is from the English habit, but, without meaning any disrepect to a great Saint, or wishing to set myself up, or taking my conscience for more than it is worth, I can only say as a fact, that I admit it as little as the rest of my countrymen: and, without any reference to the right and the wrong of the matter, of this I am sure, that, if there is one thing more than another which prejudices Englishmen against the Catholic Church, it is the doctrine of great authorities on the subject of equivocation. For myself, I can fancy myself thinking it was allowable in extreme cases for me to lie, but never to equivocate. Luther said, 'Pecca fortiter.' I anathematise the formal sentiment, but there is a truth in it, when spoken of material acts.

Fourthly, I think *evasion*, as I have described it, to be perfectly allowable; indeed, I do not know who does not use it, under circumstances; but that a good deal of moral danger is attached to its use; and that, the cleverer a man is, the more likely he is to pass the line of Christian duty.

But it may be said, that such decisions do not meet the particular difficulties for which provision is required; let us then take some instances.

1. I do not think it right to tell lies to children, even on this account, that they are sharper than we think them, and will soon find out what we are doing; and our example will be a very bad training for them. And so of equivocation: it is easy of imitation, and we ourselves shall be sure to get the worst of it in the end.

2. If an early Father defends the patriarch Jacob in his mode of gaining his father's blessing, on the ground that the blessing was divinely pledged to him already, that it was his, and that his father and brother were acting at once against his own rights and the divine will, it does not follow from this that such conduct is a pattern to us, who have no supernatural means of determining *when* an untruth becomes a *material*, and not a *formal* lie. It seems to me very dangerous, be it allowable or not, to lie or equivocate in order to preserve some great temporal or spiritual benefit, nor does St Alfonso here say anything to the contrary, for he is not discussing the question of danger or expedience.

3. As to Johnson's case of a murderer asking you which way a man had gone, I should have anticipated that, had such a difficulty happened to him, his first act would have been to knock the man down, and to call out for the police; and next, if he was worsted in

the conflict, he would not have given the ruffian the information he asked, at whatever risk to himself. I think he would have let himself be killed first. I do not think that he would have told a lie.

4. A secret is a more difficult case. Supposing something has been confided to me in the strictest secrecy, which could not be revealed without great disadvantage to another, what am I to do? If I am a lawyer, I am protected by my profession. I have a right to treat with extreme indignation any question which trenches on the inviolability of my position; but, supposing I was driven up into a corner, I think I should have a right to say an untruth, or that, under such circumstances, a lie would be *material*, but it is almost an impossible case, for the law would defend me. In like manner, as a priest, I should think it lawful to speak as if I knew nothing of what passed in confession. And I think in these cases, I do in fact possess that guarantee, that I am not going by private judgment, which just now I demanded; for society would bear me out, whether as a lawyer or as a priest, that I had a duty to my client or penitent, such, that an untruth in the matter was not a lie. A common type of this permissible denial, be it *material lie* or *evasion*, is at the moment supplied to me: an artist asked a Prime Minister, who was sitting to him, 'What news, my Lord, from France?'. He answered, '*I do not know*; I have not read the Papers.'

5. A more difficult question is, when to accept confidence has not been a duty. Supposing a man wishes to keep the secret that he is the author of a book, and he is plainly asked on the subject. Here I should ask the previous question, whether any one has a right to publish what he dare not avow. It requires to have traced the bearings and results of such a principle, before being sure of it; but certainly, for myself, I am no friend of strictly anonymous writing. Next, supposing another has confided to you the secret of his authorship: there are persons who would have no scruple at all in giving a denial to impertinent questions asked them on the subject. I have heard a great man in his day at Oxford, warmly contend, as if he could not enter into any other view of the matter, that, if he had been trusted by a friend with a secret of his being author of a certain book, and he were asked by a third person, if his friend was not (as he really was) the author of it, he ought without any scruple and distinctly to answer that he did not know. He had an existing duty towards the author; he had none towards his inquirer. The author had a claim on him; an

impertinent questioner had none at all. But here again I desiderate some leave, recognized by society, as in the case of the formulas. 'Not at home', and 'Not guilty', in order to give me the right of saying what is a *material* untruth. And moreover, I should here also ask the previous question, Have I any right to accept such a confidence? have I any right to make such a promise? and, if it be an unlawful promise, is it binding at the expense of a lie? I am not attempting to solve these difficult questions, but they have to be carefully examined.

As I put into print some weeks ago various extracts from authors relating to the subject which I have been considering, I conclude by inserting them here, though they will not have a very methodical appearance.

For instance, St Dorotheus: 'Sometimes the *necessity of* some matter urges (*incumbit*), which, unless you somewhat conceal and dissemble it, will turn into a greater trouble.' And he goes on to mention the case of saving a man who has committed homicide from his pursuers: and he adds that it is not a thing that can be done often, but once in a long time.

St Clement in like manner speaks of it only as a necessity, and as a necessary medicine.

Origen, after saying that God's commandment makes it a plain duty to speak the truth, adds, that a man, 'when necessity urges', may avail himself of a lie, as medicine, that is, to the extent of Judith's conduct towards Holofernes; and he adds that that necessity may be the obtaining of a great good, as Jacob hindered his father from giving the blessing to Esau against the will of God.

Cassian says, that the use of a lie, in order to be allowable, must be like the use of hellebore, which is itself poison, unless a man has a fatal disease on him. He adds, 'Without the condition of an extreme necessity, it is a present ruin.'

St John Chrysostom defends Jacob on the ground that his deceiving his father was not done for the sake of temporal gain, but in order to fulfil the providential purpose of God; and he says, that, as Abraham was not a murderer, though he was minded to kill his son, so an untruth need not be a lie. And he adds, that often such a deceit is the greatest possible benefit to the man who is deceived, and therefore allowable. Also St Hilary, St John Climacus, &c., in Thomassin, Concina, the *Mélanges*, &c.

Various modern Catholic divines hold this doctrine of the 'material lie' also. I will quote three passages in point.

Cattaneo: Be it then well understood, that the obligation to veracity, that is, of conforming our words to the sentiments of our mind, is founded principally upon the necessity of human intercourse, for which reason they (i.e. words) ought not and cannot be lawfully opposed to this end, so just, so necessary, and so important, without which, the world would become a Babylon of confusion. And this would in a great measure be really the result, as often as a man should be unable to defend secrets of high importance, and other evils would follow, even worse than confusion, in their nature destructive of this very intercourse between man and man for which speed was instituted. Everybody must see the advantage a hired assassin would have, if supposing he did not know by sight the person he was commissioned to kill, I being asked by the rascal at the moment he was standing in doubt with his gun cocked, were obliged to approve of his deed by keeping silence, or to hesitate, or lastly to answer 'Yes, that is the man'. In such and similar cases, in which your sincerity is unjustly assailed, when no other way more prompt or more efficacious presents itself, and when it is not enough to say, 'I do not know', let such persons be met openly with a downright resolute 'No' without thinking upon anything else. For such a 'No' is conformable to the universal opinion of men, who are the judges of words, and who certainly have not placed upon them obligations to the injury of the Human Republic, nor ever entered into a compact to use them in behalf of rascals, spies, incendiaries, and thieves. I repeat that such a 'No' is conformable to the universal mind of man, and with this mind your own ought to be in union and alliance. Who does not see the manifest advantage which highway robbers would derive, were travellers when asked if they had gold, jewels, &c., obliged either to invent tergiversations or to answer 'Yes, we have'? Accordingly in such circumstances that 'No' which you utter see Card. Pallav. lib. iii c. xi n. 23, *de Fide, Spe,* &c. remains deprived of its proper meaning, and is like a piece of coin, from which by the command of the government the current value has been withdrawn, so that by using it you become in no sense guilty of lying.

Bolgeni says,

> We have there proved satisfactorily, and with more than moral certainty, that an *exception* occurs to the general law of not speaking untruly, viz. when it is impossible to observe a certain other precept, more important, *without* telling a lie. Some persons indeed say, that in the cases of impossibility which are above drawn out, what is said is *not* a lie. But a man who thus speaks confuses ideas and denies the essential characters of things. What is a lie? It is 'locutio contra mentem'; this is its common definition. But in the cases of impossibility, a man speaks *contra mentem*; that is clear and evident. Therefore he tells a lie. Let us distinguish between the lie and the sin. In the above cases, the man really tells a lie, but this lie is not a sin, by reason of the existing impossibility. To say that in those cases no one has a right to ask, that the words have a meaning according to the common consent of men, and the like, as is said by certain authors in order in those cases to exempt a lie from sin, this is to commit oneself to frivolous excuses, and to subject oneself to a number of retorts, when there is the plain reason of the above mentioned fact of impossibility.

And the author in the *Mélanges Théologiques*:

> We have then gained this truth, and it is a conclusion of which we have not the smallest doubt, that if the intention of deceiving our neighbour is essential to a lie, it is allowable in certain cases to say what we know to be false, as, e.g. to escape from a great danger. . . .
>
> But, let no one be alarmed, it is never allowable to lie; in this we are in perfect agreement with the whole body of theologians. The only point in which we differ from them is in what we mean by a lie. They call that a lie which is not such in our view, or rather, if you will, what in our view is only a material lie they account to be both formal and material.

Now to come to Anglican authorities.

> Taylor: Whether it can in any case be lawful to tell a lie? To this I answer, that the Holy Scriptures of the Old and New Testament do indefinitely and severely forbid lying. Prov. xiii 5; xxx 8. Ps. v. 6. John viii 44. Col. iii 9. Rev. xxi 8. 27. Beyond these things, nothing can be said in condemnation of lying.

But then lying is to be understood to be *something said or written to the hurt of our neighbour*, which cannot be understood otherwise than to differ from the mind of him that speaks. 'A lie is petulantly or from a desire of hurting, to say one thing, or to signify it by gesture, and to think another thing;'[1] so Melancthon, 'To lie is to deceive our neighbour to his hurt.' For *in this sense* a lie is naturally or *intrinsically* evil; that is, to speak a lie *to our neighbour* is naturally evil . . . *not* because it is different from an eternal truth. . . . A lie is an *injury* to our neighbour . . . There is in mankind a universal *contract* implied in all their intercourses . . . *In justice* we are bound to speak, so as that our neighbour do not lose his *right*, which by our speaking we give him to the truth, that is, in our heart. And of a lie, *thus defined*, which is *injurious* to our neighbour, so long as his *right* to truth remains, it is that St Austin affirms it to be simply unlawful, and that it can in no case be permitted, *nisi forte regulas quasdam daturus es*. . . . If a lie be *unjust*, it can never become lawful; but, *if it can be separate from injustice*, then it may be *innocent*. Here then I consider

This right, though it be regularly and commonly belonging to all men, yet it may be *taken away* by a superior right intervening; or it may be lost, or it may be hindered, or it may cease, upon a greater reason.

Therefore upon this account it was lawful for the children of Israel to borrow jewels of the Egyptians, *which supposes a promise of restitution, though they intended not to pay them back again*. God gave commandment so to spoil them, and the Egyptians were divested of their *rights*, and *were to be used like enemies*.

It is lawful to tell a lie to children or to madmen; because they, having no powers of judging, have no *right* to truth; but then, *the lie must be charitable and useful*. . . . *If a lie be told*, it must be such as is *for their good* . . . and so do physicians to their patients. . . . This and the like were so usual, so permitted to physicians, that it grew to a proverb, 'You lie like a doctor;'[2] which yet was always to be understood in the way of charity and with honour to the profession . . . To tell a lie for

---

[1] 'Mendacium est petulanter, aut cupiditate nocendi, aliud loqui, seu gestu significare, et aliud sentire.'

[2] Mentiris ut medicus.

charity, to save a man's life, the life of a friend, of a husband, of
a prince, of a useful and a public person, hath not only been
done at all times, but commended by great and wise and good
men. . . . Who would not save his father's life . . . at the charge
of a *harmless lie*, from the rage of persecutors or tyrants ? . . .
When the telling of a truth will certainly be the cause of evil to a
man, though he have right to truth, yet it must not be given to
him to his harm. . . . *Every* truth is no more *justice*, than every
restitution of a straw to the right owner is a duty. 'Be not over-
righteous,' says Solomon. . . . If it be objected, that we must
not tell a lie for God, therefore much less for our brother, I
answer, that it does not follow; for God needs not a lie, *but our
brother does.* . . . *Deceiving* the enemy by the stratagem of
actions or *words*, is *not properly lying*; for this supposes a
conversation, of law or peace, trust or *promise* explicit or
implicit. A lie is a deceiving of a *trust or confidence.* – Taylor,
vol. xiii pp. 351–71, ed. Heber.

It is clear that Taylor thought that veracity was one branch of
justice; a social virtue; under the second table of the law, not
under the first; only binding, when those to whom we speak have
a claim of justice upon us, which ordinarily all men have.
Accordingly, in cases where a neighbour has no claim of justice
upon us, there is no opportunity of exercising veracity, as, for
instance, when he is mad, or is deceived by us for his own
advantage. And hence, in such cases, a lie is *not really* a lie, as he
says in one place, 'Deceiving the enemy is *not properly* lying.'
Here he seems to make that distinction common to Catholics, viz.
between what they call a *material* act and a *formal* act. Thus
Taylor would maintain, that to say the thing that is not to a
madman, has the *matter* of a lie, but the man who says it as little
tells a formal lie, as the judge, sheriff, or executioner murders the
man whom he certainly kills by forms of law.

Other English authors take precisely the same view, viz. that
veracity is a kind of justice – that our neighbour generally has a
right to have the truth told him; but that he may forfeit that right,
or lose it for the time, and then to say the thing that is not to him is
no sin against veracity, that is, no lie. Thus Milton says,

Veracity is a virtue, by which we speak true things to him *to
whom* it is equitable, and concerning what things it is suitable
for the *good of our neighbour* . . . All dissimulation is not

wrong, for it is not necessary for us always openly to bring out the truth; that only is blamed which is *malicious* . . . I do not see why that cannot be said of lying which can be said of homicide and other matters, which are not weighed so much by the *deed* as by *the object and end of acting*. *What man in his senses will deny* that there are those whom we have the best of grounds for considering that we ought to deceive – as boys, madmen, the sick, the intoxicated, enemies, men in error, thieves ? . . . Is it a point of conscience not to deceive them ? . . . I would ask, by which of the commandments is a lie forbidden ? You will say, by the ninth. Come, read it out, and you will agree with me. For whatever is here forbidden comes under the head of injuring one's neighbour. If then any lie does *not* injure one's neighbour, certainly it is not forbidden by this commandment. It is on this ground that, by the judgment of theologians, we shall acquit so many holy men of lying. Abraham, who said to his servants that he would return with his son . . . the wise man understood that it did not matter to his servants to know that his son would not return, and that it was at the moment expedient for himself that they should not know . . . Joseph would be a man of many lies if the common definition of lying held; also Moses, Rahab, Ehud, Jael, Jonathan.

Here again veracity is due only on the score of *justice* towards the person whom we speak with; and, if he has *no claim* upon us to speak the truth, we *need* not speak the truth to him.

And so, again, Paley:

A *lie is a breach of promise*; for whoever seriously addresses his discourse to another tacitly promises to speak the truth, because he knows that the truth is expected. Or the *obligation* of veracity may be made out from the direct ill consequences of lying to social happiness . . . There are *falsehoods* which are not *lies; that is, which are not criminal*. [Here, let it be observed, is the same distinction as in Taylor between *material* and *formal* untruths.] 1. When no one is deceived . . . 2. When the person to whom you speak has no *right* to know the truth, or, more properly, when little or no inconveniency results from the want of confidence in such cases, as *where you tell a falsehood to a madman* for his own advantage; to a robber, to conceal your property; to an assassin, to defeat or divert him from his purpose . . . It is upon this principle that, by the laws of war, it is allowable to deceive an enemy by feints, false colours, spies, false intelligence . . . Many people indulge, in serious discourse, a habit of fiction or exaggeration . . . So long as . . . their narratives, though false, are *inoffensive*, it may seem a superstitious regard to truth to censure them *merely for truth's sake*. [Then he goes on to mention reasons *against* such a practice, adding] I have seldom known any one who deserted truth in trifles that could be trusted in matters of importance. – Works, vol. iv, p. 123.

Dr Johnson, who, if any one, has the reputation of being a sturdy moralist, thus speaks:

'We talked,' says Boswell, 'of the casuistical question – whether it was allowable at any time to depart from *truth*.' Johnson: 'The general rule is, that truth should never be violated; because it is of the utmost importance to the comfort of life, that we should have a full security by mutual faith; and occasional inconveniences should be willingly suffered, that we may preserve it. There must, however, be some exceptions. If, for instance, a murderer should ask you which way a man is gone, you may tell him what is not true, because you are under a previous obligation not to betray a man to a murderer.' Boswell: 'Supposing the person who wrote Junius were asked whether he was the author, might he deny it ?' Johnson: 'I don't know what to say to this. If you were *sure* that he wrote Junius, would you, if he denied it, think as well of him afterwards ? Yet it may be urged, that what a man has no right to ask, you may refuse to communicate; and there is no other effectual mode of preserving a secret, and an important secret, the discovery of which may be very hurtful to you, but a flat denial; for if you are silent, or hesitate, or evade, it will be held equivalent to a confession. But stay, sir; here is another case. Supposing the author had told me confidentially that he had written Junius, and I were asked if he had, I should hold myself at liberty to deny it, as being under a pevious promise, express or implied, to conceal it. Now what I ought to do for the author, may I not do for myself ? But I deny the lawfulness of telling a lie to a sick man for fear of alarming him. You have no business with consequences; you are to tell the truth. Besides, you are not sure what effect your telling him that he is in danger may have; it may bring his distemper to a crisis, and that may cure him. Of all lying I have the greatest abhorrence of this, because I believe it has been frequently practised on myself.' – Boswell's Life, vol. iv p. 277.

There are English authors who allow of mental reservation and equivocation; such is Jeremy Taylor.

He says, 'In the same cases in which it is lawful to tell a lie, in the same cases it is lawful to use a mental reservation.' – Ibid. p. 374.

He says, too, 'When the things are true in *several senses*, the not explicating in *what sense* I mean the words is not a criminal reservation . . . But 1, this liberty is not to be used by inferiors, but by superiors only; 2, not by those that are interrogated, but by them which speak voluntarily; 3, not by those which speak of duty, but which speak of grace and kindness.' – Ibid. p. 378.

Bishop Butler, the first of Anglican authorities, writing in his grave and abstract way, seems to assert a similar doctrine in the following passage:

> Though veracity, as well as justice, is to be our rule of life, it must be added, otherwise a snare will be laid in the way of some plain men, that the use of common forms of speech generally understood, cannot be falsehood; and, in general, that there can be no designed falsehood without designing to deceive. It must likewise be observed, that, *in numberless cases, a man may be under the strictest obligations to what he foresees will deceive, without his intending it.* For *it is impossible not to foresee*, that the words and actions of men in different ranks and employments, and of different educations, *will perpetually be mistaken by each other*; and it cannot but be so, whilst they will judge with the utmost carelessness, as they daily do, *of what they are not perhaps enough informed to be competent judges of*, even though they considered it with great attention. – *Nature of Virtue*, fin.

These last words seem in a measure to answer to the words in Scavini, that an equivocation is permissible, because 'then we do not deceive our neighbour, but allow him to deceive himself.' In thus speaking, I have not the slightest intention of saying any thing disrespectful to Bishop Butler; and still less of course to St Alfonso.

And a third author, for whom I have a great respect, as different from the above two as they are from each other, bears testimony to the same effect in his 'Comment on Scripture', Thomas Scott. He maintains indeed that Ehud and Jael were divinely directed in what they did; but they could have no divine direction for what was in itself wrong.

Thus on Judges iii 15–21:

> 'And Edhud said, I have a secret errand unto thee, O king; I have a message from God unto thee, and Ehud thrust the dagger into his belly.'

Ehud, indeed, says Scott, had a secret errand, a message from God unto him; *but it was of a far different nature than Eglon expected.*

And again on Judges iv 18–21:

> 'And Jael said, Turn in, my lord, fear not. And he said to her, When any man doth inquire, Is there any man here ? thou shalt say, No. Then Jael took a nail, and smote the nail into his temple.'

Jael, says Scott, is not said to have promised Sisera that she would deny his being there; she would give him shelter and refreshment, but not utter a falsehood to oblige him.

APPENDIX B

Note on Liberalism (1865)

Liberalism

I have been asked to explain more fully what it is I mean by 'Liberalism', because merely to call it the Antidogmatic Principle is to tell very little about it. An explanation is the more necessary, because such good Catholics and distinguished writers as Count Montalembert and Father Lacordaire use the word in a favourable sense, and claim to be Liberals themselves. 'The only singularity,' says the former of the two in describing his friend, 'was his Liberalism. By a phenomenon, at that time unheard of, this convert, this seminarist, this confessor of nuns, was just as stubborn a liberal, as in the days when he was a student and a barrister.' – Life (transl.), p. 19.

I do not believe that it is possible for me to differ in any important matter from two men whom I so highly admire. In their general line of thought and conduct I enthusiastically concur, and consider them to be before their age. And it would be strange indeed if I did not read with a special interest, in M. de Montalembert's beautiful volume, of the unselfish aims, the thwarted projects, the unrequited toils, the grand tender resignation of Lacordaire. If I hesitate to adopt their language about Liberalism, I impute the necessity of such hesitation to some differences between us in the use of words or in the circumstances of country; and thus I reconcile myself to remaining faithful to my own conception of it, though I cannot have their voices to give force to mine. Speaking then in my own way, I proceed to explain what I meant as a Protestant by Liberalism, and to do so in connexion with circumstances under which that system of opinion came before me at Oxford.

If I might presume to contrast Lacordaire and myself, I should say, that we had been both of us inconsistent – he, a Catholic, in calling himself a Liberal; I, a Protestant, in being an Anti-liberal;

and moreover, that the cause of this inconsistency had been in both cases one and the same. That is, we were both of us such good conservatives, as to take up with what we happened to find established in our respective countries, at the time when we came into active life. Toryism was the creed of Oxford; he inherited, and made the best of, the French Revolution.

When, in the beginning of the present century, not very long before my own time, after many years of moral and intellectual declension, the University of Oxford woke up to a sense of its duties, and began to reform itself, the first instruments of this change, to whose zeal and courage we all owe so much, were naturally thrown together for mutual support, against the numerous obstacles which lay in their path, and soon stood out in relief from the body of residents, who, though many of them men of talent themselves, cared little for the object which the others had at heart. These Reformers, as they may be called, were for some years members of scarcely more than three or four Colleges; and their own Colleges, as being under their direct influence, of course had the benefit of those stricter views of discipline and teaching, which they themselves were urging on the University. They had, in no long time, enough of real progress in their several spheres of exertion, and enough of reputation out of doors, to warrant them in considering themselves the *élite* of the place; and it is not wonderful if they were in consequence led to look down upon the majority of Colleges, which had not kept pace with the reform, or which had been hostile to it. And, when those rivalries of one man with another arose, whether personal or collegiate, which befall literary and scientific societies, such disturbance did but tend to raise in their eyes the value which they had already set upon academical distinction, and increase their zeal in pursuing it. Thus was formed an intellectual circle or class in the University — men, who felt they had a career before them, as soon as the pupils, whom they were forming, came into public life; men, whom non-residents, whether country parsons or preachers of the Low Church, on coming up from time to time to the old place, would look at, partly with admiration, partly with suspicion, as being an honour indeed to Oxford, but withal exposed to the temptation of ambitious views, and to the spiritual evils signified in what is called the 'pride of reason'.

Nor was this imputation altogether unjust; for, as they were following out the proper idea of a University, of course they suffered more or less from the moral malady incident to such a pursuit. The very object of such great institutions lies in the cultivation of the mind and the spread of knowledge: if this object, as all human objects, has its dangers at all times, much more would these exist in the case of men, who were engaged in a work of reformation, and had the opportunity of measuring themselves, not only with those who were their equals in intellect, but with the many, who were below them. In this select circle or class of men, in various Colleges, the direct instruments and the choice fruit of real University Reform, we see the rudiments of the Liberal party.

Whenever men are able to act at all, there is the chance of extreme and intemperate action; and therefore, when there is exercise of mind, there is the chance of wayward or mistaken exercise. Liberty of thought is in itself a good; but it gives an opening to false liberty. Now by Liberalism I mean false liberty of thought, or the exercise of thought upon matters, in which, from the constitution of the human mind, thought cannot be brought to any successful issue, and therefore is out of place. Among such matters are first principles of whatever kind; and of these the most sacred and momentous are especially to be reckoned the truths of Revelation. Liberalism then is the mistake of subjecting to human judgment those revealed doctrines which are in their nature beyond and independent of it, and of claiming to determine on intrinsic grounds the truth and value of propositions which rest for their reception simply on the external authority of the Divine Word.

Now certainly the party of whom I have been speaking, taken as a whole, were of a character of mind out of which Liberalism might easily grow up, as in fact it did; certainly they breathed around an influence which made men of religious seriousness shrink into themselves. But, while I say as much as this, I have no intention whatever of implying that the talent of the University, in the years before and after 1820, was liberal in its theology, in the sense in which the bulk of the educated classes through the country are liberal now. I would not for the world be supposed to detract from the Christian earnestness, and the activity in religious works, above the average of men, of many of the persons in question. They would have protested against their being supposed to place reason before faith, or knowledge before devotion; yet I do consider that they unconsciously encouraged and successfully introduced into Oxford a licence of opinion which went far beyond them. In their day they did little more than take credit to themselves for enlightened views, largeness of mind, liberality of sentiment, without drawing the line between what was just and what was inadmissible in speculation, and without seeing the tendency of their own principles; and engrossing, as they did, the mental energy of the University, they met for a time with no effectual hindrance to the spread of their influence, except (what indeed at the moment was most effectual, but not of an intellectual character) the thorough-going Toryism and tradition-ary Church-of-England-ism of the great body of the Colleges and Convocation.

Now and then a man of note appeared in the Pulpit or Lecture Rooms of the University, who was a worthy representative of the more religious and devout Anglicans. These belonged chiefly to the High-Church party; for the party called Evangelical never has been able to breathe freely in the atmosphere of Oxford, and at no time has been conspicuous, as a party, for talent or learning. But of the old High Churchmen several exerted some sort of Anti-liberal influence in the place, at least from time to time, and that influence of an intellectual nature. Among these especially may be mentioned Mr John Miller, of Worcester College, who preached the Bampton Lecture in the year 1817. But, as far as I know, he who turned the tide, and brought the talent of the University round to the side of the old theology, and against what was familiarly called 'march-of-mind', was Mr Keble. In and from Keble the mental activity of Oxford took that contrary direction which issued in what was called Tractarianism.

Keble was young in years, when he became a University celebrity, and younger in mind. He had the purity and simplicity of a child. He had few sympathies with the intellectual party, who sincerely welcomed him as a brilliant specimen of young Oxford. He instinctively shut up before literary display, and pomp and donnishness of manner, faults which always will beset academical notabilities. He did not respond to their advances. His collision with them (if it may be so called) was thus described by Hurrell Froude in his own way. 'Poor Keble!' he used gravely to say, 'he was asked to join the aristocracy of talent, but he soon found his level.' He went into the country, but his instance serves to prove that men need not, in the event, lose that influence which is rightly theirs, because they happen to be thwarted in the use of the channels natural and proper to its exercise. He did not lose his place in the minds of men because he was out of their sight.

Keble was a man who guided himself and formed his judgments, not by processes of reason, by inquiry or by argument, but, to use the word in a broad sense, by authority. Conscience is an authority; the Bible is an authority; such is the Church; such is Antiquity; such are words of the wise; such are hereditary lessons; such are ethical truth; such are historical memories, such are legal saws and state maxims; such are proverbs; such are sentiments, presages, and prepossessions. It seemed to me as if he ever felt happier, when he could speak or act under such primary or external sanction; and could use argument mainly as a means of recommending or explaining what had claims on his reception prior to proof. He even felt a tenderness, I think, in spite of Bacon, for the Idols of the Tribe and the Den, of the Market and the Theatre. What he hated instinctively was heresy, insubordination, resistance to things established, claims of independence, disloyalty, innovation, a critical, censorious spirit. And such was the main principle of the school which in the course of years was formed around him; nor is it easy to set limits to its influence in its day; for multitudes of men, who did not profess its teaching, or accept it peculiar doctrines, were willing nevertheless, or found it to their purpose, to act in company with it.

Indeed for a time it was practically the champion and advocate of the political doctrines of the great clerical interest through the country, who found in Mr Keble and his friends an intellectual, as well as moral support to their cause, which they looked for in vain elsewhere. His weak point, in their eyes, was his consistency; for he carried his love of authority and old times so far, as to be more than gentle towards the Catholic Religion, with which the Toryism of Oxford and of the Church of England had no sympathy. Accordingly, if my memory be correct, he never could get himself to throw his heart into the opposition made to Catholic Emancipation, strongly as he revolted from the politics and the instruments by means of which that Emancipation was won. I fancy he would have had no difficulty in accepting Dr Johnson's saying about 'the first Whig'; and it grieved and offended him that the 'Via prima salutis' should be opened to the Catholic body from the Whig quarter. In spite of his reverence for the Old Religion, I conceive that on the whole he would rather have kept its professors beyond the pale of the Constitution with the Tories, than admit them on the principles of the Whigs. Moreover, if the Revolution of 1688 was too lax in principle for him and his friends, much less, as is very plain, could they endure to subscribe to the revolutionary doctrines of 1776 and 1789, which they felt to be absolutely and entirely out of keeping with theological truth.

The Old Tory or Conservative party in Oxford had in it no principle or power of development, and that from its very nature and constitution: it was otherwise with the Liberals. They represented a new idea, which was but gradually learning to recognize itself, to ascertain its characteristics and external relations, and to exert an influence upon the University. The party grew, all the time that I was in Oxford, even in numbers, certainly in breadth and definiteness of doctrine, and in power. And, what was a far higher consideration, by the accession of Dr Arnold's pupils, it was invested with an elevation of character which claimed the respect even of its opponents. On the other hand, in proportion as it became more earnest and less self-applauding, it became more free-spoken; and members of it might be found who, from the mere circumstance of remaining firm to their original professions, would in the judgment of the world, as to their public acts, seem to have left it for the Conservative camp. Thus, neither in its component parts nor in its policy, was it the same in 1832, 1836 and 1841, as it was in 1845.

These last remarks will serve to throw light upon a matter personal to myself, which I have introduced into my Narrative, and to which my attention has been pointedly called, now that my Volume is coming to a second edition.

It has been strongly urged upon me to reconsider the following passages which occur in it: 'The men who had driven me from Oxford were distinctly the Liberals, it was they who had opened the attack upon Tract 90,' p. 245, and 'I found no fault with the Liberals; they had beaten me in a fair field,' p. 252.

I am very unwilling to seem ungracious, or to cause pain in any quarter; still I am sorry to say I cannot modify these statements. It is surely a matter of historical fact that I left Oxford upon the University proceedings of 1841; and in those proceedings, whether we look to the Heads of Houses or the resident Masters, the leaders, if intellect and influence make men such, were members of the Liberal party. Those who did not lead, concurred or acquiesced in them — I may say, felt a satisfaction. I do not recollect any Liberal who was on my side on that occasion. Excepting the Liberal, no other party, as a party, acted against me. I am not complaining of them; I deserved nothing else at their hands. They could not undo in 1845, even had they wished it (and there is no proof they did), what they had done in 1841, when I had already given up the contest for four years, and my part in it had passed into the hands of others, then some of those who were prominent against me in 1841, feeling (what they had not felt in 1841) the danger of driving a number of my followers to Rome, and joined by younger friends who had come into University importance since 1841 and felt kindly towards me, adopted a course more consistent with their principles, and proceeded to shield from the zeal of the Hebdomadal Board, not me, but, professedly, all parties through the country – Tractarians, Evangelicals, Liberals in general – who had to subscribe to the Anglican formularies, on the ground that those formularies, rigidly taken, were, on some point or other, a difficulty to all parties alike.

However, besides the historical fact, I can bear witness to my own feeling at the time, and my feeling was this – that those who in 1841 had considered it to be a duty to act against me, had then done their worst. What was it to me what they were doing in the matter of the New Test proposed by the Hebdomadal Board ? I owed them no thanks for their trouble. I took no interest at all, in February, 1845, in the proceedings of the Heads of Houses and of the Convocation. I felt myself *dead* as regarded my relations to the Anglican Church. My leaving it was all but a matter of time. I believe I did not even thank my real friends, the two Proctors, who in Convocation stopped by their Veto the condemnation of Tract 90; nor did I make any acknowledgment to Mr Rogers, nor to Mr James Mozley, nor, as I think, to Mr Hussey, for their pamphlets in my behalf. My frame of mind is best described by the sentiment of the passage in Horace, which at the time I was fond of quoting, as expressing my view of the relation that existed between the Vice-Chancellor and myself.

'Pentheu,
Rector Thebarum, quid me perferre patique
Indignum cogas ?' 'Adimam bona.' 'Nempe pecus, rem,
Lectos, argentum; tollas licet.' 'In manieis et
Compedibus, sævo te sub custode tenebo.' (*viz. the* 39
Articles.)

'*Ipse Deus, simul atque volam, me solvet.*' Opinor,
Hoc sentit: *Moriar. Mors ultima linea rerum est.*

I conclude this notice of Liberalism in Oxford, and the party which was antagonistic to it, with some propositions in detail, which, as a member of the latter, and together with the High Church, I earnestly denounced and abjured.

1. No religious tenet is important, unless reason shows it to be so.

> Therefore, e.g. the doctrine of the Athanasian Creed is not to be insisted on, unless it tends to convert the soul; and the doctrine of the Atonement is to be insisted on, if it does convert the soul.

2. No one can believe what he does not understand.

> Therefore, e.g. there are no mysteries in true religion.

3. No theological doctrine is any thing more than an opinion which happens to be held by bodies of men.

> Therefore, e.g. no creed, as such, is necessary for salvation.

4. It is dishonest in a man to make an act of faith in what he has not had brought home to him by actual proof.

> Therefore, e.g. the mass of men ought not absolutely to believe in the divine authority of the Bible.

5. It is immoral in a man to believe more than he can spontaneously receive as being congenial to his moral and mental nature.

> Therefore, e.g. a given individual is not bound to believe in eternal punishment.

6. No revealed doctrines or precepts may reasonably stand in the way of scientific conclusions.

> Therefore, e.g. Political Economy may reverse our Lord's declarations about poverty and riches, or a system of Ethics may teach that the highest condition of body is ordinarily essential to the highest state of mind.

7. Christianity is necessarily modified by the growth of civilization, and the exigencies of times.

Therefore, e.g. the Catholic priesthood, though necessary in the Middle Ages, may be superseded now.

8. There is a system of religion more simply true than Christianity as it has ever been received.

Therefore, e.g. we may advance that Christianity is the 'corn of wheat' which has been dead for 1800 years, but at length will bear fruit; and that Mahometanism is the manly religion, and existing Christianity the womanish.

9. There is a right of Private Judgment: that is, there is no existing authority on earth competent to interfere with the liberty of individuals in reasoning and judging for themselves about the Bible and its contents, as they severally please.

Therefore, e.g. religious establishments requiring subscription are Anti-christian.

10. There are rights of conscience such, that every one may lawfully advance a claim to profess and teach what is false and wrong in matters, religious, social, and moral, provided that to his private conscience it seems absolutely true and right.

Therefore, e.g. individuals have a right to preach and practise fornication and polygamy.

11. There is no such thing as a national or state conscience.

Therefore, e.g. no judgments can fall upon a sinful or infidel nation.

12. The civil power has no positive duty, in a normal state of things, to maintain religious truth.

Therefore, e.g. blasphemy and sabbath-breaking are not rightly punishable by law.

13. Utility and expedience are the measure of political duty.

Therefore, e.g. no punishment may be enacted, on the ground that God commands it: e.g. on the text. 'Whoso sheddeth man's blood, by man shall his blood be shed.'

14. The Civil Power may dispose of Church property without sacrilege.

Therefore, e.g. Henry VIII committed no sin in his spoliations.

15. The Civil Power has the right of ecclesiastical jurisdiction and administration.

Therefore, e.g. Parliament may impose articles of faith on the Church or suppress Dioceses.

16. It is lawful to rise in arms against legitimate princes.

Therefore, e.g. the Puritans in the 17th century, and the French in the 18th, were justifiable in their Rebellion and Revolution respectively.

17. The people are the legitimate source of power.

Therefore, e.g. Universal Suffrage is among the natural rights of man.

18. Virtue is the child of knowledge, and vice of ignorance.

Therefore, e.g. education, periodical literature, railroad travelling, ventilation, drainage, and the arts of life, when fully carried out, serve to make a population moral and happy.

All of these propositions, and many others too, were familiar to me thirty years ago, as in the number of the tenets of Liberalism, and, while I gave into none of them except No. 12, and perhaps No. 11, and partly No. 1, before I began to publish, so afterwards I wrote against most of them in some part or other of my Anglican works.

If it is necessary to refer to a work, not simply my own, but of the Tractarian school, which contains a similar protest, I should name the *Lyra Apostolica*. This volume, which by accident has been left unnoticed, except incidentally, in my Narrative, was collected together from the pages of the 'British Magazine', in which its contents originally appeared, and published in a separate form, immediately after Hurrell Froude's death in 1836. Its signatures, α, β, γ, δ, ε, ζ, denote respectively the authorship of Mr Bowden, Mr Hurrell Froude, Mr Keble, myself, Mr Robert Wilberforce, and Mr Isaac Williams.

There is one poem on 'Liberalism', beginning 'Ye cannot halve the Gospel of God's grace'; which bears out the account of Liberalism as above given. Another upon 'the Age to come',

defining from its own point of view the position and prospects of
Liberalism, shall be quoted *in extenso*.

> When I would search the truths that in me burn,
>   And mould them into rule and argument,
> A hundred reasoners cried — 'Hast thou to learn
>   Those dreams are scattered now, those fires are spent?'
> And, did I mount to simpler thoughts, and try
>   Some theme of peace, 'twas still the same reply.
>
> Perplexed, I hoped my heart was pure of guile,
>   But judged me weak in wit, to disagree;
> But now I see, that men are mad awhile,
>   And joy the Age to come will think of me;
> 'Tis the old history — Truth without a home,
>   Despised and slain; then, rising from the tomb.

APPENDIX C (1866)

I

The Church of England

There is, perhaps, no other institution in which the English have shown their love of compromise in political and social affairs so strikingly as in the established national Church. Luther, Calvin and Zwingli, all enemies of Rome, were equally the enemies of one another. Of other Protestant sects the Erastians, Puritans and Arminians are also different and hostile. But it is no exaggeration to say that the Anglican ecclesiastical Establishment is an amalgamation of all these varieties of Protestantism, to which a considerable amount of Catholicism is superadded. The Establishment is the outcome of the action which Henry VIII, the ministers of Edward VI, Mary, Elizabeth, the Cavaliers, the Puritans, the Latitudinarians of 1688, and the Methodists of the Eighteenth Century successively brought to bear on religion. It has a hierarchy dating from the Middle Ages, richly endowed, exalted by its civil position, formidable by its political influence. The Established Church has preserved the rites, the prayers and the symbols of the ancient Church. She draws her articles of faith from Lutheran and Zwinglian sources; her translation of the Bible savours of Calvinism. She can boast of having had in her bosom, especially in the seventeenth century, a succession of theologians of great learning and proud to make terms with the doctrines and practices of the primitive Church. The great Bossuet, contemplating her doctors, said that it was impossible that the English should not one day come back to the faith of their fathers; and De Maistre hailed the Anglican communion as being destined to play a great part in the reconciliation and reunion of Christendom.

This remarkable Church has always been in the closest dependence on the civil power and has always gloried in this. It has ever regarded the Papal power with fear, with resentment and with aversion, and it has never won the heart of the people. In this it has shown itself consistent throughout the course of its existence; in other concerns it has either had no opinions or has constantly changed them. In the sixteenth century it was Calvinist; in the first half of the seventeenth it was Arminian and quasi-Catholic; towards the close of that century and at the beginning of the next it was latitudinarian. In the middle of the eighteenth century it was described by Lord Chatham as having 'a papistical ritual and prayer-book, Calvinist articles of faith and an Arminian clergy'.

In our days it contains three powerful parties in which are embodied the three principles of religion which appear constantly and from the beginning of its history in one form or another; the Catholic principle, the Protestant principle, and the sceptical principle. Each of these, it is hardly necessary to say, is violently opposed to the other two.

Firstly: the apostolic or Tractarian party, which is now moving in the direction of Catholicism further than at any other time, or in any previous manifestation; to such an extent, that, in studying this party among its most advanced adherents, one may say that it differs in nothing from Catholicism except in the doctrine of Papal supremacy. The party arose in the seventeenth century, at the courts of James I and Charles I; it was almost extinguished by the doctrines of Locke and by the ascent to the throne of William III and the House of Hanover. But in the course of the eighteenth century its principles were taught and silently transmitted by the 'non-jurors', a sect of learned and zealous men who, preserving the episcopal succession, separated themselves from the Church of England when summoned to take the oath of fidelity to William III. In our day it has been seen to revive and form a numerous and increasing party in the Church of England, by means of the movement started by the writings entitled: *Tracts for the Times*, (and thence called Tractarian,) of which there is such constant mention in this book.

Secondly: the Evangelical party which maintains all the biblical societies and most of the associations for protestant missions throughout the world. The origin of this party may be traced back to the puritans, who began to show themselves in the last years of Queen Elizabeth's reign. It was almost entirely thrown out of the Church of England at the time of the restoration of Charles II in 1660. It took refuge among the dissenters from that Church and was expiring little by little when its doctrines were revived with great vigour by the celebrated preachers, Whitfield and Wesley, both pastors of the Anglican Church and founders of the powerful sect of the Methodists. These doctrines, while creating a sect outside the established Church, exercised at the same time an important influence in the bosom of that Church itself, and developed there little by little until it formed the evangelical party, which is today by far the most important of the three schools which we are trying to describe.

Thirdly: the Liberal party, known in previous centuries by the less honourable name of *Latitudinarian*. It broke off from the quasi-Catholic party, or Court party, in the reign of Charles I, and was fed and extended by the introduction into England of the principles of Grotius and of the Arminians of Holland. We have already referred to the philosophy of Locke as having had an influence in the same direction. This party took the side of the revolution of 1688, and supported the Whigs, William III, and the House of Hanover. The spirit of its principles is opposed to extension and proselytism; and, although it has numbered in its ranks remarkable writers among the Anglican theologians, it had had but few votaries until ten years ago, when, irritated by the success of the Tractarians, taking advantage of the conversion of some of their principal leaders to the Roman Church, and aided by the importation of German literature into England, this party suddenly came before the public view and was propagated among the best educated classes with a rapidity so astonishing that it is almost justifiable to believe that in the coming generation the religious world will be divided between the Deists and the Catholics. The principles and arguments of the Liberals do not even stop at deism.

If the Anglican communion were composed solely of these three parties it could not exist. It would be broken up by its internal dissensions. But there is in its bosom a party more numerous by far than these three theological ones – a party which, created by the legal position of the Church, profiting by its riches and by the institutions of its creed, is the counter weight and the chain which secures the whole. It is the party of order, the party of Conservatives, or Tories as they have hitherto been called. It is not a religious party, not that it has not a great number of religious men in its ranks, but because its principles and its *mots d'ordre* are political or at least ecclesiastical rather than theological. Its members are neither *Tractarians*, nor *Evangelicals*, nor *Liberals*;

or, if they are it is in a very mild and very unaggressive form; because, in the eyes of the world their chief characteristic consists in their being advocates of *an Establishment* and of *the Establishment*, and they are more zealous for the preservation of a national Church than solicitous for the beliefs which that national Church professes. We said above that the great principle of the Anglican Church was its confidence in the protection of the civil power and its docility in serving it, which its enemies call its *Erastianism*. Now if on the one hand this respect for the civil power be its great principle, the principle of Erastianism is, on the other hand, embodied in so numerous a party whether among the clergy or the laity, that the word 'party' is scarcely adequate. It constitutes the mass of the Church. The clergy in particular — Bishops, Deans, Chapters, Rectors — are always distinguished by their Toryism on all English questions. In the seventeenth century they professed the divine right of kings; they have ever since gloried in the doctrine: 'The King is the head of the Church;' and their after-dinner toast: 'The Church and the King' has been their formula of protestation for maintaining in the kingdom of England the theoretical predominance of the spiritual over the temporal. They have always testified an extreme aversion for what they term the power usurped by the Pope. Their chief theological dogma is that the Bible contains all necessary truths, and that every Christian is individually capable of discovering them there for his own use. They preach Christ as the only mediator, redemption by His death, the renewal of man by His Spirit, the necessity for good works. This great assembly of men, true representatives of that English common sense which is so famous for its good as for its evil consequences, mostly regard every kind of theology, every theological school, and in particular the three schools which we have tried to portray, with mistrust. In the seventeenth century they combated the Puritans; at the close of that century they combated the Latitudinarians; in the middle of the eighteenth century they combated the Methodists and the members of the Evangelical party; and in our own times they have made an energetic stand at first against the Tractarians and today against the Liberals.

This party of order in the Established Church has necessarily many subdivisions. The country clergy, rejoicing in great ease, in intimate relations with the county gentlemen of their neighbourhood and always benevolent and charitable, are much respected, and beloved by the lower classes on account of their position, but not for the influence of their doctrine. But amongst ecclesiastics who enjoy great revenues and have not much to do (such as the members of the Cathedral chapters), many have long since deteriorated in the pursuit of their personal advantage. Those who held high positions in great towns have been led to adopt the habits of a great position and of external display, and have boasted in formal orthodoxy which was cold and almost entirely devoid of interior life. These self-indulgent pastors have for a long time been nick-named 'two-bottle orthodox', as though their greatest religious zeal manifested itself in the drinking of port wine to the health of 'the Church and King'. The pompous dignitaries of great town parishes have also been surnamed the 'high and dry' school or Church.

It still remains for us to explain three words which are in opposition to each other and which will find their place in this book: High Church; Low Church; Broad Church. The last of these denominations offers no difficulty: the word 'broad' answers to that of 'latitudinarian', and by Broad Church is understood the Liberal party. But the denominations of High and Low Church cannot be understood without explanation.

The doctrine appellation of 'High Church' signifies the teaching which aims at asserting the prerogatives and authority of the Church; but not so much its *invisible* powers as its privileges and gifts as a *visible* body; and, since in the Anglican religion these temporal privileges have always depended on the civil power, it happens accidentally that a partisan of the High Church is almost an Erastian; that is to say, a man who denies the spiritual power pertaining to the Church and maintains that the Church is one of the branches of the civil government. Thus, a Calvinist may be a partisan of the High Church, as was Whitgift, Archbishop of Canterbury in the reign of Elizabeth, and as was also Hooker, the Master of the Temple, at any rate during his youth.

The Low Church is obviously the opposite to the High Church. If then the High Church party is the party which upholds the Church and the King, the Low Church party is the one which anathematises that Erastian doctrine and considers it anti-Christian to give the State any power whatsoever over the Church of God; it was thus that formerly the Puritans and the Independents preferred Cromwell to King Charles. Today, however, since the Puritans have ceased to exist in England, the

denomination of Low Church has ceased to represent an ecclesiastical idea, and designates a theological party, becoming
synonymous with the Evangelical party. In consequence, an
analogous change has taken place in the meaning of the name
'High Church'. Instead of denoting solely the partisans of the
'Church and the King', or the Erastians, it has come to have a
theological signification and to denote the semi-Catholic party.
Thus it often happens in our own days that even the Tractarians
are called partisans of the High Church, although they began by
denouncing Erastianism, and although, in their early days, they
were violently opposed at Oxford by the High Church party or
Established Church.

II

The University of Oxford

The University of Oxford has been the intellectual centre of England ever since the Middle Ages. Six centuries ago Paris alone surpassed it as an ecclesiastical school and it was the mother of the theologians, Scotus, Alexander of Hales, and Occam. Even in those times it was a kind of representative of the political parties of the nation. An old rhymed couplet gives evidence of that:

Chronica si penses, cum pugnant Oxonienses
Post paucos menses volat ira per Angligenenses.

In the centuries following the Reformation, Oxford has always been the headquarters of the Tory or Conservative party, which has been described above as the most considerable in the Established Church. It was there that the Protestant reformers, Cranmer, Ridley and Latimer, were burnt alive in the time of Queen Mary; it was there that King Charles I found his most steadfast support against his Parliament. It was there that the non-jurors and other supporters of the Stuarts sought a refuge for their opinions when the House of Hanover had taken possession of the kingdom; and, while remaining eminently conservative in its religious and political teaching, it has nevertheless so completely sustained the intellectual vigour of its first ages, that, even in the course of the last century, it has given birth to each of the three theological parties that exist today in the Established Church, and to which the conservative spirit which so specially characterizes it, is naturally so opposed. The Evangelical party of today owes its origin to Whitfield and Wesley, who, towards the middle of the last century, began their religious life as Oxford students. Oxford was again, as this volume proves, the sole mother and nurse of Tractarianism; and the Liberalism which today inundates the English intelligent classes sprang rather from Oxford than from any other source.

Let us proceed to its academic constitution. There, too, Oxford has preserved this character of the Middle Ages which nearly all the continental universities have lost. It comprehends a certain number of separate societies which bear the distinctive names of *colleges* and *halls*, and each of which has its separate and independent rights and privileges. Its position cannot be better described than by comparing it to the political constitution of the United States of America. Just as the different States are, or have hitherto been, independent within their proper limitations and are nevertheless included in the dominion of the republic, so each of the Oxford colleges is a separate corporation legally and actually independent of all the others, although they are all constituent parts of the same university. These colleges were in the beginning inns or *hostels* intended for the reception of students who had come from afar. Little by little they took the form of separate societies, and, obtaining the patronage of important people, whether ecclesiastics or nobles, they acquired a legal existence (*status*) and were richly endowed. Other colleges have their origin in the monasteries with which the university was abundantly provided. Today there exist about twenty colleges and five halls. The difference between a college and a hall is that the college is a corporation possessing endowments and having its own complete administration, and that the hall is not a corporation. Mention is made in this work of Oriel College, founded in 1326 by King Edward II; of Trinity College, founded in the sixteenth century on the site of a Benedictine house; of Pembroke College, whose origin is more modern; and of Alban Hall, the antiquity of which goes back further than that of the two first. The corporate rights of a college rest with a head and with Fellows, whose position answers to that of the Dean and Canons of a cathedral. And this head is designated by different titles, such as Provost of Oriel, President of Trinity, Master of Pembroke, and Principal of Alban Hall. The head of the university itself is the Chancellor, who is generally a great nobleman, or a considerable statesman, elected to the position by the members of the university. The three most recent Chancellors have been Lord Grenville, so celebrated in the beginning of the history of this century, the Duke of Wellington, and Lord Derby, now the head of the Conservative party. The acting governor of the university is the Vice-Chancellor who is chosen, according to custom, from among the heads of the colleges in turn and holds his office for four years.

NOTES

p. 87 Secretum meum mihi: 'My secret is my own' (Isaiah 24: 16); words sometimes used by St Philip Neri, founder of the Roman Oratory, to his fellow oratorians, as an admonition to the effect that their relationship with God, and the graces they had received from Him, were not to be bruited about.

p. 89 The doctrine of final perseverance: the teaching that those who are predestined to eternal life receive the gift of persevering, after conversion, in the way of life necessary to salvation. Calvin maintained that God would not permit the elect to fall away; Catholic versions of the doctrine of predestination, however (beginning with Augustine), maintain that free will remains and that individual effort is therefore necessary to salvation.

p. 90 Thomas Scott of Aston Sandford (1747–1821): Biblical commentator. Rector of Aston Sandford, Bucks (1801–21). His book *Force of Truth* (1779), is a kind of Protestant *Apologia*, or History of his mind, describing the stages by which he moved from Unitarianism to Calvinism.

Antinomianism: the doctrine that Christians are freed from the observance of moral laws, derived from a misreading of St Paul's teaching that man is justified only by faith in Jesus Christ and not by obedience to the law of the old covenant. Some versions of this early heresy conveniently gave free reign to sexual licence, a problem which directly confronted St Paul.

p. 94 Butler, Joseph (1692–1752): Bishop of Durham, 1750. Author of *The Analogy of Religion, Natural and Revealed, to the Constitution and Course of Nature* (1736), a major defence of supernatural religion against the deism and rationalism of the 18th century.

p. 95 Anti-Erastianism: Erastianism is the doctrine of the subordination of the ecclesiastical to the secular power. As Newman says here, this heresy was particularly opposed by the Oxford movement; he came to believe that the Church of England was preponderantly and unavoidably Erastian in character: as he put it in 1866 'this remarkable Church has always been in the closest dependence on the civil power and has always gloried in this' (see page 399).

p. 96 Arianizing, Bishop Bull's *Defensio*, ante-Nicene: The ante-Nicene Church (i.e. the Church in the period before the Council of Nicaea) was, according to some writers, tainted by the Arian heresy that Christ was not divine and was subordinate to the Father. Bishop George Bull (1634–1710), however, claimed in his *Defensio Fidei Nicenae* (1685) that the ante-Nicene Church was, on the contrary, perfectly orthodox. Newman at this period was in his own words 'drifting in the direction of the liberalism of the day'; this was consistent with his particular admiration for the ante-Nicene Church and a feeling that the articles of the (Nicene) creed were too clearly defined; all this made accusations of 'Arianizing' not wholly inexplicable. Theological liberalism in Oxford seems always to have tended to the view that Arius's views are compatible with Christian belief; a century and a half later, the then Regius Professor of Divinity gave a series of notorious lectures arguing that far from being a heresiarch, Arius was a Father of the Church like any other. See note to p. 106.

p. 97 Petition to Parliament against the Catholic claims: In 1929, Convocation (the governing body of Oxford University) once more passed a petition against Catholic emancipation. The Tory government led by the Duke of Wellington – in which Peel was a prominent member – responded to fears of civil war in Ireland by passing the 'Roman Catholic Relief Act'. Peel was well aware of feeling in the University (which he represented in Parliament); he had hitherto always defended the established Church (which felt itself under threat now that Catholics could be members of Parliament) and had hitherto opposed Catholic emancipation. Newman felt that Peel had betrayed his constituents by this U-turn in policy and opposed his re-election to the University seat: it would, he wrote, be humiliating 'to have a Rat our member'.

p. 98 Numquam minus solus, quàm cùm solus: never less alone than when alone.

p. 99 Keble, John (1782–1866): The son of an Anglican clergyman, Keble showed his brilliance at Oxford, first as an undergraduate at Corpus Christi then with his election to an Oriel fellowship at the age of 19. He was ordained priest five years later and was content to spend most of his life in pastoral work as a country clergyman. In 1827 he published *The Christian Year*, a volume of poems. He was elected professor of poetry at Oxford, a position he held for the next ten years. In 1845, he preached his famous Assize sermon, which is generally held to mark the beginning of the Oxford movement. His influence on the movement was not only intellectual but moral, and derived chiefly from his great and evident personal holiness.

p. 103 Richard Hurrell Froude (1803–36): Froude, says Dr Sheridan Gilley, 'was the type of right-wing intellectual counter-revolutionary perhaps more common on the continent than in Britain, where conservatives usually like to consider themselves stupid.' He possessed great wit and charm; his brother, the historian J. A. Froude (who abandoned the Oxford movement when Newman seceded, becoming a friend of Kingsley), wrote after his early death from tuberculosis that he had never seen anyone 'in whom the excellences of intellect and character were combined in fuller measure.' He brought Newman under the influence of John Keble, and because of this and his own character and intellect is himself one of the key influences on Newman's life. With Newman, he wrote the 'Lyra Apostolica', and contributed three of the *Tracts for the Times*. Newman himself gives the best account of his influence over him. His 'Literary Remains', which included such unvarnished sentiments as 'Really I hate the Reformation and the Reformers more and more', aroused public hostility towards the Oxford movement.

p. 106 'The Battle of Arianism'; 'Athanasius, the champion of the truth': Arius (ca 250–ca 336) denied the Divinity of Christ; the battle between his followers and those of Athanasius (in which the latter was in the end victorious, though at one time reputedly the only bishop in Christendom to uphold the doctrine) is generally thought of as one of the pivotal conflicts of the early Church. Athanasius led an uncertain existence as bishop of Alexandria, being alternately deposed and restored depending on the vagaries of imperial politics. He was appointed bishop of Alexandria in 328 (having attended the Council of Nicea three years earlier); because of his defence of the Council's teaching that Christ is of 'one substance with the Father' he was deposed as bishop and exiled in 336; he returned in 337 but in 338 was forced once more into exile. He was restored once more in 346; deposed in 356; remained in hiding in the desert until 361, was exiled again in 362; returned in 363; was exiled again in 365; returned finally in 366 and conducted a campaign for Nicene orthodoxy, which was finally and definitively victorious at the Council of Constantinople in 381, largely as a result of Athanasius's courageous and unflagging struggle over the years. Newman had a deep and enduring devotion to him.

p. 107 δαιμόνια: The Greeks believed in *daimonia* or *daimones*, spiritual beings intermediate between gods and men. Similar beliefs were held within Judaism in the New Testament period. Christians are enjoined in 1 Jn 4:1 to test such spirits, to see whether they are of God.

p. 109 Incessu patuit dea: 'In her step the goddess was revealed' (*Aeneid* 1: 405)

p. 112 exoriare aliquis [nostris ex ossibus ultor] (Aeneid 4: 625): 'From my bones may some avenger rise up'

p. 115 Erastianism: See anti-Erastianism, note to page 95.

p. 128 τῷ τέλετ πίστιν φέρων: resting his hopes on the event.

p. 131 Dr Pusey: After Newman's 'defection', the uncontested leader of the movement; those Tractarians who remained in the Church of England tended to paint a contrast between his deep spirituality and steadfast character and – it seemed to be implied – consequent unreliability. Thus, Bishop Samuel Wilberforce, in his review of the *Apologia*, wrote that: 'whilst Newman was pouring forth with exuberant fertility controversial tracts and essays, and travelling through the land on the curious missions he describes in his "Apologia" . . . Dr Pusey was reaching far more profoundly, by the devotional tone of all he put forth, the inner religious heart of the Church.'

I used to call him σ μέγας: 'The great one.'

p. 140 Justification: 'I thought that the Anglican Church followed Melanchthon . . .' In the *Essay on Justification*, Newman contrasts the Roman position – according to which

Justification is seen as 'a *change, passage,* or *motion* of the soul from one state to another' (St Thomas Aquinas) – with the Continental Protestant understanding (i.e. that of Luther), according to which the word applies not passively to the human soul but to the '*act* on God's part, whereby he justifies the sinner. Melanchthon used the word in both senses; – so do our Homilies . . .'; thus, as in Tract XC, Newman looks to the *Book of Homilies* here to establish normative Anglican doctrine.

p. 142 **In extenso:** here, 'in full'.

p. 146 **In medias res:** in the middle of the subject, in the thick of the question.

p. 152 **Ex animo:** 'from the soul', i.e. with absolute conviction.

p. 155 **Infandum dolorem** (*Aeneid* 2, 3): unspeakable sorrow. Aeneas replies to Queen Dido's request for a description of the fall of Troy: 'Infandum [regina iubes renovare] dolorem', O queen, you are asking me to renew an unspeakable sorrow.

p. 162 **Fortes fortuna adjuvat:** 'fortune favours the brave'.

p. 167 **Quod semper, quod ubique, quod ab omnibus:** '[That which was believed] always, everywhere and by all' (St Vincent of Lérins).

p. 170 **de jure divino:** by divine law

p. 172 **I was a Monophysite:** As with other doctrinal controversies (e.g. the Donatist schism) which Newman saw as dramatically illustrating the position of Anglicanism in the nineteenth century, the doctrine itself is not in question. The (heretical) Monophysites (as opposed to the (orthodox) Diophysites, who believed that the Incarnate Christ had two natures, Human and Divine) held that Christ had only divine nature. Eutyches held an extreme form of the doctrine, to which the Monophysites were opposed. Thus, Newman suggests that the difference between the Eutychians and the Monophysites is like that between the extreme Protestantism of the Continental reformers and their descendants, and the more moderate beliefs of the Anglican reformation. The point, here and elsewhere, is that 'Rome was where she now is'.

Delirus senex: demented old man.

p. 173 Anathema to a whole tribe . . . perish the names. . . : In brief, this passage means that if remaining an Anglican entails (as at this point it is beginning to appear to Newman) that he would have to set himself in opposition to the Fathers of the Church, then Anglicanism has to be rejected, whether it means the clear protestantism of Cranmer, Ridley, Latimer and Jewel – in any case repudiated by Newman and his followers – or the teachings of the Caroline divines. These were in general more inclined in a Catholic direction, but nevertheless differed from Roman teaching in important particulars. Bramhall rejected the doctrine of transubstantiation; Ussher, a patristic scholar and a divine of great holiness, was nevertheless inclined to Calvinism; Jeremy Taylor was violently anti-Roman – his works *Dissuasive from Popery* (1664) and *The Real Presence . . . proved against . . . Transubstantiation* demonstrate the clear limits of the 'Catholic' tendencies of the Caroline divines both in their sacramental doctrine and in their dissociation from Catholic Christendom. Stillingfleet was a latitudinarian who published anti-Roman writings; so did Barrow, whose best known work was entitled *Treatise on the Pope's supremacy*.

p. 174 The Donatists: See note to p. 172. The Donatists claimed that the unworthiness of a minister of the sacraments invalidated the sacrament he administers; the Catholic Church has always taught that the validity of sacraments cannot be affected by the mental or moral condition of the minister.

Securus judicat orbis terrarum: Newman's rendering was 'The universal Church is in its judgements secure of truth.' Some years later, he gave the following explanation to an Anglican correspondent:

> 'Securus judicat orbis terrarum – "the Christian commonwealth judges without misgiving." That is the maxim . . . on which all depends. The Christian commonwealth is one organized body – from time to time local disturbances rise in it – branches of it rise up separately from the rest, and claim to be heard in matters of discipline or doctrine – they appeal to the Fathers – so did the Donatists, so did the Arians, the Monophysites, the Protestants, the Anglicans – but the Christian State, Commonwealth, Kingdom judicat securus, has the right, the power, the certitude of deciding the rights and the wrongs of the matter.'

The full text quoted in Wiseman's article was 'Quapropter securus judicat orbis terrarum, bonos nos esse qui se dividunt ab orbe terrarum in qua parte orbis terrarum.' Wiseman translated this: 'Wherefore, the entire world judges with security, that they are not good, who separate themselves from the entire world, in whatever part of the entire world.' Wiseman's article applied Augustine's principle as a judgement on Anglicanism's separation of itself from Catholic Christendom: of the Donatists, he remarks that: 'the very circumstance of one particular Church being out of the aggregation of other Churches, constituted these judges over the other and left no room for questioning the justice of the condemnation.'

p. 174 Tolle, lege: 'Take and read': The divinely revealed words which prompted Augustine to read Romans 13: 13–14.

p. 176 Under the blows of St Leo: Leo refuted the arguments of Eutyches, who denied that the humanity of Christ was of the same nature as our own, and can be seen as the founder of Monophytism even though he was later opposed by the Monophysites as too extreme (see note to p. 172); he was exiled at the Council of Chalcedon. Leo's condemnation of Eutychianism here is put together with Augustine's condemnation of the North African Donatists: together they 'pulverize' the Via media, not because of any Donatist or Eutychian tendency in Anglicanism, but because a small part of the Church has no authority to judge the whole.

p. 177 Papa: Pope.
Christi Vicarius: Vicar of Christ.
Sacer interpres: Consecrated expounder.
Sceptra gerens: Ruling authority.
Genius loci: The creative spirit or vital energy belonging to a particular place.

p. 186 experimentum crucis: an actual proof from experience which involves personally suffering the consequences.

p. 193 Arians and Semi-arians: For Arianism, see note to p. 106 above. Semi-arianism was the teaching of a group of theologians gathered around Basil of Ancyra in the mid-fourth century; they held a doctrine of Christ's nature which was a kind of *via media* between Arianism and orthodox Catholic belief. Again, the doctrine itself is not in question and the point Newman is emphasizing is that only Rome is consistent.

p. 195 Confession of Augsburg (1530): The official standard of Lutheran belief.

p. 202 Torres Vedras: A Portuguese town in the vicinity of a fortified retreat, used by Wellington as a fall-back position in the Peninsular war.

p. 208 Bp Bull's theology 'the only one on which the Church of England could stand': When asked by French clergy why, having defended as vigorously as he did – in such works as the *Judicium Ecclesiae Catholicae* – the truth of Catholic doctrine, he did not become a Catholic, Bull wrote a forthright reply entitled *The Corruptions of the Church of Rome*.

p. 210 Socinianism: The beliefs of Socinus, the Latin name of two Italians of the 16th C, Lelio Francesco Sozini (1525–62) and his nephew Fausto Paolo Sozzini (1539–1604). Both were hostile to the doctrine of the Trinity; Fausto led a group of Italian Unitarians from 1579 until his death. The dominant beliefs of the Socinians were the abiding goodness of human nature and opposition to the doctrines of original sin, the atonement and eternal punishment.

p. 218 Non in dialectica complacuit Deo salvum facere populum suum: It has not been pleasing to God to accomplish his people's salvation by logic.

p. 220 Di mi terrent et jupiter hostis: 'It is the Gods who frighten me, and Jupiter's enmity' (*Aeneid* 12, 895)
Ubi lapsus? quid feci?: 'Where was the fault? What did I do?'

p. 227 In malam partem: in a noxious sense, in the wrong way.

p. 235 ἄνομος: 'The lawless one'.

p. 238 crux: cross, difficulty.
In rerum natura: In the natural order of things.
solus cum solo: lit., solitary [being] with solitary [being], or as Newman puts it here, 'face-to-face', without intermediary.

p. 239 Vincent of Lérins. Best known for his defence of tradition (see 167n), Vincent nevertheless maintained that the final ground of Christian truth was Holy Scripture, and that the Church's authority was to be called on only when its correct interpretation was uncertain. Hence his attraction for Anglicanism.

Southwest Airlines
Open Seating

51

SITLER / EDWARD
PNR: HUM8UY
APR 14
234 MANCHESTER NH
    to BALTIMORE WASHNTN
1239 BALTIMORE WASHNTN
    to ORLANDO INTL

00001016321375

B

p. 245 Ussher, Jeremy Taylor, Barrow: see note to p. 173.
Valeat quantum: How much does it mean, how much is it worth?

p. 246 Laud on tradition: Laud argued that the Roman and Anglican Churches were both parts of the Church Catholic, whose tradition was the key to the understanding of Scripture. The proof of Scripture's divine origin, Laud said, was twofold: 'The first is the tradition of the Church of the Apostles themselves, who delivered immediately to the world the word of Christ: the other, the Scripture itself.' The tradition of later ages has authority because it conforms with Apostolic tradition.

p. 252 Victrix causa diis placuit, sed victa Catoni: 'The cause of the victors was pleasing to the Gods, but the defeated [was pleasing] to Cato.' A reference by Lucan (who apparently thought more highly of Cato than of the Gods) to Pompey's defeat at the hands of Caesar.

p. 257 in extenso: at length, in full.

p. 264 argumentum (pl. argumenta) **ad hominem:** a proof or argument drawn from personal circumstances or principles.

p. 271 Obliviscere populum tuum et domum patris tui: 'forget your own people and your father's house' (Psalm 44 [45]).

p. 279 Credenda: 'Things to be believed'; articles of faith.

p. 282 depositum: that which is entrusted; a heritage.
ipse dixit: innate authority.
Ex animo: from the soul, with complete conviction.

p. 287 pomoeria: boundaries, limits.

p. 289 Origen, Theophilus, John Chrysostom, Pope Vigilius: Among other unorthodox teachings, Origen emphasized the independence of Father, Son and Holy Spirit as 'three hypostases' – this was held to be incompatible with belief in the unity of God. Theophilus expelled his supporters from Egypt; they appealed to John Chrysostom, bishop of Constantinople. Theophilus stirred up local malcontents against John, and succeeded in obtaining his deposition and exile.
Vigilius obtained the Papacy having promised his help to restore the deposed Monophysite Patriarch Anthimus and condemn the Council of Chalcedon; the legitimate Pope,

Silverius, was deposed by force, and Vigilius declared Pope in his place. Having become Pope, however, Vigilius reneged on his agreement, refused to reinstate Anthimus, and reaffirmed Chalcedonian orthodoxy.

p. 291 Illi in vos saeviant [qui nesciunt cum quo labore verum inveniatur, et quam difficile caveantur errores]: Newman apparently expects his readers to recognize this quotation (from *Contra Epistolam Manichaei Quam vocant Fundamenti*), since he gives only the first four words of it. He gives his own free and expansive rendering: 'Let them be fierce with you who have no experience of the difficulty with which error is discriminated from truth, and the way of life is found amid the errors of the world.'

p. 293 exceptio probat regulam: the exception proves the rule.
remora: delay, hindrance.
St Leo: His 'one point of doctrine' was important, however; he pronounced that Christ had two distinct natures, human and divine.

pp. 293–5 In these pages, Newman shows how the infallibility of the Church encourages rather than repressing intellectual ferment, and how, inside the context provided by the Church's teaching authority, partly unsound authorities can harmlessly contribute to the Church's intellectual life. He gives examples of Church Fathers still honoured, though in some respects not wholly sound, as well as of the forbearance of the Church even when serious heresy is in question.

Tertullian was one of the great Fathers of the Church, despite tendencies to Stoic materialism and Montanism, an apocalyptic heresy of the latter half of the second century. **Origen** (ca. 185–253) combined orthodox theology with personal intellectual speculations which were not accepted by the church (see 289n). **Hilary of Poitiers** (315–67), though a militant foe of Arianism (see 106n), had tendencies towards a Monophysite (see 172n) view of the person of Christ. **Ambrose**, bishop of Milan (339–97), a great hero of the faith, was influenced by the partly heterodox Origen. The orthodox Jerome (340–420) refuted Origen and Pelagius; but he drew on the chronicles of Eusebius (ca 260–ca 340), who did not believe in the Divinity of Christ (being on the side of the Arians against Athanasius).

The infallible edicts of the Church arise out of this ferment. In this process, 'individual reason was paramount'; Newman lists individual contributions to the formation and defence of the Church's teaching: **Anselm** (1033–1109) defended the doctrine that the Holy Spirit proceeds from the Son as well as from the Father (the 'filioque' clause of the Nicene creed) at the Council of Bari (1098); **St Bonaventura** (1221–74) constructed the dogmatic and philosophical basis for later conciliar deliberations; **Alphonsus Salmeron** (1515–85) contributed to the Church's collective thinking on the doctrine of justification, the sacraments and other important questions. Belief in an infallible authority, says Newman, has not destroyed the independence of the mind; the Church has been generally slow to intervene in doctrinal matters. Pope **Zosimus** (elected 417) at first gave latitude to the heresiarch **Pelagius** (4C–5C) who denied the doctrine of original sin and held that man can be saved by his own virtue independently of the grace of God; but when it was necessary, he pronounced an official condemnation of Pelagianism (in 418). **Pope St Gregory VII** (ca 1020–85) was patient with the heretical views of **Berengarius** (ca 999–1088) on the real presence of Christ in the Eucharist, which led to a more precise definition of the doctrine at the Council of Rome (1079). Gregory forbade punitive measures against Berengarius.

p. 297 Disciplina arcani: The discipline of secrecy, whereby in the early Church reserve was exercised in making public Christian doctrines which might be misunderstood.

p. 300 argumentum ad hominem: See note to p. 246.

p. 304 Natalis Alexander (1639–1724)   A Dominican Church historian with Jansenist sympathies. See Appendix A, p. 365.

p. 304 Cardinal [Hycinthe] Gerdil (1718–1802):   Dogmatic and moral theologian. See quotation in Appendix A, p. 364.

THE CONTEMPORARY RESPONSE

On the day Newman began work on the *Apologia*, the historian and Catholic Sir John Acton (later Lord Acton) wrote to Newman to ask him to defend not only himself but also the integrity of the Catholic clergy as a whole. It had been noted, Acton said, that he had not done this in his original pamphlet; and there had been those who had explained this failure on the ground that Newman found it difficult to defend the Catholic Church's love for truth. So far, Acton suggested, the controversy had tended to vindicate Newman, but not the Church. Newman replied: 'you may be sure I shall go as far as ever I can.'

Newman's aim, then, was twofold: to vindicate himself, and in doing so to vindicate the Catholic Church. How successful was he in the event? It is easier to answer the question if we confine it to Newman's defence of his own integrity. According to Newman's first biographer Wilfrid Ward, 'cultivated opinion was perhaps better represented by the *Saturday Review* than any other journal. And the note struck by the *Saturday* on this subject when it reviewed the book as a whole, was echoed almost universally.' Ward's remarks refer to the public estimation of Newman himself (Newman's theological arguments were not generally accepted) and the *Saturday's* reaction is an interesting example of the willingness, even the appetite, of the Victorians to admire outstanding personal merit where it had been demonstrated, even in those whose opinions they were incapable of sharing:

A loose and off-hand, and, we may venture to add, an unjustifiable imputation, cast on Dr Newman by a popular writer more remarkable for vigorous writing than vigorous thought, has produced one of the most interesting works of the present literary age. Dr Newman is one of the finest masters of language; his logical powers are almost unequalled, and, in one way or other, he has influenced the course of English thought more perhaps than any of his contemporaries. If we add to this the peculiar circumstances of his reappearance in print, the sort of mystery in which, if he has not enveloped himself, he has been shrouded of late years, the natural curiosity which has been felt as to the results on such a mind of the recent progress of controversy and speculation, and the lower interest which always attaches to auto-biographies and confessions and personal reminiscences, we find an aggregate of unusual sources of interest in such a publication. Moreover, Dr Newman was not only the guide of many strong minds, but he appears as the apologist for a change in his own religious belief. Converts, or perverts, to use an ugly if not offensive neologism, have always something to account for; and accusations of treason, insincerity, and double dealing in all great changes of opinion, whether political or religious, are so easily made, and with such difficulty met, that it requires something more than the surface improbability of interested motives in any given case to account for, and still more to justify, what vulgar minds will always brand as an act of desertion. In Dr Newman's case the imputation of such lower motives was singularly misplaced. All that an ambitious mind could claim he had gained. He was, as far as mere intellect went, the acknowledged head of religious thought in this country. He had a following in the chief home of English education such as Oxford had never known. Be the Church of England what it may, to be the first mind in that Church, to inherit its traditions, to be its champion against all comers, to have the conviction of a special mission, not so much for infusing a new spirit into it as for recalling its ancient functions, and this under the animating conviction that he was but following in the steps of the doctors and saints of all time – to have this to do, and to be doing it surrounded and animated by the cheers and confidence of friends, zealous, high-spirited, and self-sacrificing, and, moreover, to be doing it with a considerable amount of success – all this was certainly motive enough to keep John Henry Newman in his place. He had everything to lose, and nothing to gain, by a transfer of his allegiance. The value, therefore, of the present publication is not as a vindication of the autobiographer's personal sincerity and pureness of motive – for such was not required – but rather as a curious and most interesting chapter in psychology, and, in a secondary degree, as a valuable contribution from the most trustworthy source to the inner history of the Church of England in very momentous times.

The general approbation for Newman himself, however, did not necessarily extend to an acceptance of the integrity of Catholicism as such, though the temperature of the ingrained anti-Popery displayed by these first criticisms rises and falls from one journal to another. It was not to be expected, for instance, that the staunchly Protestant *North British Review* would have any truck with Newman's insistence on the Catholic Church's love of truth, though it was very willing to make an exception in Newman's case. 'Many men, thank God, are better than their theories', could be taken as a brief summary of many of the reviews. The doctrinal problems involved in 'the lawfulness of equivocation' aroused particular suspicion:

> If the Romish doctrines regarding equivocation remained as abstract doctrines, there would perhaps be little to be said against them. But, unfortunately, in intercourse with Protestants, they start at once into active and most mischievous life. Following his arrogant theory as to the exclusive possession of truth by his Church, the Romanist finds no difficulty in regarding Protestants as the swine before whom pearls are not to be cast; as children, or madmen, who are to be habitually treated, on religious subjects at least, with 'economy'. 'Silence', 'evasion', 'playing upon words', 'material lying', all the many forms of simulation and dissimulation, are allowable in dealing with the outer barbarians; nay, they are positively praiseworthy, if used with the design of 'saving a soul'; in other words, of making a proselyte. Not that every Romanist would condescend to these arts. We have not the least suspicion, for instance, that Dr Newman himself would. Many men, thank God, are better than their theories. But this is what the Romish theories necessarily lead to; and many a family throughout the land can sadly testify that this is the Romish practice.

To give a full account of the fifty or sixty reviews that appeared would be a massive operation. The general message they convey, however, is clear enough. 'The conclusion to be drawn from these reviews', comments Fr Vincent Ferrer Blehl S.J., 'is that Newman indeed has vindicated his honesty but at what a price!' The price was that in order to be able to give Newman his due, reviewers tended to portray him as a tragic figure, a 'fallen angel but still an angel,' whose subjectivity and religious sentiment have led him to be enslaved by dogma. But the immediate reaction of those who represented the various strands of mid-Victorian intellectual opinion may be deceptive. The very fact that Newman himself was able to emerge from the shadows, that for the first time since the Protestant Reformation a major Catholic intellectual figure had not only defended his Church, but had gained massively in public stature by doing so, constitutes a landmark in the history of Catholicism in England. Looking back, R. H. Hutton wrote in 1890 that the *Apologia* was 'a book which, I venture to say, has done more to break down the English mistrust of Roman Catholics, and to bring about a hearty good fellowship between them and the members of other Churches, than all the rest of the religious literature of our time put together.'

To give a representative selection of the contemporary critical reactions to the controversy would require a separate substantial volume. I have chosen articles from four of the major periodicals (ideologically opposed to each other, but unanimous both in their admiration for Newman and in their resolute anti-Popery) from which to provide extracts of sufficient length to begin to 'get the feel' of these critics.

R. H. Hutton in *The Spectator*

Though the change in Newman's fortunes was massively consolidated by the reviews which appeared after the *Apologia* had appeared, it had already begun even before he had decided to write it. Newman's original pamphlet, reprinting his correspondence with Kingsley and giving his own satirical reply, appeared on 12 February 1864. Almost immediately, on 20 February, appeared the first part of a two-part review by Richard Holt Hutton, one of the great literary critics of the Victorian age. Hutton was to publish one of the most perceptive full-length studies of Newman; but already he is showing signs of a subtlety of critical insight (as well as of theological instinct) which was to be unmatched by any of the other reviewers. This review, entitled 'Father Newman's Sarcasm', is generally thought to have been the turning point for Newman after years of frustration and misunderstanding, and he wrote to Hutton to express his gratitude for it.

Mr Kingsley has just afforded, at his own expense, a genuine literary pleasure to all who can find intellectual pleasure in the play of great powers of sarcasm, by bringing Father Newman from his retirement, and showing not only one of the greatest of English writers, but, perhaps, the very greatest master of delicate and polished sarcasm in the English language, still in full possession of all the powers which contributed to his wonderful mastery of that subtle and dangerous weapon. Mr Kingsley is a choice though, perhaps, too helpless victim for the full exercise of Father Newman's powers. But he has high feeling and generous courage enough to make us feel that the sacrifice is no ordinary one; yet the title of one of his books, 'Loose Thoughts for Loose Thinkers', represents too closely the character of his rough but manly intellect, so that a more opportune Protestant ram for Father Newman's sacrificial knife could scarcely have been found; and, finally, the thicket in which he caught himself was, as it were, of his own choosing, he having rushed headlong into it, quite without malice, but also quite without proper consideration of the force and significance of his own words. Mr Kingsley is really without any case at all in the little personal controversy we are about to notice; and we think he drew down upon himself fairly the last keen blow of the sacrificial knife by what we must consider a very inadequate apology for his rash statement.

'Mr Kingsley,' Hutton continued, chooses 'not so much to think as to *splash up* thought, dregs and all . . . in one's face'; he then gave a summary of Newman's pamphlet, ending with a quotation of the splendid satirical passage in which Newman parodied Kingsley's arguments. His conclusion anticipates the general verdict that was to emerge when the *Apologia* itself came to be reviewed later in the year: 'that the whole justice of the matter seems to us on Dr Newman's side, that Mr Kingsley ought to have said, what is obviously true, that on examining the sermon no passage will bear any colourable meaning at all like that he put upon it.'

Yet, as other writers were to do, Hutton goes on to wonder whether Newman's retribution is not 'more than adequate'. Newman, he wrote, shows 'little desire to conceal that sense of . . . scorn which the habit of his mind in judging all human weakness by inflexible dogma has made part of the very essence of his marvellous insight into human frailty.' Thus, in appearing to criticize Newman's undue severity, Hutton paradoxically justifies it. He goes on to speak of Newman's 'cruelty' and 'sarcasm'; but he makes it plain that he is using the words in a special sense, not to imply any personal viciousness in Newman's character, but rather to indicate that a man like Newman, 'who has conceived a view of life resting, as he thinks, on the Spiritual Rock' will tend to have – if he is 'more intellectual than sympathetic' – 'views of life . . .' which 'have veins of mockery running through them in every direction.'

Even here, though, Hutton is not condemning Newman as unsympathetic; as he says later in this fascinating article, Newman's own writings show 'that a layer of very fine and delicate and generous sympathies overlying a deep and imperturbable scorn . . . is a still deeper source of knowledge of human nature.' Modern writers on Newman, some of whom tend to be squeamish about his invective and to suppose that controversialist instincts and holiness are incompatible – have much to learn from Hutton's robust analysis:

> This little discussion brings clearly home to us that one of the greatest secrets of Dr Newman's wonderful power is an intellectual basis for his mind of that peculiar hardness tending to cruelty which most easily allies itself with a keen intellectual sense of the supernatural. The finest balances, we know, are rested on a knife-edge, and so the finest intellectual sense of the valuelessness of things transient, often seems to be rested on a knife-edge so keen that it would cut through all human feelings, rather than on that charity which St Paul says is the highest and rarest of supernatural gifts. Father Newman's views of life, with all their delicate insights, wonderful shading, and beautiful perspective, have veins of subdued mockery running through them in every direction, – mockery such as a man who has conceived a view of life resting, as he thinks, on the Spiritual Rock, and who has learnt to triumph over the superficial softness of temporary phenomena, would, if more intellectual than sympathetic, be likely to cherish. The supernatural view, if acting on the intellect chiefly, leads to sarcasm, – and sarcasm is the greatest of Dr Newman's controversial weapons.

Hutton now goes on to quote from one of Newman's uninhibited lectures on *Difficulties of Anglicans* (1850) (Lecture 8: 'The Social State of Catholic Countries no Prejudice to the Sanctity of the Church'):

> In one of those lectures to his Puseyite brethren in which he used to pierce them so sharply, though so tenderly in manner, with every species of raillery, Dr Newman contrasted very strikingly the secular Protestant-Government view of things, – the sort of view Lord Palmerston would take, – with the sacerdotal Catholic view, – the sort of view Pio Nono would take, – and a more characteristic illustration of his peculiar power of sarcasm we do not remember: – 'Look at your poor-houses, hospitals, lunatic asylums, and prisons – how perfect are their externals! What skill and ingenuity appear in their structure, economy, and administration! They are as decent, and bright, and calm as what our Lord seems to name them – dead men's sepulchres. Yes! They have all the world can give, – all but life, all but a heart. Yes! you can hammer up a coffin; you can plaster a tomb; you are nature's undertakers, you cannot build it a home. You cannot feed or heal it; it lies like Lazarus at your gate full of sores. You see it gasping and panting with privations and penalties; and you sing to it, you dance to it, you show it your picture-books, you let off your fire-works, you open your menageries. Shallow philosophers, is this mode of going on

so winning and persuasive that we should imitate it?' Who cannot hear the ring of mockery with which the father of the Oratory laughs at the efforts of the world to patch up a decent and presentable show of earthly comfort? There is the same under-current of scorn in his most touching and tender addresses and appeals. Who that has ever read it does not remember that masterpiece of cruel oratorical effect in the sermon, written after his conversion, on 'Neglect of the Divine Calls and Warnings', in which he describes the vain pleas of a lost soul against the condemnation of Christ, 'I have had a conscience, I have a cultivated mind', &c, and then returns to consider all that may be said on earth of the wretch thus undergoing his final sentence of eternal torture? 'Men talk of him from time to time, – they quote his words, perhaps they even raise a monument to his name, or write his history. 'So comprehensive a mind! such a power of throwing light on a perplexed subject, and bringing conflicting ideas or facts into harmony!' or, 'It was the saying of a very sensible man'; or, 'A great personage whom some of us knew'; or, 'It was a rule with a very worthy and excellent friend of mine, now no more'; or, 'Never was his equal in society, so just in his remarks, so lively, so versatile, so unobtrusive'; or, 'I was fortunate to see him once when I was a boy'; or, 'So great a benefactor to his country and his kind'; 'His discoveries so great'; or, 'His philosophy so profound'; O vanity! vanity of vanities, all is vanity! What profiteth it? what profiteth it? His soul is in hell. O ye children of men, while thus you speak, his soul is in the beginning of those torments in which his body will soon have part, and which will never die!'

We see from this how cruel the spiritual imagination taken alone can be, – how it may almost delight to feed on the thought of the unreality of human things, and to represent to itself God's rule as one huge sarcasm on man's doings. It is often said, – with only partial truth, – that sympathy is the root of the deepest knowledge of human nature. We believe Dr Newman's writings show, as Mr Thackeray's writings in some sense, though a very different sense, show also, – that a layer of very fine, and delicate, and generous sympathies overlying a deep and imperturbable scorn, – the ripple of a sea that moves with every breath of human feeling above a bright and burnished mirror which reflects these ripples with a sort of sarcastic immobility, – is a still deeper source of knowledge of human nature. You must have the motionless depth beneath the waves, or you will not *keep* the image of the feeling as it first flashed across the mind. The difference between Dr Newman's sarcasm and the satire of a satirist like Thackeray lies in the *principle* which underlies and connects together the delusive shows of life. With the satirist the point of view which is the true focus of all his perspective is the bitterness of life's broken promises, the tinsel of its deceptive virtues. He sympathizes the more keenly with each rising emotion, *because* he knows it will be disappointed, or shattered, or exhausted soon. The keen intellectual reflector in which all the transient phases of human feeling are gathered together and mirrored shows them as unsubstantial bubbles in the moment of bursting. With Dr Newman the underlying feeling is somewhat different, – not a sense of the bitterness of death, but a positive delight of the imagination in watching the unseen prevail over the seen, Eternity swallow up the upstart growths of time, the angry breakers of human passion and vanity subside into the unfathomed sea. He follows every change of the human heart with a sort of pitiful tenderness, under which there runs a current of hidden triumph in the power of the Catholic faith and dogma to override all human ties, and dissolve all human joys and griefs by the power of its mightier affinities. The sarcasm of the theological imagination, taught by long meditation on dogma to emulate that 'terrible strength of mind' in considering human suffering which a popular preacher once attributed to God, and so steeled, to some extent, against anything deeper than a profoundly pitiful sympathy, is the ground-work of Dr Newman's greatest literary power.

Sir James Fitzjames Stephen in *Fraser's Magazine*

Sir James Fitzjames Stephen, brother of the sceptical Leslie Stephen, was a barrister and a frequent contributor to the reviews. He had defended one of those tried in the ecclesiastical courts on a heresy charge in the *Essays and Reviews* case (the defendants were found guilty, but afterwards acquitted on appeal). *Essays and Reviews* (1860) was a collection of essays by seven authors, including Benjamin Jowett, Mark Pattison and Frederick Temple, written from a strongly liberal point of view. The book attracted little attention until it was violently attacked in the *Quarterly Review* by Bishop Samuel Wilberforce (also one of the reviewers of the *Apologia*). Newman took no public part in the controversy, though encountering Pattison (formerly one of his supporters) on a train, he protested at its unsettling effect on the faith of ordinary people. Sir James Fitzjames Stephen's involvement was one of conviction; he held precisely the inflexibly anti-dogmatic liberal views Newman detested, and the following year attacked the *Note on Liberalism* which appeared in the *Apologia*'s 1865 edition (see p. 385). Stephen was to return to the attack on Newman 15 years later; Newman's reaction on that occasion was that 'it is no good our disputing; it is like a battle between a dog and a fish.' Stephen's review of the *Apologia* in *Fraser's Magazine* is a good example of classic English intellectual anti-Popery.

> The controversy between Dr Newman and Mr Kingsley has raised questions of infinitely greater importance than any which relate to the combatants themselves. Of the details of the controversy we do not mean to speak. Each disputant is fully able to take care of himself, and nothing is more difficult than to give a compressed account of a dispute in such a way as to do justice to both sides, or indeed to either. The main questions at issue are of a different character. They are deeply interesting to the community at large. And upon those questions, all transitory and personal matters being waived, we feel deeply that Mr Kingsley was right, though he expressed himself incautiously and clumsily; and that Dr Newman was wrong, though he managed his cause with great skill. . . .
>
> If, and in so far as, Mr Kingsley meant to 'call him a liar,' as Dr Newman says he did, we think he was wrong. Neither Dr Newman's life nor his writings sustain such a charge.
>
> There is, however, another question between the parties. Besides vindicating his individual moral character, Dr Newman attempts to meet another and a wider charge. In his general answer to Mr Kingsley, he says that many Protestants start with the suspicion 'that our creed is actually set up in inevitable superstition and hypocrisy.' He, on the contrary, affirms that this is not so; that the system of Romanism 'is in no sense dishonest', and that its 'upholders and teachers, as such, have a claim to be acquitted in their own persons of that odious imputation.' Of course no one makes these imputations in the terms in which Dr Newman states it. No doubt many Roman Catholics, especially those who have been born and brought up in it, hold their creed without superstition or hypocrisy; but Dr Newman's account of the principles by which he has been guided, and his statement of the conclusions at which he has arrived, appear to us to prove to demonstration, that he at least – and he is surely a favourable specimen of Protestants who have become Romanists – has been brought to accept superstition by sophistry. He may be an honest man, but his system is dishonest. This distinction is plain enough. The difference between mind and mind is so great that it is hardly possible to say what may or may not be honestly believed by particular people. It is no doubt possible that evidence which most men would reject with contempt, and that arguments which to most men would seem childish, may honestly appear conclusive to others. When, therefore, it is asserted that a system is dishonest or that a man is intellectually dishonest, all that is meant is, that the system is sophistical; that the man's mind has in fact taken a tortuous course; that the arguments to which it gives way are such as might have been accepted by a mind in search, not of the truth,

but of proofs for a foregone conclusion; and that the evidence with which he has been satisfied is not such as would generally be required by reasonable men to support the propositions at which it is pointed. This of course may be morally wrong; but no one can say that it is so in a particular case: No one can pretend to dive into the mind of another person, and pass sentence upon the way in which he has managed his own intellect. Human critics can look only to results.

Newman's arguments, Stephen went on, were 'such as might have been accepted by a mind in search, not of the truth, but of proofs for a foregone conclusion'; '. . . the evidence with which he has been satisfied is not such as would generally be required by reasonable men to support the propositions at which it is pointed'; however, he continues:

It must also be observed that it is difficult to connect the notion of dishonesty in any form with Dr Newman. His *Apologia* is a winning, and in some ways, a touching book. It is full of courage and straightforwardness; every word that the author says of himself and his opinions bears upon it the stamp of truth. The vigour and spirit with which, in his old age, he stands up for his good name; the price which he sets upon the good opinion of the world at large; his anxiety to be freed from the most odious of all imputations on the character of a straightfoward Englishman; the simple dignity with which he tells the story of his life – all these things go straight to the hearts of his readers. Almost all of us, he seems to think, are to be damned to all eternity; but with amiable inconsistency he wishes for our good opinion. He would like us to think kindly of him in hell fire. *Morituros salutat*. We have no intention to say a word inconsistent with the respect due to an old and distinguished man, who appeals so manfully to the good feeling of his countrymen; but high as Dr Newman's personal character is, we cannot read his book without feeling that his theology is dangerous sophistry, calculated to serve no other purpose than that of drugging the minds of men who care more for peace of mind than for truth, and whose *ultima ratio* is found not in their reason, but in their fears or their fancies. It is the duty of every one who thinks thus, to take opportunities of proving it.

Stephen's review is very long (only a small part of it appears here), and, whether or not we accept his argument, it is at times intellectually impressive. Though it is clearly intended to be devastating, Stephen (like all the other reviewers) goes out of his way to detach his dislike of Newman's religion from his respect for Newman himself:

We should like if possible to part on friendly terms with Dr Newman. It is impossible to read his books without liking him. Much as we dislike some of his doctrines, there is nothing cruel, nothing bitter, nothing unmanly in what he writes. His mind seems to dart at its opinions in a strange, fantastic way, which sets at defiance all common notions of reasoning; but its operations suggest rather a desperate honesty run away with by a strange, sophisticated ingenuity, than anything discreditable. Where he supposes that truth leads, there he will go; but his notions of truth are positively bewildering. His opinions appear to us to be dangerous sophistry; but the man himself is better than his opinions, and his writings wring even from a hostile critic a degree of regard and respect, which are not the less sincere because he is not likely (if indeed he ever reads these pages) to care for them, or perhaps to believe that they exist. Perhaps the best thing about him is his inconsistency. He ought by all rules to be a persecutor; but he says, no doubt with perfect truth, that a Spanish *auto da fé* would have been the death of him, and that he could never have borne even to cut off a Puritan's ears. So his wonderful sermon on the Greek Church ends mercifully. The mercy stultifies the theory to which it is appended; but it is mercy, and that is better than any quantity of logical subtlety.

Bishop Samuel Wilberforce in the *Quarterly Review*

Bishop Wilberforce's attack on the liberalism of *Essays and Reviews* had included a sideswipe at Tract XC. He had been Bishop of Oxford since 1845 (the year of Newman's defection), and his brothers and many of his friends had followed Newman to Rome. He was not wholly unsympathetic to the principles of the Tractarians, but considered that they were capable of full expression within the Church of England. He thought Newman's conversion to be the result of the 'peculiarities of the individual'. His review, nevertheless, was influential in the process of Newman's rehabilitation; though he did not accept Newman's arguments for Rome (few reviewers did) he was fully convinced of his honesty and his 'undoubted genius'.

Few books have been published of late years which combine more distinct elements of interest than the 'Apologia' of Dr Newman. As an autobiography, in the highest sense of that word, as a portraiture, that is, and record of what the man was, irrespective of those common accidents of humanity which too often load the biographer's pages, it is eminently dramatic. To produce such a portrait was the end which the writer proposed to himself, and which he has achieved with a rare fidelity and completeness. Hardly do the 'Confessions of St Augustine' more vividly reproduce the old African Bishop before successive generations in all the greatness and struggles of his life than do these pages the very inner being of this remarkable man – 'the living intelligence,' as he describes it, 'by which I write, and argue, and act'. No wonder that when he first fully recognised what he had to do, he 'shrank from both the task and the exposure which it would entail. . . . It is not at all pleasant for me to be egotistical, nor to be criticised for being so. it is not pleasant to reveal to high and low, young and old, what has gone on within me from my early years. It is not pleasant to be giving to every shallow or flippant disputant the advantage over me of knowing my most private thoughts, I might even say the intercourse between myself and my Maker.'

Here is the task he set himself, and the task which he has performed. There is in these pages an absolute revealing of the hidden life in its acting, and its processes, which at times is almost startling, which is everywhere of the deepest interest. For the life thus revealed is well worthy of the pen by which it is portrayed. Of all those who, in these late years, have quitted the Church of England for the Roman communion – esteemed, honoured, and beloved, as were many of them – no one, save Dr Newman, appears to us to possess the rare gift of undoubted genius.

That life, moreover, which anywhere and at any time must have marked its own character on his fellows, was cast precisely at the time and place most favourable for stamping upon others the impress of itself. The plate was ready to receive and to retain every line of the image which was thrown so vividly upon it. The history, therefore, of this life in its shifting scenes of thought, feeling, and purpose, becomes in fact the history of a school, a party, and a sect. From its effect on us, who, from without, judge of it with critical calmness, we can form some idea of what must be its power on those who were within the charmed ring; who were actually under the wand of the enchanter, for whom there was music in that voice, fascination in that eye, and habitual command in that spare but lustrous countenance; and who can trace again in this retrospect the colours and shadows which in those years which fixed their destiny, passed, though in less distinct hues, into their own lives, and made them what they are.

Again, in another aspect, the 'Apologia' will have a special interest for most of our readers. Almost every page of it will throw some light upon the great controversy which has been maintained for these three hundred years, and which now spreads itself throughout the world, between the Anglican Church and her oldest and greatest antagonist, the Papal See.

As for Kingsley's attack, 'The only abiding significance . . . of that disagreement will be its having given cause for the production of Dr Newman's volume. . . . Professor Kingsley has added nothing here to his literary reputation. Indeed his pamphlet can only hope to live as the embedded fly in the clear amber of his antagonist's Apology'. But Bishop Wilberforce shared with his liberal antagonist James Fitzjames Stephen an inclination – notwithstanding Newman's own personal honesty – to believe in the dishonesty of the Church he had joined:

> ... the meaning of the charge against Rome generally, and pre-eminently against that influential portion of it which bears a name almost equivalent to English ears with dishonesty, seems to us to be that the Jesuits especially, and Roman Catholic divines generally, have taught their disciples to act rather on the principles of casuistry than on the dictates of conscience. Dr Newman fully admits the existence of this double rule. He reminds us that a man 'in his own person is guided by his own conscience; but in drawing out a system of rules he is obliged to go by logic'; and he most distinctly states his own rule to be the absolute rule of a sensitive conscience: nay, he ventures so far as to say that 'in this department of morality, much as I admire the high points of the Italian character, I like the English character better'. . . . It would be too difficult a task even for his eloquence to convince the world that Jesuitry is synonymous with honesty; and it must never be forgotten that the Jesuit body is the very central life of Romanism, impregnating with its own temper the vast receptive mass around it. We have no doubt that Mr Ffoulkes's judgment of the relative excellence of his old and new communions is so far correct when he says, 'I think ... that truthfulness and intelligence distinguish Anglicans.'

One of the most interesting sections of Wilberforce's review deals with the continuing influence within Anglicanism of the movement which Newman and Wilberforce's own brothers had left for Rome. He quotes at length the section in the *Apologia* in which Newman evokes his memories of such figures as Hurrell Froude, Pusey and Keble, and then continues:

> Here then was the band which have accomplished so much; which have failed in so much; which have added a new party-name to our vocabulary; which have furnished materials for every scribbling or declaiming political Protestant, from the writer of the Durham Letter down to Mr Whalley and Mr Harper; which aided so greatly in reawakening the dormant energies of the English Church; which carried over to the ranks of her most deadly opponent some of the ablest and most devoted of her sons. The language of these pages has never varied concerning this movement. We have always admitted its many excellences – we have always lamented its evils. As long ago as in

1839, whilst we protested openly and fully against what we termed at the time the 'strange and lamentable' publication of Mr Froude's 'Remains', we declared our hope that 'the publication of the Oxford Tracts was a very seasonable and valuable contribution to the cause both of the Church and the State.' And in 1846, even after so many of our hopes had faded away, we yet spoke in the same tone of 'this religious movement in our Church,' as one 'from which, however clouded be the present aspect, we doubt not that great blessings have resulted and will result, unless we forfeit them by neglect or wilful abuse.'

The history of the progress of the movement lies scattered through these pages. All that we can collect concerning its first intention confirms absolutely Mr Perceval's Statements, 1843, that it was begun for two leading objects; 'first, the firm and practical maintenance of the doctrine of the apostolical succession . . . secondly, the preservation in its integrity of the Christian doctrine in our Prayerbooks.' Its unity of action was shaken by the first entrance of doubts into its leader's mind. His retirement from it tended directly to break it up as an actual party. But it would be a monstrous error to suppose that the influence of this movement was extinguished when its conductors were dispersed as a party. So far from it, the system of the Church of England took in all the more freely the elements of truth which it had all along been diffusing, because they were no longer scattered abroad by the direct action of an organised party under ostensible chiefs. Where, we may ask, is not at this moment the effect of that movement perfectly appreciable within our body? Look at the new-built and restored churches of the land; look at the multiplication of schools; the greater exactness of ritual observance; the higher standard of clerical life, service, and devotion; the more frequent celebrations; the cathedrals open; the loving sisterhoods labouring, under episcopal sanction, with the meek, active saintliness of the Church's purest time; look – above all, perhaps – at the raised tone of devotion and doctrine among us, and see in all these that the movement did not die, but rather flourished with a new vigour when the party of the movement was so greatly broken up. It is surely one of the strangest objections which can be urged against a living spiritual body, that the loss of many of its foremost sons still left its vital strength unimpaired. Yet this was Dr Newman's objection, and his witness, fourteen years ago, when he complained of the Church of England, that though it had given 'a hundred educated men to the Catholic Church, yet the huge creature from which they went forth showed no consciousness of its loss, but shook itself, and went about its work as of old time.'

As the unity of the party was broken up, the fire which had burned hitherto in but a single beacon was scattered upon a thousand hills. Nevertheless, the first breaking up of the party was eminently disheartening to its living members. But it was not by external violence that it was broken, but by the development within itself of a distinctive Romeward bias. Dr Newman lays his hand upon a particular epoch in its progress, at which, he says, it was crossed by a new set of men, who imparted to it that leaning to Romanism which ever after perceptibly beset it. 'A new school of thought was rising, as is usual in such movements, and was sweeping the original party of the movement aside, and was taking its place'. This is a curious instance of self-delusion. He was, as we maintain, throughout, the Romanising element in the whole movement. But for him it might have continued, as its other great chiefs still continue, the ornament and strength of the English Church. These younger men, to whom he attributes the change, were, in fact, the minds whom he had consciously or unconsciously fashioned and biassed.

The *Westminster Review*

The *Westminster Review* was founded in 1825 by Jeremy Bentham, with the assistance of James Mill, as the organ of the philosophic radicals. It therefore represents the ideological polar opposite to everything Newman believed in. Pain and pleasure, Bentham held, are the 'sovereign masters' governing human conduct; 'it is for them alone to point out what we ought to do.' Representing Benthamite Utilitarianism as it does, the *Westminster*'s review nevertheless tries to sympathize with Newman: 'none are competent to form a judgement' says the reviewer, 'who do not throw themselves into the position of the man whose actions or character they seek to criticise.' This appears to have been the attitude of most of the reviewers. But here as elsewhere, the principle does not extend to sympathy with Newman's arguments:

The immediate effect of Dr Newman's 'Apologia' will be to strengthen the position of the Church of Rome as against her assailants: in the end it can scarcely fail seriously to weaken it. Both these results will follow of necessity from the mercilessly accurate reasoning which has driven one who had no liking for paper logic, to submit himself to the infallible Church. Dr Newman's system is thorough; there is no mincing of matters. We see what we are about, and are content to abide by the issue which he raises. Whether wisely or unwisely, he has made his appeal to facts. He has to account for his belief in the existence of an authoritative external guide, whose duty it is not merely to administer to men their spiritual food but to control their intellect, to set the limits of scientific discussion, 'to animadvert on opinions in secular matters which bear upon religion – on matters of philosophy, of science, of literature, of history'. In justification of this belief, he appeals not to the words of a book, or the decrees of councils, or to the consensus of tradition, but to the patent facts of society as they appear to his eye, and as he supposes that they must appear in the eyes of all.

Predictably, the reviewer launches into an attack, first on the doctrine of original sin, then on the foundations of all religious authority; whether Catholic, Protestant or Anglican, all religion is seen by this Victorian rationalist as equally absurd. The popular tradition of the whole Christian World, says the reviewer:

is committed to Dr Newman's assertions as to the present and the original state of man. Man according to this theory was once sinless, he is now sinful. He was once perfect in body as in mind: now languages, some of them scarcely articulate, betray the decay of the latter: the physical degeneracy of Africans and Polynesians attests the degradation of the former. His intellect once led him to absolute trust in God: its universal tendency now is to utter unbelief. He had once the direct guidance of God; now, of himself, he knows not whence he came or whither to turn. He is decrepit and helpless: and if ever he is to be raised out of a state generally different from that in which he was created, there is need of external interference. Of what kind shall that interference be? It cannot be natural, because by the hypothesis the course of nature has been disorganized by human sin. It must be something extraordinary, or what is called miraculous. But miracles may be either occasional and desultory, or permanent. The former may confirm the faith of those who witness or hear of them; but they involve argument. There must be something which to men shall be as constant a quantity as the air which they breathe. There must be a 'face to face antagonist,' which shall 'withstand and baffle ... the all-corroding, all-dissolving scepticism of the intellect in religious inquiries'. There must be on the earth an infallible guide, and that guide Dr Newman finds in the Church Catholic. She alone guards the sacred deposit of the faith; she alone has spoken always the same language; she alone can adapt herself to the varying wants of ages; she alone discovers instinctively the special perils of every form of society, and interposes whenever and so far as her interference may be needed. It is true that Protestants laugh these claims to scorn, and look for infallible guidance to the pages of a book, as the Ephesians bowed down before the image which fell from Jupiter. It is true also that Anglicans intrude their theory of the Church and by suitable clipping and paring and a judicious eclecticism half convince themselves that the creation of their own brains possesses a substantial reality. Here the matter is at once brought to a point; and it is the business of all who seek to overthrow the tyranny of fallacies, to see that the question is not diverted to a false issue. With the exception of a few episcopal societies in Scotland and America, no religious body professes agreement with the Church of England; and who can say what she affirms herself? It is well to point to expressions in Rubrics and Formularies; but there is not a single term which may not be held in different senses by persons and schools all of whom have an equally legal status within her pale.

Newman could hardly have been surprised by the refusal of most critics to accept his arguments for the Catholic religion; but he had vindicated his name, and he had established that Catholicism could be believed by a scholar and a gentleman. And just as his name was now restored among his former Anglican friends, so it was now freed – except for Ultramontanes like Manning and Ward, who correctly perceived Part 7 (Chapter 5) as being, in part, a repudiation of their own position – from the suspicion of unorthodoxy within the Catholic Church. His work was not only *not* seen (as the future Cardinal Bourne untypically described it) as 'egotistical' by his brother priests; on the contrary, when only the 'autobiographical' chapters had appeared (in other words, while Newman was still writing the final chapter in defence of the Catholic faith), he was already being made aware by the clergy of his own diocese that his cause was their own. The following letter, from the greatly loved Bishop Ullathorne of Birmingham – which reads at times almost like a kind of eulogy – moved Newman so much that he published it as a 'postscriptum' in the first edition; it was not only the real sign that he had achieved his objectives in writing the *Apologia*, but the beginning of the recognition and honour which he would henceforward increasingly receive among his fellow Catholics. It is fitting that this survey of contemporary reactions should end with the one that Newman probably received with greatest satisfaction, prefaced by his own introductory remarks.

Postscriptum

4 June 1864

While I was engaged with these concluding pages, I received another of those special encouragements, which from several quarters have been bestowed upon me, since my controversy began. It was the extraordinary honour done me of an Address from the Clergy of this large Diocese, who had been assembled for the Synod.

It was followed two days afterwards by a most gracious testimonial from my Bishop, Dr Ullathorne, in the shape of a Letter which he wrote to me, and also inserted in the Birmingham Papers. With his leave I transfer it to my own Volume, as a very precious document, completing and recompensing, in a way most grateful to my feelings, the anxious work which has occupied me so fully for nearly ten weeks.

Bishop's House, 2 June 1864

My dear Dr Newman, –

It was with warm gratification that, after the close of the Synod yesterday, I listened to the Address presented to you by the clergy of the diocese, and to your impressive reply. But I should have been little satisfied with the part of the silent listener, except on the understanding with myself that I also might afterwards express to you my own sentiments in my own way.

We have now been personally acquainted, and much more than acquainted, for nineteen years, during more than sixteen of which we have stood in special relation of duty towards each other. This has been one of the singular blessings which God has given me amongst the cares of the Episcopal office. What my feelings of respect, of confidence, and of affection have been towards you, you know well, nor should I think of expressing them in words. But there is one thing that has struck me in this day of explanations, which you could not, and would not, be disposed to do, and which no one could do so properly or so authentically as I could, and which it seems to me is not altogether uncalled for, if every kind of erroneous impression that some persons have entertained with no better evidence than conjecture is to be removed.

It is difficult to comprehend how, in the face of facts, the notion should ever have arisen that, during your Catholic life, you have been more occupied with your own thoughts than with the service of religion and the work of the Church. If we take no other work into consideration beyond the written productions which your Catholic pen has given to the world, they are enough for the life's labour of another. There are the Lectures on Anglican Difficulties, the Lectures on Catholicism in England, the great work on the Scope and End of University Education, that on the Office and Work of Universities, the Lectures and Essays on University Subjects, and the two Volumes of Sermons; not to speak of your contributions to the Atlantis, which you founded, and to other periodicals; then there are those beautiful offerings to Catholic literature, the Lectures on the Turks, Loss and Gain, and Callista, and though last, not least, the Apologia, which is destined to put many idle rumours to rest, and many unprofitable surmises; and yet all these productions represent but a portion of your labour, and that in the second half of your period of public life.

These works have been written in the midst of labour and cares of another kind, and of which the world knows very little. I will specify four of these undertakings, each of a distinct character, and any one of which would have made a reputation for untiring energy in the practical order.

The first of these undertakings was the establishment of the congregation of the Oratory of St Philip Neri – that great ornament and accession to the force of English Catholicity. Both the London and the Birmingham Oratory must look to you as their founder and as the originator of their characteristic excellences; whilst that of Birmingham has never known any other presidency.

No sooner was this work fairly on foot than you were called by the highest authority to commence another, and one of yet greater magnitude and difficulty, the founding of a University in Ireland. After the Universities had been lost to the Catholics of these kingdoms for three centuries, everything had to be begun from the beginning: the idea of such an institution to be inculcated, the plan to be formed that would work, the resources to be gathered, and the staff of superiors and professors to be brought together. Your name was then the chief point of attraction which brought these elements together. You alone know what difficulties you had to conciliate and what to surmount, before the work reached that state of consistency and promise, which enabled you to return to those responsibilities in England which you had never laid aside or suspended. And here, excuse me if I give expression to a fancy which passed through my mind.

I was lately reading a poem, not long published, from the MSS. De Rerum Natura, by Neckham, the foster-brother of Richard the Lion-Hearted. He quotes an old prophecy, attributed to Merlin, and with a sort of wonder, as if recollecting that England owed so much of its literary learning to that country; and the prophecy says that after long years Oxford will pass into Ireland – 'Vada boum suo tempore transibunt in Hiberniam.' When I read this, I could not but indulge the pleasant fancy that in the days when the Dublin University shall arise in material splendour, an allusion to this prophecy might form a poetic element in the inscription on the pedestal of the statue which commemorates its first Rector.

The original plan of an oratory did not contemplate any parochial work, but you could not contemplate so many souls in want of pastors without being prompt and ready at the beck of authority to strain all your efforts in coming to their help. And this brings me to the third and the most continuous of those labours to which I have alluded. The mission in Alcester Street, its church and schools, were the first work of the Birmingham Oratory. After several years of close and hard work, and a considerable call upon the private resources of the Fathers who had established this congregation, it was delivered over to other hands, and the Fathers removed to the district of Edgbaston, where up to that time nothing Catholic had appeared. Then arose under your direction the large convent of the Oratory, the church expanded by degrees into its present capaciousness, a numerous congregation has gathered and grown in it; poor schools and other pious institutions have grown up in connection with it, and, moreover, equally at your expense and that of your brethren, and, as I have reason to know, at much inconvenience, the Oratory has relieved the other clergy of Birmingham all this while by constantly doing the duty in the poor-house and gaol of Birmingham.

More recently still, the mission and the poor school at Smethwick owe their existence to the Oratory. And all this while the founder and father of these religious works has added to his other solicitudes the toil of frequent preaching, of attendance in the confessional, and other parochial duties.

I have read on this day of its publication the seventh part of the Apologia, and the touching allusion in it to the devotedness of the Catholic clergy to the poor in seasons of pestilence reminds me that when the cholera raged so dreadfully at Bilston, and the two priests of the town were no longer equal to the number of cases to which they were hurried day and night, I asked you to lend me two fathers to supply the place of other priests whom I wished to send as a further aid. But you and Father St John preferred to take the place of danger which I had destined for others, and remained at Bilston till the worst was over.

The fourth work which I would notice is one more widely known. I refer to the school for the education of the higher classes, which at the solicitation of many friends you have founded and attached to the Oratory. Surely after reading this bare enumeration of work done, no man will venture to say that Dr Newman is leading a comparatively inactive life in the service of the Church.

To spare, my dear Dr Newman, any further pressure on those feelings with which I have already taken so large a liberty, I will only add one word more for my own satisfaction. During our long intercourse there is only one subject on which, after the first experience, I have measured my words with some caution, and that has been where questions bearing on ecclesiastical duty have arisen. I found some little caution necessary, because you were always so prompt and ready to go even beyond the slightest intimation of my wish or desires.

That God may bless you with health, life, and all the spiritual good which you desire, you and your brethren of the Oratory, is the earnest prayer now and often of,

My dear Dr Newman,
Your affectionate friend and faithful servant in Christ,
+ W. B. ULLATHORNE.

SUGGESTIONS FOR FURTHER READING

Many of the themes of the Apologia are explored, often amusingly, in *Loss and Gain*, Newman's novel about the conversion of an Anglican clergyman. This is available in paperback. So are his two most important contributions to theology, the *Essay on the Development of Christian Doctrine*, and *Grammar of Assent*; Of his Anglican writings, the *Oxford University Sermons* are published by S.P.C.K., and Ignatius Press has published the *Parochial and Plain Sermons* in a one volume edition. A good general introduction to Newman is Ian Ker's excellent and comprehensive anthology *The Genius of John Henry Newman* (Oxford: Clarendon Press 1989).

After Newman's own writings, the most indispensable tool for any serious study is Fr Ker's definitive critical biography, *John Henry Newman* (Oxford: Clarendon Press 1988), which contains a detailed account both of his life and writings. The excellent analytical index makes the book a kind of encyclopaedia of Newman's thought. Another beautifully written biography is Sheridan Gilley's *Newman and his Age* (London: Darton, Longman and Todd, 1990), which is well worth reading whether you already have Ker or not. C. S. Dessain's *John Henry Newman* (London: Nelson 1966) and his book *The Spirituality of John Henry Newman* are good introductions, the former to his thought, the latter to his spirituality. One of the most easily available books about Newman, Owen Chadwick's little monograph in the Oxford University Press *Past Masters* series is tempting only because of its brevity and the reputation of its author. Ian Ker's *The achievement of John Henry Newman* examines Newman as preacher and theologian; W. D. White's *The Preaching of John Henry Newman* gives a selection of the sermons with an introductory essay.